CREOLE
NEW ORLEANS IN THE
REVOLUTIONARY
ATLANTIC
1775–1877

CREOLE

NEW ORLEANS IN THE

REVOLUTIONARY

ATLANTIC

1775–1877

Caryn Cossé Bell

LOUISIANA STATE UNIVERSITY PRESS

BATON ROUGE

Published by Louisiana State University Press
lsupress.org

DESIGNER: Mandy McDonald Scallan
TYPEFACE: Whitman

COVER ILLUSTRATION: *Port and City of New Orleans*, by Marie Adrien Persac, ca. 1858–1859. The Historic New Orleans Collection, acquisition made possible by the Clarisse Claiborne Grima Fund, acc. no. 1988.9.

Maps created by Mary Lee Eggart.

Library of Congress Cataloging-in-Publication Data

Names: Bell, Caryn Cossé, author.
Title: Creole New Orleans in the Revolutionary Atlantic, 1775–1877 / Caryn Cossé Bell.
Description: Baton Rouge : Louisiana State University Press, [2023] | Includes bibliographical references and index.
Identifiers: LCCN 2023015983 (print) | LCCN 2023015984 (ebook) | ISBN 978-0-8071-7937-6 (cloth) | ISBN 978-0-8071-8092-1 (pdf) | ISBN 978-0-8071-8091-4 (epub)
Subjects: LCSH: Allain, Helene d'Aquin. | Creoles—Louisiana—New Orleans—History. | Revolutions—Louisiana—New Orleans—History. | New Orleans (La.)—History. | New Orleans (La.)—Race relations.
Classification: LCC F379.N59 C8725 2024 (print) | LCC F379.N59 (ebook) | DDC 976.3/35—dc23/eng/20230425
LC record available at https://lccn.loc.gov/2023015983
LC ebook record available at https://lccn.loc.gov/2023015984

À mon mari,

Dennis G. Bell

CONTENTS

ACKNOWLEDGMENTS - ix

MAPS - xiii

INTRODUCTION - 1

I. REVOLUTION - 9

ONE   Roots: *From the Sun King to the Haitian Revolution* - 11

TWO   Insurgency and Invasion - 34

THREE   The Tree of Liberty - 56

II. FRENCH ROMANTICISM - 79

FOUR   Une Famille Créole - 81

FIVE   Paris in New Orleans - 118

SIX   Les Docteurs - 151

III. CIVIL WAR AND RECONSTRUCTION - 173

SEVEN   Revolution and Counterrevolution - 175

EIGHT   Reconstruction and Coup d'État - 202

CONCLUSION - 231

POSTSCRIPT - 238

NOTES - 241

BIBLIOGRAPHY - 287

INDEX - 311

ACKNOWLEDGMENTS

As I searched for documents in a remote corner of the gigantic Bibliothèque Nationale de France, a soft voice asked, "Are you Madame Bell?" Only the day before, my partner, Monsieur Bell, had discussed my research challenge with bibliothèque staffer Joël Cramesnil. Now the polite stranger who tracked me down in the library's stacks explained that reference librarian Anne Provost had copies of the requested materials in hand! Neither before nor since have I had such an exciting visit to a research institution. Thank you, Joël, Anne, and the entire staff of the BNF for the wonderful work you do.

Essential research grants from the National Endowment for the Humanities and the University of Massachusetts Lowell supported my studies in France and Louisiana. A generous scholar-in-residence grant from the Louisiana Endowment for the Humanities funded study of the Grima Family Papers at the Hermann-Grima House in New Orleans. A study of the papers offered valuable insights into the lives of both the free and enslaved members of the French Quarter household.

I am also profoundly grateful for the support of the Ethel and Herman L. Midlo Center for New Orleans Studies at the University of New Orleans. Director Mary Niall Mitchell and her predecessor, Professor Connie Zeanah Atkinson, welcomed me into the community of national and international scholars who benefit from the professional hospitality of one of the city's leading research institutions. I sincerely appreciate their collegiality and ongoing assistance. In UNO's Louisiana & Special Collections, I also have had the privilege and pleasure of working with author, librarian, and bibliographer par excellence Dr. Florence M. Jumonville. With her unerring grasp of Louisiana history, she has been a trusted research guide throughout the preparation of this book.

I owe a special debt of gratitude to Ann E. Smith Case at Tulane University's Howard-Tilton Memorial Library for her recovery of irreplaceable primary documents after a heroic search through the archives. Like the indefatigable reference librarians at France's bibliothèque, Ann's skill and determination won the day. Leon Cahill Miller and Lori E. Schexnayder at Tulane's Louisiana

Research Collection, and Mary J. Holt at Tulane's Rudolph Matas Library of the Health Sciences, provided exceptional support with the utmost efficiency and courtesy. I am also grateful to Clint Bruce, Chaire de recherche du Canada en études acadiennes et transnationales, Université Sainte-Anne, and Professor Melody Herr at the University of Arkansas for their professional guidance in the preparation of the manuscript.

Research archivist Dorenda Dupont in the Office of the Archives at the Archdiocese of New Orleans, attorney Fernin F. Eaton, and AnnaLee Pauls at Princeton's Rare Books and Special Collections in the Firestone Library assisted me at key moments in my work, putting valuable resources at my disposal. The Historic New Orleans Collection, with its extraordinary Collins C. Diboll Vieux Carré Digital Survey and other resources, was also key to the formulation of this study.

While making *Faubourg Tremé*, documentary filmmaker Dawn Logsdon graciously shared her discovery of a rare letter written by courageous nineteenth-century civil rights leader Paul Trévigne. I remain deeply indebted to Dawn and to our mutual friend and colleague, Tulane University historian Lawrence N. Powell. Larry's support was central to this book and to countless other projects throughout my academic career.

After revolutionizing the study of slavery in Louisiana, the late Professor Gwendolyn Midlo Hall graciously opened her home to me during a research visit to New Orleans. My stay with her brought many happy rewards, including an introduction to Whitney Plantation's Dr. Ibrahima Seck. My extraordinary friend will always remain my role model as a woman and a historian. Thank you, Gwen!

I extend my heartfelt thanks to Jacques Morial, Brenda Marie Osbey, A. P. Tureaud, Fatima Shaik, Mark Roudané, Clint Bruce, and Angel Adams Parham for sharing their insights and knowledge of the city's history over the years. I am grateful for their wisdom.

Anonymous reviewers for Louisiana State University Press offered invaluable insights into the manuscript's strengths and weaknesses. Their input, together with the guidance of Editor in Chief Rand Dotson, brought greater focus to the book's overall objectives, in a dynamic that led to exciting new discoveries. I also owe a deep debt of gratitude to a publishing team that included Managing Editor Catherine L. Kadair, cartographer Mary Lee Eggart, and publicist Sunny Rosen. In the final, tense stages of the publication process, copy editor Todd Manza came to the rescue. His ability to read my mind regarding narrative changes truly lifted my spirits!

This study began as a collaborative project with Professor Anne Malena in French and Translation Studies at the University of Alberta. We proposed to publish an annotated translation of Hélène d'Aquin Allain's account of her life in nineteenth-century Creole New Orleans, *Souvenirs d'Amérique et de France par une Créole* (1883). When our initial proposal proved untenable, Anne moved on to other projects while I continued the task of researching, writing, and melding her translations and insights into this history of the city. When we began, neither of us anticipated the direction the book would take. Hopefully, this monograph demonstrates the value of making Louisiana's wealth of Francophone sources accessible to English-language readers.

MAPS

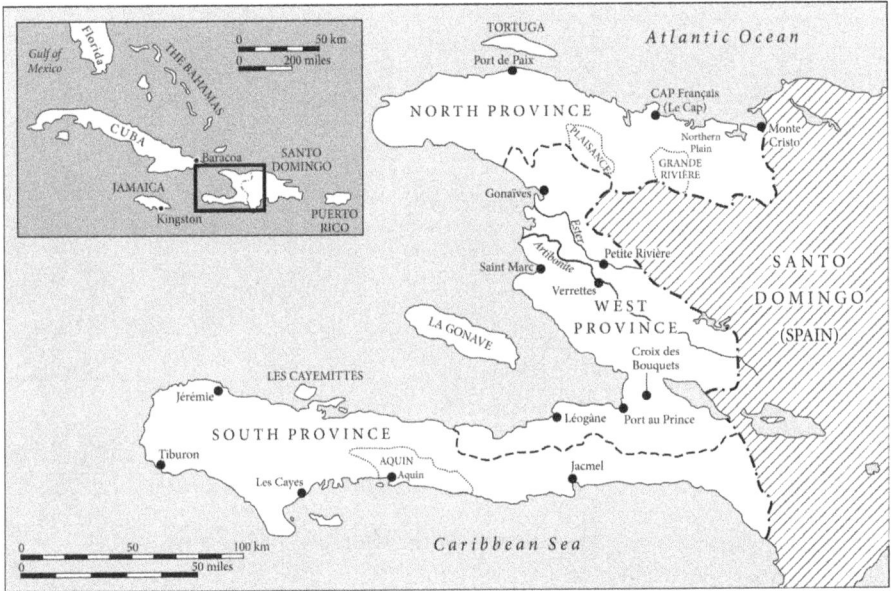

Saint-Domingue, 1789

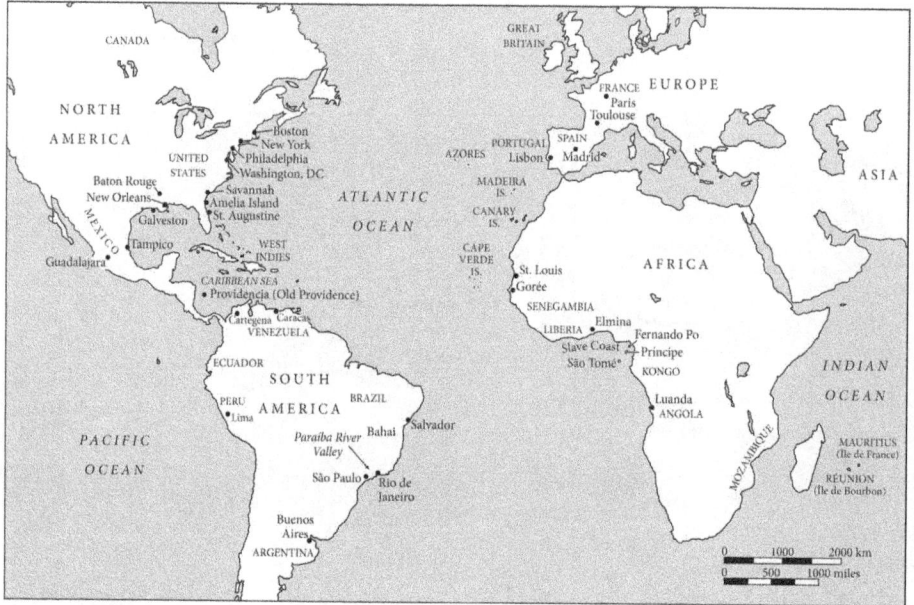

The Atlantic World, ca. 1800

DERBIGNY

CLAIBORNE

14

FAUBOURG TREMÉ

FAUBOURG SECTOR

AMERICAN SECTOR

ST. LOUIS

DUMAINE

BAYOU ROAD

13

BASIN ST.

ST. CLAUDE

12

RAMPART

MARIGNY

FAUBOURG

CANAL

BIENVILLE

DAUPHINE

ST. PETER

BURGUNDY

URSULINES

HOSPITAL

BARRACKS

ESPLANADE

1

FRENCH QUARTER

BOURBON

ROYAL

2

CHARTRES

11

LEVEE

4

5

7

10

6

8

3

9

Mississippi River

1 Mechanic's Institute	8 St. Mary's Catholic Church
2 Henry Clay Statue	9 U.S. Mint
3 U.S. Custom House	10 Allain's Home
4 La. State House	11 Slave Market
5 State Arsenal/Cabildo	12 Congo Square
6 Jackson Square	13 St. Augustine's Catholic Church
7 St. Louis Cathedral	14 French Hospital

0   0.5 miles

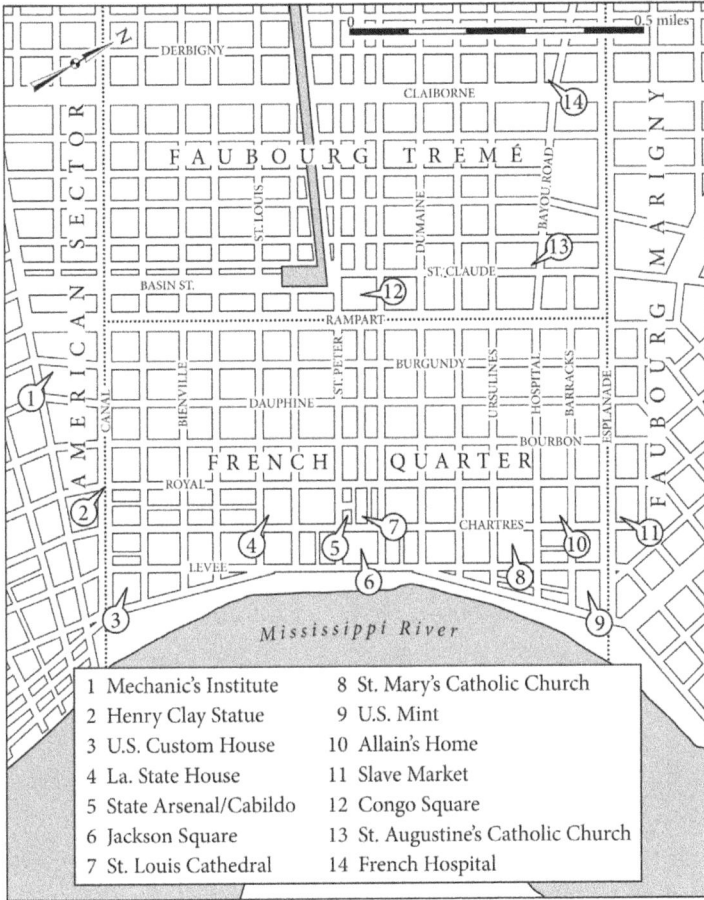

New Orleans, 1855

CREOLE
NEW ORLEANS IN THE
REVOLUTIONARY
ATLANTIC
1775-1877

INTRODUCTION

I n 1937, historian Charles Barthélémy Roussève, an Afro-Creole New Orleanian, published the first English-language history of African American Louisianians, his groundbreaking *The Negro in Louisiana: Aspects of His History and His Literature*. In his concluding "Recommendations," Roussève pressed for attention to a number of urgent objectives. He called for a "complete history of Louisiana" in which "the figure of the Negro should be drawn in true perspective, without bias, without malice." Previous histories had removed "data complimentary to the Negro as a factor in the history of the state" while others emphasized "details which vilified the black Louisianian." An unbiased state history, once achieved, should be taught objectively, Roussève wrote, so that the youth of both races "may come to look permanently upon one another as fellow-citizens who are heirs of a common past." In this way, Louisiana's youth may "fully realize that the growth and advancement of each are unavoidably conditioned by the growth and advancement of the other."[1]

In another of his recommendations, Roussève called for translations of three French-language books as a step toward making historically important sources available to Anglophone readers: Rodolphe Lucien Desdunes's *Nos Hommes et Notre Histoire* (Our People and Our History), Charles Testut's *Le Vieux Salomon, ou une famille d'esclaves au XIXème siècle* (Old Solomon, or a Nineteenth-Century Slave Family), and Hélène d'Aquin Allain's *Souvenirs d'Amérique et de France par une Créole* (Memories of America and France by a Creole), published in 1883 in Paris.[2]

In 1973, the publication of *Our People and Our History* fulfilled Roussève's call for an English-language edition of the Desdunes history of nineteenth-century Afro-Creole New Orleanians. Testut's *Le Vieux Salomon*, a historical novel depicting the horrors of slavery on a Louisiana sugar plantation, was never translated, though an important study of the abolitionist novel in *Charles Testut's "Le Vieux Salomon": Race, Religion, Socialism, and Freemasonry* offers invaluable insights into Testut's literary work and life.[3]

1

Like the Testut book, Allain's *Souvenirs* was never translated, and it faded into obscurity not long after its publication in France. A complex blending of memoir, family history, autobiography, primary documents, and excerpts from published texts, the book was intended, according to Allain, as a "written conversation" dedicated wholly to "my dear Louisiana audience."[4] Written by a woman who self-identified as a white Creole and whose French ancestors had played key roles in founding colonial slave regimes in Louisiana and Saint-Domingue, *Souvenirs* would appear to have very little to contribute to a broader understanding of the city's multiethnic history. Roussève, however, knew otherwise.

With his grounding in the city's Francophone language, culture, and history, he possessed the skills and perspective to decode Allain's personal, nearly stream of consciousness work about her family history, her life in New Orleans, and the Atlantic world she and her family traversed. He understood her insider's voice when she spoke of the free and enslaved Afro-Creoles among whom she grew to adulthood.

Roussève's inspiring call for a "complete history" of Louisiana, together with Allain's background and family history, recommended a study of the Age of Revolution's impact on the Francophone city and its environs. Chronologically extending from the American, French, and Haitian Revolutions and the wars of Latin American independence, *Creole New Orleans in the Revolutionary Atlantic* concludes with the collapse of Reconstruction in 1877, when the promise of the revolutionary age gave way to the crushing oppression of the Jim Crow era.

The city's history in the revolutionary age proceeded along a series of cascading trajectories, and though elements of the period have been recorded in numerous scholarly works—works that made the present book possible—an overall study of the city has been lacking until now. With Allain's *Souvenirs* serving as its backbone, *Creole New Orleans in the Revolutionary Atlantic* offers a comprehensive account of the tumultuous era.

Among Francophone New Orleanians, the revolutionary ethos remained a forceful presence when a diaspora of Haitian refugees, itinerant revolutionaries, French Romantic literary artists, and Paris-educated doctors sustained the republican cause. Throughout the era, multiethnic Black Louisianians (foreign and native-born, slave and free) remained revolutionary republicanism's unwavering champions. They seized upon the "bulldozer force of the revolutionary logic of rights" and never let go. Their unrelenting struggle for freedom and equal citizenship is key to this study and foundational to building a complete history of New Orleans and Louisiana.[5]

Souvenirs' author, Hélène d'Aquin Allain, arrived in New Orleans as a young child in 1836, when her parents emigrated to Louisiana from Jamaica. She grew to adulthood in the city in the heyday of French Romanticism, a complex cultural revolution that emerged in Europe in the turmoil surrounding the French Revolution. In general, the new sensibility carried Enlightenment humanitarianism forward while elevating intuition over the Enlightenment stress on reasoned ideas and rationalism. German philosopher Immanuel Kant captured the essence of the movement in the title of his influential *Critique of Pure Reason* (1781). In France, François René de Chateaubriand's *The Genius of Christianity* (1802), with his metaphysical belief in God's spiritual presence in all of creation, marked the emergence of the movement in France. In the new dispensation, reasoned ideas gave way to a spiritual/mystical vision in which the "child of nature" superseded the Enlightenment philosopher as the true holder of wisdom.

More broadly, European Romanticism's emphasis on the innate genius of all peoples spurred an intense interest in history. In this context, history writing and literary art were esteemed, with poetry demonstrating the inner genius of an individual or a people. Under Romanticism's emancipatory influence, women authors on both sides of the Atlantic forged ahead, achieving remarkable gains. In antebellum North America, they wrote their way into the ranks of the nation's best-selling novelists and short story writers. Allain's Romantic orientation is evident in her family history and her attention to the Native American, African, and African American peoples among whom she lived.[6]

In France, where the Romantic movement was closely tied to political thought and activity, its foremost exponents viewed their art form as a force for change. Thus transformed, Romanticism transcended national boundaries as well as racial, gender, and class divisions to emerge as the literary lingua franca of reformers and republican revolutionaries throughout the Francophone Atlantic. In France, Haiti, and Louisiana, Romantic writers shaped their commentary and literary works into a basis for political and social action. As we will see, all of the key features of French Romanticism were present in nineteenth-century New Orleans and exerted a profound influence on the city's Francophone community. As a member of the city's educated elite, Allain, like Desdunes and Testut, possessed a sensibility rooted in the movement's cultural worldview.[7]

Roussève and historian John W. Blassingame valued *Souvenirs* for its descriptions of West African influences in the language, songs, and proverbs of the African and Afro-Creole New Orleanians who performed the calinda, the chica, and other African dances "every Sunday in the Place Congo before large groups of spectators of every social level." Blassingame referenced Allain to document the persistence of African culture in New Orleans up to the time of the Civil War. His research persuaded him that prior to the war, Louisiana probably possessed more African dance and musical survivals than any other region of the country, a conclusion later confirmed by Gwendolyn Midlo Hall's scholarship.[8]

Writing in the 1990s, scholar Thomas Fiehrer also recognized the unique character of multicultural New Orleans and advocated for a circum-Caribbean historical model that recognized the interdependence of colonial Saint-Domingue and Louisiana. In *Souvenirs*, nearly seventy-five years earlier, Allain gave considerable force to the circum-Caribbean model and those common cultural connections.

After reading Médéric-Louis-Elie Moreau de Saint-Méry's *Description topographique, physique, civile, politique et historique de la partie française de l'isle Saint-Domingue*, a study of colonial Saint-Domingue on the eve of the Haitian Revolution, Allain marveled at the cultural similarities between enslaved Creole Saint-Dominguans and Louisiana's antebellum Afro-Creoles. Her surprise, reinforced by family folklore, led her to transcribe thirty-nine pages of Moreau's book into her own *Souvenirs*. Allain's revelation validates a phenomenon in which highly politicized Black New Orleanians, like their predecessors in colonial Saint-Domingue, were taking countless steps, both large and small, toward their own liberation. By the time of the Civil War, their revolution was well under way.[9]

Whereas Roussève and Blassingame considered Allain's book a valuable record of nineteenth-century Afro-Creole life in Louisiana, other scholars consigned *Souvenirs* to near oblivion. Because Louisianians were living under the cudgel of white supremacy by the time of *Souvenirs'* appearance, Allain did not get credit for her insights. In *The French Literature of Louisiana* (1929), scholar Ruby Van Allen Caulfeild's comprehensive bibliography made the state's Francophone writings more accessible to English-language readers. In her two-paragraph entry for *Souvenirs*, she conceded that though Allain's book was "well written," it "does not have a universal appeal because it is too definitely family history and of interest only to her close friends and members of her family." Caulfeild dealt even more harshly with Louisiana's Afro-Creole literary artists. Her reading of Armand Lanusse's *Les Cenelles: choix de poésies indigènes*, the first African American anthology of literature in the nation, convinced her that "none of them [the poems] has any great value."[10]

Edward Larocque Tinker struck a more negative blow in 1932 in his enormously influential *Les Écrits de langue française en Louisiane au XIXe siècle* (French-Language Literature in Nineteenth-Century Louisiana), an exhaustive bio-bibliography of Louisiana's Francophone literature. He described Allain's book as an "incoherent and crude collection of her memories" though he conceded that it possessed "picturesque accounts of Creole life in Louisiana"[11]

Perhaps the cruelest cut of all came in the 1964 *End of an Era: New Orleans, 1850–1860*, by Robert C. Reinders, who entirely misrepresented Allain's book. Hardly more could be expected of a twentieth-century author who agreed with Nathaniel Hawthorne that the 1850s was a decade of a "d——d mob of scribbling women." Their "tear-stained pages" and "emotional escapism," Reinders observed, "vastly outsold the Herman Melvilles." In the Northeast, however, "a few male geniuses could hold back the cackling women."[12]

As an undergraduate, historian Catherine Clinton encountered a similar attitude when she shared her discovery of Mary Boykin Chesnut's Civil War diary with a professor. He startled her with the comment, "But isn't the whole thing a hoax?" The "hoax" resulted in C. Vann Woodward's 1982 Pulitzer Prize–winning *Mary Chesnut's Civil War*. Happily, as Clinton wrote, the "hoax is over: women as well as men left important records from which a new social history of the South can and will be written."[13] Allain's *Souvenirs*, written from a circum-Caribbean/Atlantic worldview and encompassing a family history set against an age of revolutionary upheaval certainly ranks among those important historical documents worthy of serious study.

Relying upon the d'Aquin family's transatlantic kinship network and cross-racial alliances as guideposts, three distinct stages emerge between 1775 and 1877, when forward-looking New Orleanians undertook to fulfill the promise of the revolutionary age. In the interest of bringing greater coherence to the entire text, this book's eight chapters are organized under three general headings: "Revolution," "French Romanticism," and "Civil War and Reconstruction." These three broad topics highlight the major phases of the revolutionary age in the city.

The first three chapters, organized as part 1, "Revolution," extend from the early eighteenth century to 1825. Chapter 1, "Roots," documents the ancestral history of the d'Aquin family and their migration to Louisiana and Saint-Domingue, where they served in the French military and fought in the Haitian Revolution alongside the Savarys, a politically influential free family of color. Forced from Saint-Domingue in the hostilities, the allied families retreated to south Louisiana.

Chapter 2, "Insurgency and Invasion," relates events between 1804 and 1815, when itinerant revolutionaries congregated in New Orleans. They were joined in 1809–1810 by a huge influx of Haitian refugees, with the actions of a French-educated refugee judge legally fortifying the city's tripartite racial order. The presence of the itinerant revolutionaries and the refugee Francophone soldiers (both Black and white) proved decisive in General Jackson's triumph in the 1815 Battle of New Orleans.

Chapter 3, "The Tree of Liberty," documents the movements of the Haitian Revolution's Black soldiers after the 1815 Battle of New Orleans, when they rejoined other itinerant revolutionaries in the cause of Latin American independence movements. Ultimately forced by US naval forces to retreat, Savary returned to New Orleans in 1825, where he met his fellow itinerant revolutionary, the Marquis de Lafayette. The chapter's concluding pages outline the d'Aquin family's extensive web of allied families in 1840.

Under the second general heading of "French Romanticism," chapters 4 through 6 cover the period from 1825 to 1862 to document the impact of the movement on Francophone New Orleans. Chapter 4, "Une Famille Créole," centers on Allain's three-caste household and the nearby interracial church she attended with Creole women of color who shared her Catholic spirituality and her ancestral roots in Saint-Domingue/Haiti. After 1840, the neighborhood's slave markets burgeoned just steps from Allain's French Quarter home.

"Paris in New Orleans," chapter 5, explores French Romanticism's emergence in France, Haiti, and New Orleans, where the movement gathered momentum after 1815. Throughout the Francophone Atlantic, Romanticism's highly politicized orientation fueled revolutionary upheaval in Haiti and France.

"Les Docteurs," the subject of chapter 6, emphasizes the skills of New Orleans Francophone doctors who were trained at France's Paris Médicale. In a philosophy that originated in the 1789 French Revolution, the Médicale's teaching staff instilled in its students a commitment to address society's political ills as well as their patients' physical ailments.

In part 3, under the general heading "Civil War and Reconstruction," chapters 7 and 8 chronicle events between 1862 and 1877. Chapter 7, "Revolution and Counterrevolution," begins with General Benjamin F. Butler's Civil War occupation of New Orleans. Though he remained in the city for less than nine months, the term *revolution* aptly applies to the dynamic resulting from his alliance with Black New Orleanians.

Chapter 8, "Reconstruction and Coup d'État," begins with the 1866 massacre in New Orleans when Black residents gathered to petition for voting rights. The bloody events in the city and throughout the South prompted US military occupation and the ratification of the Fourteenth and Fifteenth Amendments. Together with the mounting violence, a series of catastrophic Supreme Court decisions doomed Congressional Reconstruction. A coup d'état in New Orleans in 1877 ended the prospects for the representative democracy envisioned by Black Louisianians and their allies.

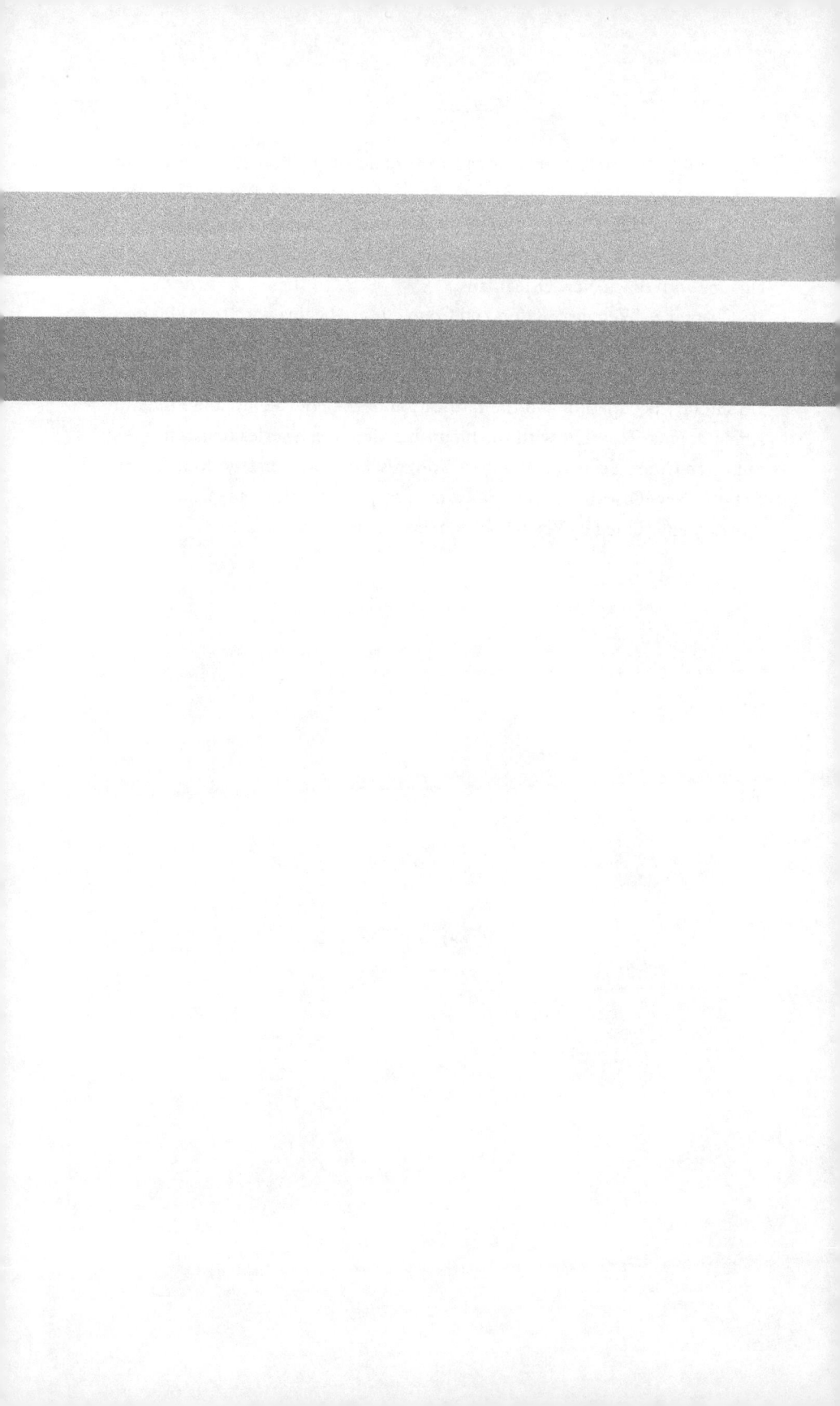

I.

REVOLUTION

Ushered in by the American Revolution, the thoroughgoing French and Haitian Revolutions sent tremors throughout the Atlantic world. While partisans of the French Revolution disseminated their ideology of freedom and equality, Haitian revolutionaries achieved an unmatched triumph in the history of the Americas. Between 1791 and 1804, they overthrew a burgeoning colonial slave regime, abolished slavery, and founded the western hemisphere's first Black nation and its second independent nation-state.

Inspired by the electrifying events in France and Saint-Domingue/Haiti, south Louisiana's free and enslaved Afro-Creoles repeatedly challenged Spain's colonial regime. Reports of sedition within the free Black militia prompted investigations, and fears of slave conspiracies forced Spanish authorities to shut down Louisiana's entire slave trade in 1796.

After the 1803 Louisiana Purchase, the Haitian diaspora's three-caste refugee population steadily increased in size until 1810, when New Orleans possessed the largest number of refugees in North America. The following year, the powerful repercussions of revolutionary Haiti reverberated once again when an enslaved *commandeur* (slave driver) led hundreds of Louisiana-born, Saint-Dominguan, and West African insurgents in the largest slave rebellion in the United States.

Just as ominously for Louisiana slaveholders, the diaspora of Haitian refugees included veteran Black soldiers who, together with their white refugee allies, had fought under the revolutionary French Republic. Over the vehement objections of white planters, the men joined the US Army in the Battle of New Orleans, where they played a decisive role in defeating the invading enemy. When the US government refused them citizenship for their service, they joined the international body of itinerant revolutionaries congregating in the city to advance republicanism in the wars for Latin American independence.

Nowhere in the United States did the French and Haitian Revolutions exert as far-reaching and enduring an influence as in south Louisiana. In the Age of Revolution, nineteenth-century Afro-Creole New Orleanians looked to the French and Haitian Revolutions as the lodestars of their aspirations.

ONE

Roots

From the Sun King to the Haitian Revolution

Building upon Allain's references to her family roots, this chapter documents the rise of the d'Aquin patriarchs to power in seventeenth-century France and the humiliating blow that drove them overseas. The debacle led three generations of d'Aquins to enlist in the French navy, where they joined the founders and inhabitants of Louisiana and Saint-Domingue. In the French military, they fought frontline battles in the Natchez wars, the Seven Years' War in Saint-Domingue, and the Haitian Revolution. In the Americas, their local and far-flung alliances ensured the survival and success of their family.

One of the most important of those military/political alliances involved Allain's great-uncle, Charles-Louis d'Aquin, free man of color Charles Savary *âiné*, and his son Joseph Savary *fils*. In Saint-Domingue, the d'Aquins and the Savarys belonged to old-line, prestigious colonial families, one white and the other a free family of color. Under the French Republic, they served as comrades in arms during the Haitian Revolution. The upheaval eventually forced the two families and their influential network of allies to retreat to New Orleans, where the revolutionary age reverberated in south Louisiana in 1811 in the largest slave revolt in North America.

* * *

"Various revolutions," Allain wrote of her family, had "destroyed their wealth, separated families, and caused all of their misfortunes."[1] The Age of Revolution repeatedly upended the lives of the d'Aquin family. A refugee herself, Allain grew up in New Orleans surrounded by survivors who regaled her with stories of an ancestral past rooted in a tumultuous Atlantic world. Neither she nor they exaggerated. The d'Aquin family history is a virtual road map of the chaotic era.

In Louisiana, d'Aquin family alliances extended to veterans of the Haitian Revolution, the Battle of New Orleans, and the independence movements in Spanish America. As a teenager, Allain counted refugees of the 1848 French Revolution among her closest friends, and as a young mother in New Orleans she lived through the upheaval of the US Civil War.

Allain arrived in the city from Jamaica as a young child, in 1836, after the British abolition of slavery in the Caribbean colony forced her family into economic exile. Her parents looked for support from an extensive Francophone kinship network—a system of family alliances that stretched from the Caribbean to Louisiana, the eastern United States, and France. In the city, relatives and friends readily welcomed them into their midst. They understood the plight of the newly arrived refugees.[2]

In her youth, Allain's thorough schooling in French Romanticism, together with her close-knit family ties and her own life experiences, fostered an intense interest in history: "Still very young, I felt a devotion to the past: to hear about the elders, to learn the names of ancestors sometimes forgotten beyond the fourth generation."[3] Throughout her life, she sought out the folkloric and material remnants of her family's past.

With family members "born, married and buried on both sides of the Atlantic,"[4] Allain's personal odyssey to reconstruct her ancestral history began at an early age and continued throughout her life as she "harvested bits of information from Saint-Domingue, Jamaica, New Orleans, Toulouse, and New York." All of her relatives, she wrote, were "of French origin except for cherished family lore claiming paternal descent from an illustrious Italian family and another, on the maternal side, making us descendants of a large Irish family."[5] Driven by her sense of history, her life experiences, and her pride in her Creole identity, she set out to chronicle her family's past and explain how she became "a child of Louisiana."[6]

The d'Aquin lore of an "illustrious Italian family" in their ancestry is accurate. Philippe d'Aquin, Allain's paternal ancestor, was the son of Antonio d'Aquino, Baron de Grotta-Minanda, whose title dated back to early medieval Capua in southern Italy. Hostilities resulting from the sixteenth-century rivalry between the French king Francis I and Holy Roman Emperor Charles V drove the Aquino family into exile. Philippe was born about 1576 in Carpentras, France, where his studies purportedly led him to convert to Judaism. In Avignon, his apparent heterodoxy scandalized his synagogue. He emigrated to Aquino in the kingdom of Naples, reconverted to Catholicism, and changed his name to d'Aquin. By 1610, he had returned to France, where his scholarly productivity opened the way to an astonishing rise to power in seventeenth-century France.[7]

In 1629, in a Latin preface and a eulogistic poem written in Hebrew, the multilingual d'Aquin dedicated his most prestigious work, the *Dictionnaire hébre-araméen* (Hebrew-Aramaean Dictionary), to Cardinal Richelieu. Having won the favor of the powerful Catholic prelate and statesman, d'Aquin obtained a royal appointment as professor of Hebrew at the Collège Royal in Paris.[8] His son, Louis-Henri-Thomas d'Aquin, studied medicine and became First Physician to Queen Marie de' Medici, the wife of King Louis XIII. In 1669, King Louis XIV (1643–1715) ennobled Louis-Henri-Thomas d'Aquin. His two sons, Antoine and Pierre, followed in their father's footsteps as physicians to France's royal family. In 1672, Antoine d'Aquin was appointed First Physician to King Louis XIV while his brother Pierre served as the king's *médecin ordinaire.*

In their rise to high office, Antoine and Pierre d'Aquin had navigated the treacherous crosscurrents of court politics with the support of the Marquise de Montespan, the influential mistress of Louis XIV. Early in the 1670s, however, Françoise de Maintenon (Françoise d'Aubigné), the governess of the king's illegitimate children by the marquise, superseded Montespan in Louis XIV's affections. The ascent of Maintenon marked the beginning of the d'Aquins' decline.

After Maintenon's morganatic marriage to the king in 1683, she maneuvered to replace Antoine d'Aquin with a courtier of her own. The campaign against him began with charges of outdated medical remedies. As his enemies piled on, he was also accused of avarice and insolent behavior toward the king. On the eve of All Saints Day in 1693, the Roi Soleil surprised d'Aquin with a lengthy and pleasant conversation. The ax fell the next day, when the Comte de Pontchartrain called on d'Aquin at his residence. The count ordered both Antoine and Pierre to leave Versailles immediately and barred them from writing to the king or attempting to meet with him.

The royal pensions the king awarded the two men could hardly compensate for the disastrous blow they had suffered. Antoine d'Aquin's disgrace is thought to have ruined his health and hastened his death, which came three years later. For his brother Pierre's enterprising offspring, however, the hugely expansionist ambitions of Louis XIV opened new avenues of advancement. The king's determination to make his nation supreme in the Americas, his creation of a formidable naval force, and his interest in France's flourishing slave colonies persuaded Pierre's son Antoine-Benoist d'Aquin, Allain's great-great-grandfather, to seek his fortunes on the other side of the Atlantic.[9]

Not long after Pierre's disgrace, France acquired the western third of the Spanish Caribbean colony of Hispaniola, renamed Saint-Domingue (present-day Haiti), in the 1697 Treaty of Ryswick. The following year, explorer Pierre Lemoyne, Sieur d'Iberville, launched an expedition from Léogane (the initial capital of Saint-Domingue) to fortify a hard-pressed French military garrison at present-day Ocean Springs, Mississippi. Iberville's successful mission tied Louisiana to colonial Saint-Domingue, with Allain's ancestor Antoine-Benoist joining south Louisiana's early colonizers. For three generations afterwards, the d'Aquins were among the founders and inhabitants of both Louisiana and its Caribbean parent colony.

As a French naval officer, Antoine-Benoist was dispatched to Fort Condé in Mobile, where he was commandant of the fortress in the 1720s. In 1726, he married Jeanne-Renée Garnier, a French native of Quimper in the seafaring region of Brittany. Though pregnant in 1728, she refused to leave her husband as Native American attacks on the French colonists escalated. She gave birth to Antoine-Pierre d'Aquin on February 29, 1729. In November, the Natchez wars began in earnest with a deadly assault on Fort Rosalie, a French fort in Natchez territory. In the protracted hostilities, Antoine-Pierre's father fought in active service under Jean-Baptiste de Bienville.[10]

Antoine-Pierre d'Aquin, like his father, served in the French navy. Posted to Saint-Domingue in 1750, he advanced through the ranks to become the colony's comptroller of naval affairs. By the time of d'Aquin's Caribbean posting, the French military relied almost exclusively on the soldiers of color who dominated the colony's security forces. At the outset of France's acquisition of the colony in 1697, governing authorities began assigning soldiers of color to its expeditionary forces. In 1733, Governor de Fayet reported that the "mulattoes do all the military service of the colony."[11] By the time of the Haitian Revolution, the status of soldiers of color remained basically unchanged.

For Afro-Creole men, military service opened the way to manumission for oneself or one's family members, economic independence, social prestige, and advancement to positions of power as commissioned officers with access to senior white authorities. After white resistance to service in the colony's armed forces culminated in an antimilitia revolt in 1768 and 1769, the presence of free soldiers of color in Saint-Domingue's military assumed even greater significance. On the eve of the Haitian Revolution, free men of color made up more than half of the colony's militia companies. The *maréchaussée* (rural police force) was made up exclusively of free Black noncommissioned officers and rank-and-file patrolmen. In addition, the men served in regular French army units and on French naval vessels. In view of the colonial military's heavy reliance on its free Black armed defenders, Officer Antoine-Pierre d'Aquin and his white cohorts necessarily cultivated mutually advantageous relationships with their subordinates of color. For the d'Aquin family, one such relationship would result in an intergenerational alliance with crucial implications for New Orleans.[12]

In 1760, d'Aquin wed Marguerite-Charlotte Bizoton, the daughter of Charles-Nicholas Bizoton, first secretary of the colony's governor, Comte de Blinac. By the time of their marriage, Saint-Domingue had developed one of the world's most profitable and deadly slave regimes. With direct access to Atlantic trade routes in the colony's North Province, planters filled the region's fertile plains with sprawling sugarcane plantations and amassed fortunes on the backs of enslaved West African workers. For the forced laborers, the consequences were devastating.

One-third to one-half of Africans, weakened by the trauma of their kidnapping and transatlantic crossing, perished during the first three to eight years after their initial arrival in the colony. For those who survived, conditions worsened after 1760, as planters increasingly relocated to France. In the absence of a property owner who might have checked the excesses of a hired agent, the psychological and physical violence accelerated. Over the course of the colony's existence, Saint-Domingue's slave population never reproduced itself. By the time of the Haitian Revolution, two-thirds of Saint-Domingue's slave workers were African-born.[13]

Antoine-Pierre and Marguerite-Charlotte reaped their profits from the cotton and indigo crops cultivated by their enslaved laborers in the West Province. On their Grande-Place and Petite-Place plantations in the jurisdiction of Saint-Marc, a port city surrounded by a fertile plain on the Artibonite River, the couple raised a large family of eight children and were reputed to be among the wealthiest planters in le bas d'Artibonite (lower Artibonite) district.

In terms of social standing, the d'Aquins ranked among Saint-Domingue's most respected eighteenth-century colonial families. By the time of the Haitian Revolution in 1791, however, patriarch Antoine-Pierre had been living in France for more than a decade. Family history fell surprisingly silent regarding his whereabouts. Not until 1870, after traveling to France, did Allain uncover the circumstances surrounding her great-grandfather's fate. In a startling discovery in a French archive, she learned of his near-death experience and his medical exile in France. His debilitating injuries occurred during the reign of King Louis XV (1715–1774) when the Seven Years' War (1756–1763) and its repercussions threatened the colony.

In the tumultuous years surrounding the war, Antoine-Pierre had been dispatched to Aquin, a port settlement founded by his family in the South Province, the colony's least developed region. His wife and three young children accompanied him to the town, where on March 24, 1771, Marguerite-Charlotte gave birth to Charles-Pierre, Allain's grandfather. With its proximity to British Jamaica, Aquin and its neighboring settlements were especially vulnerable to attack. Antoine-Pierre may have been injured during the war, when the British blockaded the French colonies, seized Guadeloupe and Martinique, and threatened Saint-Domingue.

His wounds also may have occurred during the postwar years, when French imperial officials proposed mandatory service for all free men in the despised colonial militia, a change that whites denounced as "slavery." Free Black militiamen, perceiving in the onerous new policies a far-reaching legal and social campaign to divide colonial society by race rather than by family and wealth, feared a "return to slavery." In the South and West Provinces, the government decrees provoked colonists to take up arms in the 1768–1769 militia revolt. The most violent opposition in the South Province occurred near Aquin in the port town of Torbeck. Antoine-Pierre d'Aquin, a career officer responsible for enforcing imperial policy, may have suffered the wrath of the South's angry colonists.[14]

Whatever the circumstances, Officer d'Aquin was nearly killed in a military engagement. He suffered "seventeen wounds and [was] left buried in a ditch for fifteen minutes. Taken out of there half dead with his skull cracked by a sword, he never fully recovered his health." He spent the remainder of his time in Saint-Domingue on his West Province properties in the lower Artibonite region, where "he became unreasonably obsessed with embellishing and improving his plantation[s]; he tried to channel a river and spent so much money that his wife [Marguerite-Charlotte Bizoton], very reluctantly . . . took away his control of their common funds. Soon the air of France was deemed necessary by doctors." He was dispatched to Toulouse in the south of France around 1778 and awarded a pension of 3,000 livres by King Louis XVI. Once again, he "threw money out the window," with the result that the French government threatened to reduce his subsidy. At that point, a Toulouse relative of Saint-Dominguan merchant Pierre DuBourg intervened on d'Aquin's behalf.[15]

The DuBourg/d'Aquin family alliance, it appears, had begun in Aquin during the Seven Years' War, when both families lived in the South Province town. Pierre DuBourg's son, Louis William DuBourg, the future Bishop of Louisiana and the Two Floridas, and Allain's grandfather, Charles-Pierre, were both born in Aquin, in 1766 and 1771, respectively. In Toulouse, the alliance prompted a member of the DuBourg family to take up Pierre-Antoine's cause. According to Allain, "Mme la Présidente du Bourg" safeguarded Antoine-Pierre's pension and likely arranged for his residence in an Albi monastery in the Languedoc region of France, where he died in 1801.[16]

Allain's maternal great-great grandparents, Etienne Marafret Lessard and Hélène Fasende, like Antoine-Benoist d'Aquin and Jeanne-Renée Garnier, began their quest for wealth and influence in colonial Louisiana. Lessard's skill in trading with the Native Americans in present-day Rapides Parish proved highly lucrative. In 1770, Spanish governor Alejandro O'Reilly appointed him commandant of the Rapides district. When their daughter was born, the couple named her Hélène Lessard. Thus, Hélène d'Aquin bore the name of her maternal forebears.[17]

When Hélène Lessard came of age, she married Pierre Desmortiers. In Saint-Domingue, the couple prospered as coffee planters in the Plaisance and Grande Rivière Parishes in the colony's North Province. Much of the world's sugar and coffee passed through the colony's most important port city, the nearby Cap Français.[18]

The d'Aquin and Desmortiers family fortunes, like the enormous wealth of Saint-Domingue itself, derived from the labor of enslaved West Africans and their descendants. By the time of the 1789 French Revolution, the Caribbean colony's 405,500 slave workers constituted approximately 90 percent of Saint-Domingue's total population, with another 21,808 free people of color nearly equaling a population of 27,717 whites. In an age of mounting democratic fervor, planter riches like those of Allain's predecessors rested upon a dangerously fragile foundation.

Two years after Parisian masses stormed the Bastille in 1789, enslaved Saint-Dominguans dealt the colony a staggering blow when they assaulted the heart of the regime in an attack that commenced the Haitian Revolution. In one of the most sweeping revolutions in modern history, their actions transformed the colony's enslaved majority into free and independent citizens, created the second independent nation in the Americas, and lifted the hopes of enslaved men and women throughout the Americas. Their 1804 victory marked the beginning of the end of slavery in the western hemisphere.[19]

On August 22, 1791, Boukman "Zamba" Dutty, a charismatic slave leader, signaled the onset of the revolution with a lightning military strike near the port city of Cap Français. His well-coordinated assault, planned and executed through the agency of *vaudoux* (voodoo), swept through the colony's North Province "like a torrent." By early September, most of the plantations in the wealth-producing province's twenty-seven parishes, including the Desmortiers's coffee-growing properties in Plaisance and Grande Rivière, had been destroyed. Allain's family barely escaped rebel forces.[20]

Drawing on her grandmother Marie-Anne-Elisabeth Desmortiers's family recollections, Allain narrated the events surrounding the escape of her great-grandmother Hélène Lessard Desmortiers, her grandmother Marie-Anne-Elisabeth, and Dédé-Sophie, her grandmother's enslaved childhood companion:

One of her [Hélène Lessard Desmortiers's] daughters, my grandmother [Marie-Anne-Elisabeth Desmortiers], had been given a young *négrite* [Dédé-Sophie] as a present according to the custom of the colonies; the girls may have been born on the same day since they were the same age. This child was one of the faithful *nègres* who had warned their masters, hurriedly and at their own risk, that the murderers were coming. While the latter massacred, pillaged, and set fires, the poor women fled through the fields, hidden by the tall cane and protected by devoted servants who would have shielded them with their bodies.[21]

They reached what was most likely the Grande Rivière, where a rescue boat awaited them. When the enslaved men and women who had led their enslavers to safety realized they were to be abandoned, a desperate scene ensued: "Immediately, shrill cries rise from the group of faithful blacks who disappear and must, in turn, seek rescue in the tall grasses and the bays on the coast."[22] Only the slave child Dédé-Sophie remained at the water's edge:

A young négresse [Dédé-Sophie] is left alone on the shore: she calls
to her little mistress [Marie-Anne-Elisabeth Desmortiers], she wants
to follow her, she begs that they take her also . . . "pour piti mam'zelle
blanc là . . . mo oulé couri, avé li . . . li mo piti maîtresse!" [for the little
white mademoiselle . . . I want to go with her . . . She's my dear little
mistress!]. The sailors don't hear her or don't understand. Ferocious
cries warn of the approaching rogues who have just set fire to the plantation. . . . Desperate, the child throws herself into the water and swims
toward the fleeing fugitives. The brave sailors, touched by this sight and
moved by my grandmother's tears—I imagine her reaching out to her
poor servant—change course and, with a few vigorous strokes of their
oars, reach the small black body of the valiantly advancing girl.[23]

The sailors plucked Dédé-Sophie from the sea and rowed to the rescue vessel.
The two young girls would remain together for the rest of their lives.

The rescue ship, once under way, was overtaken by Spanish pirates, the
"scum of the sea." The fate of the prisoners "promised to be horrible. Men
killed, women sold to plantations on the island of Cuba to till the land like
slaves." They were rescued, however, when a British warship overtook the pirate vessel, freed the prisoners, and transported Marie-Anne-Elisabeth Desmortiers, Dédé-Sophie, and the other refugees to Kingston in the British colony of Jamaica.[24]

In Saint-Domingue, the 1791 insurrection soon spread to the West Province's lower Artibonite region, where Allain's great-grandmother, Marguerite-
Charlotte Bizoton d'Aquin, had managed her large family and two plantations
after her husband's departure. As with the Desmortiers household, their enslaved workers alerted the d'Aquins to the approach of rebel forces. They fled,
it appears, to the Artibonite River which formed the southern border of one
of their plantations:

My great-grandmother, Mme d'Aquin, aided by devoted nègres, fled
with her children. She managed to reach the shore and to board a British rowboat ready to rescue the fugitives, but her two sons, in spite of
following her closely, were not so lucky. Pierre, the eldest and a navy
guard, was shot by the howling hordes. The rescue boat had to get away
. . . and my grandfather was left alone between his brother's corpse and
the sea into which he did not hesitate to plunge.[25]

Pierre-François, an aide-de-camp to General Viscount de Fontanges in nearby Saint-Marc, died instantaneously. His brother, Charles-Pierre (Allain's grandfather), barely escaped: "An excellent swimmer, he dove with determination, taking off his overcoat which, afloat on top of the water, drew the nègres' attention and gave him some breathing space. Diving again, he took off his vest and fooled the bandits once again, and so on, letting his clothes attract the bullets that fell all around him while he swam toward the British ship." In their flight, Allain concluded, Marguerite-Charlotte Bizoton d'Aquin's "numerous [eight] children, at least seventeen they say," were dispersed. As a consequence, Allain speculated, "we must have cousins in New York and undoubtedly, in other cities of the American Union."[26]

After Allain's maternal grandmother, Marie-Anne-Elisabeth Desmortiers, escaped to Jamaica with her family and Dédé-Sophie, she was wed at a very young age to her first cousin, François-Raymond-Alexis Desmortiers. She saw little of her husband, who was studying in Europe. When the French Revolution brought an abrupt halt to his education, he was assigned to Saint-Domingue as a French officer. He perished in the Haitian Revolution after drinking from a spring poisoned by insurgents.

Widowed at the age of fourteen, Marie-Anne-Elisabeth Desmortiers was soon remarried to a fellow refugee, Dr. Jean-Paul Daron. In Saint-Domingue, he and his brother Dr. George-Paul Daron were French military surgeons, and though they and the Desmortiers family had escaped the revolution, they had not escaped its repercussions. Inspired by the initial 1791 revolt in Saint-Domingue's North Province, enslaved Jamaicans included songs of the rebel assault in their arsenal of resistance, an arsenal that included, as elsewhere in the Caribbean, poison. In Jamaica, Marie-Anne-Elisabeth Desmortiers's half-brother, Georges Martin des Pallières, and her brother-in-law, Dr. George-Paul Daron, suffered the same fate as her first husband. Slave insurgents poisoned both men. Their actions portended the advance of revolutionary aspirations in the British Caribbean.[27]

In revolutionary Saint-Domingue, meanwhile, the youngest brother of Allain's grandfather, Charles-Louis d'Aquin, remained in the colony after his family's 1791 flight. Born in the port city of Saint-Marc in Saint-Domingue's West Province in 1777 and destined to follow his father and brothers into colonial military service, he was only fourteen when the revolution began. After the departure of his mother and other members of his family, he served as an officer in the French National Guard. D'Aquin and his neighboring planter allies apparently believed, like most slave owners, that the revolution was only a temporary crisis. They fully expected to retain their properties and resume their business affairs when the rebellion subsided.

In the West Province, as in Aquin and other frontier regions, conditions yielded mixed-race families of European men and African women whose off-spring were accepted as French colonists to the extent that they prospered as planters and soldiers. At the time of the revolution, extensive racial mixing in the West Province would explain why the d'Aquin family and other prop-ertied whites exercised a relative degree of flexibility on racial issues, with Saint-Marc being counted among the colony's least prejudiced districts. Pop-ulation distribution and security considerations also played a role in the area's racial dynamics. The West possessed 168,000 slaves and the most evenly bal-anced free population in the colony, with twelve thousand free people of color and fourteen thousand whites. And as elsewhere in the French colony, the d'Aquins and other members of the white ruling elite relied almost exclusively on free men of color for their safety.[28]

At some distance from the ruthlessly capitalistic sugar plantations worked by armies of slave laborers on the colony's northern plain, the west part of the island initially escaped the massive 1791 slave revolt that swept the North Province. Notwithstanding the rebel assault on one of the d'Aquin family's plantations, the Artibonite slave regime remained largely intact during the Haitian Revolution's early years. The majority of slaves continued to work the area's plantations, and most of the planters returned—if they had ever even left. In the Petite Rivière region, members of the d'Aquin family, as well as allied families on neighboring properties, such as the d'Eynauts (also Deynaut or Deynaud) and branches of the Rossignol-Desdunes families, among others, remained on their plantations.

The Artibonite slave resistance initially took the form of work stoppages and violations of plantation discipline. In at least two instances, slave laborers in the region forced their despised managers off the premises and replaced them with Black managers of their own choosing, the free men of color Enard and Philipeau. In a 1792 letter to the absentee owner of the indigo and sugar plantations, Madame de Mauger, in France, the enslaved asserted their rights in the extraordinary turn of events created by the 1791 revolt: "We are slaves and your subjects, and we give ourselves over to work as we should, but hu-manity must interest itself in our fate."[29]

In the new revolutionary context, free men of color in the West and South

Provinces likewise challenged their oppression. They demanded equality and attacked the colony's racial hierarchy in a series of hard-fought political and military engagements. Led by the skilled political strategist Pierre Pinchinat and military commanders André Rigaud and Louis-Jacques Bauvais, both educated in France, their successes produced results.

Their victories, together with the revolution's increasing momentum in the north, persuaded white conservatives to approve the Concordat of October 1791 proclaiming full racial equality for "citoyens de couleur." Though fierce resistance continued, the accord won converts among wealthy rural whites and conservative men of color desperate to protect their plantations. By December 1791, Saint-Marc's governing body had concluded that "only a perfect union between the white citizens and the citizens of color" could spare Saint-Domingue from "dangers that may bring about its complete ruin."[30]

The Artibonite's free signatory of color to the Concordat, Charles Savary *aîné* (Sr.), a native of Saint-Marc,[31] joined veterans of the American Revolution André Rigaud, Alexandre Pétion, and Louis-Jacques Bauvais, along with other influential leaders of color, in signing the agreement. Savary's action led to the creation in spring 1792 of an interracial self-governing body, the Conseil de Paix et d'Union de Saint-Marc, encompassing the Saint-Marc, Petite Rivière, Vérettes, and Gonaïves Parishes. With Savary as Saint-Marc's mayor, the alliance of slaveholding whites and free men of color achieved a temporary reprieve from revolutionary upheaval.[32]

In the Artibonite, a long-standing mutually beneficial relationship existed between Mayor Savary, a lieutenant colonel in the French army in his late fifties, and Charles-Louis d'Aquin and his family. Both Savary and d'Aquin were natives of Saint-Marc and descendants of prestigious, old-line colonial families. In prerevolutionary Saint-Domingue, the strength of patronage relationships between free officers of color and their white military superiors had favored the advancement of men of color. Now, Savary's military leadership and astute political skills in a world turned upside down would benefit the young d'Aquin and his family in the new, revolutionized circumstances. Savary's sons, Joseph Savary *fils* (Jr.) and Belton Savary, together with Sylvain (Silvano) d'Aquin, a Saint-Marc-born free man of color, fortified the network.

The extent of racial mixing in Saint-Domingue's West Province, together with subsequent events, points to kinship ties between Sylvain and the d'Aquin family. The reciprocal links between the Savary and d'Aquin families persisted even after the Haitian Revolution forced them all into exile. In Louisiana, their combined talents would prove decisive in the region's defenses. The d'Aquin/ Savary alliance remained consequential for the rest of the men's lives.

In November 1792, when the French Republic's new civil commissaire, Étiénne Polvérel, arrived in Saint-Marc, military leaders of color like Mayor Savary exerted a dominant political influence in the region. In their patronage relationships with lower-class people of color and the enslaved, the colony's military officers of color, the leading manumitters of slaves, were well-positioned to assume leadership roles in the tumultuous circumstances.

Their success made a favorable impression on both Polvérel and Léger Félicité Sonthonax, two of the three French commissaires tasked with implementing an April 4 decree signed into law by Louis XVI. The new mandate granted full citizenship rights to free people of color. Polvérel, assigned to govern the West Province, was impressed by Savary's allegiance to republican France and his support for the commissaire's gradualist plans for slavery's abolition.[33]

Polvérel's all-encompassing approach to general emancipation involved freeing enslaved people who enlisted in the French army and those who remained on sequestered plantations. On the rural properties, the newly liberated laborers would work for a share of the profits, acquire a voice in the management of the plantations, and share the use of animals, land, and buildings with their former enslavers. In a detailed agricultural code, Polvérel spelled out work schedules, distribution of profits, and economic penalties for violations of employment. At the same time, he extended a general invitation to planters like the d'Aquins and d'Eynauts to voluntarily liberate their slaves. In the West, plantation owners ostensibly acquiesced.

In the end, administrative chaos and military necessity doomed Polvérel's efforts in the North and West Provinces. In the more remote South Province, however, the commissaire's agricultural system would later prove highly effective under General André Rigaud, whom Polvérel named interim governor-general of the province upon his 1794 departure for France. By 1796, however, the stability Rigaud had achieved in the South Province aroused the suspicions of French commissaire Sonthonax, who feared the South Province's increasing independence and suspected Rigaud of reestablishing slavery. When Sonthonax dispatched provocateurs to the region, plantation workers rioted against the agitators. Until 1799, plantation profits from the South Province supported Rigaud's military operations and the province's political stability.

On August 29, 1793, with France's military hold on Saint-Domingue nearing collapse, Sonthonax proclaimed immediate emancipation in the North Province in a bid to persuade the region's insurgent slaves to join the French war effort. Earlier in the year, the revolutionary French Republic had declared war on Britain and Spain. On October 31, Polvérel liberated the slaves in the South and West Provinces, thereby ending slavery in all of Saint-Domingue. In February 1794, revolutionary France abolished slavery throughout its colonies.[34]

During the 1790s, the commissaires' actions reverberated throughout the United States, with white refugees excoriating them in newspapers from Boston to South Carolina. The despotic actions of the two "republican traitors," a white exile in New York contended, had turned their world upside down by favoring free men of color over whites and abolishing slavery. The attacks continued into the nineteenth century. In Louisiana, in 1810, a group of planter exiles persuaded the Superior Court of the Territory of Orleans to disbar attorney Pierre Dormenon, a white refugee himself. As an ally of Polvérel and Sonthonax, the planters alleged, Dormenon had "headed, aided and assisted the negroes of St. Domingo [Haiti], in their horrible massacres, and other outrages against the whites, in and about the year 1793."[35]

In early 1793, Spanish forces swept into the colony in the North Province while British invaders attacked the South Province at Jérémie. With the November approach of British and Spanish armies, Mayor Savary's Conseil de Paix et d'Union disintegrated, with a majority of wealthy whites and planters of color capitulating to the British. Another faction of free Black slaveholders and poorer people of color surrendered to the Spanish owing to Spain's comparatively liberal racial policies.

During the crisis, Savary called a parish meeting, which was dominated by 150 of the poorer residents of color. They refused to accept British rule on the basis of their "manifested desire to remain French subjects and to continue under the ancient standard of that nation." The showdown ended when the British sailed into the harbor. The rank-and-file soldiers manning the Saint-Marc garrison, desperate for pay and supplies, had little choice but to capitulate. Their officers, including Savary it appears, refused to surrender and fled the city to join the republican resistance. The British raised the Union Jack over Saint-Marc on December 12, 1793.[36]

Deposed Mayor Savary and d'Aquin, a second lieutenant in a dragoon company in 1794, fought the invaders in the French Republic's desegregated National Guard. They and their allies were among the staunch French republicans who defended the Artibonite region from British and Spanish forces. By the fall of 1794, their forces had succeeded in dislodging the Spaniards and holding their ground against the British. However, by May 1797, when the British evacuated the region through the heavily damaged port of Saint-Marc, the Artibonite had been reduced to a no-man's-land. The devastation and a looming civil war persuaded Charles-Louis d'Aquin and most of his neighbors to evacuate. At least two planters, members of the Desdunes-Poincy and Desdunes-Lachicotte families, refused to leave. They were later killed when Jean-Jacques Dessalines's revolutionary army swept through Petite Rivière in resistance to Napoleon Bonaparte's campaign to restore slavery to Saint-Domingue.[37]

Prior to 1797 and Bonaparte's rise to power, d'Aquin's status as a young officer under the French Republic would appear to have put him on the side of freedom and equality. France's revolutionary government abolished slavery in all its colonies in 1794, declared all men of color (freedmen as well as free men) to be citizens, and eliminated racial labels. Under the authority of the French National Guard, officers like d'Aquin commanded men of color as well as the whites who served alongside them. Until overcome by foreign invaders, d'Aquin may even have been among the planters who, together with Mayor Savary, favored Commissiare Polverel's gradualist plan of emancipation. As he prepared to emigrate to Louisiana, however, d'Aquin readied as many as twenty-five enslaved workers for departure. For d'Aquin, as for his planter family, economic self-interest trumped the French Republic's founding ideals. In New Orleans, he would continue to rely on enslaved laborers to advance his economic interests.

In 1798, d'Aquin and his fellow refugees left Saint-Domingue on a ship bound for Louisiana, in seas swarming with English, Spanish, and US freebooters who preyed upon fleeing refugees. As in the experience of the Desmortiers family, their vessel was overtaken by pirates. In the case of the d'Aquins, the renegade ship was a British corsair. Typically, the Englishmen who captured their vessel would have robbed them of their material possessions and their slaves. It is unlikely that the d'Aquin party was an exception to the rule. Most French refugees who escaped to North America were robbed at least once by British pirates. Instead of permitting the captive vessel to continue to Louisiana, the corsairs forced it into Jamaica.[38]

In exile in Kingston, the social center of the island's Saint-Domingue population, Charles-Louis d'Aquin reunited with his mother, Marguerite-Charlotte d'Aquin, and his siblings. On May 25, 1801, he married his Petite Rivière neighbor Célinie Adelaïde d'Eynaut. And at the request of his brother Charles-Pierre d'Aquin, he acted as the Catholic *parrain* (godfather) for Charles-Pierre's first son and Allain's father, Louis-Charles d'Aquin, born in 1801 in Kingston.

Early in 1804, Charles-Louis d'Aquin once again set out for Louisiana, aboard a ship carrying his mother, Marguerite-Charlotte Bizoton (Allain's great-grandmother), and a large company of more than two dozen family members, including his two brothers Pierre-Thomas and François-Louis and his sister Elisabeth-Charlotte-Antoinette "Bonne" d'Aquin, the widow of Jean Louis de Rossignol-Desdunes. Charles-Louis's sister-in-law, Marie-Josephine Alix d'Eynaut, and her husband, Théodat Camille Bruslé, as well as allied members of the Rossignol-Desdunes family, also joined the large company of passengers setting out for Louisiana. Charles-Louis's eldest surviving brother and Allain's grandfather, Charles-Pierre, remained in Jamaica for the rest of his life.[39]

At the time of their departure from Jamaica, the d'Aquins' transatlantic familial and social network, together with its economic and institutional ties, extended from the Caribbean to Louisiana, the US Atlantic seaboard, and France. Their ancestral roots in colonial Louisiana, along with the support of their fellow exiles and sympathetic Creole Louisianians, would enable the d'Aquins to rebound from their reduced circumstances. They would also benefit from events in France, where six thousand exiled planters clamored for government indemnification of their losses in the Haitian Revolution. The d'Aquin, Desmotiers, Daron, DuBourg, and allied families would be awarded compensation after 1825, when French King Charles X slapped a massive indemnity of 150 million francs on the new nation of Haiti.

In the hemisphere's second independent nation, where revolutionaries had ended slavery in the preeminent achievement of the Age of Revolution, the costs were disastrous. Historian Laurent Dubois has aptly characterized the indemnity as "a fine for revolution." The king made full recognition of the new nation's independence contingent upon payment of the indemnity to France. The sum included the capital invested in the planters' former slaves as well as their plantations. The crippling payments impoverished the new nation and led to a cycle of indebtedness to French banks that lasted into the twentieth century.[40]

By the time d'Aquin and his wife set out for New Orleans, the revolutionary tide had swept deep into south Louisiana. After 1790, republican partisans blanketed the region, appearing "in the smallest outposts, among the clergy, in all the city's taverns, and among the immigrant merchant community. They were French, Saint-Dominguan, and locally bred. They were white, brown, and black. Their precise contact with and influence among the slaves, though unknown, was a source of numerous nightmares." By July 1793, Spanish authorities had deported sixty-eight Frenchmen suspected of fomenting rebellion.[41]

Within the free Black militia, defiant expressions of solidarity with French and Saint-Domingue revolutionaries were an equally troubling development for colonial officials. In New Orleans in 1791, Spanish authorities questioned an officer in the Spanish colonial militia, free man of color Pierre Bailly, for praising Saint-Domingue's Black revolutionaries. Bailly was reportedly awaiting word from Saint-Domingue to strike a blow like the insurgent attack on Cap-Français. In 1794, Bailly's seditious "tirades" and admiration for "the maxims of the French rebels" landed him in prison in Havana for two years.[42]

In 1795, a series of slave conspiracies ensued, with the revolutionary contagion spreading to Pointe Coupée, where the discovery of a conspiracy prompted a fearful observer to conclude: "If our information is correct, the Saint-Domingue insurrection did not have a more violent beginning." Local authorities uncovered plots at Opelousas post in February 1795 and in Pointe Coupée and along la Côte des Allemands (the German Coast) in February, March, and April 1796. Petitions from "countless inhabitants" forced Spanish authorities to shut down the entire slave trade in 1796.[43]

The victory of revolutionaries in the 1804 independence of Haiti set off another series of incidents in south Louisiana. More than a hundred planters in Pointe Coupée complained of a "spirit of Revolt and mutyny" among their slaves. In New Orleans, police arrested a white Saint-Dominguan for inciting free men of color and slaves to burn the city and massacre whites.

From 1791 onward, as events in Louisiana clearly demonstrated, the phenomenon identified by historian David P. Geggus as the "Haitian influence" had an immediate impact well beyond the borders of Saint-Domingue. "Nothing remotely comparable in magnitude or outcome," Geggus concluded, "had happened before in an American slave society. The French Revolution proclaimed the ideals of liberty and equality, but the Haitian Revolution showed African Americans that these ideals could be won by force of arms." In New Orleans and its environs, the revolution's seismic repercussions would reverberate throughout the nineteenth century.[44]

All too familiar with the forces impacting Louisiana, refugees Charles-Louis d'Aquin and Célinie Adelaïde d'Eynaut resolved to remain in the city. Charles-Louis's ancestral roots in the region, his extensive web of family, military, and business alliances, Louisiana's slave economy, and the prospect of opportunity after the 1803 Louisiana Purchase contributed to their decision. In an early step toward rebuilding his life in a new home, Charles-Louis enlisted in the Bataillon d'Orléans, a volunteer white militia reorganized in 1805 by the territorial legislature. Not coincidentally, d'Aquin family ally Pierre-François DuBourg commanded the battalion. He was the son of Pierre DuBourg and brother of Louis William DuBourg, the future Catholic bishop of Louisiana.

Pierre-François DuBourg's efforts to extend his network of business and political alliances were well under way when Charles-Louis enlisted in the elite Francophone battalion. Like the d'Aquins, the DuBourgs were refugees of the Haitian Revolution, had owned property in Petite Rivière, and were allied to the Bruslé family. In New Orleans, Pierre-François DuBourg was, by 1804, a successful businessman with a stake in the African slave trade and influence in high places.

Barely a year after the US Senate's ratification of the Louisiana Purchase, DuBourg requested territorial governor W. C. C. Claiborne's permission to disembark between forty and sixty Africans in Baton Rouge. Claiborne agreed to the request on a conditional basis despite a March 1804 congressional ban on the importation into the territory of slaves from foreign countries. As Claiborne explained to Secretary of State James Madison, DuBourg was a "respectable Merchant" who could be expected to abide by the federal government's ultimate decision in the matter.[45]

DuBourg's efforts to extend his financial interests through family alliances proved especially successful when he married his young daughter Louise Elizabeth Algaé DuBourg into the family of French-born Marius Pons Bringier, the patriarch of one of Louisiana's wealthiest planter families. Seeking fortune and influence, the two ambitious men had immigrated to Louisiana from the Caribbean and enlisted in the region's military forces. After arriving from Martinique in 1783, Bringier served Spain as an officer in Louisiana's provincial army, and by 1805 DuBourg commanded the city's Bataillon d'Orléans.

Abbé William DuBourg sealed the DuBourg–Bringier alliance when he negotiated the betrothal of Pierre-François DuBourg's nine-year-old daughter, Louise Elizabeth Algaé, to Bringier's seventeen-year-old son, Michel Doradou Bringier. The agreement occurred not long after the teenager first met the young girl in 1807. Arranged marriages, a common practice among Catholics in the Caribbean as well as New Orleans, ensured that property and other assets remained within allied French-speaking families and their descendants.

In 1810, the DuBourg–Bringier alliance deepened when Pierre-François joined with Marius Pons Bringier's French son-in-law, Noel Auguste Baron Jr., to found the DuBourg & Bringier firm, a business in which the two men acted as commission agents for the region's planter elite. In 1812, at the time of now fourteen-year-old Algaé DuBourg's marriage to twenty-two-year-old Doradou Bringier, Abbé William DuBourg's dramatic rescue of Marius Pons Bringier's eldest son reinforced family ties. Authorities in Spanish Mexico had arrested Paul-Louis Bringier, seized his substantial Mexican estate, and condemned him to death. The draconian sentence likely stemmed from his association with Mexico's independence movement. Abbé DuBourg, acting through the offices of the Catholic Church, secured Paul-Louis Bringier's release in exchange for a large ransom.[46]

Not surprisingly, the DuBourg–Bringier alliance extended to the d'Aquin family. In 1810, patriarch Marius Pons Bringier stood as godfather at the baptismal font for Charles-Louis d'Aquin and Céline Adelaïde d'Eynaut's baby girl, Marie Thérèse. In some instances, affluent godparents like the Bringiers would virtually adopt their godchildren, thereby assuming financial responsibility for the child's upbringing and education. For enslaved infants in colonial New Orleans, godparentage occasionally led to freedom when slaveholders stood as their godparents. As with marriage, godparentage sustained the cohesiveness of Francophone populations.[47]

Despite Charles-Louis d'Aquin's association with highly successful businessmen like Pierre-François DuBourg and Marius Pons Bringier, his own business dealings proceeded along a chaotic trajectory. Soon after his arrival in New Orleans, he acquired a number of French Quarter properties on Toulouse and Royal Streets, possibly with the aim of launching a brokerage firm. Buying, selling, and managing properties yielded sizable fortunes for astute nineteenth-century businessmen. Whatever d'Aquin's inclinations, his frequent financial reversals doomed his future as a broker.

One of his initial ventures, in 1804, involved the purchase of a large bakehouse on the corner of Royal and Dumaine Streets, equipped with "all the belongings and constructions and bakery utensils." At the time, bakeries were one of the city's most lucrative businesses and a number of investors had achieved considerable wealth within only a few years. A bakery in the residential and commercial heart of the French Quarter promised a quick return. For d'Aquin, however, the quick return didn't materialize.[48]

In the midst of an 1807 citywide upsurge in arson attacks and slave escapes, the d'Aquin bakehouse burned. In the fiery chaos, enslaved bakery workers Théodore and Télémaque fled. The desperate twenty-four-year-old Télémaque, of the "Congo nation," escaped chained to "un nabot," with a burn to his left knee. The flight of the two men, together with the fire, nearly ruined d'Aquin. Facing bankruptcy, he attempted a partnership with Claudius Guillaud that guaranteed fresh bread from the "best flour that can be procured." In 1808, when the second bakery failed, d'Aquin's creditors seized the business.[49]

With the support of his extensive family network, d'Aquin rebounded from his loss to confront a new challenge. Beginning in May 1809 and through the early months of 1810, more than ten thousand Saint-Dominguan refugees nearly doubled the size of the city after Spain expelled them from Cuba. Skilled craftsmen, both white and free workers of color, constituted a large proportion of the new arrivals, with artisan bakers among the most common category of tradesmen. Their presence introduced a more competitive phase of the bakery business.[50]

Enslaved refugee field workers also made their presence felt. Within a year of the enormous migration, the Haitian Revolution's impact reverberated once again when hundreds of Saint-Dominguan, African, and Louisiana plantation workers revolted. They were likely emboldened by events in the Viceroyalty of New Spain (Mexico) in 1810, where just four months earlier the Catholic priest Miguel Hidalgo led a popular revolt that achieved an impressive victory against royalist forces at Guanajuato. On December 6, Hidalgo proclaimed the abolition of slavery from the Palace of Government in Guadalajara. The sensational news spread rapidly through communication networks developed by Gulf Coast slaves. Approximately a month after Hidalgo's proclamation, enslaved Black insurgents likewise struck a blow for freedom in south Louisiana.[51]

On January 8, 1811, on the German Coast's volatile sugarcane plantations, Charles, an enslaved *commandeur* widely believed to be of Saint-Domingue origin, led a rebellion on the east bank of the Mississippi River, just thirty-five miles upriver from New Orleans.[52] Though he was enslaved on the Deslondes Plantation, owned by widow Anne Baude Paumet Deslondes, Charles launched the rebellion from the sugar plantation of Manuel Andry, the largest slaveholder in St. John the Baptist Parish. At the head of an insurgent army of enslaved Louisianians, Saint-Dominguans, and West-Central Africans like the Congolese leader Jupiter, Charles led his army south after killing two whites. The insurrectionists surged forward with shouts of "On to Orleans!," with as many as five hundred men and women joining their march.[53]

Panicked white residents of the upriver parishes entered New Orleans with descriptions of their escape from "a miniature representation of the horrors of St. Domingo." The threat of attack prompted Governor Claiborne to place the city under martial law. In the crisis, he accepted the services of the port's merchant seamen. His actions with regard to the officially abandoned battalion of color are less clear. In correspondence to Secretary of State James Madison, Claiborne claimed that he had accepted the services of one company of free Black militiamen and placed them under the authority of Pierre-François Du-Bourg, the commanding officer of the white Bataillon d'Orléans.

Claiborne's letter noted that the militiamen of color "performed with great exactitude and propriety a Tour of duty," suggesting that the men had helped to suppress the revolt. But as historian Kenneth R. Aslakson observes, the militiamen probably never left New Orleans. Rather, Claiborne's praise was intended to soothe the fears of the national government. Their assignment, Aslakson convincingly concludes, involved "simply standing on guard and being prepared to defend the city." With regard to the merchant seamen, Claiborne assigned a contingent of the men to the city while another company of mariners joined the troops of US Army general Wade Hampton, the commander in chief of US troops in the Southern Division. Hampton, the owner of a number of Louisiana plantations, set out on the evening of January 9 to suppress the rebellion.[54]

The insurgents, armed with farming tools and only a few guns, were no match for their opponents. On January 11, the local militia and US Army troops captured Charles and crushed the rebellion, less than three days after it began. The on-the-scene report counted sixty-six slaves killed, seventeen missing, and sixteen taken prisoner, noting that patrols were still finding "beaucoup de cadavres" (many corpses). Charles's captors subjected him to a savage execution in which his hands were severed and his thighs were shot through to break his legs. While still alive, he was rolled in straw and set ablaze. His body was decapitated and his head was sent to Manuel Andre's Woodlawn plantation, where the revolt had begun.[55]

In London, the *Times* expressed horror at the extent of the carnage: "They shot every man of colour that came in their way; the slaughter was immense."

Commentary in a Louisiana newspaper shed light on the nature of the ferocious white backlash: "We are sorry to learn that a ferocious sanguinary disposition marked the character of some of the inhabitants. Civilized man ought to remember well his standing, and never let himself sink down to a level with the savage; our laws are summary enough and let them govern."[56]

Claiborne addressed two pleas of leniency to St. Charles parish tribunal member Jean-Noël Destrehan in the ensuing prosecutions. As the governor was aware, the grisly punishments meted out to Vincent Ogé and his allies in their failed 1790 revolt in Saint-Domingue had driven the volatile slave colony toward revolution.[57] When Claiborne did not receive a reply from his first letter, he forwarded a second on January 19, calling once again for restraint: "Justice, policy, our future safety required that the guilty should suffer; for the sake of humanity however it is greatly to be desired, that the list of the guilty may not be found still greater. . . . I have therefore only to repeat to you, that in all cases where crcumstances suggest the exercise of mercy a recommendation to that effect from the Court and Jury, will induce the Governor to extend to the convict a pardon."[58]

Destrehan did not reply. In the end, twenty-one suspected rebels were convicted and executed. Their corpses were decapitated and the severed heads were exposed on pikes at intervals from the German Coast to New Orleans to terrorize enslaved laborers into submission. The horrific violence resolved nothing. Slave resistance in St. John the Baptist and St. Charles Parishes on Christmas Eve 1811 sent panicked whites into flight once again, while Black New Orleanians exhibited "a disposition to rise in Insurrection."[59]

In strife-ridden south Louisiana, the 1811 revolt, together with cycles of arson attacks, slave escapes, conspiracies, and other forms of resistance, contributed to the current of white fear that was endemic to the region as long as slavery lasted. Memories of the 1811 slave revolt also ran deep within the German Coast's African American communities. In 1923, elderly Black residents of the region "related the story of the insurrection of 1811 as they heard it from their grandfathers." In present-day Louisiana, the insurgency's German Coast descendants still commemorate the men and women whose resistance to slavery produced the largest slave rebellion in the United States. Despite the savagery with which their revolt was suppressed, their cause endured.[60]

Another measure of revolutionary Haiti's impact in the 1809 migration involved the entry of Saint-Dominguan soldiers of color who had fought under the French Republic—a category of male refugees especially feared by white, slaveholding Louisianians. In response to their concerns, Governor Claiborne insisted on strict enforcement of an 1807 ban on the entry of all free Black males fifteen years and older, under the threat of severe penalties, including enslavement. Despite the restrictive measures, a large number of free Black veterans of revolutionary Haiti entered the region in the turmoil surrounding the influx of thousands of refugees.[61]

Their numbers included former French republican officer Joseph Savary *fils*, the son of Charles Savary, and the garrison he commanded in the Haitian Revolution. Under the French Republic, Savary had advanced to the rank of lieutenant colonel after d'Aquin's departure. In the ensuing 1799 civil war between Toussaint Louverture and André Rigaud, Louverture's conquering army forced seven hundred of Rigaud's republican soldiers into exile in Cuba. Savary's veteran garrison included men like Sévère Courtois, Marcelin Guillot, and other soldiers who were as committed to the republican cause as their commanding officer.

When Spanish authorities expelled the men from Cuba in 1809, Savary and his troops entered Louisiana through Barataria, a settlement just west of the mouth of the Mississippi River, where buccaneers Jean and Pierre Lafitte staged attacks on coastal shipping. The Lafitte brothers also transported refugees from Cuba to Louisiana, and it's likely that Savary and his men were among their passengers. After arriving, they moved westward into the Attakapas region, an area geographically linked to the Barataria enclave.[62] From there, the highly motivated veteran soldiers would go on to join overland and overseas expeditions in support of Spanish American revolutionaries. In New Orleans in the midst of those campaigns, the men would play a crucial role in defeating invading British forces in the War of 1812, under the leadership of the man they chose as their commanding officer, Charles-Louis d'Aquin.[63]

TWO

Insurgency and Invasion

Many of them [in the Battalion of Free Men of Color] have
extensive connections and much property to
defend and all seem attached to arms.
—Governor William C. C. Claiborne to
General Andrew Jackson, 1814

From throughout the revolutionary Atlantic, itinerant revolutionaries aspiring to a new world order congregated in New Orleans between 1804 and 1815. Their numbers included French republican refugees, Spanish American insurgents, republican corsairs, and free Black veterans of the Haitian Revolution whose revolutionary idealism pitted them against Europe's global powers. From Louisiana, they supported the Latin American independence movements.

Their presence coincided with a massive 1809–1810 influx of three-caste Haitian refugees who doubled the size of the city and reinforced Louisiana's tripartite Latin European racial order. When the territorial legislature attempted to impose a two-tiered race regime, relegating all Black Louisianians (both slave and free) to one of the South's harshest slave codes, a remarkable French-educated refugee judge fortified the three-tiered racial order. The dispute and its aftermath reveal an influential interracial refugee coalition that would exert an exceptional influence on ensuing events.

In the run-up to the Battle of New Orleans, General Jackson swept aside vehement objections to the recruitment of free Black soldiers. Having fought the British in the Haitian Revolution, First Major d'Aquin and Second Major Savary commanded the Second Battalion of Free Men of Color. In coordination with the white Francophone Bataillon d'Orléans, they struck a decisive blow against British forces as the enemy advanced on New Orleans.

* * *

Beginning in British North America in 1775, the revolutionary tsunamis criss-crossing the Atlantic swept high-minded exiles in all directions in the intercon-nected world of North America, Europe, the Caribbean, Africa, and Spanish America. With "their multiple and ever-shifting allegiances," according to his-torian Janet Polasky, these itinerant revolutionaries "transcended the bound-aries of the nation-state." Like the majority of refugee revolutionaries, they aspired to a new world order based on the ideals of liberty and natural rights. In New Orleans and its environs, exiled free Black veterans of the Haitian Rev-olution, disenchanted refugees of postrevolutionary France, Spanish American insurgents, and les corsairs de la liberté responded to what the French Rev-olution's Jacques-Pierre Brissot described as "le cri universel de la liberté."[1]

In the two decades after 1804, when Polasky's study ends, the revolutionary travelers who congregated in south Louisiana fit the profile of her "cosmopolitan revolutionaries." In the ongoing Age of Revolution, they recognized that new and emerging nations could not stand alone in a world dominated by Europe's global powers. It was their "holy cause," as Joseph Savary's comrade in arms Sévère Courtois viewed their objective, "to establish Independence in all the Universe." They joined in the struggle against Spain and Great Britain, anticipating that they themselves would achieve equal citizenship in return for their services.[2]

In southwest Louisiana, Savary, Courtois, and their armed corps of exiled republican soldiers found common cause with José Bernardo Gutiérrez de Lara, an unrelenting revolutionary in the cause of Mexican independence. Gutiér-rez, a former blacksmith and merchant, was a veteran of the 1810 Hidalgo re-volt led by the Catholic priest Miguel Hidalgo y Costilla. In 1812, he proposed to oust the Spanish from the province of Texas. Savary and his men marched overland with Gutiérrez in the most successful of six expeditions launched from Louisiana. After capturing San Antonio, Gutiérrez proclaimed the in-dependence of Texas and announced his intention to liberate all of Mexico.

The presence in the insurgent army of Savary's contingent of African American veterans of the Haitian Revolution raised alarm in the United States and prompted Anglo-American observers to attack Gutièrrez's legitimacy in newspapers and pamphlets in the Texas borderlands and Louisiana. In August 1813, diminished by the bad press, the expedition suffered a Spanish counter-attack that ended the short-lived Texas republic and forced the army out of Mexico. Undaunted in defeat, Gutiérrez continued his resistance to Spanish rule until 1821, when Mexico achieved its independence.[3]

Upon his return to Louisiana in 1813, Savary boldly announced his presence by offering to put a force of five hundred free soldiers of color in the service of Mexican insurgents, under the command of General Jean-Joseph-Amable Humbert, a fellow veteran of the Haitian Revolution. Like Savary, Courtois, and their comrades in arms, General Humbert had served in the French republican army in Saint-Domingue. He was a product of revolutionary France's 1793 *levée en masse*, or conscription, when a peasant from the Vosges region, like himself, could achieve promotion for success on the battlefield. Humbert rose rapidly through the ranks, and in 1798 he landed a French force in Ireland in support of the United Irish uprising. He marched ashore with pamphlets addressing the Irish as "citizens of the world" and announcing the "moment of breaking your chains [has] arrived." Humbert's combined Franco-Irish army defeated the English at the Battle of Castlebar and proclaimed the short-lived provisional government of the Republic of Connaught.

Back in France, however, Humbert's outspoken republicanism offended his commander in chief, Napoleon Bonaparte, who dispatched him to the Caribbean. In Saint-Domingue, General Victor Emanuel Leclerc, the head of the expedition, accused the republican officer of consorting with subversive elements. Fed up with Humbert's political radicalism, Bonaparte relieved him of his command. Upon his arrival in New Orleans in 1813, the French general espoused the cause of republican insurgents in Latin America and organized an expedition in support of Mexican revolutionaries in Spanish Texas.[4]

The city's Irish immigrants, ever grateful for Humbert's 1798 invasion of Ireland in support of the United Irish rebellion, gave him a hero's welcome. A spokesman for the Irish community, William Theobald Wolfe Tone, whose father, Theobald Wolfe Tone, paid with his life for his United Irish leadership, applauded the "intrepid and magnanimous Humbert," whose "name is dear to Ireland." Educated under the French Republic, the younger Tone fought, like Humbert, under Napoleon. Tone, Dr. William Flood, a "severe republican," and Jean Blanque, a former official of the French Republic, responded enthusiastically to the general's support for republican insurgents in the present-day nations of Colombia, Mexico, and Venezuela. They cheered Humbert and "those of all countries who honour the brave, and who sympathize in the feelings of a people struggling against their oppressors."[5]

In November 1813, Humbert led his New Orleans allies into Spanish Texas, where he proclaimed a Mexican republic in exile, with Spanish revolutionary Juan Mariano Picornell elected president. Lacking financial and military support, the new regime quickly failed. Back in New Orleans in 1814, Humbert assumed the office of general-in-chief of Mexico's republican armies and presided over a Mexican government in exile that included Paul-Louis Bringier. In the fall, with British forces advancing on New Orleans, Humbert, Savary's forces, Mexican field marshal Don Juan Pablo de Anaya, and Gutiérrez prepared to take part in the city's defenses. Like Gutiérrez, Anaya was a veteran of Hidalgo's 1810 revolt, the first significant blow for Mexican independence and slavery's abolition in New Spain.[6]

After Napoleon's 1814 surrender and a temporary respite from hostilities in Europe, the British turned their attention to their war with the United States. Instead of conquest, the British proposed to inflict a blow that would force their American adversary to seek peace on any terms. By mid-November, an expedition was under way to invade the nation through the Gulf of Mexico and seize control of the Mississippi River valley with the support of disaffected Native American, French, and Spanish recruits. Dominance of the river, the British calculated, would open a link to Canada and reduce the United States to an island hemmed in by their navy.[7]

With the prospect of war looming, the well-connected Pierre-François DuBourg, now an executive in the Compagnie de Navigation d'Orléans and the Compagnie d'Assurance, served as adjutant and inspector general on Governor Claiborne's staff. DuBourg's wealthy son-in-law, Doradou Bringier, and Doradou's brother, Paul-Louis Bringier, enlisted in Captain Jean-Jacques Chauveau's volunteer cavalry company. Officer Charles-Louis d'Aquin commanded a white company of *chasseurs* (light infantry soldiers) in the celebrated Bataillon d'Orléans until the fall of 1814, when sustained opposition to the city's militiamen of color erupted into a fierce public debate.[8]

The storied Latin European militia corps, a free Black institution revered by the city's African American community, originated in the 1720s when the French Company of the Indies organized semimilitary units of slaves for security purposes. At the time of the 1729 Natchez massacre, Governor Étienne Périer turned to the men for military support, promising them their freedom in return for their service. The nucleus of Louisiana's free Black militia arose from their fighting effectiveness during the campaign.

In 1739, during expeditions against the Native Americans, Governor Jean-Baptiste de Bienville's army included La Compagnie des Mulâtres et Nègres Libres de cette colonie de la Louisiane, a company of fifty free Black soldiers in the troops organized for the expedition. By the end of the French regime, the men represented a "regular company" of soldiers with their own officers, who had achieved freedom through their military service. After Spain acquired Louisiana in 1763, Alejandro O'Reilly incorporated the militiamen into the colony's security forces as the Militia Corps of Free Morenos and Pardos.

In 1779, when Spain officially sided with the American revolutionaries, the militiamen and enslaved Black New Orleanians enlisted in Governor Bernardo de Gálvez's international army. The multiethnic troops dealt the British stunning defeats at Baton Rouge, Mobile, and Pensacola. Their victories blocked enemy advances in the North American West and South. In return for their service, the governor freed the enslaved soldiers and honored the veteran militiamen with pay and commissions in the militia of color. The men and their community maintained a keen sense of pride in their ancestral legacy of military service under France and Spain.[9]

At the time of the 1803 Louisiana Purchase, the presence of three hundred Afro-Creole militiamen assembled in the Place d'Armes in the formal cession ceremonies alarmed General James Wilkinson, territorial cocommissioner with William C. C. Claiborne. He found the "formidable aspect of the armed Blacks & Malattoes [sic] officered and organized painful and perplexing." Anticipating such concerns, President Thomas Jefferson had prescribed a policy of pacification, with a view to the military corps' ultimate extinction. He directed that the "militia of colour shall be confirmed in their posts, and treated favorably, till a better settled state of things shall permit us to let them neglect themselves."[10]

As Wilkinson and Jefferson acknowledged, the battalion of self-motivated and highly disciplined free Black soldiers represented a formidable challenge. No other United States territory or state possessed an armed corps of free militiamen of color commanded by African American officers. On their own initiative, the Afro-Creole soldiers had escaped the institutional malaise that generally afflicted Spanish Louisiana's white militiamen. They were far from inclined to "neglect themselves" under their new US government. They took decisive action.

Their representatives presented Claiborne with a petition in January 1804 relating their history of achievement in the region's colonial defenses, emphasizing their military service in the American Revolution. And they identified themselves as "free citizens of Louisiana." On instructions from Washington, Claiborne responded diplomatically but took no action until early June, when he suddenly replaced the battalion's senior leaders with white officers and barred the enrollment of new recruits. The militiamen objected. Above all, they expressed their desire to be "commanded by people of their own color."[11]

On June 21, in an action designed to pacify the men and their community,

Claiborne presented the battalion with a stand of colors. They were not appeased. In early July, Afro-Creole leaders challenged their exclusion from a citizens' meeting in which white New Orleanians proposed to draft a memorial to Congress asserting their rights. In response, the men of color proposed to draft their own congressional petition to "consult as to *their* rights." Their assertiveness infuriated their white opponents, who demanded punishment of the document's author.[12]

Claiborne, always conscious of potential revolutionary upheaval in the Caribbean, convened a meeting with influential leaders of color and persuaded them to abandon their plans. The anger of the "white inhabitants was so roused" that he feared violence and recalled "that the events which have Spread blood and desolation in St. Domingo [Saint-Domingue] originated in a dispute between the white and Mulatto inhabitants, and that the too rigid treatment of the former, induced the Latter to seek the support and assistance of the Negroes." The governor was determined not to provoke the city's Black majority of approximately 3,105 slaves and 1,556 free people of color in a total urban population of 8,475 residents.[13]

Meanwhile, the city's white militiamen and their allies took great offense at Claiborne's cautious approach to the African American battalion. They criticized the governor for "putting up with their [the militiamen's] disrespectful refusal of the [white] officers whom he had appointed as their adjutants." Their spokesman, planter and merchant Daniel Clark, expressed outrage when Claiborne provided the free Black soldiers with a color standard ahead of the white military unit. Their anger prompted the governor to order a guard around the parade ground when he presented the militiamen of color with their ensign. With the establishment of the first territorial legislature in October 1804, the corps' white opponents retaliated by omitting the battalion from the militia act, thereby inactivating the unit.[14]

Between 1804 and 1807, Claiborne's security concerns and his increasingly favorable opinion of the Afro-Creole militia persuaded him to press the legislature for the corps' recognition. For their part, the territorial assembly, dominated by conservative French- and English-speaking slaveholders, ignored the governor's repeated requests. They viewed all free people of color as the "natural allies" of the enslaved. To prevent the possibility of another "Santo Domingo," they proposed to legally suppress the free community of color. For them, the presence of a free Afro-Creole militia was intolerable.

In 1806, absent the mediating influence of the Spanish colonial regime, the lawmakers enacted one of the South's harshest and most sweeping slave codes. Modeled on the Anglo-American two-tiered racial order, the Louisiana statutes aimed to relegate all people of African descent, the freeborn as well as the enslaved, to a degraded and separate caste. Confronted with a legislature fiercely committed to a draconian slave code, and a free Black community equally committed to citizenship and their historical rights, Claiborne looked to an unlikely source to resolve the dilemma. His ally was an 1804 refugee of the revolutionary Caribbean, Louis Moreau-Lislet.

Born in Saint-Domingue, Moreau-Lislet completed his legal studies in France and returned to the French Caribbean colony in 1793 in the midst of the Haitian Revolution. In his homeland he worked as an attorney, and by 1800 he held an official position under the revolutionary French Republic as a judge, where he served in Port Republicain (Port-au-Prince) and Le Cap (Cap Français). When Jean-Jacques Dessalines conquered the French army in August 1803, Moreau-Lislet made his way to Cuba and settled in Louisiana in 1804, where he would renew his ties to a network of refugees that included the d'Aquin, Brulé, Savary, DuBourg, Bringier, Faget, Roudanez, and Tureaud families.

Soon after his arrival, Claiborne immediately recognized that the newcomer's fluency in Spanish, French, and English, together with his legal expertise, fitted him for deciphering the confusing babel of civil law and common law ordinances and procedures written in English and mixed with those of France and Spain. Moreau-Lislet's impact on the legal system was immediate. His success in untangling territorial Louisiana's multilingual civil procedures elevated him to a leadership role in formulating a legal order rooted in both Roman civil law and English common law. In 1806, Claiborne appointed him first judge on the critically important New Orleans City Court, and in 1808 he was the principal author of the Louisiana *Civil Digest*.

Moreau-Lislet's 1809 judicial decision in a case impacting Louisiana's free people of color, and his connections to revolutionary France and Haiti, may have inspired an attempt to discredit him. On August 18, 1809, the *New York Herald* reported that the jurist had been Tousssaint Louverture's secretary and a grand master in a Saint-Domingue Masonic lodge for men of color. The newspaper offered no evidence to support the claims, and the revelations appear to have had no ill effect on Moreau Lislet's professional career. With regard to his social life, he achieved the rank of Grand Master of the Grand [Masonic] Lodge of Louisiana in 1818.

In the 1809 legal proceeding *Adéle v. Beauregard*, as the case mistakenly became known, Adéle Auger, a woman of color, sued Frederick Beaurocher for his claim that she was his slave. In his decision, the judge ruled that "persons of color" may have "descended from Indians on both sides, from a white parent, or mulatto parents in possession of their freedom. Considering how much probability there is in favor of the liberty of those persons, they ought not to be deprived of it upon mere presumption." The decision swept aside the legislative requirement that free people of color carry freedom papers to document their status. In the larger scheme of things, however, the judge's enormously influential ruling guided judicial and legislative decisions up the end of the antebellum era, thereby reinforcing the Latin European colonial model of a three-tiered racial order—a racial order in which enslaved Louisianians were left to suffer one of the South's harshest slave codes.[15]

Barred from militia service, denied citizenship, refused participation in the political life of the state, and prohibited from jury service by Louisiana's legislative branch of government, the city's Afro-Creole community directed their energies to the state's judiciary, with remarkable results. Under the blended Latin European civil law and Anglo-American common law legal system, they exercised many of the rights of citizens. They could possess property, make contracts, testify in all types of cases, even against whites, and enjoy the right to trial by jury. By the mid-nineteenth century, New Orleans possessed the South's largest number of free Black property owners and the most active and educated professional elite.

At the time of Moreau-Lislet's ruling in *Adéle v. Beauregard*, a huge three-caste influx of Saint-Domingue refugees into New Orleans in 1809–1810 reinforced the city's Latin European racial and cultural order. Building upon a favorably disposed judiciary, long-standing patronage relationships, interracial kinship ties, and military alliances that had originated under the Latin European regimes in both Saint-Domingue and Louisiana, the state's free people of color excelled. And though the legislature repeatedly attempted to undermine the rights of the free population of color during the first half of the nineteenth century, the Louisiana judiciary refused to budge.[16]

In 1807, the disagreement between the governor and the legislature took a violent turn when Daniel Clark, Louisiana's territorial delegate to Congress and one of Claiborne's most implacable political enemies, seized upon the issue of the free Black militia to humiliate the governor. In remarks on the floor of the US House of Representatives in December 1806, Clark took personal credit for the peaceful transfer of the Louisiana Territory when, he asserted, his leadership of a volunteer military force proved decisive. The white militiamen he commanded "had offered their services to the United States" but had been disregarded by Claiborne, whose "preference [was] given to another corps [the battalion of color]."[17]

The governor did not learn of the delegate's congressional remarks until shortly after Clark returned to the city on May 20, 1807, when they appeared in the *Orleans Gazette* in incendiary terms: "The militia of this territory [under Claiborne] had been neglected; they were totally unorganized, they had seen a black corps preferred to them and a standard publicly given it, whilst their own repeated offers and wishes to be employed in their country's services had been rejected." Claiborne took especial offense at Clark's charge that he had favored the militia of color over the white soldiers. He demanded a retraction. When Clark refused, the governor challenged him to a duel. On June 8, the two men met in Spanish territory at Fort Bute de Manchac in West Florida, where Claiborne "received a ball which passed through my right thigh about ten inches below the hip, and made a considerable contusion in my left [leg]." Clark walked away from the *affaire d'honneur* unscathed.[18]

By the time Claiborne fully recovered from the duel, he confronted an even larger nonwhite majority. As a consequence of the 1809–1810 refugee influx, the city's percentage of African Americans, both slave and free, had increased from 56.8 percent in 1805 to 63.3 percent in 1810. Recognizing the necessity of pacifying an even larger population of free men of color, some of whom were veterans of the Haitian Revolution, Claiborne continued his efforts to incorporate the existing battalion of men of color into the territory's militia structure.

The legislature reluctantly relented after the United States declared war on Great Britain on June 12, 1812. In the wartime overhaul of the militia system, lawmakers authorized the governor to form a Battalion of Free Men of Color limited to 256 soldiers. With some modifications, Claiborne essentially reactivated the battalion of soldiers he had inherited from the Spanish regime. Still, the militia's enemies considered the unit a dangerous presence, and when the theater of war shifted from the North to the Southeast in 1814, tensions escalated once again.[19]

With the threat of an attack on New Orleans mounting in the late summer of 1814, Claiborne wrote to Major General Andrew Jackson, the commanding officer of US forces in Louisiana, the Mississippi Territory, and Tennessee, recommending the recruitment of three hundred to four hundred more free men of color. The governor proposed the action on the basis of a meeting on August 11 with the existing unit's Afro-Creole officers and their white commanders, Colonel Michel Fortier *père* (senior), a wealthy merchant, and Major Pierre Lacoste, a sugar planter in St. Bernard Parish. The aged Fortier, having fought alongside the battalion of color in Bernardo de Gálvez's campaigns against the British in the American Revolution, was well aware of their combat effectiveness.

During their discussion, the officers of color pledged their loyalty and estimated that as many as six hundred more free men of color might be recruited, on the condition that they be deployed in Louisiana. The officers were referring to former French republican officer Joseph Savary and his fellow veteran soldiers of the Haitian Revolution. Their enlistment, the free Black officers explained, would "give great Satisfaction, and excite their greatest zeal in the cause of the United States." Clearly alarmed, the governor diplomatically evaded their request and immediately ordered, "without delay," a census of all free adult men of color in New Orleans and its vicinity. The government's treatment of the men, Claiborne wrote to Jackson, "at the Present Crisis is an Enquiry of Importance; If we give them not our confidence, the Enemy will be encouraged to entrigue and to corrupt them."[20]

From Mobile, Jackson replied on August 22 with full support for Claiborne's recruitment recommendation. The general welcomed the expressions of loyalty and patriotism voiced by the men and their officers. In light of the governor's positive assessment and the patriotic declarations of the men themselves, he "would not hesitate in recommending that the corps be augmented." Jackson proposed increasing the size of each company by one hundred men. He could not, however, guarantee that the battalion's deployment would be confined to Louisiana. Jackson, like Claiborne, also recognized the tactical necessity of enlisting the men in Louisiana's defenses.[21]

In September, Claiborne's concerns shifted to rumors of a British-inspired slave revolt. He informed both the mayor's office and the New Orleans City Council of the threat and urged Mayor Nicolas Girod to issue a proclamation alerting New Orleanians to the danger of foreigners and suspicious strangers. The mayor seized upon the governor's directive to take direct aim at the thousands of Saint-Dominguan émigrés of color who had more than doubled the city's free Afro-Creole population in the 1809–1810 refugee movement. In a proclamation issued on September 16, Girod called for a crackdown on foreigners, and "especially free people of colour" who had "introduced, and still do frequently introduce themselves into this city." Such people, the mayor declared, had entered Louisiana in defiance of the 1807 law that prohibited "the emigration of free negroes and mulattoes into the territory of Orleans."[22]

Anyone who could not "prove instantly they were free, shall be arrested by the patroles, constables, watchmen or any other white person and brought to the police jail." For good measure, Girod quoted the statute's threat of enslavement. The proclamation appeared regularly in the Louisiana Courier/Courrier de la Louisiane. At the same time, the city council approved a seven-member Committee of Defense—a committee for whom the 1811 slave revolt loomed large. Its high-profile membership included US District Judge Dominick Augustine Hall; David B. Morgan, state legislator and brigadier general of the state militia; Jacques Philippe Villeré, major general of the state militia; and Jean-Noël Destrehan, a state senator and former president of the territorial legislature. In the 1811 slave revolt, Villeré was the commanding officer of the territorial militia and Destrehan's plantation had been the focal point in the interrogation and summary trials of the accused captives. With the ostensible purpose of coordinating security measures with the governor, the committeemen and their allies lobbied aggressively against arming free men of color.[23]

By the end of October, the campaign of intimidation had proved effective. The exodus of free Saint-Domingue émigrés of color was under way, with large numbers immigrating to Cuba. Given the makeup of the tribunal, the threat of being caught up in the dangerous dragnet undoubtedly persuaded some native-born Louisianians to join the refugee movement. As intended, the flight also dealt a blow to Claiborne's recruitment efforts. The "great emigration to Cuba of free people of Colour" with "many others to follow," the governor wrote to Jackson, "will much operate against your [recruitment] plan, But it is nevertheless believed that several Companies may be raised."[24]

In the midst of the crisis, a furious dispute erupted over Jackson's intention to increase the ranks of the city's African American men-at-arms. Claiborne cryptically referred to the uproar as an "unfortunate misunderstanding between the officers" of the Battalion of Free Men of Color. The disagreement, Claiborne wrote to Jackson on October 17, had excited "much Interest" and a "Court of Enquiry" was investigating the matter. The confrontation originated in Jackson's enthusiasm for recruiting three hundred to four hundred more soldiers of color to be drawn from Savary's veteran soldiers of the Haitian Revolution.

Claiborne warned Jackson "that many excellent citizens will disapprove the policy you wish to observe towards the free people of Colour." Even with an enemy invasion threatening, "respectable citizens" could not be persuaded to enlist more African American soldiers. The argument that the men might be recruited by the British if the United States rejected their pledge of loyalty made no headway with the opposition. Given the depths of white distrust,

Claiborne feared the dissolution of the existing battalion, for "limited as it is, [the battalion] excites much distrust, and I should not be surprised, if at the insuing legislature, an attempt should be made to put it down."

Jackson's recruitment policy, opponents insisted, was tantamount to putting guns into the hands of their British enemies. Representatives of the Committee of Defense warned the governor that if the men remained in post-war Louisiana with their "Knowledge of the use of Arms, and *that pride of Distinction*, which a soldier's pursuits so naturally inspires, they would prove dangerous." They viewed Jackson's plan advisable only if accompanied by a guarantee that the recruits would be deployed outside of the state and permanently barred from returning to Louisiana at the war's end, an unacceptable condition for the free soldiers of color.[25]

Conversely, those who supported the general's policy insisted that distrusting and disrespecting the men was more likely to drive them into the arms of the enemy. To ensure the allegiance of men of color, they argued in favor of increasing the ranks of the militiamen and putting the men on an equal footing with white soldiers. Charles-Louis d'Aquin appears to have been the most forceful proponent of this position—a position that landed him at the center of the "unfortunate misunderstanding" referenced by Claiborne in his October 17 letter to General Jackson.

D'Aquin's steadfast advocacy of the free soldiers of color with whom he had fought under the French Republic in the Haitian Revolution provoked the fury of his Committee of Defense adversaries. They and their Anglophone allies attempted to ruin him by charging that he was himself a man of color, a disastrous accusation in Louisiana's racial hierarchy. The claim arose from d'Aquin's close association with the Savary family and his likely kinship ties to Sylvain d'Aquin, a free Black veteran of the Haitian Revolution. In response to the 1814 uproar, the military convened a court of inquiry to resolve the matter.[26]

On October 15, 1814, Jackson's dispatches arrived from Mobile at the height of the furor over the recruitment of the free Black soldiers. In his communications, the general sided with d'Aquin and Claiborne. His decisive action prolonged the life of the First Battalion of Free Men of Color and opened the way for the recruitment of Savary's soldiers. In a proclamation addressed to "Louisianians," Jackson called upon "all Frenchmen," "all Americans," and "all freemen" to unify against the invading British, their "natural and sworn enemy." Any man who "refused to defend his rights when called upon by his government deserves to be a slave and must be punished as an enemy to his country." The general closed his address with an equally forceful statement fully authorizing the governor "to organize any volunteer company, battalion or regime which may proffer its services under this call."[27]

Jackson, like Claiborne, viewed the enlistment of free men of color as a tactical imperative. He agreed with the governor that to distrust the men would "make them your enemies." By placing confidence in them, "you engage them by every dear and honorable tie to the interest of the country [that] extends to them equal rights and priviledges with white men." The new recruits would "make excellent soldiers," and he directed Claiborne to publish his accompanying proclamation "To the Free Coloured Inhabitants of Louisiana," in which Jackson called on them to "defend all which is dear in existence." He invited his "brave fellow Citizens" and "sons of freedom" to enroll in the US Army. In return, every "noble hearted generous brave freeman of colour volunteering to serve during the present contest with Great Britain, and no longer, there will be pd. the same bounty in Money and lands, now received by the white Soldiers of the United States."[28]

Jackson assured Claiborne that he would send one of his aides to enlist recruits and pay their bounty if the governor succeeded in raising a regiment, battalion, or company. In response, Claiborne reported that several companies might be recruited from among the free Saint-Domingue émigrés of color since they would most likely be "desirous to join the army." At the same time, the weary governor regretted the nearly three-week delay of the general's instructions: "I should have been happy to have laid it *earlier* before the people." By the end of October, he feared the ongoing flight of free people of color to Cuba would shrink the number of potential recruits.[29]

Jackson reached the city on December 1, having concluded that New Orleans was the target of the anticipated British invasion. He immediately set out to inspect the city's defenses with Arsène Lacarrière Latour, a French topographer whom he appointed major and principal engineer to the Seventh Military District. After a failed 1801 attempt to reclaim his Saint-Domingue property, Latour had fled the war-torn colony just ahead of the French army's 1803 surrender to the British. He escaped to Cuba, where the Lafitte brothers were ferrying refugees to Louisiana. Upon his arrival in New Orleans, he worked on maps of the city and its coastal environs. In November 1814, Edward Livingston, Jackson's trusted Louisiana liaison, recommended Latour to the general on the basis of his integrity, his fluency in both French and English, and his expertise as a military engineer. As his credentials indicate, Latour's skills would be an important factor in Jackson's victory.

Within days of his arrival, Jackson reviewed the city's venerated Bataillon d'Orléans. After observing the white battalion's maneuvers, Jackson praised Charles-Louis d'Aquin and the other officers for the unit's "exact discipline" and skills in troop movements that were "rarely attained by veterans." Soon afterwards, Jackson's praise notwithstanding, d'Aquin was abruptly removed from his bataillon post as the captain of the company of *chasseurs* he had commanded up to that time.[30] Apparently, the court of inquiry investigating the dispute over the recruitment of free men of color took disciplinary action against him. He was reassigned to the First Division of the Louisiana Militia with his brother-in-law Lieutenant Camille Bruslé. Though the mayor's office and the Committee of Defense may have taken satisfaction from his demotion, d'Aquin would prove to be a trusted and highly effective officer in Jackson's army.[31]

With the British bearing down on the city, Jackson hastily patched together a heterogeneous, multiethnic fighting force of approximately 3,500 to 4,000 Louisiania and Saint-Domingue Creoles (both Black and white), Anglo-Americans, Frenchmen, Spaniards, Irishmen, Italians, and Choctaw Native Americans. Influential New Orleanians even persuaded the general to accept the services of the Lafitte brothers, smugglers Jean and Pierre, and their interracial company of renegade buccaneers.[32]

After Kentucky militiamen began arriving in the city on December 1, a quatrain in the Creole patois entitled "Kaintock" (Kentuckian) originated in the run-up to the British attack. The verse conveyed the inevitable ethnic tensions while immortalizing d'Aquin and his bakery:

'Mericain coquin,
Billé en Naquin
Voleur de pain
Chez Michie D'Aquin

(American rogue,
Dressed in nankeen,
Stealer of bread
From Monsieur d'Aquin!)[33]

Two thousand more Kentuckians arrived on January 4, 1815, marching through the city shivering and barely clothed. Their alleged reputation for stealing bread might have grown out of their desperate circumstances. In the two months that followed the battle, nearly one thousand Kentucky and Tennessee soldiers perished of disease in hospital tents.[34]

As Jackson considered the possible routes of a British invasion, Latour advised him that Lake Borgne was the enemy's most likely point of entry. He was right. On December 13, within two weeks of the general's arrival, US Navy gunboats sighted the British armada at the entrance to Lake Borgne. Jackson assigned Major General Jacques Philippe Villeré, the commanding officer of the district between Lake Borgne and the Mississippi, the task of obstructing the waterways leading to the river. On December 17, Jackson specifically ordered the obstruction of Bayou Bienvenue with felled trees and shrubs to prevent the British from reaching the Mississippi River. The next day, Major Gabriel Villeré, Major General Villeré's son, who had been assigned to guard the waterways connecting his father's Mississippi River plantation to the bayou, acknowledged receipt of the order. Three days later, Major Villeré posted a small militia detachment on Bayou Bienvenue to watch for the approach of the enemy. He did nothing to obstruct the bayou or the other passages as Jackson had ordered.

With the British threatening the panic-stricken city, General Jackson declared martial law on December 16, 1814, and ordered a *levée en masse* forcing every able-bodied man, regardless of race or nationality, to serve in the city's defenses. On the same day, the United States Army officially mustered the First Battalion of Free Men of Color into service with an aggregate strength of 353 men including their officers. Jackson dispatched the men to a defensive position at the confluence of Bayou Sauvage and Chef Menteur Pass to block the British from invading across the Gentilly plain.[35]

When the general ordered the enlistment of another battalion of free men of color, former French officers Joseph Savary *fils* and his father, Charles Savary *aîné*, immediately raised a volunteer battalion. Latour, Jackson's loquacious chief engineer, had undoubtedly recommended such an action on the grounds that the "gallant" Savary *fils* "had acquired an honourable and distinguished reputation in the wars of St. Domingo."[36] And though Charles Savary's age and infirmities prevented him from taking up arms, his "patriotism was manifested on every occasion," according to Jackson, in rallying the Second Battalion of Free Men of Color "to a faithful and brave defense of the country." The fighting force the two men organized comprised the garrison Joseph Savary had commanded in the Haitian Revolution and included Courtois, Marcelin Guillot, and other soldiers who had accompanied Savary in the

Gutiérrez campaign. On December 19, the Second Battalion of Free Men of Color was mustered into the US Army with an aggregate strength of 256 men. Within forty-eight hours, the men were ready for active service.[37]

Jackson readily bowed to the new battalion's request to have Charles-Louis d'Aquin assigned to their unit as its commanding officer. Many factors played a role in their choice, including their experience as republican comrades in arms in the Haitian Revolution, d'Aquin's staunch advocacy of their recruitment, and their shared hatred of the British. In addition, long-standing personal, professional, and political alliances forged in colonial and revolutionary Saint-Domingue influenced their decision.

Upon d'Aquin's appointment to first major of the Second Battalion, Jackson personally named Savary to the grade of second major, making him the first African American to hold that post in the US Army. The battalion's highly disciplined, battle-tested soldiers, like their commanding officers d'Aquin and Savary, had served in the French Republic's National Guard in the Haitian Revolution. In Saint-Domingue, the men had fought invading British and Spanish armies in the Artibonite valley, and some proportion of the soldiers had seen action in Gutiérrez's Mexican expedition. As Jackson anticipated, the combat-ready battalion would prove decisive in the impending struggle.

Camille Bruslé joined his brother-in-law, First Major d'Aquin, in the new battalion as a third lieutenant. The unit's newly recruited officer corps also included Captain Marcelin Guillot, Major Savary's brother Sergeant Belton Savary, Sergeant Major Sévérè Courtois, and First Lieutenant Sylvain d'Aquin. Lieutenant d'Aquin fits the profile of mixed-race descendants of long-standing colonial families in prerevolutionary Saint-Domingue who were included in their white family's social network. After apparently emigrating to New Orleans with the d'Aquin family in 1804, he married well, prospered as an artisan, and owned slaves. In 1807, he married into the prominent Carrière family, whose free patriarch of color, Noel Carrière, was decorated for his service against the British under Bernardo de Gálvez in the American Revolution. As an officer in the Second Battalion, Sylvain d'Aquin distinguished himself against the British in the 1815 Battle of New Orleans. In 1820, he supported a household of eight individuals, including an enslaved man and woman. Sometime within the next ten years, he settled upon an occupation as a mason and bricklayer.[38]

On December 22, the English arrived at an unobstructed Bayou Bienvenu, approximately twelve miles below New Orleans, and captured the militia sentries at the bayou's observation post. The next day, a British advance force of approximately 1,800 soldiers proceeded undetected up Bayou Mazant and Villeré Canal to the Mississippi River. In disobeying Jackson's orders to blockade Bayou Bienvenu and its connecting waterways, Major Gabriel Villeré had exposed the city to a surprise enemy invasion. He was later court-martialed for his negligence.

The British seized Jacques Philippe Villeré's plantation less than eight miles below the city and captured his son, Major Villeré, with his entire detachment of thirty militiamen. The evidence indicates that Villeré purposely ignored his instructions to obstruct the canal. Waterways like the route from Lake Borgne to his father's plantation were ideal pathways for smugglers in pirogues to transport contraband goods to plantations. Other planters were known to engage in the highly lucrative contraband trade. In addition, Major General Jacques Philippe Villeré, the commanding officer of the state militia, was well acquainted with smugglers Jean and Pierre Lafitte. The inescapable conclusion appears to be that the Villerés deliberately disobeyed Jackson's orders.[39]

Upon learning of the invading enemy's presence within striking distance of the city, Jackson ordered an immediate attack. Among the troops converging on his headquarters, Jackson noted the rapid approach of the Bataillon d'Orléans: "Ah! There come the brave Creoles." Trotting closely behind the white unit, d'Aquin's battalion impressed the general as "a gallant and effective force, well officered, and capable of any service."[40] In a coordinated assault, the two units would fully validate the general's impressions. When the last of his troops had passed in review, Jackson mounted his horse and galloped south to the Villeré plantation to lead his army in battle.

The nighttime frontal assault by 2,131 American troops caught the British entirely by surprise. The astonished invaders soon recovered. With the arrival of reinforcements, they threatened to outflank the Forty-Fourth US Infantry on Jackson's right at the levee road on the Mississippi River. At this crucial moment, Plauché's Bataillon d'Orléans, Daquin's Second Battalion, and Captain Pierre Jugeant's Choctaw Indians fought back the enemy's advance in a decisive echelon formation. Under heavy fire and in hand-to-hand fighting, the combined forces came close to forcing the surrender of a British regiment.

In the first major battle, the skill and ferocity with which the American army fought achieved a psychological victory. Their actions convinced the British commanding officer, General John Keane, that Jackson's army numbered as many as fifteen thousand troops. More concretely, the Americans had advanced deep into the enemy encampment before darkness, gun smoke, and a thick river fog forced a halt to hostilities. The successful two-hour assault produced an army of eager veterans, set the English back several days in a delay that bought valuable time to build a defensive line, and likely saved New Orleans.[41]

In the final battle on Sunday, January 8, 1815, a British force of seven thousand soldiers launched a frontal assault on Jackson's army of three thousand troops concentrated at fortifications along the Rodriguez Canal, which extended from the Mississippi at one end to a swamp east of the river at the other end. Jackson positioned Plauché's Battalion d'Orléans near the center of his defensive line. Immediately to Plauché's left, Lacoste's and d'Aquin's battalions of color protected the largest artillery gun in Jackson's defenses. At six o'clock in the morning, Lieutenant General Sir Edward Michael Pakenham prematurely signaled his British troops to attack. Under withering artillery and musket fire, however, the troops faltered and fled. When Packenham rushed forward to reverse the headlong retreat, he was mortally wounded. The main assault lasted less than an hour and cost the British its commander and two thousand casualties, with the Americans suffering approximately seventy-one losses.

After the firing ended at 8:30 a.m., British sharpshooters began picking off US soldiers who left their defensive positions to help the wounded and take prisoners. Major Joseph Savary and a detachment of his men readily volunteered to clear the field of the enemy snipers. Though suffering heavy casualties, including Savary's brother, Sergeant Belton Savary, the unit dispatched the shooters. Sergeant Savary died of his injuries two days later. Savary's daring maneuver in the last significant skirmish of the battle added further martial luster to the reputation of his commanding officer, Major d'Aquin, and the Second Battalion of Free Men of Color. Exultant at his victory, the rapturous Jackson is reputed to have embraced Savary on the battlefield in a spontaneous show of camaraderie.[42]

Jackson's jubilation at his army's stunning victory on the east bank gave way to shock at the news of General David B. Morgan's rout on the west bank of the Mississippi. Morgan, using poor judgment in anticipation of the January 8 assault, had ignored military engineer Latour's advice and extended his line to an indefensible position. It wasn't the first time Morgan had performed below par. In the first major engagement on December 23, his timidity at English Turn prompted Sergeant Jonathan Rees to contemptuously refer to the general as "an old woman." Positioned in the enemy's rear, Morgan had refused to attack without orders from Jackson but finally relented when he could no longer restrain his men.

Under British assault on January 8, Morgan's army crumbled, abandoning its artillery to the British and exposing Jackson's east bank position to sweeping gunfire. Upon recognizing the threat to his right flank, Jackson immediately directed General Humbert to cross the river with four hundred men and take command. Humbert eagerly embraced the opportunity to strike at Pakenham, a former battlefield adversary who had forced the surrender of his undermanned Franco-Irish army at the Battle of Ballinamuck during the 1798 rebellion led by the Society of United Irishmen.[43]

When Humbert arrived on the east bank, however, the Anglo-American officers refused to recognize the French general's authority; he was "an unnaturalized foreigner" and only "an American should command Americans."[44] Fortunately, the British decision to retreat resolved the debate and assured an American victory. Hardly had the shooting ended when an infuriated Jackson expressed his incredulity in an address to the troops on the east bank of the river. "No words can express the mortification I felt at witnessing the scene exhibited on the opposite [west] bank." He attributed their actions to the "want of discipline, the want of order, a total disregard to obedience, and a spirit of insubordination, not less destructive than cowardice itself." Such behavior, he concluded, were the causes "which led to the disaster, and the causes must be eradicated, or I must cease to command."

Referring to Humbert's treatment, Jackson growled his disapproval: "Private opinions, as to the competency of officers, must not be indulged and still less expressed; it is impossible that the measure of those who command should satisfy all who are bound to obey, and one of the most dangerous faults in a soldier is a disposition to criticise and blame the orders and characters of his superiors." He dispatched General William Carroll to take command of Morgan's position.[45]

General Carroll also presided over the military court of inquiry investigating the rout of Morgan's army. Without mentioning the general specifically, the members of the court pointed to the "officer immediately commanding" and found fault in "the manner in which the force was posted on the line, which they [members of the court] consider exceptionable." Morgan, instead of concentrating his troops along one defensive line between an impassable woodland and the Mississippi River as Latour had recommended, had divided his army in defensive lines along two canals while leaving an unguarded space in his main line of defense. Taking advantage of those gaps, the British troops rapidly overran Morgan's defenses. The incompetent general escaped the tribunal's censure.[46]

For the failure of the Villerés to obstruct Bayou Bienvenue, Major Gabriel Villeré was tried by court-marshal for negligence, on March 15. In their decision, the court declared that "Major Villeré appears to have performed his duty, from the moment he was left in command under the order of major-general [Jacques Philippe] Villeré, with zeal and fidelity; and that the circumstances of his surprise and capture by the enemy, . . . might have occurred to the most vigilant officer." Gabriel Villeré was honorably acquitted of all charges.[47]

In the fall of 1814, Major General Villeré, Brigadier-General Morgan, and the other five members of the city council's Committee of Defense had fought a determined campaign against the presence of African American soldiers in the city's armed forces. The committee had threatened to dissolve the First Battalion of Free Men of Color and fought the creation of a second battalion on the grounds that their use of arms would make the men a "dangerous" presence. When d'Aquin defended the men, the committee attempted to discredit him in an attack that led to his dismissal from the prestigious white Bataillon d'Orléans.

In fact, the two preeminent officers of the state militia had proved to be the weakest links in the city's defenses. Villeré's negligence had exposed the city to a surprise attack and the possibility of capture. Morgan's incompetence and his staff's Francophobia had threatened Jackson's astonishing victory by opening his entire defensive line to being enfiladed by British fire from the west bank. Another member of the city's Committee of Defense, US District Judge Dominick Augustine Hall, though posing no danger during hostilities, proved to be a costly nuisance.

After the January 8 defeat of the British, Jackson refused to end martial law until official notification of the Treaty of Ghent arrived. When state lawmaker Philip Louaillier attacked the general's stringent restrictions in the *Courrier de la Louisiane,* Jackson had the lawmaker arrested on March 5. In solidarity with Louaillier, Judge Hall issued a writ of habeas corpus freeing the lawmaker from prison. In response, Jackson accused the judge of "abetting and exciting mutiny within my camp" and ordered his arrest. By the evening of March 5, both men were behind bars in the city's military barracks. When news of the Treaty of Ghent's February 17 ratification arrived on March 13, Hall was allowed to resume his duties as a federal judge.

On March 31, in *United States v. Andrew Jackson,* Judge Hall took his revenge by charging the general with contempt of court for ignoring the writs of habeas corpus in the arrests of Louaillier and himself. On the grounds that the proceedings were unconstitutional, Jackson refused to answer the judge's interrogatories. Hall charged Jackson with contempt once again and fined him $1,000. Jackson complied with the Hall's sentence and paid the fine.[48]

By comparison, d'Aquin, Savary, and the two battalions of free men of color, men who Villeré, Morgan, Hall and other Committee of Defense members had considered a "dangerous" presence in the city, had executed Jackson's battlefield commands with precision and success. Writing to Secretary of War James Monroe within days of the December 23 battle, Jackson described the debacle at the Villeré plantation and referenced the presence of "the two hundred men of colour (chiefly from St. Domingo) raised by colonel Savary and acting under the command of major Daquin." Savary's volunteers (the Second Battalion of Free Men of Color), the general continued, "manifested great bravery."[49]

Both battalions of free soldiers of color, the general continued, had "not disappointed the hopes that were formed of their courage and perseverance in the performance of their duty." Their officers, "Majors Lacoste and Daquin, who commanded them, have deserved well of their country." Officer Savary's conduct, Jackson continued, "has been noticed in the account rendered of the battle of the 23d, and that officer has since continued to merit the highest praise." Speaking specifically of Major d'Aquin's battalion, Major Latour agreed wholeheartedly with Jackson's emphasis on the corps' "brilliant display of valour."[50]

In his public call to arms in September 1814, Jackson proclaimed the United States "the only Country on Earth where every Man enjoys freedom, where its blessing are alike extended to the poor, and Rich, calls on you to protect these rights. . . . The individual who refuses to defend his rights when called by his Government, deserves to be a slave." For enslaved men and women on Louisiana plantations, the irony in Jackson's appeal certainly struck a bitter note. For them, the hope of freedom came from the English invaders. In 1814, British vice admiral Sir Alexander Cochrane had issued a proclamation offering liberation, resettlement, and land grants in the British Caribbean to men who enlisted in the English military. The offer included their families.

On the Jacques Philippe Villeré, Pierre Lacoste, and neighboring plantations, approximately two hundred enslaved Louisianians sided with the English. On the Villeré plantation alone, fifty-two men, women, and children fled. Their escape succeeded, and though they achieved neither equality nor full freedom in the Caribbean, they secured a better way of life for themselves and their children. In twenty-first-century Trinidad, their descendants continue to commemorate their courageous act of self-liberation.[51]

Nor did Lousiana's African American veterans achieve true freedom after their defense of the city. Tensions flared within weeks of the conflict when Major Savary refused to march his men out of New Orleans. White hostility to the soldiers' continued presence likely prompted Claiborne to recommend the deployment of Savary and his men to a remote outpost at Chef Menteur Pass. The governor justified the assignment on the grounds that nearby planters would not volunteer their slaves to widen and deepen the fortification's ditches. Savary defied the order.

As combat troops who had demonstrated their patriotism and effectiveness on the battlefield, the men considered the assignment an insult. Major d'Aquin, their commanding officer, explained their objections: "[When] I asked why they refused to obey, they replied that they wanted to make known to the General [Jackson] that they would always be willing to sacrifice their lives in combat in defense of their country as had been demonstrated but preferred death to the performance of the work of laborers that was demanded of them." D'Aquin concluded with an apology: "I am very sorry, Mon Generalle for being unable upon this occasion to carry out the wishes of the government."[52] Though clearly angered by Savary's defiance, Jackson uncharacteristically ignored the breakdown in military discipline.

In mid-March, Savary, Courtois, Guillot, and twelve other Saint-Domingue officers of d'Aquin's battalion pressed further ahead with a petition of grievances addressed to Jackson. They implored him to protect them from the "ordinary course" of state laws exposing them "to the most humiliating vexations." They sought from either the general or President Monroe a guarantee of protection that would put them "beyond a prejudice which always existed in this country." Such an "act of Justice" would "save them [the soldiers] from future insult."[53]

Though the state and US government fulfilled Jackson's promise of equal pay and land bounties, the men never experienced the status of "fellow Citizens," the term of address with which Jackson had appealed to them on the eve of hostilities. In another devastating blow, the white planter and merchant elite who controlled the territorial legislature renewed their efforts to end the free Black militia after the Battle of New Orleans. The unit's official termination would come in 1834. As elsewhere in the slave South, Louisiana's white slaveholding elite viewed the militiamen's presence, let alone their demands for citizenship, as a grave threat to the state's slave regime. Their implacable hostility persuaded Savary and his determined veteran soldiers to look elsewhere to fulfill the republican promise of the revolutionary age.[54]

THREE

The Tree of Liberty

In overthrowing me, you have cut down in San Domingo [Saint-Domingue]
only the trunk of the tree of liberty. It will spring up again by
the roots, for they are numerous and deep.
—Toussaint Louverture, 1802

T his chapter begins in 1815, after the Battle of New Orleans, when Major Savary and his veteran soldiers were denied citizenship. Under Savary's command, the men rejoined itinerant revolutionaries in the cause of Latin American independence. For the enslaved and free men of color, military service in the revolutionary armies promised freedom and citizenship. In Haiti, Savary secured support from Haitian president Alexandre Pétion and sailed with the French "corsair Jacobin," Louis-Michel Aury, to support insurgent forces. Their efforts eventually faltered when the US military forced their retreat in Spanish East Florida.

Savary returned to the city in 1825, where he met his fellow itinerant revolutionary the Marquis de Lafayette. Touring the United States to reinvigorate the nation's revolutionary spirit, Lafayette advocated the cause of a new "Romantic" generation of political and humanitarian activists.

This chapter concludes with an outline of the d'Aquin famly's extensive web of allied families bound by social, business, quasi-kinship, and military alliances that had evolved by 1840. Their interracial ties extended onto south Louisiana sugar plantations, where their complex network produced a new generation of freedom fighters.

* * *

In New Orleans, the spring festivities celebrating the 1815 Treaty of Ghent featured the revolutionary flags of Cartagena and the Mexican Republic alongside those of the United States, Great Britain, and other European nations. D'Aquin's bitterly disappointed Second Battalion soldiers could only have viewed the display's republican and international symbolism with profound cynicism. Having failed to achieve citizenship through military service in defense of the United States, Joseph Savary, Sévère Courtois, and other members of the battalion looked elsewhere for the vindication of their rights. Courtois, a sergeant major in d'Aquin's battalion, left Louisiana to enlist in the service of the Republic of Cartagena, where the government had abolished color distinctions and granted equal citizenship rights to free people of African descent. The province's republican fervor would also deal a blow to slavery by extending freedom to bondsmen who enlisted in the revolutionary army. Early in Latin America's struggles, African American solidarity with revolutionary forces ensured that racial equality would become an insurgent rallying cry.[1]

Like Courtois, Joseph Savary and other free veterans of color also looked to the wars of Latin American independence to achieve equal rights. When Jackson authorized General Humbert and Field Marshal Don Pablo de Anaya, a representative of Mexico's revolutionary government, to organize a small guerilla force to support Mexico's revolutionary movement, they rejoined the struggle. Major Savary and thirty-one veterans of his former battalion readily enlisted in the new unit, together with a hundred white soldiers. During the summer, Mexican revolutionary José Gutiérrez, Humbert, and their allies drew up plans to attack the Spanish arsenal at Pensacola and seize its armaments for proposed operations against Mexican royalists. Planned for the summer of 1815, the expedition was supported by the New Orleans Association, a broad and amorphous alliance of New Orleanians, from the reputable Edward Livingston to the disreputable Lafitte brothers.

Association members generally agreed upon the objective of Spain's ouster from Mexico. Beyond Spain's removal, however, no consensus existed. Whereas Humbert, Anaya, Gutiérrez, Savary, and their allies looked to an independent Mexican republic, some associates preferred a United States or French occupation. Another faction coveted the profits to be gained from Mexican resources, arms sales, and raids on Spanish shipping. Still others probably saw an opportunity to promote democratic change while advancing their own financial interests.

The association's dissonant aims and the intrigues of Spanish agents in New Orleans made a successful expedition against Mexico's royalist army illusive. By the time the Mexican Republic's ambassador, José Manuel de Herrera, arrived from Haiti in March 1816 to secure aid for the independence movement, Humbert, Anaya, and Gutiérrez had redirected their energies. Undeterred, Ambassador Herrera informed the New Orleans Association of an offer of support from Haitian president Alexandre Sabès Pétion (1770–1818) and his recruitment of Louis-Michel Aury, a former naval officer for revolutionary forces in New Granada and Cartagena.[2]

Even before Haiti split into two competing states in 1807, with Pétion in the south and Henri Christophe in the north, the southern city of Jacmel had offered refuge and aid to Latin American insurgents. Under President Pétion, the Haitian republic opened Les Cayes (Aux Cayes) to revolutionaries in Spanish America, supplying Simón Bolívar with troops, arms, and provisions on the condition that he end slavery in liberated territories. Scholar David Geggus has contextualized Pétion's actions in the following terms: "This [Pétion's] contribution to decolonization and liberation on the mainland may have been the Haitian Revolution's most enduring influence on the Greater Caribbean." He concludes, "All in all, those who did most to export liberty from Haiti were not the ex-slave rulers who dominated the north (and who continued to purchase African workers through the slave trade) but the free-born and light-skinned *anciens libres* of the south." In Louisiana, Major Joseph Savary and his fellow Saint-Dominguan veterans welcomed President Pétion's invitation and rejoined the republican struggle.[3]

Pétion's generosity in manpower and munitions extended to committed republican insurgents like Louis-Michel Aury, who enjoyed logistics support and safe harbor in Haiti. Aury, born in Paris about 1787, arrived in the West Indies in 1803 as a sailmaker and helmsman aboard a French warship. After surviving a bout of yellow fever that hospitalized him for three months, the teenage sailor aspired to join the ranks of privateer commanders sailing their own fleets on behalf of the revolutionary cause in Spanish America. Given Aury's Jacobin republicanism, France's 1804 abandonment of the French Republic for Napoleon Bonaparte's empire likely influenced his decision. He was among the earliest privateers to join the revolutionary struggle for Spanish American independence, and he made his mark. In Latin America, according to historian Pierre Force, Aury has been "recorded in the national histories of Colombia, Venezuela, and Argentina as a hero of Latin American independence."[4]

In New Orleans in 1810, he purchased his first ship. As he prepared for departure, however, a federal marshal seized his schooner on the grounds it was being refitted as a French privateer in a neutral port. The United States government, determined to avoid being drawn into European hostilities, provided that privateers violating the nation's neutrality were liable to confiscation. In Savannah, Aury suffered a more deadly setback in November when rioters destroyed the schooner in which he owned a share and attacked the vessel's crew. In view of Aury's practice of recruiting mariners of color to man his vessels, racial hostility would explain the assault's ferocity. In an 1812 letter to his family in France, he expressed his shock and outrage at the deadly violence: "I have sometimes been at scenes of horror and carnage, but never in my life have I seen a barbarous action so premeditated and so cold-blooded as that . . . That a man can cold-bloodedly butcher unfortunate fellows scattered and unarmed is in my eyes the height of cruelty, and that is what the Americans did to my sailors killing and wounding twelve."[5]

After finally acquiring his own ship in 1813, Aury sailed south to the Spanish Main, where Cartagena had declared its independence from Spain on November 11, 1811. The cosmopolitan port city would operate as a short-lived republican junta for four years. The new government awarded Aury letters of marque in June 1813, and in the ensuing months he captured a large number of Spanish ships with his fleet of four vessels. Cartagena and other colonies at war with their former rulers reserved the right to seize Spanish ships and cargoes, with privateers like Aury operating under strict rules of engagement. In the seizure of vessels, violence was to be avoided, with privateers respecting the life and property of their captives. When a ship signaled surrender by lowering its flag, the privateer dispatched a small boat to take possession of the captured vessel.

Privateers like Aury acquired their own armed vessels and operated under the authority of sovereign governments with formal authorization in the form of letters of marque, warrants authorizing the privateer to attack and seize enemy ships during warfare. Europeans had introduced privateering into the Caribbean near the end of the sixteenth century. With a demonstrated record of effectiveness in hostilities, the practice was flourishing by 1800. The greatest share of the profits from the capture of prizes (the ships and their cargoes) was divided between the government, the outfitter or investor, and the officers, with privateer sailors sharing the remainder of the booty.

Not long after his Cartagena victories, the revolutionary United Provinces of New Granada deputed to Aury command over its national squadron. In 1815, the Spanish navy and army seized upon political divisions in the United Provinces to besiege Cartagena. Outmanned and outgunned, the city's defenders withstood the blockade for three months. In December, Aury boarded two thousand starving insurgents onto his fleet of thirteen vessels. Both aided and bedeviled by gale force winds, his convoy escaped the naval cordon. At sea for nearly a month, more than half of the refugees perished from lack of water and food. In late January, Aury's scattered fleet limped into its Haitian destination, Pétion's Les Cayes refuge. Aury's heroism at Cartagena, his Jacobin republican views, and his commitment to the revolutionary cause in Spanish America won him "many admirers" as well as a reputation as an "excellent sailor, brave officer and the terror of the Spaniards."[6]

Either during his flight from Cartagena or soon after his arrival in Les Cayes, Aury rejoined Sévère Courtois, his fellow traveling revolutionary. Soon afterwards, Aury began negotiations with Herrera and his New Orleans Association backers, who proposed to first attack Tampico, a royalist port of embarkation for Mexican silver mines. Under the auspices of the Mexican Republic, Aury's reconstituted Cartagena fleet would transport and disembark the invading land force. The scheme involved a temporary staging port at Spanish Galveston. Aury accepted the offer and awaited authorization.

In New Orleans, Herrera entrusted Mexico's revolutionary flag and privateer commissions to Major Savary. As a member of a famed Saint-Domingue family, Savary needed no introduction. In 1799, if not earlier, Pétion and Savary had likely crossed paths while serving as French republican officers under General Rigaud in the War of the South during the Haitian Revolution. New Orleans Association member and privateer owner Joseph Sauvinet transported Savary to Haiti, where he conveyed the documents to Pétion. With Savary's delivery of the Mexican Republic's authorization, the Haitian president approved Aury's departure. Courtois readily joined his two allies.

On June 4, 1816, Savary and Courtois sailed with Aury from Les Cayes in a squadron of four armed schooners and two cargo vessels manned by veteran Haitian crewmen who had served alongside Aury in the siege of Cartagena. Two hundred new Haitian recruits fortified the fleet's armed forces. In this and subsequent expeditions, the multiethnic, multinational makeup of his crews attested to the authenticity of Aury's Jacobin egalitarianism. In 1815, Ignace, one of Aury's Black crewmen captured by the Spaniards, testified that the French privateer's command included "Spaniards, Englishmen, Americans, many from the colony of Guárico [a Taíno place-name used by the Spaniards to refer to Cap Français], most of them men of color." Reflecting the privateer's heavy reliance on the Republic of Haiti for manpower as well as munitions, the majority of his crewmen were Haitian sailors. His interracial officer corps, dressed in the French naval style, also reflected the strength of Haitian manpower, with men like Sévère Courtois commanding armed vessels. Notorious and feared throughout the Spanish Caribbean, the French privateer's naval crews came to be known as "los negros de Aury" (Aury's Blacks).[7]

After setting out for the Louisiana coast in June, Aury and his squadron engaged in a series of assaults on Spanish commerce. Traveling north and west, his fleet attacked Spanish ships and neutral carriers transporting Spain's cargoes. They confiscated shipments of prize goods and seized Spanish ships. By the time Aury arrived at the mouth of the Mississippi River in July, he had more than doubled his fleet. Savary disembarked in New Orleans to deliver Aury's letter of acceptance to Herrera while the French privateer delivered Spanish prizes amounting to $7,000 in gold and silver and eighteen barrels of prized cochineal in support of the Mexican expedition. The assets arrived just in time to renew the New Orleans Association's flagging interest in the project. Aury immediately sailed for Texas while Herrera, Savary, and other supporters of Mexican independence prepared to join him.

At Galveston, Aury established a base of operations for the Mexican independence movement despite a number of disastrous setbacks. In the treacherous pass to Galveston Bay, several of his vessels ran aground. His inexperienced Haitian recruits, ordered to empty the disabled vessels of their heavy artillery and prize cargoes onto little more than a sandbar, mutinied on September 7. In the ensuing struggle, the mutineers wounded Aury and barely escaped the arrival, two days later, of an interracial army of approximately 120 men, with Savary commanding forty free Black veterans of the Battle of New Orleans and Henry D. Peire, a New Orleans Associate, officering 110 white soldiers.

Savary, an aggressive and formidable veteran soldier who inspired respect, took charge of Aury's military force. He had honed his skill at transforming untrained troops into disciplined soldiers as a lieutenant colonel in command of a garrison during the Haitian Revolution. With Savary commanding his armed forces, Aury suffered no more mutinies. Until they parted ways in 1818, the two men and their allies acted upon their vision of revolutionary republicanism by supporting the insurgent cause in the wars of Spanish American independence.[8]

On September 13, Minister Herrera proclaimed the convalescing Aury the civil and military governor of the province of Texas on the authority of the Mexican Republic. Fortified by Major Savary and his free veterans of color,

Aury soon reigned supreme on land and sea. He filled all of the new province's appointive offices with his trusted Cartagenan lieutenants (an action that angered Peire's Anglo-Americans), he created an effective monetary system, and he authorized approximately twenty privateer vessels under the Mexican authority. The small settlement even boasted a printing press, with Herrera advocating Mexican independence in the only newspaper published in the province at the time. By the end of 1816, Galveston's privateering commerce in cargoes of Spanish prize goods was thriving, with the capture of a ship from Central America fetching $278,000 in silver and $500,000 in indigo.

By the fall of 1816, Aury's attention had shifted to an expedition led by Spanish liberal Francisco Xavier Mina, a distinguished veteran of the Peninsular War against France, who proposed to liberate all of Mexico. With support of statesmen in England, Haiti, and the United States, Mina's expedition represented the most ambitious attempt to overthrow Mexico's Spanish regime. Having acquired aid in Port-au-Prince, Mina arrived at Galveston Bay in late November with the aim of persuading Aury and the New Orleans Association to transport his troops farther south along the Mexican coast. In the ensuing negotiations, the associates broke with both Mina and Aury, switching their allegiance to the Lafitte brothers, who had no intention of supporting Mexican revolutionaries.

At Galveston, Mina organized his army and designated Aury the commander of his naval forces. Aury's convoy landed Mina's expedition on April 21, 1817, near the mouth of the Santander river, where they easily captured the port of Soto La Marina. The Spanish revolutionary issued a proclamation on his arrival, asking Mexicans to "permit me to participate in your glorious struggles," with the assurance that they could "count me among your compatriots." Mina achieved a number of inland victories, until royalist forces overwhelmed his army in late October. In Mexico City, a Spanish tribunal condemned him to death, and in November he died before a firing squad at Fort San Gregorio, along with twenty-five fellow insurgents.[9]

Upon Aury's return to his Texas base, the shifting sands and mixed motives at Galveston Bay persuaded him to relocate to Spanish East Florida's Amelia Island in the Sea Islands chain at the Florida–Georgia frontier. In July, he, Savary, and a combined force of approximately 130 of Aury's Cartegena veterans and Savary's Louisiana troops abandoned Galveston to the Lafitte brothers and the New Orleans Association. They set sail for Haiti to resupply and replenish their crews for a rendezvous with Aury's republican ally Gregor MacGregor.

The two men had served together at the siege of Cartagena, with the Scotsman MacGregor rising through the ranks of Simon Bolívar's army and marrying into the general's family. MacGregor was as committed to Latin American independence as Aury and he proposed to conquer Spain's strategic East Florida province. Aury, Savary, and their men planned to join him.

At Fernandina, the main settlement on Amelia Island, MacGregor had forced the surrender of the Spanish garrison in June and raised the flag of the Republic of Florida under the authority of the Venezuelan revolutionary government. By mid-August, however, newcomers Ruggles Hubbard, a New York lawyer, and Jared Irwin, a former Pennsylvania congressman, had effectively ousted MacGregor and transformed the island into a base for large-scale slave smuggling across Saint Marys River into the United States.

At the mouth of Saint Marys on September 16, 1817, Aury encountered MacGregor abandoning Amelia Island for England, where the Scotsman was laying plans for supplying Spanish American insurgents with munitions. The men met for a few hours, with MacGregor describing the disappointing fate of his East Florida expedition and the existing situation on the island. The next day, Aury's *Congresso Mexicano* sailed into Fernandina's harbor and declared Amelia Island a province of the Mexican Republic. On the basis of his commission from Herrera, Aury raised the Mexican flag three days later.

Claiming preeminence over Ruggles and Irwin, Aury assumed command of MacGregor's forces and created a temporary governing body with an admiralty court. As in Galveston, Amelia's privateering commerce flourished, with an estimated $500,000 in Spanish prize ships and cargoes passing through the island within two months. In October, two veteran intellectuals of the independence struggle in South America, Don Vicente Pazos, a Buenos Aires journalist, and Pedro Gual, a supporter of MacGregor and future Venezuelan president, arrived and began drafting a permanent founding document based on the US Constitution. Gual wrote to an ally that the "influence of the emancipation of [the] Floridas on that of Mexico, New Granada,Venezuela, Buenos Ayres, Chile and Peru, is of more magnitude than it is generaly [sic] imagined."[10]

Their constitution provided for an elective legislature with voting rights extended to every inhabitant who had resided on the island for a minimum fifteen days and swore to "support the cause of the Republic of the Floridas." After six months of service, officers and privates who served the new republic faithfully would be awarded a minimum land grant of 320 acres. As in Galveston, the settlement's printing press issued a newspaper, Fernandina's weekly *El*

Telégrafo de las Floridas, with Pazos broadcasting their republican cause under the protection of the constitution's guarantee of a free press. On November 5, 1817, "year one of independence," Aury addressed Fernandina's residents: "Citizens, we are Republicans from principle . . . We have come here to plant the tree of liberty, to foster free institutions, and to wage war against the tyrant of Spain, the oppressor of America, and the enemy of the rights of man."[11]

For slaveholders only a stone's throw from the United States border with East Florida, the new republic's promise of freedom and equality for its multiracial/multiethnic citizens posed an imminent threat. United States newspapers took especial exception to the presence of Savary's armed company of officers and soldiers. Stoking obsessive fears of the Haitian Revolution, the *Savannah Republican* described the men as "brigands who had participated in the horrors of St. Domingo."[12] John Houston McIntosh, a prominent planter whose self-styled "patriots" had attempted to oust the Spanish from East Florida six years earlier, joined in the attacks. McIntosh's diatribe of November 8, 1817, also singled out Savary and his men: "His [Aury's] great dependence however, is upon about one hundred and thirty brigand negroes—a set of desperate bloody dogs" who make the "neighborhood extremely dangerous to a population like ours and I fear if they are not expelled from . . . [Fernandina] some unhappy consequence might fall on our country. It is said they have declared that if they are in danger they will call to their aid every negro within reach. Indeed, I am told that the language of the slaves is already such as to be extremely alarming."[13]

For one paranoid contributor to the *Savannah Daily Gazette,* the international contingent of soldiers and political activists threatened a replay of the French Revolution's most extreme phase, the Terror (1793–1794): "We expect daily to see a guillotine erected in Washington Square, Fernandina and some Mexican chief holding up the reeking head of an American Citizen, exclaiming 'behold the head of a traitor.'" Maryland's *Baltimore Patriot* disparaged the egalitarian camaraderie among Aury's multiethnic sailors and soldiers: "Yes! Seated at the same table, eating the same food, drinking from the same cups and wearing the same insignias."[14] The Anglophone recruits enrolled by Irwin and Hubbard in Charleston and Savannah refused to serve with the Haitian officers and sailors—men who "insist[ed] upon equal rights and privileges with the whites, and otherwise [are] very insolent indeed, [even] so as to assume equal command." The Anglo-American whites were "so enraged at the attempt of the blacks to command them that they would have died in the contest."[15]

Joseph Freeman Rattenbury, a British veteran of the Napoleonic wars who arrived near the end of October, at the height of hostilities, blamed Aury and his "French" faction for the tensions. According to Rattenbury, Aury had "acquired his ideas of liberty in the French revolutionary school" and had surrounded himself with "the refuse of all nations, and all colours, collected from the mass of iniquity spread over the islands of the West Indies, and the Spanish Americas."[16]

On November 5, Aury restored order by declaring martial law and denouncing the "mercenaries, traitors or cowards who abandoned the cause of republicanism in the hour of danger."[17] However, the greatest threat to the fledgling republic emanated from Washington, DC, where the new president, James Monroe, viewed the United States takeover of Spanish Florida as key to his objectives of expanding the nation's boundaries and achieving hemispheric dominance. In 1812, as secretary of state, Monroe had worked with President James Madison and former president Thomas Jefferson in a covert action to acquire the Spanish possession. At that time, south Georgia's patriot forces had drawn up plans to invade East Florida and cede it to the United States as their counterparts had done in West Florida. In a letter to Secretary of State Monroe, patriot leader McIntosh provided the pretext with his vehement objection to Spain's deployment of Black troops along East Florida's boundary with Georgia. Alluding to the Haitian Revolution, McIntosh predicted that the presence of Spain's armed Black soldiers would inevitably "bring about the revolt of the slave population of the United States."[18]

Supported by US Navy gunboats and regular troops, Georgia's patriots seized Amelia Island in March 1812 and declared the independent Republic of Florida. McIntosh, the new republic's director, promptly turned the Spanish territory over to the United States while the combined land and naval forces proceeded to besiege St. Augustine. The ensuing domestic and international outcry persuaded Madison and Monroe to disavow the entire venture. The turning point came in September, when a much smaller Spanish force of Black militiamen and Seminoles ambushed a convoy of patriots and US Marines. In May 1813, Spanish troops marched back into Fernandina.[19]

Upon his election to the presidency, Monroe resumed his efforts to acquire East Florida. This time the president and his ally in the failed 1812 attempt, patriot leader McIntosh, succeeded. On December 2, 1817, in his first annual message to Congress, the president announced his plans to seize both Amelia Island and Galveston from maurauding "privateers." He dismissed assertions that Amelia Island's occupying forces had been authorized by any of Spanish America's revolutionary governments. Rather, Amelia's foreign adventurers had "assumed a more marked character of unfriendliness to us" by creating "a channel for the illicit introduction of slaves from Africa into the United States, an asylum for fugitive slaves from the neighboring States, and a port for smuggling of every kind." The president offered no evidence to substantiate his charges of slave trading and piracy.[20]

Congressional supporters of Spanish American independence rallied around US Speaker of the House Henry Clay of Kentucky, who argued in favor of neutrality and against an attack that would impede liberation from Spain. William Duane, the Pennsylvanian publisher of the *Philadelphia Aurora* and a fervent supporter of the independence cause, argued that Amelia's nascent republic had been authorized by both the Mexican and Venezuelan insurgent governments and that its survival was "essentially conducive to the promotion of their [Mexico's and Venezuela's] independence." John Rhea, a congressman of Tennessee, sponsored a resolution asking the president to furnish information regarding the nature of the Amelia and Galveston establishments.[21]

On December 23, United States naval and land forces invaded Amelia Island and raised the nation's flag in Fernandina. Aury, having wisely refrained from armed resistance, joined with Pazos, who was highly respected in Spanish America's independence movement, to author an eloquent lawyerly protest. An editorialist for Venezuela's *Correo del Orinoco* defended their position by comparing the Monroe government's aggression to that of a despot rather than the actions of "a Republican administration, of virtuous people, enemies of Spanish Tyranny and lovers of independence and the liberty of its South American brothers." The invasion was "an inexcusable scandal [and] . . . we condemn the excesses of the President of the United States."[22]

On January 10, 1818, after having presented his critics with a fait accompli, Monroe assigned Secretary of State John Quincy Adams the task of responding to the House's December request for information on both Galveston and Amelia. The documents Adams submitted dealt mainly with Galveston's Lafitte brothers, who were undeniably engaged in piracy and slave trading. Adams, who regularly referred to Spanish American privateers as pirates or "piratical privateers," submitted only one document on the subject of Amelia Island.[23]

It was planter McIntosh's November 8, 1817, letter in which the patriot leader had referred to Major Savary and his troops as "desperate bloody dogs."[24] The Adams report contained nothing to substantiate the charges of slave trading. On January 13, in an attempt to tamp down further criticism, Monroe addressed Congress to formally announce the government's takeover of the island. The action, he explained, was necessary to ensure the nation's border security. Furthermore, the "foreign adventurers" who had seized Amelia had done so without authorization from any Spanish American government.[25]

When widespread press criticism intensified, the government doubled down on its insistence that the island was a pirate haven for smuggling slaves into the United States. Pro-administration newspapers buttressed the government's position. In a February letter to the Monroe administration, Pazos defended Aury, describing him as a "worthy officer and distinguished patriot," and he deplored charges by Washington officials and US newspapers that had "confounded [him] with pirates and malefactors."[26] Pazos followed his defense of Aury with a March 6 memorandum to the US Congress. Introducing himself as a "deputed agent of the authorities acting in the name of the republics of Venezuela, New Granada and Mexico," Pazos requested that his client governments be permitted a "redress of grievances." The House refused to accept his petition.[27]

In the end, the Monroe administration's misrepresentation of Aury and his allies prevailed. The success of the presidential ploy can be gauged by its ongoing influence on present-day scholarship. In his 2015 *Privateers of the Americas*, for instance, David Head reiterates the US government's portrayal of Aury as a slave trader. The French privateer's one consistency in life, Head concludes, was his "comfort with—indeed commitment to—profiting from "the sale of his fellow human persons."[28]

In one of the most authoritative studies of Aury, scholar Stanley Faye documented only one instance of the privateer's encounter with a slave ship. The incident occurred on Old Providence, an island 120 miles off the coast of present-day Nicaragua. In 1819, after ousting the Spanish from the Caribbean island, Aury established his headquarters under the authority of the allied Chilean and Buenos Aires republics. Not long afterwards, Captain Bernardo Ferrero limped into port with two vessels—his badly damaged cruiser, the *Gavilán*, and his pirated brigantine, a slave ship with ninety captive Africans. Aury's Argentine prize court embargoed the captain's vessel, condemned the cargo of Africans, and court-martialed Ferrero. Aury, the captain complained, "insulted me, my flag and my government [Colombia], replying only unwillingly to my salute the day of my arrival . . . [and] he lured away my crew before the end of my cruise."[29] Ferrero's desperate circumstances, including the exorbitant cost of provisions, forced the *Gavilán's* captain to sell his human cargo to Aury, who incorporated the men into his armed forces.[30]

Aptly described as "le corsair-jacobin" by scholar Anne Pérotin-Dumon, who counted Aury among "les corsairs de la liberté," the French privateer sailed continuously in support of Spanish American independence movements, from the time he acquired his own privateer vessel in 1813 until his death in 1821. With privateer commissions from republican juntas in Cartagena, the United Provinces of New Granada, Mexico, Buenos Aires, and Chile, Aury's effective attacks on Spanish shipping helped weaken colonial rule. With the confiscated resources, he fortified his privateer navy, funded and transported cash-strapped insurgent armies, and launched nascent republics in Mexico, Spanish Florida, and the western Caribbean. His efforts in New Spain led the famed Mexican insurgent José María Morelos to proclaim him the first governor of Texas under the Republic of Mexico. From his base of operations on Old Providence, he continued to aid the independence cause in Spanish America. The Haitian republic was key to his far-reaching campaigns.[31]

Haiti's national life stood on the foundation of slavery's abolition, with President Pétion promoting the cause of international abolitionism. By the time Aury, Courtois, and pro-independence families fled Cartagena in 1816 for refuge in Les Cayes, Pétion had broadened his antislavery project beyond seizing offshore slave trading vessels and liberating African captives. As historian Ada Ferrer has shown, the Haitian president pressed Bolívar and other "Latin American revolutionaries toward new and more radical policies" by requiring two pledges in return for Haitian assistance.[32]

In the first instance, Pétion linked asylum and logistics support to a pledge from Bolívar to abolish slavery in the republics he was fighting to create. In a second, less well-known pledge, Bolívar agreed to bar insurgent privateers from selling captives taken from slave trading vessels. The human cargoes were to be transported to Haiti, where Pétion's free soil policy, legally enshrined in Article 44 of his 1816 constitution, offered freedom and citizenship to all Brown and Black people setting foot in the Haitian republic, regardless of their status. In view of Haitian policies and Aury's dependence on Pétion for asylum, munitions, Haitian sailors and soldiers, and other vital necessities, it seems unlikely that the corsair Jacobin would have betrayed his key patron in the manner described by Head and other historians.[33]

On Amelia Island in late December 1817, Aury remained calm with the approach of United States land and naval forces. Likely recalling the murderous dockside attack on his Black sailors in Savannah, he ordered all of his officers and soldiers of African descent to take shelter on a vessel anchored offshore. With the invasion of his nascent republic, Aury surrendered peacefully to US forces. The ship carrying Savary, Sévère Courtois, Marcelin Guillot, and their comrades in arms transported the men to safety. In early January 1818, Savary appeared in Galveston. During the summer, Aury, Courtois, and Guillot reemerged in the Caribbean, where they seized Old Providence Island from the Spanish and proposed to join revolutionary forces on the Spanish Main. By that time, Bolívar had concluded that his ties to Haiti and Afro-Caribbean privateers were a liability.

After conquering remaining Spanish forces at Santa Fe on August 7, 1819, and proclaiming the Republic of Colombia in December, President Bolívar set out to achieve international respectability and diplomatic recognition. In view of British, French, and United States hostility toward the Black republic, Bolívar moved to shut down his political ties to the Haitian nation and disavow its privateering allies. In early 1821, when Aury volunteered to incorporate his forces into the Colombian military, Bolívar issued a stinging rebuke, writing, "The Republic of Colombia has raised itself to the state of no longer needing any more privateers who degrade its flag in all the seas of the world."

Notwithstanding President Pétion's crucial support of Colombia's independence movement, the new nation's founding elite went even further in their efforts to repudiate their ties the Haitian republic. They portrayed themselves as "white, civilized, and enlightened" while shunning "the stigma of blackness, barbarism, and obscurantism associated with the Caribbean." When Aury died after an 1821 riding accident, Courtois succeeded him as Old Providence's commandant and joined the ill-fated 1823 Soles y Rayos de Bolívar revolutionary conspiracy to liberate Cuba. When the attempted revolt failed, Courtois returned to Haiti.[34]

By 1821, Savary had returned to his family in New Orleans and taken up residence in his French Quarter home at Burgundy and Hospital (present-day Governor Nicholls) Streets with his wife Eugénie Pressot (also Presand or Presot), a native, like her husband, of Saint-Marc. In return for his valor in the Battle of New Orleans, the state awarded Savary a pension that was probably the highest assigned to any Louisiana veteran of the War of 1812. His radicalism notwithstanding, Savary worked within the state's legal constraints to assist the free community of color in Louisiana's increasingly harsh caste system, a system that sought to relegate all free Black people to an inferior status,

In an era when white authorities viewed cabarets and grocery stores as sites of subversion, Savary appeared as a bondsman for taverners and store-keepers serving liquor. In at least two instances, "Uncle" Savary sponsored free teenagers of color for apprenticeships—Alfred Audige, a native of Curaçao, as a joiner/cabinetmaker, and Charles Suffren as a cooper. Decades later, during the secession crisis, the city's Catholic Church praised all of the free Black companies as the "worthy grandsons of the noble [Joseph] Savary" until the men enlisted in the US Army. Savary's profile in courage prompted one corps of Civil War soldiers to designate itself the Savary Company.[35]

Like Savary, Haiti's Pétion remained a revered figure among Afro-Creole New Orleanians. In an 1838 meeting of the Société d'economie et d'assistance mutuelle, merchant Pierre Antoine Jonau presented a portrait of the Hai-tian president to the antebellum city's most prosperous social organization. During the ceremony, Henry Chevarre, the society's president and a veteran of the Battle of New Orleans, called upon members to emulate Pétion's attri-butes: "Always observe with veneration the purity of this great man who only caused tears to fall at his death. In imitation of his virtues, we likewise unite to demonstrate our indissoluble ties." The painting of Pétion, mounted near a portrait of George Washington, remained a fixture at Société d'economie events for decades, serving as a source of pride and inspiration for the organi-zation's members.[36]

In 1789, Thomas Paine pointed out to George Washington that "a share in two revolutions is living to some purpose."[37] Savary, Aury, Humbert, Courtois, and their comrades had likewise lived to "some purpose" in their share of rev-olutions. In their support for Spanish American independence movements, they had advanced the cause of democratic change by weakening Spain's grip on its imperial dominions in the Americas. In 1825, Savary crossed paths with Gilbert du Motier de Lafayette (1757–1834), a fellow itinerant revolutionary who shared his commitment to national independence and equality. The Mar-quis de Lafayette had first joined his voice to the "le cri universel de la liberté" during the American Revolution.[38]

With an international reputation as the "hero of two worlds," Lafayette set out on a whirlwind tour of the United States (1824–1825) at the age of sixty-eight. In New Orleans, thunderous artillery fire and rapturous crowds greeted his arrival. In the midst of the weeklong processions, receptions, and other entertainments, Lafayette requested a meeting with the free Black veterans of the Battle of New Orleans. In the North and South, he had repeatedly asked to meet with African Americans, both slave and free, to remind the nation's white citizens of the significant role of Blacks in the American Revolution. His Louisiana hosts hastily organized a deputation and the men met with Lafayette on April 14, the day before his departure.

Speaking in French, the general praised the veterans for their valuable service in the War of 1812 and recalled the sacrifices of African American men during the American Revolution, when he had seen them shed their blood "with honor in our ranks for the cause of the United States." He shook hands with every member of the delegation, greeting each man, according to the *Courier de la Louisiane*, with "esteem and affection." He also chatted with Major Savary of the Second Battalion and Captain Louis (Luis) Simón of the First Battalion, having been informed by Governor Henry S. Johnson of their bravery in the New Orleans battle. Though their conversation was necessarily brief, the three men had much in common.[39]

Like Lafayette, Simón's father, Charles (Carlos) Simón, was a decorated veteran of the American Revolution who had fought under the Spanish in the Louisiana campaigns against the British. Lafayette's interest in Savary's homeland antedated the French Revolution, to the time when he joined the antislavery Société des amis des noirs (Society of the Friends of Blacks). In the early years of the revolution, he continued to press for emancipation and free Black equality in the French Caribbean, along with Jacques-Pierre Brissot, Abbé Henri-Baptiste Grégoire, and the Marquis de Condorcet.

In 1789 in France, in his capacity as the commander of the Paris National Guard, Lafayette invited Vincent Ogé and five other Saint-Domingue leaders of color to a dinner party for the visiting English abolitionist Thomas Clarkson. To Clarkson's considerable surprise, Ogé and his colleagues attended the soirée wearing Lafayette's Parisian National Guard/militiaman-as-citizen uniforms. In postrevolutionary Haiti, Lafayette supported Pétion's republic.[40]

The day after his meeting with Savary, Simón, and their fellow veterans, Lafayette shared his excitement and his disappointment with his daughters: "Mes chères amies, . . . This almost entirely French republic has something entirely piquant." However, he continued, "there is only one point to which I decidedly cannot resign myself: that is slavery, and the anti-black prejudices." Scotswoman Frances "Fanny" Wright, a close friend of the general, visited with him in the city. Wright, a political writer, abolitionist, and radical feminist, was appalled. Her visit to New Orleans was galvanizing: "Slavery I expected to find here in its horror, and truly in all its horrors it is found." The experience strengthened her resolve to remain in the United States and fight for slavery's abolition.[41]

Wright first met Lafayette in 1821, during the reactionary era of the Bourbon Restoration (1814–1830), when the marquis's faith in the French Revolution's early promise of "liberté, egalité, fraternité" led him to throw open the doors of his French residences to like-minded guests. His quasi-religious belief in freedom, equality, and national independence placed him at the center of an international network of men and women writers, political activists, and revolutionaries. His allies included a new generation of Romantic intellectuals who, like Wright, incorporated eighteenth-century notions of human rights into new forms of political and cultural expression. Until the end of his life, Lafayette advocated the presence of liberty and constitutionally protected rights everywhere and at all times in a career that, according to historian Lloyd Kramer, "brought the eighteenth-century Enlightenment and revolutions into the culture of nineteenth-century Romanticism."[42]

In their words and deeds on both sides of the Atlantic, Lafayette and Wright reinforced the Romantic movement's vitality and prospects for revolutionary change. In New Orleans, their brief presence validated French Romanticism's political ethos—an ethos that had united Savary, Humbert, Aury, Courtois, and their allies in their armed struggle for equality while linking them to nationalists everywhere in a common struggle against dynastic autocrats. Under the cover of literary Romanticism, the free veteran soldiers of color who remained in the city maintained their faith in republicanism and resisted the rising tide of white oppression. Attuned to Romanticism's liberating possibilities, they laid down their arms, seized their pens, and channeled their discontent into Romantic protest literature. In the new style of warfare, hostilities would unfold on a literary battlefield.[43]

Near the time of Lafayette's visit, the city's free Black veterans-turned-artisans founded La Société des Artisans in the mode of the Francophone Atlantic's French and Haitian *cénacles* (literary societies). In these tightly knit societies, Romantic authors shared their work, protested injustice, and formulated resistance strategies. In New Orleans as in Paris and Port-au-Prince, cénacle writers became active agents of change by assuming a broader, quasi-political role within the free Francophone communityof color.

In one of the many Afro-Creole works of protest literature authored in the city prior to 1840, an anonymous veteran with the pseudonym Hippolyte Castra attacked the treatment of free soldiers of color in the aftermath of the Battle of New Orleans. The poem, "The Campaign of 1814–15," is believed to have been recited at a Société des Artisans meeting before veterans-turned-artisans such as Sylvain d'Aquin. At the approach of the British, the author wrote, white soldiers urged men of color to "Come, let us conquer, my brothers." After their victory in "this terrible and glorious combat, all of you shared a drink with me and called me a valiant soldier." Soon, however, "fierce looks" replaced the "gracious smile" and the veteran soldiers of color became "an object of scorn."[44]

In providing a literary forum for free New Orleanians of color, La Société laid the foundation for a stellar African American literary tradition that has thrived into the present-day. With a Francophone membership that included whites as well as men of color, the organization yielded its first prodigy in the person of Victor Séjour. The aspiring young writer debuted his work before a society audience that included the refugee officers and soldiers of the Second Battalion. The artist's father, Louis Victor Séjour, was an officer in d'Aquin's unit and was, like his commanding officers d'Aquin and Savary, a native of Saint-Marc who entered Louisiana as a member of Savary's garrison in the 1809 migration. By 1822, he operated a small dry goods store. His young son's extraordinary talent impressed the organization's interracial membership and sometime between 1834 and 1836, the teenage Séjour left New Orleans for Paris.

In France in 1837, the abolitionist journal *Revue des colonies* published Séjour's "Le Mulâtre" (The Mulatto), the first short story by a United States African American author. Set in Saint-Domingue, the tale is exceptional for its straightforward depiction of slavery's horrors. In subsequent works, *Diégarias* (Jew of Seville), accepted by the Comédie Française in 1844, and *The Fortune-Teller* (1859), Séjour dramatized the dangers of multiethnic identity in a society divided by race and religion. Two other manuscripts of a protest nature, *l'Esclave* (The Slave) and a drama based on the life of abolitionist John Brown, have yet to be recovered.

In Paris, Séjour's skills as a dramatist propelled him to critical and popular acclaim. Twenty of his twenty-two plays were performed on Parisian stages between 1844 and 1875 with three of his productions being performed simultaneously in the French capital. In New Orleans where *Diégarias* was well received in 1847, white supremacists dissed a proposal to honor the playwright with a medal recognizing his success.

In his 1858 drama *Le Martyre du Coeur* (Martyrdom of the Heart), Séjour featured a Black character in a major role. The play weighed the outcomes of emancipations in Haiti, France, and the British Caribbean as models for slavery's abolition in the United States. In the end, the dramatist depicts the British model of abolition through peaceful political reform as the best way forward for North America. Séjour's artful strategy allowed him to steer clear of Napoléon III's pro-South sympathies while upholding his dedication to the antislavery cause. When Séjour died in Paris in 1874, the French memorialized his genius by burying him in the city's famed Père Lachaise cemetery.[45]

Beginning with their illegal entry into the city in 1809, Louis Victor Séjour, the Savarys, and their fellow veteran soldiers repeatedly ignored state and city laws designed to relegate them to an inferior status. The international character of La Société des Artisans, a cénacle with a politically charged mission, represented a clear and present danger to the interests of white slaveholding planters. The society's multiracial membership challenged the spirit if not the letter of local statutes restricting contact between whites and people of color. Still, conservative city and state officials refrained from a crackdown on La Société despite their intense hostility to the mere presence of the free men of color. Their caution might be attributed to the possible presence in the organization of well-connected whites like d'Aquin and his powerful allies in the refugee population.[46]

At the time of the British attack on the city, d'Aquin's close-knit Franco-phone network included Lieutenant Théodat Camille Bruslé, who had remained with his brother-in-law when d'Aquin was assigned to the Louisiana militia and then transferred to the Second Battalion of Free Men of Color. Bruslé's sister, Josephine-Charlotte Benigne, was married to Joseph Patrice DuBourg, Pierre-François DuBourg's brother. During the battle, Pierre-François DuBourg served on Governor Claiborne's staff. DuBourg was also related to the extremely wealthy Bringier family through the marriage of his daughter, Algaé DuBourg, to Michel Doradou Bringier. In 1814, Michel Doradou's brother, Paul-Louis, had served in Mexico's revolutionary government in exile alongside General Humbert. With hostilities threatening, both Bringier brothers, Michel Doradou and Paul-Louis, enlisted in Captain Jean Chauveau's cavalry company. During the battle, Michel Doradou served as General Jackson's aide-de-camp. To celebrate the victory, Bringier patriarch Marius Pons Bringier entertained Jackson and his wife, Rachel, as houseguests at his palatial White Hall plantation in St. James Parish. Over the years, the Bringier family maintained their friendship, and in 1840 the hero of New Orleans and former president visited Michel Doradou Bringier's plantation l'Hermitage, named after Jackson's Tennessee estate.[47]

Business agreements as well as Catholic marriages and baptisms fortified the d'Aquin/DuBourg/Bruslé/Bringier network. D'Aquin and Bruslé were especially close, having married the d'Eynaut sisters, Célinie Adelaïde and Marie-Josephine Alix, respectively. In 1810, Marius Pons Bringier served as the Catholic godfather at the baptism of d'Aquin's daughter, Marie Thérèse. In the same year, Pierre François DuBourg entered into a business partnership with Marius Pons Bringier's son-in-law Noel Auguste Baron Jr. D'Aquin's ties also extended to his fellow Saint-Domingue refugee Louis Moreau-Lislet. In 1808, the distinguished Louisiana jurist partnered with Marie-Josephine Alix Bruslé to act as godparents for d'Aquin's daughter, Elisabeth Josephine.[48]

At the same time, close-knit alliances born of revolution, loss, and flight were evolving on Marius Pons Bringier's White Hall plantation in St. James Parish. The intimate ties would have far-reaching consequences. In 1804, Marie Anne "Nanene" Roudanez, a refugee of the Haitian Revolution, married the wealthy widower Marius Pons Bringier in St. Mary's Church on Chartres Street in New Orleans. During the revolution, Nesterine, Roudanez's enslaved servant, had saved her life. The two women escaped to Louisiana and remained virtually inseparable for the rest of their lives. On or near the Bringier plantation, Marie Anne Roudanez's brother, Jean-Louis Roudanez, met Aimée Potens, a free woman of color and a midwife. Born in Saint-Domingue to an enslaved woman, Potens had escaped the revolution as an infant in arms.

With a reputation as a "very honorable French merchant," Jean-Louis Roudanez married Potens despite an 1808 Louisiana law prohibiting marriage between free people of color and whites. In the circumstances, the couple likely married under the religious authority of Antonio de Sedella (Père Antoine), the schismatic head of the New Orleans Catholic Church. In 1815, Potens gave birth to their first son, Jean-Baptiste Roudanez. Their second son, Louis-Charles Roudanez, was born in 1823, with Marie Anne Roudanez and Marius Ste. Colombe Bringier, Doradou Bringier's son, serving as his godparents. In the same year as his second son's birth, Jean-Louis Roudanez died, leaving the two boys fatherless.

Their father's death and their mixed-race identity notwithstanding, both Jean-Baptiste and Louis-Charles Roudanez were dispatched to France, where they were trained in engineering and medicine, respectively. Jean-Baptiste returned to Louisiana to work as an engineer and mechanic on the Bringiers' sugar plantations and other estates of the region, where his expertise in setting sugar kettles was in great demand. In antebellum New Orleans,

Louis-Charles established a thriving medical practice treating a multiracial medical clientele.

In 1803, near the time of Marie Anne Roudanez's marriage to Emmanuel-Marius Pons Bringier, another key family alliance was sealed when Bringier's daughter Elisabeth married Augustin Dominique Tureaud, a native of La Rochelle, France, and a Saint-Domingue refugee. By making a wedding gift of Union sugar plantation to the couple, Bringier forged a business as well as a family partnership. The complex web of Roudanez–Bringier–Tureaud familial, business, and interracial ties would produce three of the most important African American civil rights leaders of the nineteenth and twentieth centuries, the Roudanez brothers and A. P. Tureaud.[49]

In 1840, when General Andrew Jackson stopped at Michel Doradou Bringier's l'Hermitage plantation, his destination was New Orleans. He visited the city for the ceremonial laying of a cornerstone for a memorial marking the site of his position on the Chalmette battlefield on January 8, 1815. During the ceremony, Jackson expressed a desire to meet with the free Black veterans of the battle. City officials arranged a reception at the aged general's hotel, where the men were introduced as "the brave soldiers who fought in defense of the country under the orders of Majors Lacoste and Daquin and who now wished to pay their respects and shake the hand of their General as a token of gratitude." In the deeply moving encounter, the men recalled their experiences on the Chalmette battlefield twenty-five years earlier, when their comaraderie had defeated invading British forces.[50]

By the time of the meeting between Jackson and his former comrades in arms, both the original Battalion of Chosen Men of Color, an institution founded in 1729, and the Second Battalion had become casualties of Louisiana's increasingly harsh caste system. In 1834, the year of d'Aquin's death, Louisiana state legislators overturned the 1812 legislation providing for the First Battalion. The new law restricted service in the state militia to white citizens, while repealing all of the supplementary measures providing for the service of militiamen of color. By their actions, lawmakers had officially terminated the two free Black battalions. That same year, members of La Société, an organization founded by veterans of color, incorporated their organization in a legal action that extended its life into the twentieth century.[51]

After 1830, the implementation of an Anglo-American racial order relegating all people of color—both slave and free—to a separate and inferior caste gathered momentum. As elsewhere in the South, segregation, anti-

miscegenation laws, and the legal ostracism of racially mixed children signified the imposition of two-category pattern of racial classification. While
increasingly restrictive manumission laws curtailed the size of the free population of color, the movement toward a dual racial order aimed to reduce all
free people of African ancestry to a degraded status.

By the time of Jackson's 1840 visit, Charles-Louis d'Aquin's bakehouse,
despite its tumultuous start, had grown into a thriving family business, the
Daquin Brothers Bakery on New Levee Street (present-day South Peters). The
company, operated by François, Adophe, and Thomas d'Aquin, prospered up
to the time of the Civil War. Charles-Louis d'Aquin's daughter Marie Althée
Josephine d'Aquin enhanced the prestige of her family by her marriage to the
wealthy planter Louis de Puèch, a Saint-Domingue refugee like her father.
Althée's three children were educated in France, and their son, Ernest Auguste
de Puèch, returned to New Orleans, where he organized the city's Cotton Exchange and became its first president.

In their youth, Althée d'Aquin and her four sisters, Léocadie, Lucile,
Uranie, and Célina, were renowned in New Orleans for their beauty. Althée
d'Aquin was the favorite relative of Hélène Allain's father, Louis-Charles
d'Aquin. His cousin "won over everybody's heart" with her "fineness of mind
as well as [her] charming kindness."[52] Louis-Charles d'Aquin's close ties to
his uncle's immediate family, together with Major d'Aquin's legacy of distinguished military service and his extensive socioeconomic network, promised
a bright future for his godson, Louis-Charles d'Aquin, a failed refugee planter
from the British Caribbean. Louis-Charles d'Aquin's decision to resettle his
family in New Orleans ensured that his young daughter Hélène d'Aquin would
grow up in a city at the crossroads of the revolutionary Atlantic.

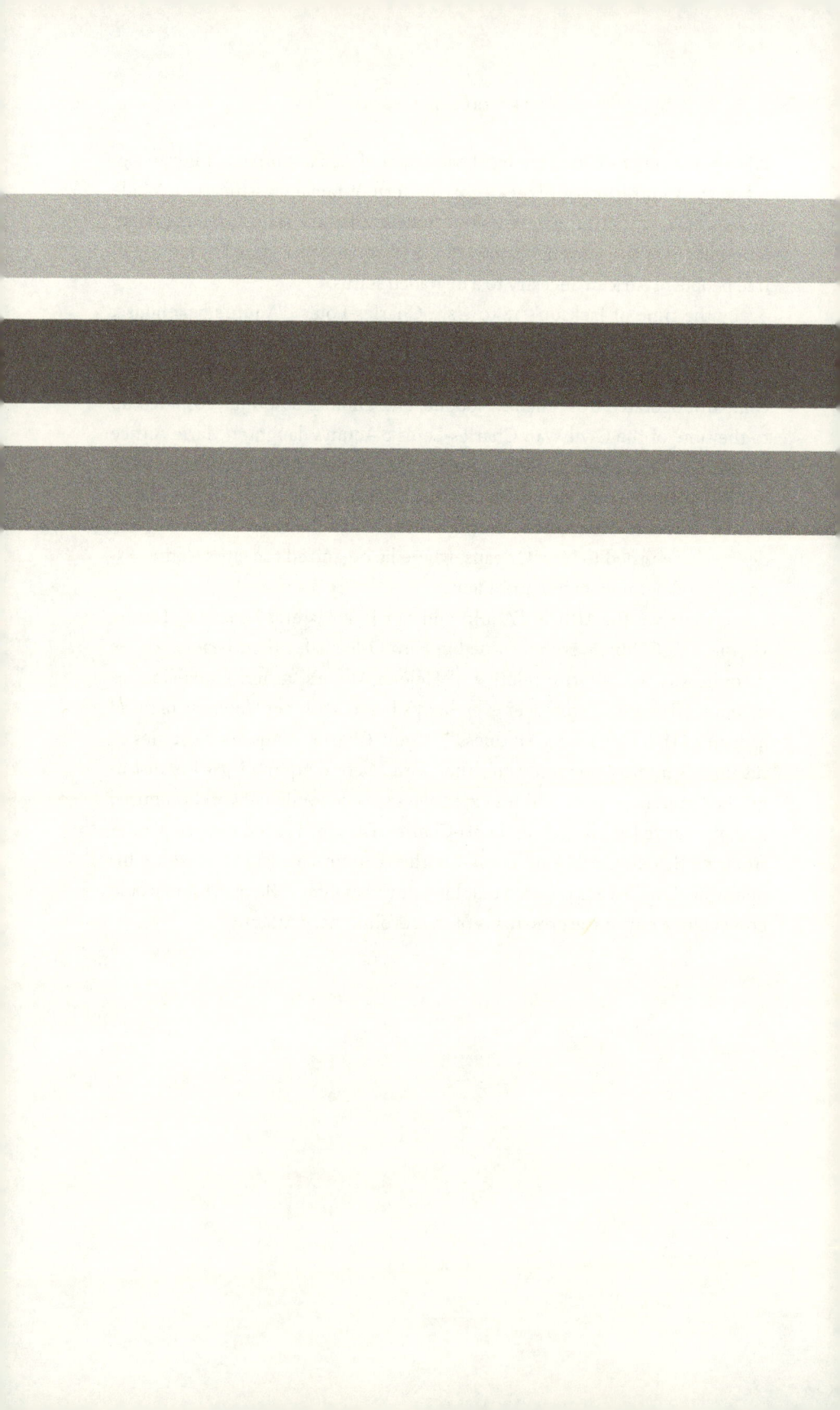

II.

FRENCH

ROMANTICISM

Internationally, Romanticism's adherents could be found in both conservative and liberal camps. Owing, however, to the highly politicized nature of French Romanticism, the movement's proponents throughout the Francophone Atlantic remained committed to fulfilling the Age of Revolution's republican promise. Their numbers included the Afro-Creole intelligentsia of New Orleans and Haiti.

Shaken by the Romantic assault, France's political and religious ramparts gave way in the 1848 French Revolution. Alphonse de Lamartine, French Romanticism's most politically active artist, and Félicité de Lamennais, Romanticism's renegade Catholic "chaplain," stood at the political forefront when France's Second Republic abolished slavery and proclaimed universal male suffrage. In New Orleans, the city's Afro-Creole intelligentsia marveled at the sight of African-descended elected representatives seated alongside Lamartine, Lamennais, and other celebrated republicans in France's Constituent Assembly. They anticipated the day when they would achieve the same freedoms and political rights in their own nation.

By the time Hélène d'Aquin Allain arrived in New Orleans in 1836, French Romanticism had already coalesced with an egalitarian philosophy of radical Catholic reform. The two movements shared a belief in the indivisibility of God and nature. For the Catholic masses, prayer served as the ethereal medium. In this new spiritual/mystical dynamic, all peoples would unite in a system of universal fraternity. The revolutionary implications of the new belief system struck a deep chord in a profoundly religious Francophone city inured to orthodox Catholicism's spirit-in-matter piety.

Allain encountered the excitement of the reform movement in her own interracial household, where her Afro-Creole companion engaged her in indelible out-of-body experiences. In her neighborhood's interracial church, she worshiped alongside free women of color who shared her ancestral roots in Saint-Domingue/Haiti and her belief in Catholicism's spiritual/mystical humanitarianism. In the city streets, she observed vaudoux's dynamism with its blending of ancient African religious beliefs, Catholicism, and Native American practices. Though personally well tutored in vaudoux's dangerously explosive power, Allain, like so many other Francophone New Orleanians, nonetheless found the slave religion's "invisible powers" irresistible.

FOUR

Une Famille Créole

U ne Famille Créole," chapter 4, recounts three-year-old Allain's arrival in New Orleans in 1836, where she and her impoverished family were taken in by relatives. Educated in the school her mother had founded to support her family, Allain fully absorbed the spiritual/mystical philosophy of Catholic reformers attempting to resuscitate the French Catholic Church in the aftermath of the French Revolution and the Napoleonic wars. Within Allain's intensely religious household, her aunt, a Catholic nun, replicated a convent cell in the loft of their home while her pious "uncle" ministered to the poor.

Allain and her family regularly attended a Catholic church where an interracial coalition of Francophone women shared their interest in Catholic reformers and aspired to found a convent. At the same time, the women discreetly elevated sacramental doctrine over racially discriminatory civil law in their religious practices. After the city's church authorities refused their two attempts to establish an interracial religious order, they founded the second order of African American Catholic nuns in the United States. Like the first Black convent, the New Orleanians traced their ancestral roots to Saint-Domingue/Haiti.

This chapter ends with a discussion of the slave markets that emerged between 1840 and 1862 within steps of Allain's home and along the pathway to her church. Her surrounding neighborhood grew into the focal point of North America's largest slave market, with thousands of human beings caught up in the merciless trade. In the antebellum South altogether, more than 2 million men, women, and children were reduced to the status of movable property and subjected to unspeakable horrors.

* * *

Three-year-old Hélène-Marie-Joseph d'Aquin arrived in New Orleans in the spring of 1836 with her father, Louis-Charles d'Aquin, her mother, Marie-Anne-Elisabeth Daron, and her three young siblings: six-year-old Henri-Charles, one-year-old Elisabeth, and infant Paul-Joseph George. Like her parents, Hélène d'Aquin was born into British Jamaica's Saint-Domingue refugee community after her grandparents fled the Haitian Revolution. Upon arriving in Kingston, her grandfather, Charles-Pierre d'Aquin, settled in Saint Thomas in the Vale with his wife, Marie-Louise-Victoire Le Bon de Lapointe.

In the island's Blue Mountains region, he managed four coffee plantations and supervised as many as thirty-four slave workers. His son Louis-Charles d'Aquin, Allain's father, was sent to France for his education. "My father," Allain wrote, "who had left Kingston at the age of twelve to attend Louis le Grand lycée in Paris, was the only boy my grandfather could afford to send to a respectable college. He taught his daughters himself."

In Paris, her father's French guardian deserted Louis-Charles in the midst of his studies. When Louis-Charles was unable to pay his fees, the headmaster evicted him from his lodgings. When his aunt Marie-Charlotte-Zélie d'Aquin Reynaud de Barbarin learned of his distress, she welcomed her brother's child "with open arms." In his aunt's home, her son Auguste befriended the young student while she and her husband, Jean-Baptiste Reynaud de Barbarin, refugees of the Haitian Revolution living in France, resolved the crisis. Louis-Charles d'Aquin returned to Louis-le-Grand and completed his education. Upon his return to Jamaica, he worked with his father managing slave plantations and courted Marie-Anne-Elisabeth Daron, Allain's mother and the daughter of Marie-Anne-Elisabeth Desmortiers and Dr. Jean-Paul Daron.[1]

Upon their arrival in Jamaica, Saint-Domingue's Francophone Catholic refugees set about forging new family networks through godparentage and marriage. For the displaced Daron and d'Aquin families, the ties were especially close. Their alliance produced a triple marriage, with Allain's father and two of his sisters marrying three of the Daron siblings; Louis-Charles d'Aquin wed Marie-Anne-Elisabeth Daron (Allain's father and mother), Eveline-Marguerite-Françoise d'Aquin wed Charles-Joseph-Edouard Daron, and Louise-Marie-Thérèse Elmire d'Aquin married Pierre-Elie-Theodore Daron. Their tightly knit kinship ties rested, however, upon shifting sands. By the time Allain's parents wed in 1827, Jamaican slavery was tottering.[2]

The Haitian Revolution had shaken the British slave regime to its foundation. Within months of the great slave revolt that drove the d'Aquin and Desmortiers families from Saint-Domingue, a Jamaican slave conspiracy marked the onset of a cascading series of plots and insurrections that in 1831 would culminate in one of the hemisphere's four largest slave rebellions. For the British government, the alternative was clear. An attenuated emancipation from above was far preferable to revolutionary emancipation from below. The English Parliament's 1833 Act of Abolition went into effect in Britain's Caribbean colonies in August of the following year.[3]

The prospect of economic ruin and emigration likely hastened the death of Allain's grandfather, Charles-Pierre d'Aquin. Six years earlier, he had buried his forty-nine-year-old wife, Marie-Louise-Victoire Le Bon de Lapointe. In 1834, just five months ahead of Britain's legal abolition of slavery, sixty-three-year-old Charles-Pierre d'Aquin died in Kingston. After burying her grandfather, Allain's family struggled to survive in the new economy. But as with slavery's destruction in Saint-Domingue, British emancipation in Jamaica forced a new generation of French-speaking planters into flight. Uprooted and impoverished, Hélène and her family looked to the Louisiana branch of their transatlantic kinship network for support.

Between 1835 and 1840, the last major wave of nineteenth-century Caribbean refugees disembarked in New Orleans. Allain, with her parents and three siblings, joined the exodus. They had "naturally turned to Louisiana" where the presence of family members and friends promised a favorable reception. Upon their arrival, they were immediately taken in by Charles-Joseph-Edouard Daron (Allain's mother's brother) and Eveline-Marguerite-Françoise d'Aquin (her father's sister). Allain's aunt and uncle had married in 1821 in Kingston before emigrating to the city.[4]

When Allain's family took up residence in the Daron's French Quarter household in the mid-1830s, they joined a large, diverse, and assertive Francophone community. Between the onset of the French Revolution in 1789 and the start of the US Civil War in 1861, thousands of free and enslaved migrants displaced by the Francophone Atlantic's revolutions, coups d'état, and royalist reactions fortified the city's Creole population of whites, free people of color, and enslaved New Orleanians. Reinforced by the massive 1809–1810 influx in equal proportions of white, free Black, and enslaved Saint-Domingue refugees, French-speaking residents refused to yield either their language or their cultural identity to the Anglo-American newcomers. Owing to their tenacity after the 1803 Louisiana Purchase, New Orleans remained the South's island of Creole culture well into the nineteenth century.

By 1830, African Americans (enslaved and free) represented 56.5 percent of the urban population in a city with a tenacious Francophone culture that surprised contemporary visitors. In *Domestic Manners of the Americans* (1832), British author Frances Trollope described New Orleans as having "much the appearance of a French Ville de Province" and noted "the large proportion of blacks seen in the streets, all labour being performed by them." French émigré and New Orleans author Charles Testut described a city that appeared little changed as late as 1852, describing "New Orleans with its First Municipality [French Quarter], a French city in an American city, that has kept, after nearly ninety years of foreign domination, boundaries as clearly defined as those of the muddy river stream that flows into the deep blue sea." For the d'Aquins, the city's thriving Francophone community, supportive family network, and slave-based economy appeared to bode well for their success. Yet their family's experiences in two failed slave regimes pointed to an unpredictable future. Transatlantic, national, and local developments contributed to that uncertainty.[5]

Carried forward from the Enlightenment, a deep current of humanitarianism gathered momentum in the nineteenth-century Atlantic world. The degradation of human beings in slavery came to be seen as alien to civilized societies. In the United States North, the new outlook coalesced in 1831 in demands for slavery's immediate abolition. Elsewhere in the western hemisphere, Chile, Central America, and Mexico had ended slavery by 1830 and the newly emergent South American Republics, with the exception of Paraguay, had provided for slavery's extinction. Current and formerly enslaved people played a crucial role in the independence struggles. Constituting between a quarter and a half of those who fought the Spaniards, they leveraged their military support into freedom and citizenship.[6]

In the United States South, a revolutionary call to action arrived from Massachusetts in the form of a pamphlet written by David Walker, a North Carolina–born free man of color living in the North. His treatise, *Walker's Appeal . . . to the Coloured Citizens of the World,* was published in Boston in September 1829 and urged people of color in the United States and around the world to unite and end their subjugation. With firsthand knowledge of the covert communication network commanded by enslaved southerners, Walker succeeded in distributing his pamphlet to New Orleans and other port cities throughout the South. His booklet arrived in Louisiana soon after its publication and fortified an ongoing struggle. Between 1829 and 1831, renewed slave resistance swept the river region from Pointe Coupée to Plaquemines Parish south of New Orleans.

In March 1829, only forty miles north of the city, enslaved workers once again revolted on German Coast plantations, and this "created a general alarm, but was speedily suppressed and two of the ringleaders hung." Though it was swiftly ended, it left an "insurrectionary spirit" in its wake. In New Orleans, an 1829 Christmas slave conspiracy was thwarted when one of the enslaved women exposed the Black conspirators. Less than three weeks later, on January 13, a large fire ignited simultaneously "on all sides of the square" left "no doubt of its being the work of malicious design." During the same month, two other conflagrations consumed "several thousand bales of cotton."

In March 1830, city authorities arrested a free merchant of color, Robert Smith, for possession of Walker's pamphlet, and early the next month two more slave leaders were executed for plotting an insurrection. In Plaquemines Parish below New Orleans, in October, a conspiracy involving free men of color and as many as one hundred slaves was discovered. Two companies of militiamen succeeded in arresting the ringleaders, who "were to be punished."

In the aftermath of the 1831 Nat Turner rebellion in Southampton County, Virginia, in which at least fifty-five whites were killed, Louisiana authorities acquired information that "the colored people in the (West Indian) Islands, had a correspondence with the Blacks of Louisiana." The communication encouraged "the insurrectionary dispositions" of the "coloured population of that city [New Orleans], and along the coast, to rise upon the white inhabitants." With fears of slave rebellion sweeping the entire region, President Andrew Jackson dispatched federal reinforcements in response to the entreaties of state officials.[7]

In New Orleans, Louis-Charles d'Aquin languished after his 1836 arrival in the city. Seemingly recognizing the perils ahead and depleted by his failure and dependence, he grew increasingly melancholic. In November, Allain's father, sapped of his vigor, died in the home of his brother-in-law and his sister, Charles-Joseph Daron and Eveline-Marguerite d'Aquin Daron, at the age of thirty-six. "I was not yet four-years old," Allain recalled, "and only six months had elapsed since my parents had left the picturesque blue mountains of Jamaica when my mother was widowed . . . Accustomed to the open air, to the freedom of life in the fields, to the rich existence of the former planters, my poor father could not bear New Orleans' climate and all the discomforts caused by his loss of independence. He left behind four orphans."[8]

The following May, Allain's one-year-old sister Elisabeth died: "Our little sister, Elisabeth, the only one who had inherited his [her father's] blue eyes, soon followed him into heaven and we were only three [children]."[9]

Death struck again in early November 1838: "Another grave was opened soon thereafter: my [maternal] grandmother [Marie-Anne-Elisabeth Daron] died of apoplexy [a stroke] on All Saints Day. She was stricken on the street while walking with me to Mass. Her last glance was for her beloved grandchild Henri [Allain's brother] who had arrived that morning from the college of Grand Coteau [Louisiana] where he had spent his first year." Allain recalled those early years in Louisiana as a time "enshrouded in sadness" when she was "bathed by her [mother's] tears as much as cared for by her hands." Rarely, she observed, did her mother smile.[10]

After the loss of her husband, mother, and one-year-old daughter within a space of two years, Marie-Anne-Elisabeth Daron d'Aquin, Allain's mother, could not conceal her grief. At the same time, however, she set about rebuilding her family's life. After her husband's death in 1836, d'Aquin joined the ranks of widowed and single French émigré women who turned to teaching to support themselves and their families. As subsequent events would show, her parents, the Darons, had made a considerable investment in their daughter's education.

A good education paid off handsomely for émigré Ann Marsan Talvande, a Saint-Domingue refugee who had fled the Caribbean for South Carolina. She founded Madame Talvande's French School for Young Ladies in the heart of Charleston. Talvande's patrons were the daughters of the region's great planters, young women like the famed diarist Mary Boykin Chesnut. Though d'Aquin did not achieve the celebrity or the stature of Talvande, she acquired a respectable reputation and financial success.

The Daron's spacious living quarters on the corner of Condé (present-day Chartres) and Quartier (present-day Barracks) Streets, with its two-story brick building divided into twelve rooms and a loft, proved ideal for d'Aquin's purposes. The compound could be accessed through a side entranceway on Barracks Street that opened onto a courtyard and a two-story brick structure at the rear of the property, with a kitchen on the lower floor and three rooms on the upper level.

D'Aquin enjoyed a considerable advantage over other aspiring educators whose straitened circumstances required them to rent rooms for their classes. Opening a school in her home gave d'Aquin the added advantage of involving her young daughter, Hélène, in her educational undertaking. While her two sons, Henri-Charles and Paul-Joseph George d'Aquin, attended the Jesuit St. Charles College boarding school in Grand Coteau, d'Aquin educated Allain in her own school. She and her young family may also have benefited from the Daron family's landlord, John McDonogh.

In December 1838, just as d'Aquin was inaugurating the Institution de Mme Vve [widow] Charles d'Aquin for female students, McDonogh, a philanthropist, veteran of the War of 1812, and slaveholder of great wealth, signed a will awarding half of his huge estate to the education of all of the city's children regardless of their racial identity. Given McDonogh's deep commitment to education and his penchant for extending low-rent, long-term leases to the needy, it's entirely possible that the D'Aquin Institute, as it was popularly known, benefited from his largesse. In 1844, the philanthropist purchased the Darons' Chartres Street residence. The property remained in McDonogh's estate until its 1859 sale. Despite the change of ownership, the D'Aquin Institute with its "splendid library for the times" maintained its space in the Daron home and achieved an "unusual degree of credit and stability" while charging students "very reasonable" fees.[11]

Though d'Aquin acquired a reputation as an educational leader in antebellum New Orleans, little is known of the institute's actual operations beyond its newspaper advertisements. Early in the school's creation, d'Aquin established a boarding school offering classes for full- and half-time boarders as well as day school students. Together with a primary school education, the institute offered an impressive range of upper-level courses in English and French rhetoric, ancient and modern history, natural philosophy, chemistry, and mathematics. Music instruction accompanied every level of education, while "sedulous care" was taken "to promote the moral as well as the physical improvement of the pupils." Though the Chartres Street location remained constant, other advertised addresses suggest that d'Aquin might have rented rooms elsewhere in the French Quarter to accommodate day school students.[12]

Beginning in the 1840s, Allain acquired her education in her mother's boarding school. With access to the D'Aquin Institute's "splendid" library, she pored over books that shaped her worldview and the arc of her life. In an educational institution created by a devout Catholic committed to the "sedulous care" of her students' moral well-being, the school library and curriculum would have included the works of the Francophone Atlantic's Catholic reformers Joseph de Maistre (1753–1821), François-René de Chateaubriand (1768–

1848), and Hugues-Félicité Robert de Lamennais (1782–1854). The plight of French Catholicism, together with the thinking and actions of student Allain, lend strong support to this conclusion.

For Francophone Catholics throughout the Atlantic world, the French Revolution and the Napoleonic era had dealt devastating blows to the Church of France, leaving the French masses demoralized, exhausted, and deeply divided. With France's 1814 Bourbon Restoration, reform-minded Catholics undertook the regeneration of the Church and of French society. The influential publications of Maistre, Chateaubriand, and Lamennais propelled them to the forefront of the movement. Their new spiritual/mystical vision of the world exerted a remarkable influence on Francophone Catholics in antebellum New Orleans.[13]

Their philosophies reflected a core concept of French Romanticism, the pantheistic belief in the indivisibility of God and nature. In this view, God's omnipresence infuses the natural world with meaning and purpose. Endowed with consciousness, human beings can interpret nature's web of sacred correspondences through the creative process. Hence, the ultimate task of human creativity is to unite the visible and the invisible by communicating with the all-encompassing sacred unity. From early childhood, Allain's experiences and education in the profoundly Catholic Daron/d'Aquin household predisposed her to this key Romantic concept.[14]

Allain was familiar with many of the works of Joseph de Maistre, though *Les soirées de Saint-Pétersburg* (The Saint Petersburg Dialogues, 1821) appears to have made the deepest impression. Maistre was a Savoyard lawyer, diplomat, and historical theorist whose mystical writings influenced French Romantic thought of the 1820s and 1830s. Maistre was, Allain wrote, "aptly named the 'Christian Plato'" and "the first philosopher I understood." For Allain and like-minded French Catholics, Maistre's theory of the historical process was central to his appeal.[15]

Key to Maistre's narrative of European history was his belief that knowledge emanates from moving souls who commune with one another. Their movement is generated by their will—a will engraved in every human heart—to discover divine law as they move through the world. In their movements, unpredictable gifts of divine grace result in bursts and starts of discovery. In combination, divine and human wills produce a history of knowledge that reveals a process of unalterable advance. Religious institutions aid the dynamic by discarding false knowledge and promoting the advance of the true.

In the process, Maistre saw history accelerating toward its inevitable culmination in global unification under Catholicism. The Catholic Church, the major mediator between state and people, would sustain good government everywhere while guaranteeing peace and gradual reform. Maistre anticipated a final age of Christian unity that would mark history's end.

Maistre considered prayer an extraordinary "law of the world" with measurable results that demonstrated a manner of reason superior to the absolutist, systematic variety developed by Enlightenment *philosophes* in their *Encyclopédie*. The spiritual will resulting from individual souls communing with each other moves the prayer and prophecy whereby they govern the world. Praying groups of souls exerted a moral force capable of causing the rise or fall of nations. Prayer could actually change the course of history. Allain could personally relate to Maistre's theology of prayer.[16]

Referring to the "communion of saints so well explained by the author [Maistre] of *Les soirées de Saint-Pétersburg*" (1821), Allain pointed to "those conversations with God, which we call prayers." With her aunt Amélie d'Aquin, a Religieuse du Sacre Coeur, in mind, Allain defended cloistered Catholic nuns and all contemplative orders by quoting French cleric Émile Bougaud: "From the depths of those closed houses and from behind the bars of their parlors, they communicate with many souls; they enlighten them, console them, encourage them, and bring them a thousand rays of sunshine."[17]

During her own childhood in New Orleans, Allain experienced an indelible out-of-body sensation under the influence of Suzanne, a free Afro-Creole member of the household. "Beneath her most beautiful black skin," she wrote, "Suzanne hid a beautiful soul." Allain related the sensation:

I remember her spirit and playful mood lighting up my childhood more than once: one of my best memories was the incredible speed with which we descended the stairs together at my uncle's, the eldest Daron, who stood in as our father then. Holding me tightly by the hand, Suzanne would pull me down, laughing loudly and almost making me fly. I was out of breath, a little scared but so happy! I felt as if some of my dreams were coming true. I used to dream often that I was floating in air. . . . I think I read in a book by the great Joseph de Maistre that this feeling is rather frequent during sleep, particularly in young people, and is the sign of the effect of the presence within us of an immortal soul which is not tied to the earth like the body.[18]

Later in life, when Allain returned to France, her admiration for Maistre led her to visit his family in Toulouse. To her delight, she met Madame J. Du-Bourg, a descendant of Joseph de Maistre's younger brother Xavier, the famed philosopher's grandson, and other members of his family.[19]

French Romantic author François-René de Chateaubriand shared with Maistre a revulsion for the French Revolution's violent excesses and believed that the Enlightenment philosophers' rationalist critique of religion had laid the groundwork for the upheaval. In the case of Chateaubriand, the revolution had taken a terrible personal toll. His elder brother, Jean-Baptiste de Chateaubriand, and sister-in-law were guillotined in the 1794 Terror, while his mother and other members of his immediate family were imprisoned.

Though the published works of both authors exerted far-reaching and lasting influence, Chateaubriand's more accessible *Génie du christianisme* (The Genius of Christianity, 1802) enjoyed enormous and immediate popularity. Like Maistre, Chateaubriand possessed a spiritual/mystical vision of a physical world suffused by God's divinity. In *Génie*, Chateaubriand wrote that "when our subject requires us to treat of the existence of God, we seek our proofs in the wonders of Nature alone." And in the overarching theme of his magnum opus, Chateaubriand insisted on Christianity's moral superiority over other religions. He pointed to the Church's centuries of artistic and poetic achievements to make his point. With his paean to the aesthetic splendors and spiritual contributions of Christianity, Chateaubriand joined Maistre in the vanguard of the literary re-Christianization campaign.[20] Both men were determined to regenerate French society and the Catholic Church. In that spirit, and because Chateaubriand's publications had a direct bearing on Allain's family history, she was introduced to his work at an early age.

The French Catholic priest Félicité de Lamennais joined Maistre and Chateaubriand in the leadership ranks of the religious reform movement with the publication of his multivolume *Essai sur l'indifférence en matière de religion* (Essay on Indifference in Religious Matters, 1817). His magnetic apologia for Christian spirituality and his incisive attacks on Enlightenment rationalism raised him from obscurity to overnight fame. "He [Lamennais] is magnificent," exclaimed the young Romantic poet Alphonse de Lamartine. He "thinks like Monsieur [Joseph] de Maistre, writes like [Jean-Jacques] Rousseau, forceful, honest, heroic, vivid, decisive, refreshing, he has it all." The book sold thirteen thousand copies in the first year, with translations appearing in all of the major European languages.[21]

Lamennais envisioned a regenerated Catholic Church led by a papacy that would, he believed, "bring everything to unity, coordinate the nations as member of a single family in a system of universal fraternity by obedience to their common Father." Bedazzled by Lamennais's all-embracing religious vision, the avant-garde of the Romantic movement fell under his spell. His circle of associates, disciples, and admirers grew to include Romanticism's crème de la crème—Alphonse de Lamartine, Alexandre Dumas, Victor Hugo, George Sand (Aurore Dupin), Franz Liszt, Augustin Sainte-Beuve, Auguste Comte, and Alfred de Vigny, among others.[22]

Together, Lamennais and Chateaubriand appeared at the forefront of Catholicism's realignment with France's intellectual elite. Victor Hugo, having been won over to the Catholic Church by Chateaubriand's *Génie du christianisme*, made his first confession to Lamennais in 1821 after reading the French priest's *Essai*. Whereas Chateaubriand's *Génie* had married French Romanticism to Catholicism, Lamennais's *Essai* transformed its author into the movement's chaplain. The marriage did not last long.

Lamennais had initially looked to government as a channel through which the Catholic papacy would transmit spiritual renewal to the exhausted and demoralized French and European masses. The 1815 Holy Alliance promised as much when European powers agreed to collaborate in the interest of a shared Christian purpose and international peace. When the agreement degenerated into a political alliance for the suppression of dissent, Lamennais denounced offenders and called on the church to confront them. The Holy See, however, was completely unwilling to rise to the occasion. The Catholic hierarchy, Lamennais recognized, was itself allied with repressive governing forces and opposed to reform and regeneration.[23]

In his socialist *Paroles d'un croyant* (Words of a Believer, 1834), Lamennais deplored "the abominable system of despotism which is developing everywhere." Equating the voice of the masses with the voice of God, he cast his lot with the people. Acting directly through them, he believed, God would bring about society's regeneration. While Pope Gregory XVI emphasized the duty of Catholics to obey their sovereigns, Lamennais enjoined the public to disobey rulers who violated the law of God.[24]

Paroles d'un croyant caused an even greater sensation than Lamennais's 1817 *Essai*, and once again, translations appeared in nearly all European languages. A papal encyclical of June 1834 condemned the heretical *Paroles* as "corrupt, wicked, and dangerous." The Paris correspondent for the London

Times credited the book with putting "weapons into the hands of the factious of every denomination. It is a fire ship launched in the midst of the moral world."[25] In France, Romantic author George Sand "revered him [Lamennais] as a saint." And social humanitarian Pierre Leroux hailed the book as "la Marseillaise du Christianisme."[26]

Lamennais believed Christianity to be the universal religion of humanity, and that it would evolve as human beings progressively rooted out all remnants of class and racial distinctions. Only through Christianity could liberty be achieved for individuals and societies. Though Lamennais broke with the Catholic Church, he retained a lifelong attachment to Maistre's spiritual/mystical beliefs. He described the advance of the anticipated regeneration in the following celestial terms: "The divine breath fills the Universe, and manifests itself everywhere in a multitude of beings who elevate themselves progressively from the most rudimentary organization, to sentiment and thought, . . . without end, without limit."[27]

These intelligent dwellers of the universe "do not drag themselves like us in a body of flesh and blood." They possess a "less heavy envelope." God had reentered "nature, his true temple," to prepare for the regeneration. The "birth of a great unity" will be possible with "religion returned to its pure essence." The regenerative dynamic would be personal and collective, terrestrial and extraterrestrial.[28]

Paroles d'un croyant marked Lamennais's dramatic metamorphosis from an advocate of monarchy and the Catholic Church to a fervent republican. He denounced France's existing political order, and his subsequent outpouring of articles and pamphlets attacking Louis-Philippe's government landed him in Sainte-Pélagie prison in 1841 for a year. After Pope Gregory XVI condemned his book, he renounced the Church and never returned.[29]

Reputed to have had a wider circulation than any book published in France since the invention of the printing press, Lamennais's *Paroles d'un croyant* crossed the Atlantic to New Orleans, where it exerted a profound influence on the city's free population of color and like-minded whites. His call for a spiritual regeneration to arise from the people and replace a compromised church and despotic government struck a deeply resonant chord. Lamennais's republican egalitarianism and religious mysticism would long outlive him at the séance tables of the city's Afro-Creole Spiritualist movement.[30]

Altogether, the Daron household shared with the surrounding Francophone refugee population a deep attachment to their Creole identity. Allain, born into a tenaciously self-sustaining refugee community in Jamaica, bore her Creole ethnicity as a badge of honor and referred to her Caribbean refugee neighbors as Creoles. The ethnic designation first emerged among Black colonists in Spanish America who coined the term *criollo* to apply to African-descended people born in the Americas. By the time the French colonized Saint-Domingue and Louisiana, the Spaniards had broadened the term's usage to apply to all native-born colonists. The French copied the Spanish model, applying *créole* to its colonial populations without reference to color. Growing up in New Orleans, Allain embraced her Latin European identity and the Creole city's loosely defined racial order. In the ensuing decades, the term *créole* and the Creole population it identified would come under increasing attack.[31]

Allain's Francophone neighbors overflowed the French Quarter's downriver boundary at Esplanade Avenue and congregated in the Faubourg Marigny. At the Chartres Street residence, Marie-Anne d'Aquin's brother, Charles-Joseph Daron, immediately stepped in to support his sister and her children. Noted for his amiability among those with whom he worked, the childless Daron proved equally winning with his niece and nephews. The Kingston-born businessman had moved to Louisiana in the early 1830s with his wife, Eveline-Marguerite d'Aquin, and entered into a partnership in an insurance firm, Kohn, Daron, and Company. He also worked as an administrative agent for the Catholic Church, and by 1850 the papacy had elevated him to the rank of Roman consul in New Orleans.

Allain and her siblings remained devoted to their uncle, who, she later wrote, "stood in as our father." Reflecting upon the plight of her family when she was an eight-year-old, Allain recalled, "We were *poor,* my mother, my two brothers, and I." Still, they were "*poor* without ever feeling destitute: we were at home under my uncle's roof, may his memory be blessed a thousand times." Allain's brother, Henri-Charles d'Aquin, expressed his gratitude to his uncle when he graduated from the École de Médecine in Paris in 1856 by dedicating his thesis "A la Mémoire de mon Père, A ma Mère, A mon Oncle, M. Charles Daron."[32]

Allain's aunt, Eveline-Marguerite d'Aquin, posed a greater challenge for the children. Not long after her marriage to Charles-Joseph Daron, she suffered a life-threatening illness that left her disabled and suffering chronic pain for the rest of her life:

I have always known my father's sister as an invalid; having contracted measles through her own carelessness six months after her wedding,

she was a valetudinarian and I would see her in her wheelchair at meal-
time, running her household, working, creating delicate objects and
artificial flowers, mostly for her oratory. For twenty-six years my uncle
loved her tenderly and faithfully, and bore witness to her suffering. She
never had children, and since she could never go into the world with
him, he never went himself. He spent no time away from her, except
for work and sheer necessity.[33]

As a child, Allain found her aunt grave and intimidating, an understand-
able disposition for a woman of Eveline-Marguerite d'Aquin's condition. Still,
the Daron home brimmed with activity: "Their [the Darons'] home was not
sad, full as it was with parents, friends, and acquaintances who gathered
around their hospitable table. There were many of us: my father had been the
eldest of eleven [sic] children, all alive at that time. Many lived there, others
came and went. The family was a small world where I learned honor, charity,
piety."[34]

Allain looked to another resident of the Daron household for her earliest
model of Catholic piety: Amélie d'Aquin, her aunt and Eveline-Marguerite
d'Aquin's sister. In the building's loft, Amélie d'Aquin replicated a Catholic
convent cell and practiced a severe Carmelite discipline of pious seclusion,
strict austerity, and self-abnegation. Before her family's emigration to New
Orleans, she had joined the Religieuses du Sacre Coeur, a cloistered religious
order in Kingston. In Louisiana, the small space she carved out for herself in
"a corner of that vast attic where we froze in winter after having suffocated in
summer" made a lasting impression on Allain.

She marveled at her aunt's attic room, "an enclosure made of roughly hewn
planks" with its window and "small wooden bed painted the color of the Carmelite order, as were the wardrobe and the washbasin, a chair, a footstool,
and altar, that's all." Inside "this charthouse [a medieval monastery] my aunt
prayed, sewed, meditated when her duties as a nurse did not keep her at her
sister's bedside or did not occupy her otherwise in the household." Despite the
rats that invaded the building's interior spaces during the night and "disturbed
her sleep and ours," Allain's aunt "would not have traded [her attic room] for
a palace."[35]

Amélie d'Aquin attended to her disabled sister and made the coffee every
morning after Suzanne prepared a "bombe full of hot water."[36] Amélie d'Aquin
went to church twice a day, and other than visiting the poor, "she never went

anywhere else." As a child, Allain enjoyed some of her happiest moments in her aunt's "privileged garret," where she would "sit low on the footstool at the feet of the recluse and listen to her speak to me of God. I studied every detail of this interior where order, peace, and detachment from worldly goods reigned supreme."[37]

Amélie remained in the Daron household to assist her younger sister until Eveline's death in 1847. As soon as "her beloved sister's ashes had turned cold," Amélie left New Orleans for the east bank town of Convent, upriver from the city. There she resumed her presence within the Sacred Heart religious community, at St. Michael's Church in St. James Parish.[38]

In the profoundly Catholic "chère maison" of her childhood, Allain revered her "uncle" Charles-Eugene Dubreuil as much as her aunt Amélie. He lived on the first floor of the residence, in a small room behind the dining room that stood at the corner of the house, fronting the intersection of today's Chartres and Barracks Streets. His father, Gaspard-François Dubreuil, a talented violinist from a wealthy French family, had lived with his wife, Marie-Thérèse-Françoise Lamarque, in Cap Français until the Haitian Revolution forced the couple's flight to Jamaica. Charles-Eugene Dubreuil was born in 1812 in Kingston, where his mother died in 1816.

Absent his ailing wife, Gaspard-François Dubreuil "would leave his small child of barely two years in the middle of a room every day, place a piece of bread in his hand and a bowl of milk on his knees, lock the door, and return only after having spent long hours giving music lessons." When news of the child's plight reached Allain's grandmother Marie-Anne-Elisabeth Daron, she persuaded the father to leave the baby with her during the day. "In the beginning, she would return him for the night, but little by little the orphan became part of the [Daron] family." In Jamaica, he was raised by Allain's mother, Marie-Anne-Elisabeth Daron, who "held him over the baptismal font" in 1813 when she and her brother Charles-Joseph Daron stood as the eighteen-month-old toddler's godparents. Dubreuil emigrated to Louisiana with the Daron family.[39]

When Allain "was old enough to reason and ask questions," her family related his history, though she "had to be told the story again to really believe that my Uncle Dubreuil is only a stranger among us." In *Souvenirs* in 1883, Allain described Dubreuil: "This pious and kind man is more than sixty years old and the same as I knew him at thirty. Always even tempered, with biblical simplicity, honesty and rare integrity, he has charitable ways which are illustrated by the welcome he gives to all the unfortunate, transforming his humble home into *l'hotel-Dieu* [the main hospital of a town] . . . It is to other disinherited people that this virtuous and modest man gives today what he received then."[40]

Suzanne and Martha, an enslaved resident of the compound, occupied rooms in the two-story slave quarters at the rear of the property. The arrangement of their living quarters typified multistoried urban slave quarters throughout the antebellum South. The general pattern placed the white family residence at the front of the property, with the separate slave quarters at the rear. This design maintained the requisite social distance between the slaveholder, the enslaved, and the free residents of color.

Owing to fire hazards, the slave quarters' first floor housed the kitchen and washroom, with the upper floors serving as living quarters. While the single rooms assigned to Martha and Suzanne may have contained a fireplace and a window, with relatively comfortable furnishings, the kitchen below exposed them to the rising heat and smoke of the fireplace, stove, and oven as well as the danger of fire. In any event, their many domestic duties kept them away from their rooms most of the time. For Martha and Suzanne, the rear building's limited accommodations offered little privacy and could hardly be considered a home.[41]

Allain's reference to Martha's "husband" presumed that the enslaved woman was married, though neither slave marriages nor slave families possessed legal standing under Anglo-American law. While Catholicism sanctioned slavery, colonial Louisiana's Latin European church officials had mandated that enslaved people should receive the Catholic sacraments, including the sacrament of marriage. Some Latin European practices still held sway in the early decades of the nineteenth century, and it's entirely possible that Martha and her husband were wed in the sacrament of marriage in St. Mary's Catholic Church on Chartres Street, an interracial congregation favored by descendants of the Haitian diaspora.[42]

Just blocks from the Daron residence, in a church that included Allain and her family, St. Mary's worshipers of all conditions and complexions met in the spirit of equality. In 1838, British visitor Harriet Martineau noted the Catholic phenomenon in St. Louis Cathedral, a place "the European gladly visits, as the only one in the United States where all men meet together as brethren. . . . Within the edifice there is no separation." All knelt together, from the "fair Scotchwoman or German to the jet-black pure African." During the sermon, the sight of the "multitude of anxious faces, thus various in tint and expression, turned up towards the pulpit, afforded one of these few spectacles which are apt to haunt the whole future life of the observer like a dream."[43]

In St. Mary's egalitarian milieu, an interracial coalition of Catholic women organized in the 1820s in response to an increasingly harsh Anglo-American slave regime. Their efforts reflected the momentum of the re-Christianization campaign in France, a movement that would exert a profound influence on the Allain household. For the St. Mary's coalition of women, the Catholic reform movement reinforced their efforts to mitigate the inhumane treatment of enslaved and free Black New Orleanians. Their humanitarianism constituted a quiet and unrelenting religious coup within the Catholic Church. Their struggles culminated in the creation of the nation's second Catholic order of African American nuns.

In 1826, French nun Marthe Fortière and her protégée, Juliette Gaudin, a free woman of color, attempted to found a branch of the Dames Hospitalière (a French religious order). The church's refusal to recognize an interracial convent did not deter Gaudin and or equally determined teenage Afro-Creole ally, Henriette Delille. Both Gaudin and Delille traced their ancestral roots to Haiti, and Catholic Church sacramental records reveal that as early as 1829 they and two allies had begun serving as *marraines* (godmothers) to enslaved and free infants of color. By 1832, their names appeared regularly in Catholic records.

Between 1834 and 1860 in St. Mary's Church, and after 1845 in St. Augustine Church in the Faubourg Tremé, Gaudin and Delille acted as marraines for dozens of enslaved and free Black children and adults. By the 1830s, their ministry extended to the sacrament of marriage. In St. Mary's, Delille witnessed the 1838 marriage of Jean Garick, a free man of color, to Loize, an enslaved woman, and in 1840 she likewise appeared as a witness in the marriage of a Frenchman to a free woman of color.

The actions of the two women and the priest who administered the marital sacraments clearly violated an 1830 state law prohibiting a free person of color from acting to "destroy that line of distinction which the law has established between the several classes of this community." A free Black violator of the statute was subject to a $1,000 fine and a three- to five-year term of imprisonment at hard labor. At the end of confinement, the transgressor would be banished from the state for life. Nonetheless, the practice continued, as when Etienne Rousselon, a French priest and founder of St. Augustine Church, married George Herriman and Louisa Eckel, a Cuban-born free woman of color, on September 4, 1846, in St. Mary's Church. Historian Cyprian Davis speculates that documented sacramental activities of questionable legality were kept out of the public record. Such an action would be grounded in the Church view that sacramental doctrine superseded civil law. Delille, Gaudin, and their allies were determined to carry that guiding principle into effect.[44]

In their daily visits to St. Mary's, Gaudin and Delille encountered French emigré Marie-Jeanne Aliquot, a devout Catholic who often frequented the church after her 1832 arrival in the city. Born in the Montpellier region of southern France, Alliquot proved to be a shrewd financier of some wealth as well as a teacher wholly committed to the education of young girls of color. She joined the two women in their ministry and they organized a second interracial religious order in 1836, the Sisters of the Presentation. By that time, however, their proposed convent and their work with the city's enslaved and free residents of color had raised concerns among civil authorities.[45]

Church officials dispatched Aliquot to Jefferson and St. John Parishes, where some Catholic planters desired religious instruction for their slaves. In 1842, Delille and Gaudin bowed to the Church hierarchy's insistence on a racially segregated religious congregation and founded the Sisters of the Holy Family, the second order of African American nuns in the United States. As in New Orleans, the women who had founded the nation's first congregation of color, the Oblate Sisters of Providence in Baltimore in 1829, were descendants of the Haitian diaspora.[46]

From childhood, Allain attended St. Mary's Church, where she likely crossed paths with Gaudin and Delille. The interests and lives of the deeply religious women overlapped in other ways. In her Chartres Street home, Allain revered her aunt Amélie, the nun in her own household, who, like her pious uncle Dubreuil, ministered to the city's poor. The Sisters of the Holy Family and the d'Aquins also shared in the long-standing support of their mutual friend Dr. Jean-Charles Faget, a devout Catholic physician of international fame who, like them, traced his ancestral roots to Saint-Domingue/Haiti.

Dellile and her Catholic allies, like the d'Aquin family, drew inspiration from Chateaubriand's vision of a regenerated church and society. In addition to France's nineteenth-century religious reformers, the interests of Delille and her sisterhood centered on the works of key humanitarian figures of the Catholic Reformation, including the Spanish mystic Teresa of Avila (1515–1582), Francis de Sales (1567–1622), and Vincent de Paul (1581–1660). In the spirit of Catholicism's sixteenth-century reform movement, women founded many new religious orders, a phenomenon closely studied, no doubt, by young women of color determined to establish their own convent.

Both the D'Aquin Institute and the antebellum Holy Family libraries possessed Chateaubriand's *Génie du christianisme*, with the convent's two-volume abridged edition designed for teaching purposes. Other books in the Holy Family collection centered on Catholicism's spiritual/mystical tradition, a topic that captivated both Juliette Gaudin and Allain.

Together with several volumes of the writings of Spanish reformer Teresa of Avila, Gaudin's personal selections included two influential French classics by Francis de Sales, *The Introduction to the Devout Life* and his *Treatise on Divine Love*. Francis de Sales's love-based mysticism would remain deeply popular in his Savoie homeland, where Joseph de Maistre, a fellow Savoyard Catholic, fully imbibed his spirituality. Throughout his life, Maistre, a religious philosopher revered by Allain and her family, would return repeatedly to Francis de Sales's writings for intellectual inspiration and spiritual consolation. Surely a conversation between Gaudin and Allain on the spiritual/mystical kinship between de Sales and Maistre would have yielded meaningful Christian fellowship.[47]

In New Orleans, the enthusiasm for seeking spiritual guidance from the works of Teresa of Avila, Francis de Sales, and Joseph de Maistre reflected the craving among believers seeking a personal path to God apart from a church and society compromised by the horrors of slavery. That craving was especially pronounced among Catholics of color, who suffered the torment of increasing racial injustice within their own church. The desire to achieve a truly catholic faith would prompt many Afro-Creole New Orleanians to seek alternatives outside of the institutional church.[48]

Acculturated to the church's Latin European religious practices, Allain remained a congregant of St. Mary's for as long as she lived in the city. She would later marry and have her infant son baptized in the church. During the Civil War, she would also have experienced the dramatic changes at St. Mary's when pro-Confederate priest Gabriel Chalon introduced a three-tiered seating arrangement assigning whites to the front of the church, people of color to the middle pews, and enslaved Catholics to the rear.

Eventually, Archbishop Francis Janssens would direct the Sisters of the Holy Family to leave St. Mary's Church altogether. Catholic Afro-Creole nun Mary Bernard Deggs bemoaned the changes: "It is only since the Civil War that this state has become so very prejudiced and the people of this city have so many hard feelings against the colored class. We have always been like one and the same family, going to the same church, sitting in the same pews, and many of them sleeping in the same bed." The actions of the church's segregationist leadership reflected the imposition in Louisiana, as elsewhere in the South, of a strictly enforced two-tiered racial order that reduced all people of African ancestry, enslaved or free, to a degraded status.[49]

During Allain's youth, however, the city's nineteenth-century Francophone population of observant Catholic slaveholders appears to have generally adhered to Latin European religious practices. Allain's description of life inside the Daron/d'Aquin household supports this view. The pious Eveline Daron taught the light-complexioned Martha to cook and instructed her in "religious principles such as prayer, duty, and catechism; she sent her to confession and allowed her to provide food for her husband though he belonged to another master." In Allain's reading of Harriet Beecher Stowe's *Uncle Tom's Cabin*, the deep Christian faith shared by the enslaved Tom and Eva, his owner's devout daughter, recalled her family's Catholic spirituality: "At my Uncle Daron's, masters and servants were part of a truly Christian family such as it should always exist."[50]

Stowe, Allain lamented, "did not put enough emphasis on the part played by these good masters." Allain knew "more than one 'Eva,'" and she "knew planters who would have willingly repeated François-René de Chateaubriand's words: 'A people whose social order is based on slavery and polygamy is a people that should be sent back to the Mongolian steppes.'" Some south Louisiana planters spoke eloquently of human rights and "were ready to make any sacrifice to reconcile their lawful interests with their humanitarianism." They shared the concerns of abolitionists. At the same time, she added, "it is unfortunately too true that there was more than one 'Legris' [Simon Legree]."[51]

In 1821, General James Wilkinson, a slaveholder himself and close friend of French-born planter Julien Poydras, characterized Francophone slaveholders in somewhat similar terms: "You cannot find any one of virtue & Intelligence who, viewing negro slavery in the abstract, & to probable results, will not condemn it as a curse. Yet yielding to Habit, indolence and ease, we approve the curse." Alarmed by Missouri's insistence on being admitted as a slave state, Wilkinson feared the breakup of the United States: "The Missourians will discover too late that opponents to the introduction of Slavery among them were their best friends." In 1822, Wilkinson moved to Mexico, where the newly independent nation had outlawed slavery.[52]

In Allain's descriptions of her Creole household, no other literary portrait matched the attention to detail given to free woman of color Suzanne. Allain wanted "our children" to know about a "devoted, loved, and respected *négresse*: Suzanne! She came very young from New Orleans, where she had belonged to one of my great-uncles, Villeras [Major Charles-Louis] d'Aquin, from whom my grandfather purchased her."[53]

In Jamaica, sometime around 1816, Charles-Pierre d'Aquin, Allain's grandfather, purchased the teenage, possibly West African, Suzanne from his brother in New Orleans. She may have been partly intended as a "gift" for seventeen-year-old Eveline-Marguerite d'Aquin, with whom Suzanne later returned to New Orleans. However, Charles-Pierre d'Aquin's wife, Marie-Louise, required assistance with her repeated pregnancies and rapidly growing family. Before her death, she gave birth to eleven children. When Suzanne arrived, the household included four children under the age of nine and a one-year-old toddler. Suzanne proved to be a vital member of the household. In an expression of his appreciation, according to Allain, her grandfather paid Suzanne for her services, despite the fact that she was his enslaved servant.

In 1828, Suzanne became even more central to the d'Aquin family when Marie-Louise d'Aquin died at the age of forty-nine, leaving three young children: eight-year-old Louise-Adèle, ten-year-old Louis-Thomas, and thirteen-year-old Louis-Jules. Prior to his own death in 1834, Allain's grandfather had provided for Suzanne's emancipation in his will in appreciation for her crucial role in his household. Allain cites the document:

I [Charles-Pierre d'Aquin] do hereby, in consideration of the good and faithful services of my *négresse*, named Suzanne, to her late Mistress [Marie-Louise-Victoire Le Bon de Lapointe], beloved wife, and to my family, recommend Her to the Kindness and benevolence of my children generally, and I do hereby also direct my executors next herein after named to set free the said *négresse*, Suzanne, when and so soon as my youngest daughter, [Louise-]Adèle, shall be able to dispense with her services.[54]

By 1836, when Allain arrived in New Orleans, Louise-Adèle d'Aquin was sixteen. By that time, Suzanne was a free woman and, it appears, a paid employee in the household:

[His] wish was respected and my aunt was still very young when Suzanne, legally free but as attached to the children she had seen grow up as if her ties had not been broken, stayed with them all her life, until she died in their arms. She only left my aunts once, forty years ago or so, to take a leisure trip to France. She was characteristically, this dear *négresse*, as intelligent, gay, and lively as she was devoted. She had taken on some of the good Parisian humour of the time.[55]

Suzanne captivated Allain with a childhood birthday gift. Allain remained grateful for Suzanne's generosity for the rest of her life: "Suzanne had good taste. . . . I will never forget a small white muslin dress with large lilac dots she [Suzanne] had given me for my birthday and which I liked very much. I was eight years old then, I think, a few years after my father's death and we were *poor*, my mother, my two brothers, and I. . . . We did not blush, therefore, to accept a small gift from the family's former slave."[56]

Suzanne's decision to marry intrigued the household. Allain recalled her betrothal: "Our interesting *négresse* was more than forty years old when she decided to get married. What madness, people whispered, how is it possible when she never wanted to be tied down and isn't young anymore?" Suzanne thought it was probably wise to find a protector for her old age and for, she said in Louisiana Creole, "tous pitis maîtrès la yé, plus capable soigné moin" (when my little masters will not be able to take care of me anymore). "Suzanne spoke French very well and only chose to use it when she wanted to impress or for a laugh."[57] Allain described the excitement surrounding the wedding:

I recall that wedding as though it were yesterday: I can still see Suzanne climbing into the coach with her fiancé, a large, very dark *nègre,* an honest and quiet man whose health would soon deteriorate and whose death would leave behind a grief-stricken widow. But none of this was foreseen on the day of the wedding and everyone was happy. A few guests, with varying shades of complexion, were received in my uncle's parlor; my aunts, especially the two youngest, Adèle and Lilia, had presided over their dear *négresse*'s toilette and joined her to welcome the guests. Whites and blacks together; my aunt Eveline wanted to be first in enjoying everything from her wheel chair. Refreshments and large trays of sweets were passed around; then, at a given signal, the newlyweds with their guests descended into the courtyard and danced, sang, and enjoyed themselves in the living quarters of Suzanne and

Martha, the cook who also opened her room to the day's festivities. The family had acquired a new member and nothing else changed in the household, where Suzanne kept working until my aunt died. She was then taken in, widowed and ill herself, by my aunt [Lilia d'Aquin], who looked after her with the most touching affection.[58]

The mature, well-dressed subject of German artist Adolph Rinck's painting *Free Woman of Color, New Orleans, 1844* bears a striking resemblance to Suzanne as she is described by Allain. The image, painted near the likely time of Suzanne's marriage, could have been intended as a gift, with the bride posing in her wedding gown. According to Allain, Suzanne was a dark-complexioned woman who wore a *tignon* in the same style as the subject of the portrait.[59] Allain described one other important similarity: "I was in a festive mood when my mother, who otherwise always kept me under her watchful eye, allowed me to tidy up Suzanne's room and wardrobes. I loved to count the beautiful madras [headscarves] she wore more or less coquettishly depending on the occasion. On Sunday and holidays, her *tignon* was done with more care, a certain way of tying the knot and to let the ends spread out in the shape of [cowrie] shells, ready for the parade."[60]

Rinck's subject is wearing a richly colored turban with knots tied in the shape of cowrie shells, exactly as Allain described Suzanne's tignon. Indigenous to the Indian Ocean, cowrie shells were valued throughout Africa. Their presence in archeological sites in Louisiana and elsewhere in the Atlantic world suggests their use in ancient African religious practices. For New Orleanians like Suzanne, the shells would have represented a cherished link to their ancestral roots in Africa.[61]

Dédé-Sophie, a West African refugee of the Haitian Revolution who fled Saint-Domingue with Allain's maternal grandmother, Marie-Anne Desmortiers, also entranced Allain. When revolutionaries attacked the Desmortiers family in Saint-Domingue, Dédé-Sophie's courage secured her a seat in a rescue boat alongside her young mistress, Marie-Anne Desmortiers. After their escape to Jamaica, where Allain's grandmother married Dr. Jean-Paul Daron, Dédé-Sophie lived "her humble existence under the grateful roof of my grandmother and her children, whom she rocked on her knee and lulled to sleep with the strange songs of the women of her country." Allain recalled how her "kind face with the scarred cheeks meaning she belonged to one of the Congo nations has been with me for as long as I can remember."[62]

After moving to New Orleans, Dédé-Sophie lived with Allain's godparents, Théodore Daron, her mother's brother, and Elmire d'Aquin, her father's sister:

> Dédé-Sophie made it obvious that she was very fond of my mother's youngest brother, Théodore Daron, who lived on a plantation in Lower Louisiana, and she spent most of her time with him; she often came to give us a kiss, however, and never failed to bring me a small bag of peeled pecans, which I found delicious. May I be forgiven this insignificant detail! Nothing is small in friendship and I was as grateful at the sight of those nuts patiently divested of their hard cover as if Dédé had given me [gold] nuggets from California.[63]

The West African woman outlived her slave owner, Marie-Anne-Elisabeth Daron, by seventeen years. In 1855, when Dédé-Sophie died, Allain regretted that her studies in France had taken her away from New Orleans, where she "had hoped to close her [Dédé Sophie's] eyes." Allain considered her a "courageous person" and penned a fascinating literary portrait of her:

> She was not tall but her bent and thin body still showed that she must have been strong. She always wore an indigo cotton dress with yellow flowers or leaves, a bit like the materials in fashion today, a gingham apron made of a cloth kerchief crossed over on the chest, and a dull madras head scarf. I must not forget her large earrings and the collection of small nuts and seeds from the Caribbean that hung from her belt with her keys like trinkets or mysterious amulets! She leaned on a stick and chewed on her gums rendered toothless with age. Her features were in no way repulsive; on the contrary, her physiognomy was grave and soft, and not devoid of intelligence. She still did small washes for my mother in exchange for tobacco money, since she smoked a pipe as conscientiously as a native from the shores of the Rhine.[64]

As Allain noted, Dédé-Sophie, like countless West Africans, bore her ancestral ethnic identity in her "country marks," her facial scarification denoting her Congolese identity. And like men and women across the vast continent of Africa, Dédé-Sophie wore amulets or charms to ward off evil spirits and protect herself from misfortune. In West Central Africa, intercessional *minkisi*, or charms, involved a "spirit-embodying" medium such as graveyard soil in a protective wrapper of some kind. Owing to the extensive importation of West Central Africans into Louisiana between 1780 and 1820, the Congolese-Angolan population achieved numerical dominance. In such circumstances, Dédé-Sophie may have encountered fellow West African Louisianians bearing distinctive country marks like her own.[65]

Both Dédé-Sophie and Suzanne made an enduring impression on the young girl. In *Souvenirs*, Allain returned their friendship and support with vividly drawn portraits in some of her best writing. No other relatives or friends are depicted with the same attention to character and detail. Through force of will and personal dynamism, the two women inscribed their place in the author's "histoire famille." Outside of the Daron household, Allain was equally fascinated by the ethnic diversity, language, music, and religion of the African-descended free and enslaved New Orleanians she encountered. Her fascination is easy to understand. United States seaports, as passageways linking Africans and African Americans throughout the Atlantic world, became the "capitals of Afro-America."[66]

Existing primary sources indicate that probably three-fourths of the twelve thousand enslaved people forced into Louisiana from 1803 to 1812 were African, excluding the 3,226 enslaved Saint-Dominguans who had experienced slavery's overthrow in the Haitian Revolution. Some proportion of the new African arrivals, when combined with the existing enslaved and free African-descended population, increased the city's Black majority from 56.8 percent of the total population in 1805 to 63.3 percent in 1810. Upon their arrival in the city during the early United States period, disembarking Africans fortified a foundational slave culture introduced under the French by the Senegambian Bambara people. After France ceded Louisiana to Spain, the new regime inaugurated a massive re-Africanization of Louisiana's existing enslaved population with people from Senegambia, the Bight of Benin, the Bight of Biafra, and Central Africa. In New Orleans, the multiethnic influx resulted in an exceptionally unified and heavily Africanized culture that remained a defining feature of the city's urban environment. During her youth, Allain bore witness to its nineteenth-century vibrancy.[67]

When she was growing up on Chartres Street in the 1840s, she later recalled, "the pretty Jackson Square in front of the [St. Louis] Cathedral did not yet exist, and neither did the double row of Pontalba houses which I saw being built. The old Spanish church had character; we heard about the venerable Père Antoine [Antonio de Sedella] and the excellent Abbé Mouni [Louis Aloysius Leopold

Moni] and the *nègres* still danced in Congo Square!"[68] Every Sunday night was "a time for celebration, and blacks and whites, slaves and masters would crowd against the strong fence that separated the dancers from the onlookers." Though Allain never saw the dancing herself, she retained a vivid memory of the distinctive sounds emanating from Congo Square on Sunday afternoons—"Dansé calinda, boudoum, boudoum! / Dansé calinda, boudoum, boudoum!"[69]—or the saying "Qué Bamboula ya pé fé!" (What noise they make!). "An obvious allusion," Allain noted, "to the din created by the Bamboula dancers."[70]

In 1819, the English-born architect and engineer Benjamin Latrobe had much the same impression of the ritual African ceremonies upon encountering the phenomenon in Congo Square. Attracted by the throbbing sound of drums while strolling on Saint Peter Street, he found that a "most extraordinary noise . . . proceeded from a crowd of five or six hundred persons, assembled in an open space or public square." The participants were "formed into circular groups" that later observers identified as representing different African nations. The music, Latrobe continued, "consisted of two drums and a stringed instrument." An elderly man playing a large cylindrical drum and another with a second, smaller drum "made an incredible noise." Though alarmed to find such a large gathering of unsupervised slaves, Latrobe found "not the least disorder among the crowd, nor do I learn on inquiry, that these weekly meeting of the negroes have ever produced any mischief."[71]

Later reflecting on her memories of Congo Square and "our Louisiana *nègres*," Allain wrote:

> Suddenly all the old Creole songs come back to me: the "Calalou" sung to the rhythm tapped loudly on the table while closing and opening one's fist, the "Tan patate la chuite na mangé li, na mangé li!" [When this potato is cooked, we will eat it], as well as some entertaining proverbs: "Tout cabinet gagnié maringuoins yo." [Everyone has troubles! Or, literally, Every cupboard is full of mosquitoes.] "Parole trop fort, mâchoire marrée." ["One keeps silent when there is too much to say."] "La terre mouillée, la pluie tombée." ["It always rains on wet earth."][72]

In addition to hearing a great deal about the dances in Congo Square, Allain heard from her mother "hundreds of times" about the stereotypical characteristics of the Congo, the Ibo, the Arada (Dahomeans), the Mondongues, and the Mina. The descriptive terms reflected the great importance slaveholding planters attached to the African origins of the enslaved. That concern drove observers on both sides of the Atlantic to develop an "elaborate lexicon" to categorize them. The slave classifications Allain learned reflected the influence of Moreau de Saint-Méry's *Description . . . de la partie française de l'isle Saint-Domingue,* a multivolume, exhaustive study of French colonial Saint-Domingue on the eve of the Haitian Revolution.

While in France in 1793, Moreau, a Caribbean-born Creole, narrowly escaped the wrath of French revolutionaries by fleeing to the United States, where he published his book in Philadelphia. His exhaustive, parish-by-parish study of the French colony counted Allain's ancestors among Saint-Domingue's noteworthy colonists, and her family kept a copy near at hand. Remarkable in its scope and detail, it remains an indispensable resource despite Moreau's deeply flawed notions of the biological and moral superiority of whites.[73]

While Moreau wrote extensively on the characteristics of Saint-Domingue's African "nations," identifying a multitude of African ethnic groups,[74] he also drew an ethnographic portrait of Saint-Domingue's colonial population, dividing it into three classes: whites, slaves, and free people of color. After dividing the overall population into a tripartite racial order, he further distinguished between those born in the colony, whom he termed "Creoles,"[75] with a cultural identity shared by both whites and Blacks—an identity distinct from individuals born in Europe or Africa. In his ethnography, Creole identity emerged as an inclusive sociocultural category shared by Saint-Dominguan-born whites and people of color, both enslaved and free.

Moreau considered Saint-Domingue his native country. According to scholar Doris Garraway, his "nationalism is expressed through an idea of creoleness that implies a degree of cultural evolution and unity underlying racial and power dichotomies." She quotes Moreau: "It would be a false idea indeed to believe that each of these three classes has its own character, which distinguished it entirely from the other two." This shared Creole culture bred a familiarity, he continues, between Creole slaves and whites, such that "being raised with whites, or under their eyes, the latter [the enslaved] attach themselves to them [the whites] in a more immediate manner."[76] In this way, slavery would be naturalized, creating nearly filial bonds between slaveholders and the enslaved. In Moreau's telling, the brutality of Saint-Domingue's slave regime is swept aside. His glaring insensitivity to the humanity of the enslaved is all the more striking in relation to his recognition that cultural transmissions ran both ways.

For instance, he documented the manner in which colonial whites appropriated African-derived cultural practices. His eyewitness accounts reveal the irresistible influence slave dances such as the calinda and the chica, and vaudoux, exerted on white Creole men and women. As he admiringly observed, the "impression that it [the chica] causes is so powerful that the African or the Creole, of whatever shade, who would watch without emotion would be regarded as having lost all but the last sparks of sensitivity." In restricted balls, Saint-Domingue white women danced both the calinda and the chica. The syncretic rites of vaudoux, combining dance with divination and sacrifice, produced an even more dramatic response. For white Creole women, according to Moreau, vaudoux elicited rapture: "In short, the dance plunges them [white women] into such a delirium that an outside spectator would believe that this pleasure has the greatest command over their souls."[77]

While the Haitian Revolution completely debunked Moreau's delusional theory of a "naturalized" slavery, his sociocultural description of a distinct Creole identity shared by both whites and Blacks and separate from those of Europeans and Africans rang true for Allain. Her reading of Moreau's *Description* "awakened within me a thousand memories of the past," she later wrote in her 1883 memoir. "I only have to quote Moreau de Saint-Méry," Allain explained, to recall "a few memories of New Orleans, a few interesting details about the *négres*, their manners and customs, and about the Creoles whom I love as one loves one's own family."[78]

She begged her readers' indulgence for including a thirty-nine-page excerpt from Moreau's *Description*. The faithfully copied transcript began with a few abbreviated entries on Saint-Domingue's Creole whites and African slaves. Allain dedicated the remaining two-thirds of the excerpted narrative to Moreau's discussion of the French colony's Creole slaves. Those passages convinced her that "our Louisiana *négres* cede nothing to those of the old colonies: dances, songs, proverbs, they inherited it all." She couldn't deny herself "this lengthy quotation because it is similar to the story of Dédé-Sophie and Suzanne," a story that mattered to Allain.[79]

Allain herself proudly self-identified as "une Créole," a cultural identity she shared with the Francophone whites and African-descended New Orleanians with whom she lived in her home and prayed in her racially mixed church. She spoke French, English, and Louisiana Creole, a language first developed by the earliest African arrivals in the French colony. She grew from a young child to womanhood in a Creole subculture in which the three castes intermingled in domestic and public spaces. In the city's streets, she ate food prepared by African American street vendors and understood the magnetic power of African drumming in Congo Square. The city's Creole subculture defined Allain's personal identity and her life in New Orleans.

The large segment of the *Description*'s text she chose to publish includes Moreau's especially valuable description of vaudoux, a syncretic diasporic religion that combined African, Creole, and European influences. His own prejudices notwithstanding, Moreau produced the first detailed description of a ritual vaudoux ceremony. The movement served as an extremely powerful cultural medium through which slaves retained their African roots, formed new alliances, and ultimately forged a revolutionary strike force. Colonial officials attempted and failed to suppress the movement, recognizing, as Moreau noted, "nothing is more dangerous than the cult of Vaudoux." In view of her family history, Allain was well aware of its power. "Tales of the stirring drama of Haiti rocked my childhood," Allain later recalled. At the age of ten, she remembered the "chill and terror I felt upon hearing about the *nègre* Vincent who, in his own words, had sold his soul to the devil."[80]

Allain's great-grandmother Hélène Lessard Desmortiers, "pistol in hand, confronted every curse; she would send Vincent into convulsions by throwing holy water on him and confront him with a kind of courage very few men had." The rebellious Vincent, according to family lore, was notorious for his "misdeeds" and died at the age of twenty. In the end, it appears, Vincent had his revenge. The vaudoux-led revolutionaries who stormed the North Province in 1791 destroyed the Desmortiers's slave plantations within a month of the Haitian Revolution's onset. Allain's great-grandmother, her grandmother, Marie-Anne-Elisabeth Desmortiers, and Dédé-Sophie barely escaped revolutionary forces.[81]

As a young girl in New Orleans, Allain recalled how she and her friends "would give a wide berth" to a large isolated building where, they had been told, "the Vaudoux gather!" She remembered her terror when she and her young companions would wander near the foreboding structure, a building "we considered an infernal den." At times, rumors circulated that when the Vaudoux danced in the night before a house, a child within the dwelling would die soon afterwards. At other times, a sudden recovery resulted from the "benevolent intervention of a *négresse*" familiar with vaudoux practices and "devoted to her masters." The derogatory rumors equating vaudoux with the magical power to either cure or destroy distorts the nature of the African-diasporic religion. Though Allain's family history predisposed her to fear vaudoux, the nature of the religion in both Saint-Domingue and Louisiana reveals a much more complex reality.[82]

Vaudoux emerged in colonial Saint-Domingue and Louisiana from the cultural backgrounds of the Fon (in present-day Benin), the Yoruba (in present-day Nigeria), and the Congo (in present-day Angola and Bas-Zaire) peoples. In both the Caribbean and Louisiana, West Africans overlaid their traditional belief systems with a veneer of Roman Catholic rituals. At the core of the vaudoux folk religion stood a West African–based spirituality with holistic healing as its primary objective. In the Afro-Caribbean, spirituality and healing were, and still are, synonymous. In eighteenth-century Saint-Domingue, vaudoux healers honed their skills on a rich heritage of African healing traditions, Caribbean pharmacopeia, and European therapies. In both Saint-Domingue and Louisiana, African-descended healers achieved astonishing results with enduring consequences.

In New Iberia, Louisiana, the case of Félicité, an enslaved woman born in Saint-Domingue/Haiti, is instructive. In September 1839, Félicité nursed Black and white patients during a yellow fever epidemic that affected nearly every family in the community. Possessed of an extraordinary ability to fight the fever, she attended tirelessly to the afflicted while comforting the dying. Félicité won her freedom for her remarkable service. At the time of her death in 1852, her former enslaver, sugar planter Frederick H. Dupérier, laid her body in state in his home. Hundreds of Black and white admirers streamed past her bier to pay their respects. In twenty-first-century Louisiana, a marker in New Iberia commemorates Félicité's heroic service.[83]

On plantations in both Saint-Domingue and Louisiana, skilled enslaved women like Félicité attained highly respected positions in the slave hierarchy in their roles as *hospitalières* (women in charge of plantation hospitals) and midwives. Saint-Domingue's slave communities also esteemed herbalists, both men and women, who prepared medicinal remedies for their bodies as well as spiritual medicine in the form of divination, charms, and spells for their souls.

In antetellum New Orleans, repeated outbreaks of cholera, influenza, consumption, typhoid, and yellow fever threatened urban residents. The biggest killer, yellow fever, struck every summer with increasing ferocity over the course of the nineteenth century, making New Orleans the deadliest city in the nation. Like their counterparts in the Caribbean, Louisiana's Afro-Creole healers blended their African healing traditions with native remedies and European therapies in response to the deadly onslaughts. Influential healers Sanité Dédé, Marie Saloppé, Betsey Toledano, Marie Laveau, Marie Glapion (Marie Laveau's daughter), Charles Lafontaine (known as Doctor Jim Alexander),[84] Jean Montanée (popularly referred to as Doctor John), and J. B. Valmour (John B. Averin)[85] attracted patients of all ethnicities and classes in a phenomenon that speaks to the efficacy of their "invisible powers."[86]

With close ties to Choctaw Native Americans, Afro-Creole New Orleanian Marie Laveau, a devout Catholic and free woman of color, achieved widespread renown for her skill as a herbalist and vaudoux adherent. The grisgris charms she created for her devotees, similar in creation to those used in Africa and Haiti, protected the wearer.[87] Laveau's humanitarian concern for her fellow New Orleanians also led her to minister to the countless sick and dying victims of the city's recurring yellow fever and cholera epidemics. Like Félicité in New Iberia, Laveau's success struck contemporaries as a supernatural power. In Laveau's case, that perception reinforced her reputation as a vaudoux priestess. She acquired a larger-than-life persona for her legendary spiritual powers—a persona that persists in the present day.[88]

The widely traveled, cosmopolitan Jean Montanée, a former slave popularly known as Doctor John, practiced herbal medicine and acquired a reputation as a "performer of miracles." He, like Laveau, remains enshrined in the city's collective memory. Near the age of fifty in 1866, he impressed a reporter as "eminently respectable," wearing Parisian-style clothing. His ebony complexion, together with his Bambara ritual scars or "country marks" extending in arching, parallel curves on either side of his face from his temples to the corner of his lips, enhanced his striking physical appearance. Montanée's success as an herbal practitioner attracted a large multiracial clientele. His affluent male and female patients made him a wealthy man. By 1870, however, a series of financial swindles had drastically reduced his fortune. In August 1885, he died in poverty. His death notwithstanding, his power to heal survived in the city's collective memory and he, like Laveau, left a lasting influence on the city's culture and history.[89]

In the hands of African descended militants, enslaved as well as free, African pharmacology and European therapies also served as powerful weapons of resistance and revolt. François Makandal, one of Saint-Domingue's most influential slave healers, applied his familiarity with tropical medicine to his herbal formulations. In his hands, herbalism in Saint-Domingue became a powerful tool of resistance through his creation of poisons. After escaping from slavery to join maroons in the colony's mountains, he became a legend among his fellow slaves, who believed he possessed superhuman powers. Even after his 1758 capture and execution, he remained a potent symbol of resistance and freedom among enslaved Saint-Dominguans.[90]

Two years after European mesmerism's 1784 introduction into Saint-Domingue, the practice reached the slave community in Marmelade Parish in the colony's North Province, with dramatic results. Large numbers of slaves, usually numbering as many as two hundred participants, deserted their plantations to attend clandestine nocturnal mesmerist assemblies led by four slave magnetizers, Jérôme, Télémaque, Jean, and Julien. Their revolutionary call for rebellion prompted a brutal crackdown that ended their magnetist activities. Still, the mesmerist gatherings fed into a building spirit of militancy that would erupt with explosive force in the 1791 slave revolution. By the time mesmerism achieved notoriety in New Orleans in the 1850s, its revolutionary potential was widely recognized. Mesmerist fervor in Saint-Domingue led Franz Anton Mesmer, the German inventor of the therapy, to boast that the Haitian republic owed its independence to him.[91]

By 1852, J. B. Valmour, a free African American blacksmith and mesmerist healer, was attracting large interracial audiences to his small Toulouse Street shop. His healing feats involved his ability to "throw the regenerative fluid." The white French emigré Joseph Barthet compared Valmour to a renowned magnetist in Pau, France, the blacksmith Laforgue, whom Napoleon III's government suppressed during its early 1850s crackdown on French magnetists. From mesmerism, Valmour assumed a leadership role as a Spiritualist healer.

In his Le Spiritualiste journal, Barthet praised Valmour as a Christlike figure who obtained "miracles of the same kind." In a rancorous feud in 1858, the conservative Catholic clergy described Valmour's healing feats as "gris-gris." The dispute prompted a police action that forced Spiritualism underground, where Valmour attracted highly motivated devotees like Henri-Louis Rey and François Louis "Petit" Dubuclet, the offspring of influential Afro-Creole families. Rey's parents, Barthélemy Rey and Rose Agnès Sacriste, had entered the city as children during the Saint-Domingue refugee movement. His father, a prosperous businessman, played a key role in developing the Marigny and Tremé Faubourgs while working to help found the Couvent School, the Sisters of the Holy Family convent, and St. Augustine Church.

After his father's death in 1852, Henri Rey's disillusionment with both church and state prompted his turn to Spiritualism. Steeped in a diverse religious culture in which out-of-body experiences proliferated, the phenomenon was not new to him. His mother, a devout Catholic, often experienced visions in which her deceased children appeared to her. Rey joined Valmour's Cercle Harmonique (Harmonic Circle), where the former French priest Felicité de Lamennais was a frequent spirit guide at their séance table. The dissident Catholic cleric's spirit communications envisioned the transformation of the material world into a mirror image of the spirit world's egalitarian republic where social and political equality reigned. Rey and his influential Afro-Creole allies looked to the future through the lens of France's revolutionary Second Republic.[92]

While the healing powers and irresistible personas of Marie Laveau and Doctor John remain fixed in Louisiana's twenty-first-century public imagination, the widespread interracial popularity of African American healers like Valmour, Laveau, Doctor John, and others posed a dangerous threat in a crisis-ridden atmosphere of mounting sectional tensions. To address the perceived insurrectionary potential of influential healers and other religious leaders of color, the city council legislated an 1858 municipal ordinance that alerted white residents to the "great and constantly growing evil [that] now exists . . . in contravention of the law and the well-being of . . . the South and the safety of the institution of slavery, by the numerous assemblages of persons of color." The statute mandated that Black Christian services be supervised by a white minister and required African Americans to obtain written permission from the mayor for all gatherings. It was too late.[93]

Effective enforcement of the ordinance proved impossible. Despite the official shutdown of their churches and lodges, the historically independent African Methodist Episcopal Church and Prince Hall Freemasonry remained intact and poised for a thriving comeback. Spiritualism's adherents met clandestinely around séance tables while vaudoux's adherents practiced their ceremonies on the shore of Lake Pontchartrain, on the banks of Bayou St. John, and under the cover of the city's swampland cypresses.[94]

In antebellum New Orleans, the vaudoux terrors Allain imagined as a youth could never compare with the human horrors unfolding in her surrounding neighborhood. Between 1840 and 1862, while she thrived within the walls of the Daron compound, the encompassing city streets and businesses grew into the focal point of North America's largest slave market. Operating under the "chattel principle," the city's slave traders reduced thousands of men, women, and children to movable personal property to be sold into slavery. In the antebellum South altogether, the sales of more than 2 million men, women, and children in interstate, local, and state-ordered sales fueled the trade's massive expansion. Of the two-thirds of a million interstate sales alone, 25 percent involved the destruction of a first marriage. Fifty percent destroyed a nuclear family, with many of the sales separating children under the age of thirteen from their parents.

In New Orleans, the debacle began just a short block from the Daron residence, at the corner of today's Chartres Street and Esplanade Avenue. It radiated into adjacent and nearby clusters of competing slave trading firms. In the 1850s, another slave trading sector developed in the city's uptown "américain" business district. By 1854, approximately nineteen slave yards operated in the two sections of the city. During the trading season, from September to May, thousands of African Americans were sold into the domestic trade from the slave pens, slave yards, and property frontages where traders displayed their human "merchandise."

The traders conducted their sales in buildings with barred windows and doors, walls as high as fifteen to twenty feet, and street signs such as "T. Hart Slaves" advertising their businesses. During the trading season, men, women, and children were lined up on the street in front of the buildings, where their presence attracted prospective buyers, antebellum visitors, and curiosity seekers. By the time an 1852 city ordinance barred the cruel spectacle from the city streets, Allain was nineteen years old and well aware of the nearby commerce in human beings.[95]

In fact, her cryptic third-person description of a scene inside a slave market suggests that she was aware of the human misery and suffering in the nearby slave yards from an early age. She wrote, "A little girl about eight or ten years old entered into one of the well-known slave markets with her mother. She left pale, trembling, tears streaming, and with her hands over her eyes crying out: 'Oh Mama! *Joseph has been sold by his brothers!*'" In her emphasized phrase, Allain is referring to the biblical Joseph of Genesis 37:2–29, whose envious brothers sold him into Egyptian slavery for twenty shekels of silver.[96]

As a devout Catholic who regularly attended St. Mary's Church on Chartres Street, Allain would also have been aware of the slave trader's yard along her walk to religious services. The yard remained active until 1862, when the US Army occupied the city, ending its operations. After that, the abandoned property passed into the hands of Gaudin and Delille's Sisters of the Holy Family. The order of African American Catholic nuns opened St. Mary's School on the site, in 1870, for young women of color. Afro-Creole Sister Mary Bernard Deggs described the property in the following terms: "No one would think of buying it for the very reason that it had previously been a [slave] trader's yard and many sins had been committed at that place, not only sins, but the most horrible crimes. It must have been the will of God that our sisters should buy the place to expiate the crimes that had been committed there."[97]

Allain hinted at her antebellum neighborhood's dangers when relating her childhood experiences with Creole women of color who sold their homemade delicacies to the district's children. Allain and her friends craved the candies and other edibles prepared by the street vendors. Allain favored Aunt Sanité and her *bâtons* (possibly a drumstick of baked fowl), "hot and fresh out of the oven." In Allain's description, "Aunt Sanité was a heavy mulatto woman, short and almost as round as the basket where were spread on a white napkin all sorts of goodies, among others those *estomacs mulâtre*, so-called probably because of their color. . . . This brave woman stood at the corner of Chartres and Bayou [Road] streets and always had the kindest smile for the children attracted by her display."[98]

Allain's concern stemmed from her awareness that women like Sanité, working in such close proximity to the slave markets, ran the risk of being taken by force and sold into slavery. Such a fate had befallen Louisiana-born Eulalie, who had been living in Pointe Coupée for decades as a free woman when kidnappers forced her, her six children, and ten grandchildren to New Orleans, where slave traders sold them at public auction. In New Orleans, Euphémie, who had been living as a free woman for more than twenty years, was likewise sold at auction with her seven children. After losing years of their lives in slavery, the two women and their families were able to sue for their freedom, with the help of neighbors and friends.[99]

During Allain's youth, one of the most publicized cases of an abducted victim forced into the New Orleans slave yards involved Solomon Northup, a freeborn African American citizen of upstate New York. In 1841, Northup traveled to Washington, DC, in pursuit of a job prospect. Two men posing as potential employers drugged him, chained him, and sold him into slavery in New Orleans. After remaining in bondage for twelve years in rural Louisiana, he secured his freedom from a notoriously brutal owner on a remote Bayou Boeuf plantation.

Northup had communicated his plight to his family with the help of Samuel Bass, an itinerant carpenter. Legal assistance owed to Northup as a free citizen of New York and documentary support from Louisiana senator Pierre Soulé, an influential member of the city's Francophone community, assured Northup's rescue from slavery. In Washington, Soulé readily supplied the necessary documentation for safe passage through the state. The senator, Northup later explained, "especially interested himself in the matter, insisting, in forcible language, that it was the duty and interest of every planter in his State to aid in restoring me to freedom, and trusted the sentiments of honor and justice in the bosom of every citizen of the commonwealth would enlist him at once in my behalf." In 1853, bearing the physical and emotional scars of his ordeal, Northup finally achieved freedom.[100]

Senator Soulé's largesse extended to other free men of color during the antebellum era. In 1840, he recommended the gifted young pianist Victor Eugène Macarty for entry to the Conservatoire de Paris, directed at that time by the brother of his friend Léon Halevy. In 1852, he furnished artist Eugène Warburg with a recommendation for study in Paris. In 1857, after Warburg sculpted a series of bas-reliefs depicting scenes from *Uncle Tom's Cabin*, commissioned by Harriet Leveson-Gower, Duchess of Sutherland, Soulé joined with the duchess and Harriet Beecher Stowe in recommending Warburg for study in Florence, Italy. Ultimately, however, the senator's efforts to navigate the tightrope between slavery and freedom doomed his political career and ruined his health. In 1870, he died a disgraced and broken man in the midst of a struggle to build a genuinely representative democracy in Reconstruction Louisiana.[101]

Though the city's thriving commerce in human beings grew into the nation's largest slave market after 1840, international, national, and local developments pointed toward slavery's demise. In the Spanish American wars of independence, emerging nations either abolished slavery outright or legislated its gradual extinction. Nineteenth-century humanitarianism, having produced an aggressive abolitionist movement in the US North, made deep inroads in New Orleans. In the city, traditional African religious beliefs in an all-powerful spirit world converged with Catholicism's spirit-in-matter piety to give potent impetus to the city's religious and political culture.

In France, the humanitarian impulse fueled an empowering philosophy of Catholic reform whereby prayerful individuals and communities of believers could achieve Christian unity and universal fraternity. This spiritual/mystical vision, articulated in France by influential Catholic reformers, was a core concept of French Romanticism. In 1848, humanitarians of all ethnic, religious, and political persuasions would take inspiration from events in France when another phase of the age of Atlantic revolutions gave concrete political expression to their egalitarian ideals.

FIVE

Paris in New Orleans

On résiste à l'invasion des armées; on ne résiste pas à l'invasion des idées.
(An invading army can be resisted but not ideas whose time has come.)
—Victor Hugo, *The History of a Crime*, 1877

French Romanticism gathered momentum throughout the Francophone Atlantic after 1815. By the time of Allain's 1836 arrival in New Orleans, when this chapter begins, the movement had achieved enormous popularity. In France, Haiti, and New Orleans, its egalitarian ethic and highly politicized orientation gave rise to a diverse avant-garde.

The Romantic activists at the forefront of the 1843 Haitian Revolution and the 1848 February Revolution in France demonstrated the movement's power as a force for change. The French Second Republic's abolition of slavery and the political empowerment of the newly liberated men made a deep and lasting impression on Black New Orleanians. They studied the new wave of revolutionary upheavals as models for their own liberation movement.

Under Romanticism's emancipatory influence, Allain and the members of her social circle aspired to join the ranks of nineteenth-century women authors. Allain gave belated expression to those aspirations by including their unpublished literary works in *Souvenirs*. She also included a pamphlet authored by her French émigré mentor, Madame Ligeret de Chazey. In the 1855 publication, Ligeret defended Creole New Orleanians from a scurrilous attack published in Paris. The ensuing controversy is detailed in the chapter's concluding pages. The incident offers insights into the *mentalité* of Francophone women on both sides of the Atlantic, mounting ethnic tensions, and the growing sectional crisis.

* * *

By the mid-1830s, when Hélène d'Aquin Allain first arrived in New Orleans and teenage prodigy Victor Séjour departed for Paris, French Romanticism's triumph in Louisiana was nearly complete. The movement's strength was readily apparent among the city's racially and socially heterogeneous residents, who had eagerly absorbed the new body of thought. French speakers of all ethnicities seized upon the Romantic ethos as a medium of artistic and/or political expression. Allain's life history and Séjour's meteoric success on Parisian stages demonstrate the profound influence of French Romanticism in Louisiana and elsewhere in the Francophone Atlantic.[1]

In antebellum New Orleans, Paul Trévigne, an educator and influential free Creole of color, captured the excitement of the movement's momentum in Louisiana in an amusing reminiscence about the phenomenon:

I recall that in the thirties, Louisiana and especially New Orleans were considered part of France. French literature was the only literature of interest. The struggle between the classicists and the Romantics overtook everyone and was as intense in New Orleans as in Paris. The advocates of the classical school could not fathom the downfall of their idols. They couldn't imagine how anyone could consider works like *Phèdra* and *Athalie, Le Cid, Mérope* and *Oreste*[2] as worthless antiquities. Thus, they sang with ironic gusto the celebrated song of Madame Fleury-Jolly[3] from which I extracted these two couplets:

I adore the renowned drama
In which the impassioned ingénue says to the hero:
"Press my bosom to your manly breast,
Flesh of my flesh, bones of my bones."

From that vulgar vernacular
We've been freed, thanks to Victor Hugo.
As for Racine and Voltaire, give it a rest!
We've had enough of them. For shame, they are rococo![4]

The 1830s literary showdown so cleverly depicted by Trévigne echoed a far more consequential confrontation in France between classical and Romantic partisans. The battle lines took shape in Paris in 1829, when Alexandre Dumas, the son of the former slave and celebrated French general Thomas-Alexandre Dumas Davy de la Pailleterie, caught classicists off guard in their Théâtre française stronghold with the staging of his Romantic historical drama *Henri III et sa cour* (Henry III and His Court). To the dismay of classicists, the relatively unknown twenty-five-year-old Dumas scored his first major success though his play had barely been publicized prior to its performance. Classicists regrouped the following year for an attack on Victor Hugo, the acknowledged leader of the Romantic literary movement. The stakes were high.

In 1830, the widely publicized staging at the Théâtre française of Hugo's play *Hernani*, with its overt declaration of Romantic principles, unleashed a storm of classicist opposition for its threat to aristocratic conventions. Hugo threw down the gauntlet in his preface to the play:

> Romanticism . . . is only . . . liberalism applied to literature . . . Liberty in Art, liberty in Society: such is the double goal toward which all consistent and logical minds should tend. . . . Liberty in literature is the offspring of political liberty. This principle is the principle of the age, and will prevail. The Ultras of every sort, Classical as well as monarchical, will in vain help each other try to restore the old regime on society and literature; every step on the path of progress in the country, every intellectual development, every step toward liberty will help to demolish all that they have built up. . . . Henceforth poetry shall bear the same slogan as politics: TOLERATION AND LIBERTY.[5]

Hernani's critics, according to the young French writer Théophile Gautier, "secretly concocted, everything short of ambush, in order to assassinate the play and finish it off—along with the new School [of Romanticism] in one fell swoop." On February 25, when the play premiered, the young "uncivilized" Romantic artists, wearing their hair au naturel as opposed to the still-fashionable wigs, made easily identifiable targets for the "respectable" classicists who pelted them with street garbage and rotten vegetables. While achieving a small tactical victory, the aristocratic classicists suffered a disastrous defeat months later when the 1830 July Revolution toppled the reactionary Bourbon regime of King Charles X.

For *Hernani*'s Romantic supporters who anticipated an affirmation of the revolutionary principles of 1789, the outcome of the revolution was bitterly disappointing. Louis-Philippe, the Duke of Orleans, was collaterally related to the Bourbons. To calm the revolutionary opposition, he pointed to his service in the 1792 republican army, proposed democratic change, and proclaimed his intention to rule as a constitutional monarch under the title of roi des Français (king of the French) rather than the autocratic roi de France (king of France). Once in power, however, he abandoned his liberal principles and worked behind the scenes to preserve his royal prerogatives and advance the interests of the upper bourgeoisie. Finding Louis Philippe's regime detestable, Romantics turned their fire on "la Monarchie bourgeoise."[6]

Nineteenth-century European Romanticism represented a profound spiritual and intellectual reorientation that, in general terms, elevated individualism, imagination, and emotion over the eighteenth-century Enlightenment's emphasis on rationalism and traditionalism. In the Romantic ideal of personhood, the individual aspired to autonomy, self-expression, and universalism. Throughout the Atlantic world, the movement's liberating impulses loosened traditional cultural conventions.

In France, the movement remained intensely focused on political matters, owing to the unfulfilled promise of the French Revolution. In Europe, the Francophone Caribbean, and Louisiana, that focus would produce a powerful resonance. The Romantic affinity of New Orleanians originated, in part, in the experiences of their eighteenth-century forebears.[7]

After the city's 1718 founding, the dependence of the French on the labor and military skills of enslaved Africans, the French colonizers' relative openness to peoples of other ethnicities, and a shortage of European women produced a permeable, creolized society in which race mixture was common and widely accepted. After the 1803 Louisiana Purchase, thousands of refugees from the Francophone Atlantic's revolutions, coups d'état, and royalist reactions fortified the city's Creole population of whites, free people of color, and enslaved New Orleanians. Thus bolstered, the city's diverse and assertive Francophone population refused to yield either their language or their cultural identity to Anglo-American newcomers. Owing to their tenacity, New Orleans remained the South's island of multiethnic, Creole culture.[8]

With the advent of French Romanticism, the Francophone city's historic culture of inclusiveness and interracialism proved especially hospitable to a Romantic sensibility that validated its multiethnic character. Creole New Orleanians' fervent embrace of French Romanticism began with the works of Chateaubriand. In 1791, while in his early twenties, the young Frenchman's restless genius and fascination with Native Americans prompted a heroic, five-month transatlantic trek to the Mississippi River at the dangerous United States frontier. After testing Rousseau's theory of "noble savages" living in a state of nature, untouched by the artificiality and corrupting influences of civilization, he returned to Europe, where he authored *Les Natchez* (1798).

Chateaubriand's historical epic centered on the 1729 war between Louisiana's French colonizers and the region's Natchez Indians. The author set the main action of the historical drama on the banks of the Mississippi, "the Nile of the wilderness," with its "forest colonnades and the pyramid tombs of the Indians."[9] Referring to the book's focus, Chateaubriand explained that he "could see no subject more interesting, especially for Frenchmen, than the massacre in 1727 [*sic*] of the Natchez colony in Louisiana. All the Indian tribes conspiring after two centuries of oppression, to restore liberty to the New World."[10]

For Hélène Allain and her family, Chateaubriand's *Les Natchez* evoked a unique sense of familiarity. Her great-great-grandfather Antoine-Benoit d'Aquin had fought in the 1729 Natchez war, and her great-grandfather Antoine-Pierre d'Aquin was born near the battlefront. Her maternal great-great grandfather Etienne Marafret Lessard had built a fortune based on his expertise in Native American language, customs, and trade patterns in central Louisiana. In New Orleans, Allain later recalled her encounters in New Orleans with the Native American "descendants of those proud Chactas sung by Chateaubriand." Her first reading of Chateaubriand's work must have been a spellbinding experience.[11]

Chateaubriand's *Atala* (1801), a novelette excerpted from *Les Natchez*, achieved enormous popular success. It and its sequel, *René*, are considered the first works of nineteenth-century French Romantic fiction. Chateaubriand incorporated the two publications into his enormously influential *Génie du christianisme* (1802), a monumental defense of Christian spirituality that married French Romanticism to Catholicism. *Génie*'s emphasis on Christianity's power to relieve the melancholy of the adolescent soul, its spiritual/mystical vision of God's immanence in nature, and its admiration for the "man of nature" (Native American) in his uncorrupted state of innocence "set a current of sympathy flowing between the author and a whole generation of young French men and women." More than any other work, according to scholar David Cairns, it was "the primer of early French Romanticism."[12]

In New Orleans as in France, devout Catholics like the d'Aquins fell under the spell of Chateaubriand's *Génie* with its glorification of Christian spirituality and its egalitarian depiction of Louisiana's indigenous peoples and history. For the city's Rouquette brothers, Adrien-Emmanuel, François-Dominique, and Térence, life imitated art. Their perspectives and lives demonstrate the ways in which French Romanticism fostered mutual respect, sociability, and collaboration among multiethnic Louisianians. For Louisiana slaveholders, however, the phenomenal success of Chateaubriand's "handbook" of early Romanticism raised concerns. They recognized the new movement's subversive potential. The Rouquette brothers' artistry and actions confirmed their fears.

Their French father, Dominique Rouquette, emigrated to New Orleans in 1800, where he married Louise Cousin, the Creole daughter of a wealthy landholding family. He fought under Jackson in the Battle of New Orleans and bequeathed his love of literature and his library of 1,300 books to his young sons before his 1819 suicide. The Rouquette brothers spent much of their youth at their family's rural residences in Orleans and St. Tammany Parishes. They roamed the outlying woodlands with their Choctaw playmates on Bayou St. John in New Orleans and Bayou Lacombe on the north shore of Lake Pontchartrain. Educated in New Orleans and Paris, they became ardent devotees of Chateaubriand.

Adrien, the most noteworthy of the brothers, went the furthest in modeling his life after the Romantic heroes of Chateaubriand's *Atala* and *René*. After passing his examinations in France in 1833, he returned to Louisiana to seek his own "Atala," Chateaubriand's idealized Indian maiden. Among the Choctaw, he purportedly fell in love with the chief's daughter, Oushola (Songbird), and proposed marriage. Tragedy struck on the eve of their wedding, when the Indian princess died of consumption. At the urging of his family, the despondent Adrien returned to Paris to study law. In France, he abandoned his law books to express himself creatively in the manner of Chateaubriand, Lamennais, and Alphonse de Lamartine, his Romantic heroes.[13]

Under their influence, he published his first book in 1841, a critically acclaimed collection of poems entitled *Les Savanes, poésies américaines* (The Prairies: American Poems). The French Romantic poet Auguste Brizeux proclaimed Adrien " the bard of Louisiana, the Ossian of America, and France includes you among its poets." In England, poet Thomas Moore described him as "the Lamartine of America" and declared that "*Les Savanes* breathes the fragrances of the forest."[14]

After savoring his success, Adrien returned to New Orleans, where his fervent Catholicism and penchant for mysticism led him to enter the priest-hood in 1845. He continued to write, and in 1848 he revealed the intensity of his mystical religiosity in an English-language book entitled *Wild Flowers, Sacred Poetry*. He had drawn his inspiration from the secluded natural beauty of Bayou Lacombe, where "the spirit of *one* I knew not, I saw not, but dearly felt and will never forget, a mystic and inwrapping spirit breathed within me."[15]

In St. Louis Cathedral, his impassioned sermons impressed his congregation until 1850, when he made powerful enemies by preaching against slavery. With the church's approval, Abbé Rouquette left the city for missionary work among the Choctaw, not far from his childhood home on Bayou Lacombe. With the approach of the Civil War, he remained steadfastly anti-secessionist. He considered the secession movement a "monstrous farce . . . played by most wicked actors." Though "others may doubt, others may despair," Rouquette believed "in the youth and strength of our great republican nation."[16]

In 1879, he published an imitation of Chateaubriand's *Atala* entitled *La nouvelle Atala ou la fille de l'esprit* (The New Atala or the Spirit's Daughter) under his Choctaw name, Chahta-Ima (One of Us). As in Chateaubriand's novelette, *La nouvelle Atala* was a tribute to Native Americans, who, Abbé Rouquette wrote, "resemble the heroes of Homer and Ossian; their simplicity is as admirable as their openness and their pride." When he died in the city's Hotel Dieu hospital in 1887, a silent gathering of Choctaw tribesmen surrounded his bed and just as silently followed his funeral procession to St. Louis Cemetery.[17]

Chateaubriand's egalitarian artistry exerted an equally profound influence on Abbé Rouquette's two brothers, Dominque and Térence. For them, however, their alliances with the city's Afro-Creole intelligentsia provoked an angrier reaction.

Dominique, a Romantic literary artist like his younger brother Adrien, showed great promise. In Paris in 1839, he published *Meschacébéenes* (Mississippians), a book of Romantic poetry devoted to Louisiana. Victor Hugo, Pierre-Jean Béranger, and numerous other French writers praised the publication and predicted a bright future for its author. Instead of basking in the Parisian limelight of his literary success, however, Dominique almost immediately returned to New Orleans, where his bohemian lifestyle and extravagances reduced him to a hand-to-mouth existence.

A subsequent book of poetry, *Fleurs d'Amérique* (American Flowers), published in the city in 1856, portrayed Louisiana's Choctaw Indians as a people living in an unspoiled state of nature. In the book, he invited the "young poets of France" to visit Louisiana's forests, where nature had revealed herself to Chateaubriand and where "she will have for you, as for him, flowers, harmony, new flora, / Come, Nature gives to the poets, as to the birds, sustenance and refuge and asks only for songs in return!" Parisian critics applauded *Fleurs d'Amérique* as enthusiastically as they had praised *Meschacébéenes*.[18]

In Louisiana, however, Dominique's fellow New Orleanians viewed his bohemianism and his literary art with increasing contempt. As he advanced in age, he turned for refuge to Nathalie Formento Populus, a journalist, poet, and educator who belonged to the city's Creole literati of color. She was the offspring of an influential Italian surgeon and Félicia Mélot, a woman of color. Before leaving the city, Populus's father acknowledged her as his child and arranged a first-rate education for her at an elite French Quarter private school.

Like Victor Séjour, the city's celebrated literary artist, she attended the Vieux Carré's Académie Saint-Barbe for wealthy free children of color. Both she and Séjour studied under the tutelage of Michel Séligny, the school's founder. Séligny was himself a skilled author whose numerous literary works appeared in the city's leading Francophone periodicals. Populus maintained a lifelong friendship with her headmaster until his death in Paris in 1868.[19]

After passing her examinations, Populus taught at the Institution Catholique des orphelins indigents (Catholic Institute for Indigent Orphans), a school for free children of color. The school was popularly known as the Couvent School after its benefactress, Marie Justin Camaire, an African-born ex-slave who married Bernard Couvent, a prosperous member of the city's Afro-Creole community. The school attracted leading members of the city's free Creole intelligentsia, including Populus, who won la Médaille du Professeur from the French government in recognition of her instructional services. She shared Dominique's passion for French literature. Over coffee in her kitchen, he would read his poetry aloud and they would discuss the famed French writers they both knew and loved. Creole historian Edward Larocque Tinker described their encounters based on his interviews with Populus: "The pleasant music of the French parlor soothed him, he forgot his age and his isolation. He imagined himself in Paris in the act of debating the questions raised by the great intellects of 1830. She admired the man of letters; she didn't criticize him for his way of life or his neglected clothing."[20]

Populus also shared her passion for French literature with her fellow instructors at the Couvent School. The teaching staff included Armand Lanusse, Joanni Questy, and Paul Trévigne, the city's leading writers and activists of color. Her friend Dominique Rouquette was undoubtedly well acquainted with her colleagues, given their mutual literary interests and Rouquette's family ties. Térence Rouquette, Dominique's younger brother, collaborated with Lanusse and Questy in 1843 on the creation of *l'Album littéraire: Journal des jeunes gens, amateurs de littérature* (The Literary Album: A Journal of Young Men, Lovers of Literature). Other participants included French émigrés Eugene Supervielle and Jean-Louis Marciacq; the latter was the white director of a school for free children of color. The first known African American literary magazine in the United States, *l'Album* featured commentary, works of fiction, and poetry.[21]

Just as Juliette Gaudin, Henriette Delille, and Marie Jeanne Aliquot had found when they struggled to organize an interracial convent of Catholic nuns, the racial makeup of *l'Album*'s creators and contributors violated an 1830 state law mandating severe penalties for violating the caste distinctions that separated the "several classes" of society. Even more dangerously, the journal's vehement attacks on "the sad and awful condition of Louisiana society" violated an 1830 state law barring all reading materials tending to agitate the free Black and slave populations, under penalty of imprisonment or death.[22] The extreme severity of the laws understandably prompted some contributors to withhold their identities. Even so, a number of literary artists, including Armand Lanusse, Joanni Questy, Camille Thierry, and Térence Rouquette, boldly signed their poems and short stories.

In an unsigned introductory essay, "Horrors of the Day," a writer deplored the decline of the nation's revolutionary ideals. The spectacle of rampant greed, unrelieved poverty, and institutionalized injustice "grips our heart with deep sorrow, showering grief over all our thoughts, filling the soul with terror and despair." If one were allowed to express oneself freely, the writer continued, "how many truths would be revealed!"[23]

In an article titled "Crime Everywhere" in the August issue of *l'Album*, a writer continued the attack on conditions in Louisiana. The author lamented the British rise through "the triumph of the material through callous genius," and the decline of the moral legacy of the American revolutionary leaders Benjamin Franklin and George Washington. In earlier times, voices had arisen to "celebrate the benefits of liberty, this maiden of heaven by which each is a king on earth." Now, under English influence again, tyranny and chaos prevailed.[24]

After a reader charged *l'Album*'s staff with instigating revolution, the short-lived journal ceased publication. As *l'Album*'s critic certainly recognized and feared, New Orleans was especially susceptible to the highly politicized turn Romanticism had taken throughout the Francophone Atlantic. Spurred on by the sense of an unfinished revolution, a generation of Romantic poets, novelists, and dramatists in France, Haiti, and Louisiana saw their art form as a force for change growing out of the revolutionary heritage.

In France, Victor Hugo, Alexandre Dumas, Félicité de Lamennais, Alphonse de Lamartine, and other leading French intellectuals joined their demands for freedom of expression to the broader struggle for political equality and social justice. By their actions, France's foremost Romantic exponents linked the movement's egalitarian ethic to the Age of Revolution. Thus transformed, Romanticism transcended national boundaries as well as racial, gender, and class divisions to emerge as the literary lingua franca of reformers and republican revolutionaries throughout the Atlantic world. In France, Haiti, and Louisiana, Romantic writers shaped their commentary and literary works into a basis for political and social change. In Haiti, nearly simultaneous with *l'Album's* debut in New Orleans, one of the earliest manifestations of political Romanticism occurred with the 1843 Haitian Revolution.

During the 1830s, a new generation of Haitian intellectuals organized cénacles and circulated their own Romantic literary art and commentary in which they advocated social and political reforms. In 1835, Haiti's leading Romantic writers—the Nau brothers Ignace and Emile, the Ardouin brothers Coriolan and Beaubrun, and Beauvais Lespinasse—founded in Port-au-Prince a literary society modeled after the cénacle de l'Arsenal in Paris, founded by Alphonse de Lamartine, Victor Hugo, and Alexandre Dumas.[25]

They were supported by Port-au-Prince political activists Joseph and Juliette Courtois, who had launched a weekly journal, *Feuille du Commerce,* to challenge the authoritarian presidency of Jean-Pierre Boyer. Under the previous president, Alexandre Pétion, Joseph Courtois had worked for the return of Haitian exiles who had settled in France. He and Juliette also opened a coeducational secondary school, the Maison d'Éducation. After the Courtoises acquired a printing press, they joined Boyer's opposition and founded *Feuille du Commerce* in 1825. Sévère Courtois, Joseph's brother, had shipped the printing machine to the couple from Colombia. Sévère, an itinerant revolutionary with Joseph Savary and Louis-Michel Aury, and a veteran officer in d'Aquin's battalion in the Battle of New Orleans, was also a privateer veteran in the Spanish American struggle for independence. Sévère Courtois understood the power of the printed word freely expressed. Together with other opposition newspapers, the Courtoises's *Feuille du Commerce* would play a key role in undermining Boyer's despotic regime.

In 1822, Boyer, a former general who succeeded Alexandre Pétion to the presidency in 1818, sparked widespread outrage when he ordered the arrest of a number of senators in the nation's Chamber of Deputies, with one of the men condemned to death and executed. Boyer's unpopularity mounted after 1825, when he entered into an agreement with Charles X to pay France a staggering indemnity to compensate exiled French planters. Demonstrators at the national palace shouted, "Long live independence! Long live freedom of the press! Long live the constitution! Down with despotism, tyranny and tyrants!" Boyer declared the opposition seditious, and in 1831 he arrested a number of his critics for their commentary in the Courtoises's *Feuille du Commerce*. Joseph Courtois himself was jailed for defaming the president. During her husband's confinement, Juliette Courtois continued to publish. In her role as an editor and contributor, she acquired a reputation as Haiti's first woman journalist.[26]

In September 1842, in response to Boyer's renewed attacks on elected representatives, the president's republican opposition organized the Society for the Rights of Man and the Citizen and issued a call to arms. In the 1843 Haitian Revolution, insurgent republican leaders managed to forge an urban–rural alliance and recruit General Charles Rivière-Hérard to lead revolutionary forces. Boyer, having lost the support of his army, fled on February 13 aboard a British ship bound for Jamaica. Less than two months later, on April 1, the date of President Alexandre Pétion's birth, the revolutionary leadership installed a provisional government with Hérard as president. On December 30, Haiti's Constituent Assembly approved a new constitution providing for a democratic republic. It provided for freedom of speech, public assembly, and the right of petition. It ensured a free press and mandated the gradual implementation of a system of free primary public education, while also declaring the equality of all religions. The document, similar in many respects to the US Constitution and its Bill of Rights, differed from that document in one foundational way: it condemned slavery.

During the nearly ten months it took the Constituent Assembly to hammer out its new charter, General Hérard was handing out military offices, enlarging the size of his army, and defying the mandates of the new civilian government. In the end, however, the 1843 revolutionaries proved unable to carry their republican blueprint into effect. "The bitter paradox of Haitian history," scholar

Mimi Sheller observed, "is that its successful revolutionary struggle left the new republic with all the tools for democracy but one, and that the most fundamental—subordination of the military to civil control."[27] Still, at home and abroad, the Haitian nation remained a potent symbol of Black freedom and independence as well as a model of a successful anti-colonial revolution.

The 1843 revolt foreshadowed a wave of insurrections sparked in Europe by the 1848 French Revolution. The overthrow of France's July Monarchy set off upheavals from Denmark to the Adriatic Sea, from the Rhine River to Central Europe, and from the Baltic Sea to Croatia. On the evening of his February 24 abdication, Louis-Philippe paced up and down in a trancelike state repeating, "Like Charles X! Like Charles X!" The day before, angry republican firebrands and distressed workers in Paris had confronted government forces on the Boulevard des Capucines, where soldiers opened fired. Scores of demonstrators were either killed or wounded. As the melee spread, Parisians threw up barricades throughout the central districts of the city. The roi des Français had no choice but to vacate his office.[28]

On the morning of the king's abdication, various factions approached Alphonse de Lamartine, a skilled orator, for leadership. From his sickbed, he rushed to the Chamber of Deputies, where he and his political allies forced the proclamation of the nation's Second Republic. At the outset of the 1848 French Revolution, he joined with nine other republican leaders to set up a provisional government, pending a national April election for a Constituent Assembly on the basis of universal male suffrage. In rapid succession, they abolished titles of nobility, the death penalty for political offenses, and press censorship, unleashing a flood of newspapers. In Paris alone, more than four hundred papers appeared between February 1848 and the end of December, with women voicing their priorities in *La Tribune des femmes*, *La Voix des femmes*, and *l'Opinion des femmes*.

The provisional government, with a number of leading members of the Société pour l'Abolition de l'Esclavage (Society for the Abolition of Slavery) represented in its leadership, named abolitionist Victor Schoelcher president of the Commission on Slavery. On April 27, the government approved the commission's abolition decree. It provided for the unconditional abolition of slavery at the end of two months, with all liberated adult males acquiring the right to vote. In the French Caribbean, the emancipation edict had an electrifying effect. Thousands of slaves in Guadeloupe and Martinique abandoned the plantations.

When Schoelcher was elected to the Constituent Assembly, he joined Félicité de Lamennais in the legislature's Montagne (Mountain), a faction in the assembly that identified as republican socialists. In the abolition struggle, the former French priest had authored the most damning religious attacks on slavery. In his widely read publications, he wrote that "the essence of slavery is the destruction of the human personality." At "certain times, and in certain countries, man has become the property of man; he has become an article of traffic; he has been sold and bought, like a beast of burden. . . . Brethren have said to brethren: We are not of the same race as you; our blood is purer. You and your offspring are destined to serve us forever." However, he wrote in biblically inflected prose in his influential 1834 *Les Paroles d'un croyant*, "we are one, for our brethren are one with us, and we are one with our brethren. God hath made nor small nor great, nor masters nor slaves, nor kings nor subjects, He hath made all men equal."[29]

In France's new Constituent Assembly, Lamennais was chosen to serve on the committee to draft a new constitution. In that role, he argued for decentralization of government, with political autonomy for local communes, separation of church and state, free and universal education, and graduated taxes. His positions attracted interest but they were not retained as a basis for discussion. Discouraged, he resigned after two months. Worse was to come.

In a grudging concession to republican socialists in the provisional government, political republicans had authorized the creation of National Workshops. The workshops did nothing to address the evils industrial wage earners suffered in the form of long hours, poor pay, job insecurity, and unemployment. Instead, the workshops became little more than a relief agency for the unemployed, whose numbers ballooned from twenty-five thousand needy workers in mid-March to nearly two hundred thousand idle men in a Parisian population of a million. By mid-June, the workshops could no longer accommodate the men enrolled in the project.

The 1848 Constituent Assembly elected in April on the basis of universal male suffrage, by a majority voting population of provincial bourgeois and landowning peasants, was equally unsympathetic to the working class. When the assembly moved to dissolve the National Workshops, the city's laboring class resisted. In response, the government proclaimed martial law, and the "Bloody June Days" from June 24 to 26 ensued. The workers' barricades were no match for the French army's artillery and greater numbers. A ferocious suppression followed, with at least ten thousand insurgents killed. The young professed communist Karl Marx described the February revolution as the *"beautiful* revolution," and the June Days as the *"ugly* revolution, the repulsive revolution."[30]

The catastrophe convinced the Constituent Assembly to centralize power in the hands of a strong president to be elected immediately on the basis of universal male suffrage. Candidate Louis Napoléon Bonaparte, the nephew of Napoléon Bonaparte, expressed solidarity with the common people and promised order and stability. He benefited enormously from the "Napoleonic legend" that had been growing for twenty years out of a nostalgia for an epic era in French history. In 1836, the completion of the Arc de Triomphe with its commemoration of the victories of the French Revolution and the Napoleonic Wars stoked memories of the nation's former greatness. Misguided artists and intellectuals fueled the dangerous illusion. In 1830, Victor Hugo penned "À la Colonne," showering Bonaparte with extravagant praise in his tribute to the Vendôme Column commemorating the French victory at Austerlitz. In "Le Retour de Napoléon" (1841), New Orleanian Victor Séjour authored an equally grandiose paean to the return of Napoléon's remains from St. Helena to Paris in 1840 for interment in Les Invalides.

Lamartine warned against the Napoleonic legend and even attempted to prevent Louis Napoléon from crossing the French border under the terms of an 1832 law that banned the Bonaparte family from France. His efforts proved completely futile. In December 1848, Bonaparte was elected president of France in an enormous landslide, with 5.4 million of the 7.3 million votes cast.[31]

Expressing his own alarm at the "rise of the Prince Président to power," Lamennais worked to defend the republic against its enemies' attacks. When he was reelected in May 1849 to represent the department of Seine, he shared his excitement with his confidante in New Orleans, Éléonore Bénard Ligeret de Chazey: "I have been elected by Paris. Pray to God that he will give me the strength I need to fulfill my duties." With Louis Napoléon Bonaparte waiting in the wings, Lamennais's return to the legislature's Mountain to vote with the republican socialists was short-lived.[32]

At the outset of the 1848 French Revolution, republican enthusiasts in New Orleans greeted news of the Second Republic with speeches, processions, and banquets, amid repeated choruses of "La Marseillaise." The city's French partisans and their Anglophone supporters, led by Senator Pierre Soulé, a political refugee of Charles X's repressive regime, drew up a series of resolutions to congratulate the people of France on their victory over tyranny. They praised the provisional government's declaration of universal male suffrage and its labor policy, a worthy plan, they wrote, to "protect the rights of the worker and assure him of the greatest possible prosperity." Invoking the spirit of the 1789 French Revolution, New Orleanians proclaimed the principles of "liberté, égalité, fraternité" in their approval of the resolutions by public acclamation. Public ceremonies for insurgents killed in the revolution began in St. Louis Cathedral.[33]

The *New Orleans Courrier de la Louisiane* rejoiced that in "all the cities of the North, the establishment of the French Republic has been greeted with ecstasy, and a multitude of resolutions have been addressed to the Provisional Government." When South Carolina senator John C. Calhoun and his proslavery Whig and Democrat allies opposed a Senate proclamation commending the French people on the establishment of their new republic, the *Courrier* bemoaned their "disgraceful backwardness."[34]

Fully aware of the revolutions in France and the French Caribbean, Romantic author Armand Lanusse chose 1848 to launch the opening of the Couvent School. Three years earlier, the indefatigable Lanusse had published a book of poetry, *Les Cenelles: choix de poésies indigènes* (Mayhaws: A Selection of Indigenous Poems). As with *l'Album littéraire*, a journal whose publication coincided with the 1843 Haitian Revolution, Lanusse once again took the lead in creating a pioneering African American publication with provocative undertones. *Les Cenelles* was the nation's first African American anthology of literature. Taken together, *l'Album littéraire* and *Les Cenelles* contain all of the major components of the Romantic style and thought that swept the Francophone Atlantic world in the nineteenth century. Quoting republican proponents Alphonse de Lamartine, Félicité de Lamennais, Alexandre Dumas, and Victor Hugo in the two publications, contributors signaled their admiration for four of France's most politically active authors.[35]

In his role as an educator at the Couvent School, Lanusse directed a highly politicized faculty with teaching assistants educated in France and Haiti. Together with Lanusse, who shared his Haitian ancestry with his colleagues and students, they educated the next generation of activists. For the Desdunes brothers, Pierre-Aristide and Rodolphe-Lucien, the Age of Revolution bore directly on their lives. Second-generation New Orleanians with ancestral roots in Haiti, the two boys were born in the midst of a new wave of revolutionary upheavals. Their Couvent School instructors incorporated the Haitian Revolution of 1843 and the 1848 French Revolution into their history studies and emphasized French Romanticism's power as a force for change.

In an apt description of the school, historians Donald E. DeVore and Joseph Logsdon designated it "the nursery for revolution in Louisiana." In their studies, the Desdunes brothers were eager protégés and readily embraced Romanticism's political use of art and history to teach lessons in the present and the future. In view of their Haitian identity, their familial ties to the Caribbean, and the oppression they suffered under Louisiana's increasingly repressive slave regime, the brothers wholeheartedly embraced the teachings of their Couvent School professors. They would grow up to join the leadership ranks of Louisiana's advocates for revolutionary change.

For the two young boys, their instructors, and Black New Orleanians, the stunning events of the French Revolution stood out as an inspiring new milestone. After proclaiming the French Second Republic, literary artist Alphonse de Lamartine and his republican allies abolished slavery and proclaimed universal male suffrage. In 1848, all African-descended men in France's Caribbean colonies elected representatives to the Second Republic's interracial National Assembly. For Black New Orleanians, France's 1848 February Revolution would remain the lodestar of their aspirations for freedom and political equality.[36]

Shocked by events in France, the French Caribbean, and Louisiana, white slaveholding southerners expressed alarm. On a fact-finding mission through the South in January 1849, South Carolinian H. W. Conner described his impressions to his state senator, John C. Calhoun: "I fear for Louisiana. New Orleans is almost Free Soil in their opinions. The population is one half Northern Agents, another 1/4 or 1/3 are Foreigners. The remnant are Creoles who cannot be made to comprehend their danger until the negroes are being taken out of the fields. . . . Louisiana will be the last if at all to strike for the defense of the South."[37]

Calhoun may also have been aware of the significant proportion of the city's Afro-Creole community who traced their ancestral roots to Haiti and maintained their familial ties to the western hemisphere's first independent Black nation. In 1823, Battle of New Orleans veteran Louis Séjour visited his native Haiti with his eleven-year-old son, Ruojès-Louis Séjour, while his six-year-old brother, Victor Séjour, remained at home. As a child, New Orleans poet Pierre-Aristide Desdunes had traveled to Haiti with his father during the 1850s despite an 1831 Louisiana law prohibiting free people of color from returning to the state if they visited the West Indies. New Orleans writer Nelson Desbrosses, an esteemed healer and Spiritualist medium, spent a number of years in Haiti studying vaudoux. Like the Séjour and Desdune families, he returned to the antebellum city without incident.[38]

Calhoun and his allies no doubt felt a considerable sense of relief at subsequent events in Haiti and France. In both nations, republican aspirations for a constitutional government had culminated in dictatorships—that of Emperor Faustin I (Faustin-Élie Soulouque) in Haiti in 1849 and of Emperor Napoléon III (Louis-Napoléon Bonaparte) in France in 1852. In 1851, Bonaparte had crushed the Second Republic, intentionally choosing December 2, the anniversary of his uncle's stunning victory at Austerlitz, for his own sweeping triumph. He dissolved France's National Assembly, arrested scores of left-wing legislators and political leaders, proclaimed a state of siege by marching heavily armed troops into Paris, and promised an election to sanction his putsch.

When Victor Hugo's name appeared prominently on an incendiary flyer urging Parisians to resist on the grounds that "Louis-Napoléon is a traitor. He has stolen the constitution. He has perjured himself. He is an outlaw," Bonaparte offered a reward of 25,000 francs for the capture of Hugo dead or alive. Hugo fled, leaving behind a trunk of unfinished manuscripts, including Les Misérables. A year later, Bonaparte proclaimed the Second French Empire.[39]

In New Orleans, political activist Prosper Barousse joined the thousands of political exiles of the Francophone Atlantic's revolutions, coups d'état, and royalist reactions who entered the city between the 1789 French Revolution and the 1861 outbreak of the United States Civil War. During his sojourn in New Orleans between 1839 and 1844, Barousse won the respect of the city's Francophone literati with his impassioned Romantic writings. A "fiery republican" with socialist leanings, he returned to Paris where he took part in the 1848 French Revolution. Napoléon III's seizure of power forced him into flight. In 1852, he arrived in New Orleans, where he and his new wife, Marie Barousse, were welcomed with open arms by French-born Louisiana senator Soulé, an enthusiastic supporter of the republican cause who had fled repression ahead of the 1830 French Revolution.[40]

Armentine Soulé, the senator's wife, introduced Marie Barousse into Louisiana society, while Creole socialite Nancy Bouny invited the young woman, an aspiring French writer, to present a lecture on French literature in her lavish residence. Bouny's renowned salon regularly attracted the Francophone community's Creole elite, including the Olivier, Gardeur, Pitot, Canonge, Baquié, Grima, and d'Aquin families, among others. The 1852 winter evening event was no less impressive. Allain described "a glittering assembly" that included her closest friends, Bouny's daughters Zélie and Nancy, and French émigré Éléonore Ligeret de Chazey and her two daughters, Gladys Faget and Antonia. Marie Barousse's lecture was well received, and Bouny, admired for her wit and generosity, delighted Allain and her other guests with her famed *gombo filé* (filé gumbo). Before long, however, the d'Aquin, Soulé, Bouny, Ligeret de Chazey, and other Fancophone families would deeply regret their hospitality. Within a few years of the literary gala, two of Bouny's guests, lecturer Barousse and Allain's friend Éléonore Ligeret, would be at the center of a bitter transatlantic controversy.[41]

Like Prosper Barousse, Ligeret, as she signed her name, and her family fled Paris in the political turmoil surrounding the 1848 French Revolution. She was an erudite and cultured woman whose attentive father, a French provincial attorney, had overseen her education. She married an eminent Parisian physician, Dr. Jacques-François Ligeret de Chazey, and moved to Paris in 1838 after her husband was appointed to a post in King Louis-Philippe's government. In Paris, the influential couple mingled with the French avant-garde.

Éléonore Ligeret studied art with the director of the Ecole Impériale de Dessin, artist Jean-Hilaire Belloc, who despite his republicanism had been appointed to his position by the influential Marie-Adélaïde d'Orléans, the king's sister. Together with Félicité de Lamennais, Ligeret's social circle extended to Belloc's wife, the Romantic author and translator Louise Swanton-Belloc; author Adélaïde de Montgolfier, whose father, Étienne, together with his brother Joseph de Montgolfier, invented the *montgolfière* (hot air balloon); and exiled Polish refugee Ludwik Mieroslawski. Itinerant Polish revolutionaries like Mieroslawski were active across Europe in the 1848–1849 "Springtime of the Peoples." In return for their contributions to the revolutionary movements, they aspired to win support for the independence of Poland.[42]

Lamennais's 1834 *Paroles d'un croyant* (Words of a Believer), dedicated to the "tremendous revolution which is going on at the heart of human society," captivated Ligeret. Possessed, herself, of a profound religious sensibility, she considered Lamennais a "prophet, an apostle, a martyr for the truth." For Ligeret as for George Sand, his book was a revelation. For its author, it was a critical milestone. Published in Paris, the book created a sensation, running to more than one hundred editions and translated into virtually every European language. Admirers hailed the *Paroles d'un croyant* as "la Marseillaise du Christianisme."[43]

Paroles d'un croyant marked Lamennais's dramatic metamorphosis from an advocate of monarchy and the Catholic Church to a fervent republican. In the book, he denounced France's existing political order and broke with the Church. Pope Gregory XVI condemned the book. Lamennais's subsequent outpouring of articles and pamphlets attacking Louis-Philippe's government landed him in Sainte-Pélagie prison in 1841 for a year, with a fine of 2,000 francs.[44]

Lamennais's blending of social justice with spiritual renewal in *Paroles d'un croyant* appealed to Ligeret's sociopolitical aspirations as well as her devout religiosity. She immediately set about authoring a feminist response entitled *Paroles d'une femme* (Words of a Woman). Soon after her first meeting with the famed Romantic writer, she asked him to appraise her manuscript. His egalitarianism, however, did not extend to women's rights.

Though Ligeret's study revealed "real talent," "exceptional powers of observation," and "vivacity and uncommon elegance of expression," he found her argument for women's legal rights flawed. "It seems to me," he wrote, "that alongside your tableau of the suffering of women in marriage, one could set forth another which would be no less true, a tableau of the suffering of men." There was no doubt, he concluded, that women would "improve their position in the family and in society as they improved themselves morally and intellectually." Whatever Ligeret's reaction to Lamannais's disappointing critique, their friendship thrived.[45]

Ligeret's life in Paris ended abruptly at the outset of the 1848 French Revolution, when the king abdicated and revolutionaries proclaimed a republic. The new provisional government stripped her husband of his office despite his republican sympathies. Alarmed by his sudden dismissal in the midst of the revolutionary struggle, Ligeret and her family prepared to leave France. Before their departure, they attempted to bid Lamennais farewell at his residence. He wasn't home and regretted missing them. It would have been their last adieu. Ligeret, her husband, and their twenty-year-old daughter Antonia arrived in New Orleans aboard the *Anna* on November 27, 1848. In New Orleans, they joined the household of their eldest daughter, Gladys, and her husband, Dr. Jean-Charles Faget, a native of the city who, like Allain, was descended from refugees of the Haitian Revolution.

From the United States, Ligeret poured out her sorrows to Lamennais. She was appalled by slavery and longed to return to France. In an 1849 reply to her bleak accounts of life in Louisiana, Lamennais was, he confessed, very disturbed by everything you tell me of the country in which you live; a dismal country, indeed, in which, to again meet a human being and the feelings that God has endowed him with, one must seek him among the poor slaves, away from the stupidly arrogant race which calls itself and believes itself civilized, and which, in forgetting its Christian principles, is more barbarous than the *sauvages* [Native Americans] that it tracks and hunts in the vast deserts of the West.[46]

His sympathetic letters and grim descriptions of the ongoing turmoil and suffering in strife-torn Paris did nothing to ease Ligeret's homesickness. They continued to correspond until the Romantic writer's death. His last letter to Ligeret was dated January 8, 1854. He died on February 27. On his deathbed, he refused to see a priest and expressed his "unshakable faith in the future triumph of his ideas." He was buried, as he wished, in a common, unmarked grave with those for whom he had fought.[47]

For Ligeret and thousands of New Orleanians, events took a disastrous turn for the worse in 1853, when the city suffered the deadliest yellow fever epidemic in its history. Between May and December, it's estimated that between eight thousand and eleven thousand residents, 10 percent of the city's population, perished. French émigré Prosper Barousse succumbed to the pestilence. By the time of his death, his wife, Marie Barousse, had begun to work with another French writer, Manoël de Grandfort, in a collaboration that had raised Creole eyebrows. In November, they produced a diminutive, short-lived weekly journal, *Le Coup d'œil* (The Blink of an Eye), to which Barousse contributed articles, including at least one serialized romance fiction featuring a woman protagonist.

In early 1854, she further breached the Francophone community's social mores when she married Grandfort within six months of her husband's death, a period of mourning considered "scandalously brief." At the same time, the couple attempted another literary journal, *Les Moissonneurs* (The Reapers), which promised the serial publication of Madame de Grandfort's novel *Un Amour d'outre-tombe* (A Love from Beyond the Grave). In March, after the second journal failed, the Grandforts returned to France.[48]

A little over a year after the Grandforts' departure for Europe, Allain and her mother boarded a ship for the transatlantic crossing. The d'Aquin boarding school's success enabled its founder, Marie Anne Elisabeth d'Aquin, to temporarily close her establishment for the 1855–1856 school year and accompany her daughter Hélène d'Aquin to France to complete her education at the Sorbonne. Their friend Ligeret no doubt used her influence to have Allain enrolled in summer art classes at the Ecole Impériale de Dessin in Paris. Both Ligeret and her daughter Antonia had studied under the school's director, artist Jean-Hilaire Belloc, before emigrating to New Orleans.

At the time of the Ligeret de Chazey family's arrival in Louisiana in 1848, five of Antonia Ligeret de Chazey's miniature paintings were being exhibited at the Salon de Paris. In an act of kindness that endeared her to the d'Aquin family, Antonia presented the d'Aquins with a "beautiful" miniature of Allain's older brother, Henri-Charles d'Aquin, who was studying medicine in France. Antonia Ligeret's generosity endeared her to Allain, who came to consider her friend, "after my mother, the most influential person in my life." Allain's ties to Antonia and the Ligeret de Chazey family would deepen further when Hélène d'Aquin married Frédéric Constant François Joseph Allain, a protégé of Ligeret's son-in-law Dr. Charles Faget.[49]

In Paris in 1855, Allain entered into the company of some of France's most forward-thinking intellectuals. She studied art under Jean-Hilaire Belloc, who affectionately dubbed Allain his "water color painter" and invited her to join the Bellocs' social circle. She chatted with her art instructor's wife, Louise Swanton-Belloc, whose French translations of Lord Byron, Maria Edgeworth, Harriet Beecher Stowe, and other English-language writers reinforced Romanticism's strength and vitality in France. Allain met Adélaïde de Montgolfier, Swanton-Belloc's collaborator, who shared her lifelong friend's concerns for women's rights. Allain also developed a fondness for the distinguished French violinist Charles Eugene Sauzy, under whom Ligeret's daughter Gladys Faget had studied music.

Louise Swanton-Belloc supported an array of social and republican causes, including slavery's abolition, women's equality, the independence of Greece, Ireland, and Poland, prison reform, and the repeal of capital punishment. In the United States, she contributed articles to the *Liberty Bell*, an abolitionist publication founded in 1839 by Maria Weston Chapman, a key ally of William Lloyd Garrison. When Chapman visited Paris, Swanton-Belloc helped her organize a French branch of the American Anti-Slavery Society. In 1853, when Swanton-Belloc translated Harriet Beecher Stowe's abolitionist masterwork for readers in France, Stowe praised the translator in the following terms: "Madame Belloc has written, assisted by her friend Mademoiselle Montgolfier, the best French translation of *Uncle Tom's Cabin*."[50]

After passing her examinations and taking leave of the Bellocs at the Ecole

Impériale, Allain returned to New Orleans in 1856, where her mother boasted the addition in her institute's coming school year of a "special course for ladies and young girls presented by a *demoiselle* graduated from the Sorbonne."[51] Unfortunately, a series of disasters that had befallen French-speaking New Orleanians overshadowed Marie Anne Elisabeth d'Aquin's good news and Allain's debut as an education professional. When Allain and her mother returned from France, Creole New Orleans was in crisis.

During the 1850s, with sectional tensions mounting and the threat of war looming, the city's English-speaking leaders accelerated their efforts to "Americanize" the slave South's largest city and port. In the struggle, they tapped into deep-seated Anglo-American perceptions of Creoles as intellectually inferior and degenerate owing to linguistic, racial, and cultural amalgamation.[52] In a series of fiercely contested political maneuvers that began in 1850, les Américains finally triumphed, after decades of struggle.

In the riotous 1855 alderman race, white supremacists took aim at George Pandelly, a Creole elected in 1853 to the city's Board of Assistant Aldermen. He was descended from one of Louisiana's oldest and most distinguished Creole families. His father-in-law, Alexander Dimitry, was a widely respected spokesman for the Creole community. In the political challenge to Pandelly's alderman seat, Victor Wiltz, a self-described "steward" of the South's white supremacist orthodoxy, charged that Pandelly's maternal family tree included ancestors who were not "free white persons." Pandelly sued his accuser for "slanders uttered by defendant [Wiltz] to the prejudice of his [Pandelly's] social and political standing." The ensuing 1854 trial, in which Pandelly's ancestry was publicly scrutinized, created a sensation and drew large crowds to the Presbytère, where the case was tried. The ruinous contest forced Pandelly to resign his key political post, giving his Anglo-American opponents control of the legislative branch of city government.[53]

In the run-up to the 1858 mayor's race, an armed "vigilant committee" of hundreds of Creoles, Irishmen, and Germans seized the state arsenal in the Cabildo and encamped on Jackson Square. They touted the mayoral candidacy of Creole New Orleanian P. G. T. Beauregard and demanded oversight of the forthcoming election, protesting a pattern of voter intimidation and fraud. When neither they nor their opponents would agree to back down, the *New Orleans Times-Picayune* declared the city on the verge of civil war. The election proceeded peacefully, however, with Anglo-Americans winning the mayor's office and gaining complete control of city government.[54]

Perhaps reflecting on the Creole/Anglo-American political struggle for control of New Orleans and the city's Francophone literary culture, an 1856 editorial directive in Richmond, Virginia's, *Southern Literary Messenger* set forth "the duty of southern authors" to create a southern literature that would defend slavery and end "the unholy citadel erected by the slander, fanaticism, and malignity of . . . [the South's] enemies."[55] In Paris, as if on cue, the inscrutable Madame de Grandfort anticipated the *Messenger*'s literary call to arms with a proslavery, semifictional travel book that coincided with the political crises in New Orleans.

After returning to France in 1854, Grandfort authored *Fleurs Américaines* (American Flowers), which included a vicious attack on Francophone New Orleanians. Upon its initial arrival in New York in January 1855, *Fleurs Américaines* was advertised as a semifictional book authored by "Marie Fontenay," a pseudonym for Grandfort. The publication prompted a harsh rebuke from the columnist for "The Editor's Easy Chair" at *Harper's New Monthly Magazine*. "We have," the reviewer concluded, "thrust our pen through this bit of foolery belonging to Madame Fontenay . . . to show the overgrown conceit, as well as ignorance, of very many French travelers among us."[56]

When *Fleurs Américaines* was reissued later in Paris in spring 1855, it debuted under a new title, *l'Autre monde* (The New World), authored by Marie Fontenay, with "Mme Manoël de Grandfort" given in subscript. In the second edition of *l'Autre monde* (1857), Mme Manoël de Grandfort alone appeared as the author. Perhaps encouraged by the New York magazine's lengthy denunciation, Grandfort decided to dispel any ambiguity involving her authorship. In taking full credit for *l'Autre monde*, she likely aspired to duplicate the lucrative success of English writer Frances Trollope, who had created an international sensation in 1832 with *Domestic Manners of the Americans*. In a thinly veiled attack on Trollope, Grandfort purported to dismiss the "fashion of English travelers who take part in addressing insults to Americans because they are a commodity that sells well in London bookstalls."[57]

The English author based *Domestic Manners* on a journal she kept as she traveled in the United States for nearly four years, suffering business failure and humiliating poverty. Trollope's candid observations made the book one of the most popular travel accounts about the new nation. At the same time, its acerbic commentary enraged many North American readers. Its critics notwithstanding, *Domestic Manners* went through four editions within a year of its debut.[58] Trollope's success brought wealth and opened the way for a remarkable literary career in which she published more than one hundred books, including the first antislavery novel, *The Life and Adventures of Jonathan Jefferson Whitelaw* (1836). Her dramatization of slavery's cruelties foreshadowed Harriet Beecher Stowe's *Uncle Tom's Cabin* (1852) and won converts to the abolitionist cause.

If Grandfort's ploy failed to produce comparable literary success, it nonetheless produced ample rewards. Though a reviewer for *Harper's* considered *l'Autre monde* "a very queer book," the writer conceded that Grandfort "in her portraiture of American manners certainly out-Trollopes Trollope."[59] Like *Domestic Manners, l'Autre monde* created an international uproar, went through several transatlantic editions, and launched its author onto a successful, lifelong writing career. Both books also benefited from the public popularity of travel journals. In purpose and content, however, Trollope's humane if unflattering portrait of North American life bore no resemblance to *l'Autre monde's* horrific attack.

l'Autre monde also bolstered the cause of Anglophone southerners who viewed the city's French Romantic movement as a dangerous breach in the South's intellectual *cordon sanitaire*. In the book, Grandfort denigrated the humanitarian ethos of both French and northern Romanticism in favor of the movement's southern counterpart—a Romantic vein that glorified the South's slave-based society and fortified its white supremacist status quo.

Her slashing caricatures of abolitionism, feminism, Romanticism, socialism, and other nineteenth-century -isms gave voice to the South's loathing for its critics in Europe and the North. It appears likely, given the scope of Grandfort's attack, that she was recruited and even compensated by southern ideologues who were as determined to refashion the city and the region's literary culture as they were to revolutionize its political landscape.

Among Anglophone southerners, the prevalence of French-language publications in New Orleans was a cause for great concern. As late as 1850, most of Louisiana's literary works were written in French, and though Sir Walter Scott was enormously popular among the city's English-speaking community, he had little influence on French writers. Indeed, the English language as a literary medium did not supplant French until after the Civil War.[60]

In *l'Autre monde's* opening pages, Grandfort takes direct aim at Chateaubriand, whose enormously popular *Atala* and *René* introduced Louisianians to Romanticism. Her protagonist, Julien, in part a caricature of the famed French author, sets out from France in the early 1850s to visit the United States. The free-spirited young traveler realizes his "poetic dreams" of dwelling among the "Florida Indians," roaming "with the fugitive slaves in Louisiana," and seducing "a beautiful Wisconsin damsel on the shores of Lake Michigan." But as his journey unfolds, Julien becomes disillusioned. Even the shores of the Mississippi River are disappointing, for he discovers that "those magnificent landscapes promised by the poet of the *Natchez*" were instead a "dull horizon" that had been "transformed into a brilliant spectacle purely by the melodious imagination" of Chateaubriand.[61]

Oddly for a cosmopolitan French visitor, his disenchantment takes on a rabidly pro-southern character as he assails the South's most despised northern -*isms*. Over a third of the book targets feminism, a movement closely aligned with abolitionism—another subject of repeated attacks. Few of the reform and humanitarian movements inspired by Romanticism's sweep through the North and Europe are spared. Feminism's Lucy Stone and Amelia Bloomer; abolitionism's Frances Trollope, the Duchess of Sutherland, and Harriet Beecher Stowe; utopian socialism's Robert Owen and Charles Fourier; and Romanticism's Chateaubriand and Lamartine, among other reform-minded activists, are ridiculed.[62]

In a chapter entitled "New Orleans and Slavery," Julien describes how his thinking is completely revolutionized in a city "that yellow fever, rattlesnakes, and the rogues of all nations overrun." Horrified at the mélange of peoples, languages, and social customs he encounters, he expresses revulsion at the "hideous patois" he hears in a "hybrid society composed of all colors and all nationalities." His experiences transform him from an abolitionist sympathizer who "had wept over Mrs. Stowe's pages" to a virulent white supremacist espousing the antebellum South's "positive good" theory of slavery.[63]

On a French Quarter street, Julien finds Lolotte, a proud, finely dressed Black woman, "frightful." He is shocked when he overhears an enslaved flower peddler explain that her friend Lolotte "has a good husband, my dear! He is white—Monsieur Dolphe!" Julien is also taken aback at the demeanor of enslaved women: "Nothing equals the vanity and insolence of these *creatures*, and I have often been astonished at the kindness shown them by créole [white] women."[64]

Julien's impressions of Francophone white women are similarly negative. They are, he explains, poorly educated, with "minds generally of an inferior level; the subject of their conversations always dull and insipid—all of which defects arise from too frequent contact with their *négresses*, with whom—a grave error—they are too familiar." Julien finds Creole slave masters as permissive as slave mistresses. He is astonished to learn of a forthcoming slave soirée organized "by their master's permission, and that, too, in his own home!"[65]

In Louisiana's rural parishes, where women's education is infinitely more neglected than that of their city sisters, "the *créoles* on the plantations frequently use no other tongue than the *patois des négres.*" Their "lack of intelligence and manner is so great that even their pretty faces have a stupid, ugly look." And as for "morality or religion, the *créoles,*" to Julien's dismay, "exhibit an indifference that even the illustrious Lamennais did not foresee. The larger number are born, live and die, without having known the meaning of baptism, the Mass, or first Communion."[66]

An encounter with runaway slaves persuades Julien that all African-descended Creoles were "subject only to ignoble and repulsive instincts," and it is these beings on whom "a pitiful philosophy [abolitionism] would bestow the name of men, and whom it would raise to our level!" Even wealthy free Creoles of color, though educated in the best northern schools, preferred living in a country where "they are constantly humiliated, instead of emigrating to France or England, for example, where the same rights and privileges as the whites enjoy, would be granted to them."[67]

l'Autre monde's 1855 Anglophone translator, New Orleanian Edward C. Wharton, noted the "sensation created among the Creoles of this State . . . and the notice taken of the French original by most of the newspapers of the country." But Grandfort's venomous concluding paragraph in her essay "La Nouvelle-Orléans et l'esclavage" went too far for Wharton, who excluded the passage from his translation. "How deplorable in America," Grandfort exclaimed in her own voice, "is the familiarity that *whites* bring to bear in their relations with the other race! Do not some go all the way there to unite with *mulâtresses* and *quarteronnes*? That, a union? What sacrilege! That has the same name on both continents; a name which applies to the greatest of crimes in all countries: *bestiality!*"[68]

Creolization, with its multiracial, multilingual, and assimilationist ethos, had left the French influence "in the frozen hearts" of Francophone Louisianians "like something dead." Northern abolitionism with its threat to slavery and white supremacy posed an equally menacing danger, and the author addressed the crisis directly, having dispensed with Julien's fictional character three essays earlier. In her concluding polemic, "Protestantism, Equality and Liberty in the United States," she attacked a northern Protestantism that had consecrated "the doctrine of Equality, by putting itself at the head of the Abolition move-ment." Abolitionism kept the country in constant turmoil with "terror sown in the South, fanaticism aroused in the North, hatred spread everywhere. *The sin of slavery* must be punished even if it means the death of the master."[69]

Disunion endangers the nation as "the South daily becomes more and more separated from the North which has become the pillager of her re-sources and the enemy of her institutions. Protestantism cares not for these threatened dangers. The *négres* must become the equals of the whites," even if that meant the destruction of the nation. In its current state, a "deformed" American society must be stopped from gaining a "footing in Europe." Such an outcome would result in "the raising in our public squares four bare walls in the middle of which a tedious *reverend* in a white cravat" would preach doctrines that "neither you nor I can ever forgive for having inspired and given birth to the sensitive 'Uncle Tom.'"[70]

Almost simultaneous with *l'Autre monde*'s 1855 Paris debut, a New York publisher issued a Francophone edition and a New Orleans firm published Wharton's English-language manuscript under the title *The New World*. Se-rialized versions also appeared in the New York journal *Semaine littéraire du Courrier des États-Unis* (Weekly Literary Courier of the United States) and the influential New Orleans Francophone newspaper *l'Abeille* (The Bee). *l'Autre monde* went through several transatlantic editions and launched its author upon a successful, lifelong writing career in France.[71]

In New York, French political exile Albert Fabre refuted Grandfort's char-acterization of Creoles in the *Semaine littéraire*. In New Orleans, an anony-mous pamphleteer generally sided with Grandfort but also attacked Creoles in *l'Inconnue à Mme de Grandfort et à Madame L**** (Anonymous to Mme Grand-fort and Madame L[igeret]). In another pamphlet, *l'Ombre de Mme de Grand-fort* (The Shadow of Mme Grandfort), author L. d'Ambruménil singled out Grandfort in a critique in the *New Orleans Times-Picayune* that was described as a "clever review."[72]

In d'Ambruménil's sixty-page pamphlet, the author seized upon the rumors surrounding the death of Grandfort's husband Prosper Barousse and her mar-riage to Manoël de Grandfort to depict *l'Autre monde*'s author as a vampire-like monster. The French narrator, like Grandfort's Julian, sets out from France for Louisiana. Along the way, his traveling companion, a well-educated, brave, and devoted friend, is reduced to a trembling, "pale and agitated" wreck when he catches a glimpse of a terrifying specter. "Did you see that woman?" he asks the narrator. "She is my dark phantom; she is the evil genius of whom I have spoken."

Later that night, the narrator's tormented friend receives a letter from the mysterious woman requesting a large sum of money. "I am mad, as mad as a March hare," his companion exclaims, "to assist such a woman, and with her ninth husband . . . Poor husbands, they end up in the grave. She uses them up quickly and finds another just as rapidly. The burial today; tomorrow the grieving; the day after tomorrow the quest for suitors who draw lots for her. . . . There is little that accords with divine, civil or social laws; but she knows only one law, that of her own desires and whims." Despite the woman's scandalous behavior, the narrator realizes that his distraught companion is helpless to resist her power. The poor man forwards the money, he explains, "to help her publish, and lay the foundation for fame or fortune."[73]

When the two men finally arrive in New Orleans, they stumble upon a copy of *l'Autre monde*. With the discovery, the narrator learns that the book's author is none other than Marie de Grandfort, the evil genius who torments his friend. His anguished companion confesses how, as a youth, he had fallen in love with Grandfort only to be caught up in the whirlwind of her "fictional and double life, as shallow in France as in America, with its equally depraved flirtations." He learns too late, he explains to the narrator, that Grandfort possesses "dissolute instincts that invent torments to rip open a man's chest, tear out his heart, squeeze the blood from it drop by drop, dissect it bit by bit, fiber by fiber, until robbing her victim of the power to recognize his own damnation."[74]

In d'Ambruménil's telling, the monstrous "Marie" is capable of any villainy to achieve her ends. He employs his vampirish character to point up Grandfort's hypocrisy and ruthlessness. For one thing, Grandfort hardly fit her own ideal of womanhood. While she demanded that other women be confined to the home and hearth to bear and raise children, she herself aspired to a career as a writer. She was exactly the kind of self-made professional woman she railed against in her addresses and writings.

In d'Ambruménil's concluding chapter, the tormented French traveler reflects on his impressions of the United States and its political economy. In the final paragraph, however, he returns to the subject of his obsession: "What has become of Mme De Grandfort? What has become of Marie? . . . We are leaving for the bayous. While studying the labyrinth that Lafitte made so famous and the archipelago of islands where the Gulf of Mexico murmurs, I will tell you the rest of the story."[75] The sequel, it seems, never appeared in print.

l'Autre monde horrified Allain and her fellow Creole New Orleanians, a population that had welcomed Grandfort into its midst. A profound sense of betrayal engulfed the community. In referring to the book twenty-seven years later, Allain could not bring herself to mention the book's title or its author.[76] As a Creole New Orleanian and a thoroughgoing Romantic, she was one of Grandfort's targets. Allain spoke the "hideous patois" of the Creole city's "hybrid society" and delighted in the festivities when her family welcomed free woman of color Suzanne's Afro-Creole wedding party into their home.

Ligeret de Chazey, one of Allain's most influential mentors, took up the cause of the city's French-speaking community in an anonymous pamphlet published in New Orleans in 1855, *Les Créoles. Réponse à Madame de Grandfort.* Allain later included Ligeret's entire pamphlet in her *Souvenirs* as an expression of her admiration and gratitude. She also published a number of poems, prayers, and brief stories authored by both Ligeret and her daughter Antonia.[77]

Though Ligeret was an émigré, her ties to the city's Creole community ran deep by the time of *l'Autre monde*'s publication. In *Les Créoles* she rallied to the defense of her friends and family and reminded Grandfort that the city's Francophone community had "welcomed, loved, and protected you [Grandfort] in the land of exile!"[78]

She knew Grandfort, she informed her readers, "as Mme Barousse, when she bore the honorable name," and she was also familiar with the sketches of Creole women Grandfort had authored for the journal *Le Coup d'œil.* The author of those essays and the Grandfort she knew did not write *l'Autre monde.* Instead, Ligeret insisted, "through imprudence, through thoughtlessness, she lent her name to this publication, she did not write it."[79]

Other reviewers joined Ligeret in questioning the book's provenance. The columnist for "The Editor's Easy Chair" in *Harper's* pointed out that the author's first pseudonym, Marie Fontenay, had been replaced by "another title, to wit, 'Madame Manoël Grandfort.' There is however, shrewd reason to suspect that this even is a misnomer, and the veritable note-taker in our country was a male adventurer."[80] The anonymous author of the pamphlet *l'Inconnue* drew the same conclusion: "All of the ideas with which her [Grandfort's] *Autre monde* is imbued were hatched in a masculine brain; they have been transmitted to Mme de Grandfort, who has artfully embellished them with festoons and embroidery: it is she who has given them their glossy finish."[81]

Ligeret and other critics were clearly justified in questioning *l'Autre monde*'s origin, with its aggressive defense of southern slavery and its "positive good" argument that no person of color, whether enslaved or free, was fit for freedom. Moreover, Grandfort's damning attack on race relations in Francophone New Orleans reflected a decades-long campaign to sabotage a suspect multiethnic urban population—a population with a history of interracial alliances and an intense loyalty to a shared French heritage. That heritage included one of the proslavery South's most despised -isms, Romanticism with a conscience.

Still, Grandfort clearly had a hand in authoring l'Autre monde's extensive attacks on northern feminists. In an 1855 Parisian newspaper editorial, she complained bitterly of being persistently ridiculed for her writings and addresses by "female legislators who, adorned with a pipe and trousers [Bloomerites], propose to actively reform the world to their advantage." She suffered such abuse "because I have repudiated the demand of all those rights which would only end in making a woman a sexless and unattractive being; because I have said and repeat that our only place is in the home; that there was at one time a title, a right and a duty for us: maternity!"[82]

Ligeret refuted the book's contention that Francophone New Orleanians displayed an indifference to religion "that even the illustrious Lamennais did not foresee."[83] In New Orleans, Ligeret insisted, both Protestants and Catholics attended faithfully to their religious obligations. How could it be otherwise, she asked, "in a city ceaselessly decimated by death, where epidemics of cholera, yellow fever, pernicious fevers, [and] scarlet fever rage with such violence and often compete with one another?"[84]

As for l'Autre monde's scurrilous depiction of free and enslaved Creole women on Louisiana's rural plantations, Ligeret observed that Grandfort had never been invited to a plantation. This slight was the likely reason for her insulting and misguided remarks. If she had visited a plantation, she would have met well-educated slave mistresses who, though "unable to stop slavery" attempted to "soften it with all their might," and yes, when consoling the elderly or a mother who had lost a child, "they speak with charming grace in the créole patois, this sweet and native language."[85]

In describing her own stay with a planter family, Ligeret also voiced her admiration for an elderly négresse who made regular morning visits to the plantation:

[They called her] a hospitalière; they gave her white bread, wine, [and] meat for the convalescents. This good woman, in her practice of attending to the sick, resembled a Sister of Charity. She would follow the doctor's orders with a good deal of sense and came twice a week, knew all about fevers and remedies, served as a mid-wife for the young *négresses*, loved her patients like a mother, and her heartfelt intelligence would shame Mme de G*** for the hatred and disdain she heaps on an oppressed, lowly race to which we owe protection and indulgence precisely because of its subordination.[86]

African American women like the *hospitalière* Ligeret observed in south Louisiana performed the bulk of health care work on plantations throughout the South.[87] Owing to the critical role they played in the health care needs of the enslaved work force, Anglophone planters referred to them as nurses, "doctresses," or midwives. Still, planters generally portrayed the women's healing work as menial labor even while they feared their autonomy and influence. Such does not appear to have been the case with the remarkable caregiver Ligeret encountered, who, it seems, was respected for her work and had acquired some degree of freedom.[88]

In the afternoon, Ligeret continued, the women gathered in the *salon* to sew and read aloud, though their literary interests differed dramatically from those of their Anglophone counterparts. For proslavery southerners, Scottish novelist Sir Walter Scott best expressed their Romantic sensibility. They identified with the fictional knights and aristocrats of Scott's novels and took considerable pride in comparing their civilization of enslaved workers and sprawling plantations to feudalism's medieval heroes, manors, and serfs. Captivated by Scott's fiction, the South developed a vein of Romanticism that glorified its slave-based society, fortified its white supremacist status quo, and fostered the notion of a separate southern nationality. Scott's influence led Mark Twain to declare that "Sir Walter had so large a hand in making Southern character, as it existed before the war, that he is in great measure responsible for the war."[89] In the 1850s, a visitor to a Mississippi plantation observed that "the ladies of our household read, were fond of [Sir Walter] Scott. He is a favorite of the South. Of the manners and scenes in his novels, one is much reminded among this people."[90]

In Ligeret's experience on a Creole plantation in Louisiana, she and her companions met to read, but "in truth, it was not the novels and articles by authors of Mme de Grandfort's predilection, but instead we read *Les Paroles d'un croyant* [The Words of a Believer], *Le Livre du peuple* [The Book of the People], *Une Voix de prison* [A Voice from Prison], by M. de Lamennais, a writer so pure, so profound, and so uplifting."[91] In view of *Les Paroles d'un croyant's* denunciation of slavery, its condemnation by an 1835 papal encyclical, and its later description as "a lyrical version of the *Communist Manifesto*," it's surprising that Ligeret's pamphlet didn't rouse southern censors—censors who likewise would have condemned Lamennais's profound influence on the city's multiethnic, Francophone religious and political culture.[92]

Owing to the revolutionary nature of Lamennais's titles, Allain omitted them from her own otherwise faithful transcription of Ligeret's pamphlet in her 1883 book, *Souvenirs*. Lamennais's *Les Paroles* marked the former French priest's complete break with the Catholic Church and his advocacy of republicanism, socialism, and abolitionism in the cause of the disenfranchised and dispossessed. Instead of citing Lamennais's works, Allain exercised her own form of censorship and substituted for them the more benign works of Pascal, Racine, Lamartine, and other French authors. She judged accurately the white Francophone community's increasing conservatism in the 1880s and likely acted to shield her friend's reputation as well as her own.[93]

Nearly simultaneously with the book's 1855 debut in Paris, a New Orleans publisher issued Wharton's English-language version, suggesting a transatlantic collaboration. The translation, coming on the heels of the racially charged Pandelly case and in the midst of a high-stakes political showdown in the Creole/américain rivalry, was a windfall for the city's Anglophone faction. Given Grandfort's brief residence in New Orleans, the book's proslavery orthodoxy, and the circumstances surrounding its publication, it appears highly likely that the book had at least two authors, and maybe more. Ligeret's suspicions as well as those of other critics appear to have been well founded.

l'Autre monde's sensational distortions of the city's Francophone population succeeded in attracting international attention.[94] By driving the stake of racial division into the heart of the multiethnic city, Grandfort achieved the celebrity and international attention she craved. Whether she was acting alone or in concert with white supremacist southerners, the result was the same. *l'Autre monde* dealt a devastating blow to the nation's dwindling island of blended Francophone peoples and cultures. Creole New Orleanians paid dearly for Grandfort's treachery.

Lamennais, the "chaplain to the Romantic movement" and Ligeret's religious mentor and confidant, counseled social justice through religious devotion and moral renewal. In that spirit, Ligeret concluded *Les Créoles* with an appeal: "Ah! We mustn't slander each other in this way! . . . All men are brothers, all must love one another and raise themselves through charity closer to God who is all love and charity."[95]

Neither d'Ambrumél's vengeful satire nor Ligeret's plea for fellowship could repair the damage. Creole New Orleans suffered devastating divisions in the 1850s, with white Creoles bowing to the xenophobia and white supremacy of their fellow southerners.[96] The d'Ambrumél and Ligeret pamphlets faded quickly into obscurity as the deepening rift between North and South drove the United States toward the Civil War.

While Ligeret was defending Creole New Orleanians against Grandfort's *l'Autre monde,* her son-in-law Dr. Charles Faget was waging a relentless research campaign against yellow fever. His battle involved defending science-based medical research while arguing against "states' rights medicine." His humanitarianism originated in his unerring commitment to Catholicism's universalist ideals, a religiosity reinforced by his medical school education in Paris, where physician revolutionaries conceived a new philosophy of healing rooted in the 1789 French Revolution's rallying cry of "liberté, égalité, fraternité."

SIX

Les Docteurs

Chapter 6 chronicles events between 1830 and 1860, when Allain's brother Dr. Henri-Charles d'Aquin, her husband, Dr. Frédéric-Marie-François Allain, her family friend Dr. Jean-Charles Faget, and Faget's Afro-Creole colleague, Dr. Louis-Charles Roudanez, obtained their doctorates at the Paris Médicale, a huge medical complex in the heart of the French capital. In a philosophy that originated in the 1789 French Revolution, the Médicale's teaching staff instilled in its students a commitment to address society's political ills as well as their patients' physical ailments.

Upon their return to New Orleans, they remained steadfast in their commitment to the Médicale's guiding principles. Together with courageous medical researchers like Allain and d'Aquin, Faget fought the city's deadly yellow fever epidemics throughout his medical career, operating on two fronts. On the first front, he developed a vital diagnostic tool for identifying the viral infection and saving lives. On the second, he fought critics of his science-based medicine as well as doctors who practiced "states' rights medicine," a brand of medical malfeasance rooted in white supremacy and proslavery orthodoxy.

During the Civil War and Reconstruction, Faget's colleague Dr. Roudanez waged an equally courageous civil rights campaign in the struggle to revolutionize race relations in Louisiana and the nation. The careers of the two men and their allies serve to illustrate the profound currents of humanitarianism and political idealism that fueled the struggle for revolutionary change in New Orleans.

* * *

In January 1838, Charles Sumner, a Massachusetts attorney in his twenties traveling Europe, experienced a revelation during his visit to the sprawling health complex known as the Paris Médicale, in the heart of the city. While attending a lecture at the Sorbonne, his attention drifted to the medical students in the spacious hall. The lecturer "had quite a large audience," Sumner noted, "among whom I noticed two or three blacks, or rather mulattos—two-thirds black perhaps—dressed quite à la mode and having the easy, jaunty air of young men of fashion." The ease with which the young students of color interacted with their white peers startled Sumner and he watched them closely: "They were standing in the midst of a knot of young men, and their color seemed to be no objection to them. I was glad to see this, though with American impressions, it seemed very strange. It must be then that the distance between free blacks and whites among us is derived from education, and does not exist in the nature of things."[1] The scene of interracial camaraderie proved transformational. Sumner's awakening would lead to his own interracial alliances and a campaign to revolutionize race relations in his own country.

Sumner's experience at the Paris Médicale reveals the extent to which France's medical professionals had institutionalized the egalitarian and democratic ideals of the revolutionary era. At the outset of the 1789 French Revolution, physicians democratized and modernized their profession by opening it to all qualified men regardless of their wealth or background. They replaced Latin with French as the language of instruction, they waived tuition fees for foreign students, and their theorists forged a new philosophy of medicine. In 1789, author Sabarot de l'Avernière equated the physician's alleviation of physical suffering with the priest's spiritual salvation of the soul.

Onto this elevated notion of a physician's calling, François Lanthenas, an interior minister in the French First Republic, grafted the vision of doctors as political saviors. In *De l'influence de la liberté sur la santé* (The Influence of Liberty on Health, 1792), he wrote, "Who, then, should denounce tyrants to mankind if not the doctors, who make man their sole study, and who, each day, in the homes of poor and rich, among ordinary citizens and among the highest in the land, in cottage and mansion, contemplate the human miseries that have no other origin but tyranny and slavery?"[2]

Challenges such as Lanthenas's transformed the medical profession into one of the most politically progressive occupations in France. Jules Guérin, the French editor of a widely read medical journal, observed that the entire profession was "essentially liberal and republican" by the mid-nineteenth century. Remarkably, between 1870 and 1914, under the Third Republic (1870–1940), 358 physician-legislators sat in the Chamber of Deputies and the Senate. France's revolutionized medical arts, like French Romantic literary art, would have far-reaching consequences. The lives of four of its Louisiana graduates, Jean-Charles Faget, Louis-Charles Roudanez, Frédéric-Marie-François Allain, and Henri-Charles d'Aquin, illustrate the profound currents of humanitarianism and egalitarianism fueling democratic change in New Orleans and throughout the Atlantic world.[3]

Between 1830 and 1860, Faget, Roudanez, Allain, and d'Aquin were among the thousands of French and international students who flocked to Paris's medical mecca owing to French expertise and egalitarian idealism. The number and quality of the city's hospitals, the excellence of its faculty, the variety of its specialties, the opportunity to examine women patients (examinations rarely permitted in the United States), and the abundance of cadavers for dissection guaranteed that its graduates would be at the forefront of medical science. France was pioneering the science of modern medicine in the Paris Médicale, an assemblage of hospitals, doctors, nurses, technicians, and the illustrious Faculté de Médecine de Paris. A student's entry into the Parisian health system with its thirty teaching hospitals, including the Hotel Dieu, St. Louis, and the Salpêtrière, ensured the best available medical education. And as with the French Romantic literary movement, the Médicale would produce its share of humanitarian and political activists.[4]

Dr. Jean-Charles Faget was a New Orleans–born Creole whose parents fled the Haitian Revolution. His French grandfather, Jean Faget, was a baker in Marmande in southwestern France when he migrated in 1770 to Saint-Domingue. His son Jean-Baptiste Faget was born in Port-de-Paix on the west coast of the North Province, where he married Marguerite Antoinette Laraillet. In the port city, Jean-Baptiste Faget was a merchant, a ship's captain, and a Freemason in a brotherhood valued among mariners who risked the constant threat of attack on the high seas.

In the West Indies and elsewhere in the Americas, pirates might "rob and hang all without distinction of religion." Still, according to the Frenchman interviewed by Lafayette's secretary Auguste Levasseur during their visit to the United States in the mid-1820s, the "robbers of the sea" had "a particular respect for freemasons, whom they almost always treat like brothers." Many mariners claimed to owe their lives and prosperity to a "masonic sign timely made under the scimeter of robbers of the sea."[5]

In 1802, the Fagets fled the Haitian Revolution and settled in Cuba, where Faget resumed his career as a merchant mariner. At the time of Haitian independence in 1804, Faget joined his voice to those inveighing against attacks on shipping along the Cuban coast by "los negros rebeldes de Santo Domingo" (the Black rebels of Saint-Domingue). Commercial traders denounced violent assaults on their maritime crews, while Spanish authorities reported the capture of slave ships bound for Cuba and the liberation of their human cargoes by Haitian authorities.[6]

In 1809, the Fagets joined the mass migration to New Orleans, where Jean-Baptiste Faget advanced quickly to a high Masonic office in the Francophone community's influential Grande Loge de la Louisiane. In the War of 1812, he served as a field musician in the city's white militia unit, the Battalion d'Orléans, under the command of Major Jean Baptiste Plauché. During hostilities, a British officer observed how American soldiers "were kept continually in a state of excitement by the bands of martial music," and after the Americans repulsed an assault by the British on December 28, they celebrated to the strains of "Yankee Doodle" and "La Marseillaise." Later in life, Faget would join with other prominent New Orleanians to found the New Orleans Philharmonic Society.[7]

His son, Jean-Charles Faget, was born in the city in 1818 and was educated by the Jesuits as a young child. When he reached adolescence, his mother, Marguerite Laraillet Faget, accompanied him to Paris, where he was enrolled in 1830 in the Collège Rollin. Upon his graduation in 1837, he entered the College of Medicine of the University of Paris, where he graduated in 1845 magna cum laude. In 1844, ahead of his graduation, he married Gladys Ligeret, the daughter of Éléonore and Dr. Ligeret. Soon after completing his studies, Dr. Faget and his new wife moved to New Orleans, where their young friend Hélène d'Aquin Allain described Gladys Ligeret as a refined woman of "great beauty." The deeply religious Catholic couple would have thirteen children.[8]

By 1845, when Dr. Jean-Charles Faget returned to New Orleans from France, French-educated doctors in antebellum Louisiana were performing pathbreaking work in the field of obstetrics. Beginning in 1820, the pioneering French doctor François-Marie Prévost, another refugee from the Haitian Revolution, achieved remarkable results. In one dramatic instance, he performed a cesarean section on an enslaved woman whose deformed pelvis made a vaginal delivery impossible. Absent all but the most rudimentary of surgical instruments, Prévost saved the mother and delivered the baby safely. When his patient became pregnant a second time, he performed another successful surgery, which both the mother and infant survived. In an 1881 study of eighteenth- and nineteenth-century cesarean sections in the *American Journal of Obstetrics*, the author noted that the "success of the Caesarean operation upon the slave women on the plantations of Louisiana has been very remarkable" with the "skill of her French surgeons and associates [having] had much to do with it."[9]

Dr. Faget's broad-minded humanity led him to join in the innovative work in obstetrics by introducing the use of chloroform during childbirth. Whereas surgical anesthesia gained in popularity after its 1846 introduction into the operating room, its use in obstetrics met with staunch resistance. Religious and medical conservatives opposed its introduction in the delivery room in observance of the biblical mandate that "in sorrow shalt thou bring forth children" (Genesis 3:16). Under their influence, the new therapy remained largely out of the reach of most women, even women of wealth, education, and talent.[10]

In Louisiana, Faget pioneered the use of chloroform in the delivery room and advocated its use in medical journals in Paris and New Orleans. As in his contemporaneous and voluminous studies of yellow fever, he bombarded his critics with clinical studies. Between 1868 and 1876, Faget introduced the public as well as doctors to his method of administering chloroform during childbirth, writing newspaper articles in l'Abeille de la Nouvelle-Orléans/New Orleans Bee. To reach Anglophone as well as Francophone readers, Faget's colleague Dr. F. Gaudet translated his essays into English. In Paris in 1880, a collection of Faget's published research papers appeared in an eighty-six-page booklet entitled l'Art d'apaiser les douleurs de l'enfantement (The Art of Easing Suffering in Childbirth). While Faget's information campaign may not have satisfied his critics, his advocacy added considerable weight to the medical argument for a more humane approach to women's suffering in childbirth.[11]

According to his younger colleague and friend, Dr. Edmond Souchon, Faget was a tall man of striking physical appearance with a high forehead and long, "grizzly" black hair combed straight back. Throughout the year, the intensely religious doctor dressed in the manner of a Catholic priest. In the winter, he wore a long black coat attached at the neck with a clip and a silver chain, together with a low-crowned silk hat. In the summer, he traded his winter headgear for a black straw hat of the kind customarily worn by priests. He even spoke, Souchon remarked, in the soft and gentle tone of a Catholic cleric. When the retiring and modest Faget arrived in New Orleans in 1845, the city possessed a "galaxy of distinguished men, most of them graduates of Faculté de Médecine de Paris." The newcomer advanced rapidly to the fore to achieve fame on both sides of the Atlantic.

The admiring Souchon considered Faget's character ideal, "for besides his great medical ability, he had splendid qualities of heart and mind . . . He was a consistent Christian and always a thorough and honorable gentleman." Like Hélène d'Aquin Allain and countless other Francophone Catholics, Faget's profound religiosity was influenced by philosopher Joseph de Maistre. In 1855, Faget began his *Etudes sur les bases de la science médicale et exposition sommaire de la doctrine traditionnelle* (Studies on the Foundations of Medical Science and a Summary Account of Traditional Doctrine) by referencing Maistre.

In the voluminous book's dedication to Jean-Bruno Cayol, a distinguished elder physician at the Faculté de Médecine, Faget quoted Maistre: "Moral affinities are a law of nature like those of the physical order." Basing his philosophy on the indivisibility of God and nature, Maistre maintained that spiritual enlightenment promoted science. Religious belief, though not indispensable to scientific advance, nonetheless encouraged science, since love of God was humanity's best means of knowledge. Judging from the scope of his medical science and the intensity of his devout Catholicism, Faget acted upon Maistre's philosophy with profound conviction.[12]

Faget's astonishing work ethic and medical genius did not carry over into his financial affairs. He had very little interest in the ledger side of his practice. He was, Souchon observed, "a poor charger, a bad collector, [and] no investor at all." For Faget, the well-being of his patients was of far greater concern than his financial statement. His medical practice reveals a man committed to the humanitarian side of medicine. His interactions with a new order of Afro-Creole Catholic nuns sheds light on another aspect of his humanitarianism.[13]

Near the time of his return to New Orleans in 1845, Faget visited the Sisters of the Holy Family in their Faubourg Tremé neighborhood. Three years earlier, the Catholic women of color had won authorization for their religious community. Not long afterwards, they moved into the "cradle" of their African American convent on Bayou Road, where the Creole Catholic postulants were officially received into the order, took their first vows, and wore their first habits. There, in the convent's infancy, Sister Mary Bernard Deggs later wrote, "our good old Dr. Faget" was "the first to offer his services to our dear sisters on Bayou Road." Deggs, who entered the religious community in 1873, knew the supportive physician, who would visit when "called to see someone who was sick and needed him."[14] In nearby St. Augustine Church in 1852, Delille, Gaudin, and Josephine Charles took their formal vows.[15]

Faget remained attentive to the congregation's medical needs throughout his life, in a religious community that included "Sister Aliquot" (Marie-Jean

Aliquot), the order's French-born ally and supporter. Just as the Sisters of the Holy Family had once given priority to sacramental law over civil law, they also brushed aside the church's prohibition against an interracial convent and embraced Aliquot as one of their own. Between her visits to outlying plantations east of New Orleans, Aliquot made the Bayou Road convent her home. She remained in the residence with her "sisters" in the spirit of their Catholic faith until her death during the Civil War. She died on January 1, 1863, the day on which President Abraham Lincoln issued the Emancipation Proclamation.

Faget shared his commitment to the Sisters of the Holy Family with Dr. Louis-Charles Roudanez, a major benefactor of the convent and an influential member of the city's Afro-Creole community. Faget and Roudanez possessed large biracial practices, and both men had fully absorbed the Faculté de Médecine's humanitarian emphasis on a holistic approach to medical-political healing.[16]

In his youth, Roudanez, whose maternal grandmother was a slave, was sent from St. James Parish to attend school in New Orleans. After completing his early education, he was sent to France, where he earned a bachelor of letters in 1847 and a bachelor of science in 1849. In Paris at the outset of the 1848 French Revolution, Roudanez was among the multitude of students who joined the resistance at the barricades to witness what Karl Marx described as the "*beautiful* revolution."[17]

The February revolutionaries who forced the abdication of Louis-Philippe, proclaimed the Second Republic, abolished slavery, and provided for universal male suffrage made a profound impression on Roudanez. Though he was not among the tens of thousands of Polish, German, Hungarian, and Italian political refugees who rushed to their home countries to fight for change in the Springtime of the Peoples, he fully embraced the lessons of the awe-inspiring events he witnessed in revolutionary Paris.[18]

Roudanez acquired his doctorate in medicine in 1853 from the Faculté de Medicine de Paris, where he studied under a number of the institution's medical luminaries. He was especially grateful to Professors Jean-Baptiste Bouillaud and Philippe Ricord and thanked them for the "extraordinary kindness with which they have chosen to honor me." A brilliant orator, Ricord sought to further democratize the Faculté de Medicine in 1848 by empowering students to elect the Faculté's dean. Bouillaud, a bold champion of the 1848 Revolution, counted republican/socialist leaders Louis Blanc, Hippolyte Carnot, and Alexandre Ledru-Rollin among his allies.[19]

In addition to Roudanez, Bouillaud mentored Puerto Rican student Ramón

Emeterio Betances, another extraordinary protégé of mixed-racial ancestry, for whom the 1848 French Revolution was a transformative experience. Betances, like Roudanez, completed his medical studies in Paris determined to address the political ills of his homeland as well as his patients' maladies. Like many Afro-Creole New Orleanians, he lionized Haitian president Aléxandre Pétion, who he believed embodied "the living spirit of the French Revolution in the Caribbean."

Returning to Puerto Rico in 1855, Betances worked tirelessly to treat the victims of a cholera epidemic while also engaging in clandestine activities to undermine slavery. Spanish authorities forced him into exile for his abolitionism and his leadership in the first armed revolt against Spanish rule in 1868. He lived most of the remainder of his life in exile in France, where the nation's republican elite welcomed the physician–political activist into their ranks.[20]

Upon completing his degree, Roudanez returned to the United States equally determined to revolutionize his homeland. Before returning to Louisiana, he enrolled at Dartmouth College in New Hampshire, where he earned his second medical degree in 1857. The following year, he returned to New Orleans, where he opened a lucrative medical practice treating Black and white Creole families. At the same time, he married Célie Saulay, with whom he would have eight children. Barely had Roudanez settled into his new life in the city when the November 8, 1860, election of Abraham Lincoln sparked the nation's secession crisis. In the ensuing catastrophe, Roudanez would excel as a physician–political activist in his work as a courageous civil rights leader and the founder of two pioneering African American newspapers. His publications would attract national and international attention during the Civil War and Reconstruction.[21]

Dr. Louis-Charles Roudanez's attendance at the Faculté de Médecine de Paris overlapped with the presence of two fellow New Orleanians, medical students Henri-Charles d'Aquin and Frédéric-Marie-François Allain. In Louisiana, Dr. Faget's study of yellow fever had impressed the two younger men while they attended classes at the Medical Department of the University of Louisiana (present-day Tulane University). D'Aquin and Allain were also friends in a social network that included Hélène d'Aquin, Henri d'Aquin's sister. Upon his graduation in 1850, Henri d'Aquin sailed for France to complete his medical education in Paris.

As an undergraduate at the Faculté de Médecine, d'Aquin counted Alfred-Armand-Louise-Marie Velpeau among his favorite Parisian professors. Velpeau's partiality to American students made him popular with aspiring doctors like d'Aquin. Reflective of the French Revolution's democratizing influence, Velpeau rose from his lower-class background as the son of a blacksmith in a rural village to become a professor of clinical surgery at the Faculté de Médecine, where he wrote the surgical textbook most widely used by students. When he was elected chair of France's prestigious Académie des Sciences in 1843, he thanked his peers and remarked, "I should never have believed, gentlemen, that I should one day rise so high, setting out as low as I did."[22] Reflecting on Velpeau's background and skills, another nineteenth-century graduate of the Faculté de Médecine, physician and author Oliver Wendell Holmes, would later observe of Velpeau that "a good sound head over a pair of wooden shoes is a good deal better than a wooden head belonging to an owner who cases his feet in calf-skin."[23]

Student d'Aquin, a protégé of Faget, chose for his doctoral thesis a topic that overlapped with the research of his mentor. D'Aquin's "Parallèle du typhus et de la fièvre typhoïd" (A Comparison of Typhus with Typhoid Fever) compared the two infectious diseases in a method similar to Faget's comparison of yellow fever and pernicious malaria, a study that saved lives. During the 1840s, both typhus and the increasingly dangerous typhoid fever began appearing with greater frequency in New Orleans with the migration of Irish immigrants and American migrants through the region during the nation's westward migration.

As typhoid fatalities mounted, Louisiana doctors fiercely debated whether the disease belonged to a unity of fevers (an outdated one-fever notion) or should be identified as a separate entity. With Faget's work no doubt in mind, d'Aquin settled on a comparative study of the two diseases. With the completion of his degree in 1856, he returned to the city, where he joined Faget in braving yellow fever, malarial fevers, and other infectious diseases. And like Faget, d'Aquin added a new chapter to Louisiana's obstetrical history.[24]

In 1867, he and another physician, Dr. D. Warren Brickell, were called in on the case of a woman unable to deliver vaginally. Her attending physician's failed attempt to remove the baby through dismemberment persuaded the two doctors to undertake a cesarean section. They saved the patient's life in a procedure involving the suturing of the uterus with silver wire. Their decision to suture the uterus was only the third of its kind in the United States and the first in which doctors used silver wire sutures. The Creole woman reported good health ten years later. She was the first white woman to undergo a cesarean section in Louisiana.[25]

Typically, surgeons did not suture the uterus in cesarean surgeries, resulting in fatal hemorrhaging or infection. A mid-nineteenth-century survey of several studies in the United States demonstrated an appalling mortality of 50 percent to 85 percent of patients. With improvements in the aseptic technique and other innovative procedures like those of d'Aquin and Brickell, cesarean surgery began to improve appreciably in the late nineteenth century.[26]

In Paris, at the Faculté de Médecine, d'Aquin's friend Frédéric Allain singled out Dr. Alphonse-François-Marie Guérin from among the professors he acknowledged in his 1855 doctoral thesis. Their kindred fellowship originated in their shared Briton ethnicity. Allain's father, Dr. Pierre Allain, was born in Bourseul, a commune in the Côtes-du-Nord (present-day Côtes-d'Armor) Department in Brittany, northwestern France. A slaveholding physician, Dr. Pierre Allain practiced medicine in Plaquemines and St. Charles Parishes and crisscrossed the Atlantic on visits to his French family. His wife, Félicité Caroline Pepe, was born in New Orleans and gave birth to Frédéric during an 1831 sojourn in Bourseul. Growing up in Louisiana, Frédéric Allain's interest in his father's profession persuaded him to attend medical school. Among his University of Louisiana peers, he was popularly known as "Briton," a nickname he favored, owing to his pride in his Brittany roots.[27]

Dr. Guérin was born in the small Brittany city of Ploërmel in 1816. His father was a low-level court functionary who died in 1822, leaving his widow to raise six-year-old Alphonse and his seven-year-old brother. Guérin remained ever mindful of his modest origins and his struggle to join the elite corps of surgeons in the Faculté de Médecine. Envisioning the dawning of a new era, he welcomed the 1848 French Revolution and the Second Republic, proclaiming "liberté, égalité, fraternité" as his motto. He remained a dedicated republican throughout his life, and during Louis-Napoléon's December 2, 1851, coup d'état, he hid a number of prominent republican leaders in his home to prevent their arrest by Bonparte's police. In the bloody 1871 urban battle between the Parisian Communards and the Army of Versaille, Guérin resolutely confronted the soldiers at the entranceway to the St. Louis Hospital to protect his wounded Communard patients. "In the name of humanity," he demanded, "I summon you to withdraw!" They obeyed. Guérin's idealism and humanitarianism made a considerable impression on his New Orleans protégé.[28]

At the time of Allain's graduation from medical school in 1855, Hélène d'Aquin was in Paris with her mother to complete her own education at the Sorbonne. Already a member of Allain's social circle, she likely joined her brother

Henri-Charles and their friends to celebrate Frédéric's achievement. The happy event in Paris is a mark of the considerable success and happiness Hélène d'Aquin enjoyed during the 1850s. Despite "the deceitful pages written by a traveling French woman" (Grandfort) and increasingly ominous developments in the United States, she completed her education in France, began her teaching career on her return to Louisiana, and fell in love with Dr. Frédéric Allain.[29]

With his diploma in hand in 1855, Dr. Allain returned to New Orleans to practice medicine and court Hélène d'Aquin. Dr. Henri-Charles d'Aquin arrived in the city the following year to join with Faget in studying the deadly seasonal epidemics of yellow fever. By 1855, Faget was in the midst of studying fever symptoms among Creole children. His appointment in 1853 as the attending physician at the Asile des Orphelins (Orphans Asylum), Faget later wrote, had opened "a field of extremely valuable research." His important findings would mark a number of key milestones in fever research.[30]

Dr. Allain followed in the footsteps of his mentor by assuming the office of attending physician at the Asile de la Société française (French Society Asylum), a post Faget had held ten years earlier, after completing his own medical education in Paris. The Asile de la Société française, popularly known as the French Hospital, was founded by La Société française de bienfaisance et d'assistance mutuelle de la Nouvelle-Orléans (The French Benevolent and Mutual Aid Society of New Orleans). La Société française was one of a series of nineteenth-century benevolent societies designed to assist newly arriving immigrants. Organized in 1839 and incorporated in 1843, the organization appears to have been the first such society to establish a permanent hospital. The French Hospital opened its doors in 1844 on Bayou Road in the Faubourg Tremé.[31]

The Société's founding document reflected the revolutionary republicanism of Pierre Soulé, the most charismatic and high-profile founding member of the Francophone coalition. The Castillon-born Soulé was a Freemason and republican agitator who fled France after the government of Charles X ordered his arrest. The politically ambitious Soulé arrived in Louisiana in 1826, set up a law practice, and soon achieved high office within the ranks of the city's freemasons. In 1828, he married Armentine Mercier, the offspring of one of the city's most prominent Creole families. Her two brothers, Armand and Alfred Mercier, were both Paris-educated doctors and civic activists.[32]

Reflecting Soulé's influence, the Société's 1843 founding constitution drew upon French Freemasonry and republican ideals. Ignoring the usual model for a benevolent society, Soulé looked to France's "secret societies" as its organizational blueprint. He envisioned the society establishing links to like-minded national and international organizations. Société historian Félix Limet alluded to the mounting revolutionary fervor brewing in Europe in the 1840s in explaining Soulé's thinking: "Bear in mind that it was 1848 at the time and that the eminent man who was president of the Society, Monsieur Pierre Soulé, was a political man."

Limet points to the first article of the document to highlight the 1843 document's political character: "Article I.—The association has for its purpose the physical, moral and political improvement of its members. To lend mutual assistance and aid in misfortune; to encourage the good in one and all through counsel and by example; to mutually encourage the acquisition of rights which assure the liberty of man in every country; . . . such are the primary obligations that the society members agree to among themselves."[33]

After Soulé's 1848 election to the US Senate prompted his resignation from the Société's presidency, members modified the original charter. In the revised 1852 constitution, Article I was stripped of its political connotations and the term *fraternity* in the founding document was replaced with the word *charity*. In the evolving national schism of the 1850s, the Société's decision to adopt a politically neutral position demonstrated sound judgment. Though it could not completely divorce itself from the looming political maelstrom, the benevolent society proved highly successful in its humanitarian mission.[34]

Faget advanced that mission in his work on the staff of the French Hospital and in his dedication to yellow fever research, the city's overriding health concern. His studies convinced him that the affliction was caused by the entry into the body of a microorganism. Because the fever emanated from dockside areas, he correctly surmised that the deadly microbe was carried into the city by foreign shipping. On the basis of his findings, he advocated for the infectious school of thought, arguing that the disease was not spread directly from person to person. Dr. Charles François Deléry, a leading spokesman for the contagionist school, insisted that yellow fever was communicated from one person to another as in the case of contagions like influenza.

In another departure from old-school medical thinking, Faget insisted that many patients were being mistakenly diagnosed with yellow fever when they were actually infected with what he identified as a *fièvre paludéenne* (malarial fever). The new school and the old school, according to Dr. Souchon, engaged in "interminable *polemiques*" as they "broke their lances against one another, and enunciated their theories and related the facts they had as proofs." To support his findings, Faget published a stream of research papers, attracting national and international attention. He was a delegate to the 1855 Fifth National Quarantine and Sanitary Convention in Philadelphia, and when his book *Etudes sur les bases de la science médicale* was published in Paris the following year, the Société de Médicine de Caen awarded him a gold medal.[35]

The intense disputes between the Faget faction and Deléry's allies stemmed from profound differences over politics and race as well as medicine. As the antebellum sectional crisis drove the North and South apart, conservative southern professionals closed ranks in defense of slavery. The movement gave rise to the theory of states' rights medicine, championed in New Orleans by its foremost proponent, Dr. Samuel A. Cartwright. In 1848, the fire-eating, Virginia-born physician moved to the city to promote this brand of medicine rooted in white supremacy and proslavery orthodoxy.

Cartwright argued that the South's unique disease environment warranted a brand of medicine separate from that of the North. Furthermore, Cartwright insisted that fundamental physiological differences between the races required separate medical therapies for the two groups. To drive home his racist theories, he concocted a category of "social diseases" specific to Black southerners, such as "drapetomania," a condition that caused slaves to run away, and "dysaesthesia aethiopis," a disease that produced knavish behavior. In New Orleans, Cartwright found forceful proponents for his southern brand of medicine. Physicians who refused to fall in line came under mounting attacks. In the contest, Dr. Faget and his colleagues were on the wrong side of the sectional divide.[36]

Deléry and his proslavery New Orleans allies distrusted organizations like La Société française de bienfaisance and its French Hospital. They understood that the North's abolitionist movement and the abolition of slavery in the 1848 French Revolution originated in the powerful currents of humanitarianism and republicanism sweeping the nineteenth-century Atlantic world. La Société's 1843 founding charter, melding Soulé's admiration for the revolutionary cause of "liberté, égalité, fraternité" with the society's humanitarian mission, could only be seen as subversive of the slave South's interests. Proslavery whites remained suspicious and hostile despite the organization's decision to remove Soulé's politically provocative language from its constitution.[37]

Deléry responded to Soulé's leadership in the outpouring of support for the 1848 French Revolution by authoring his 1849 *Étude sur les passions* (A Study of the Passions). Reflecting on the seismic impact of revolutionary upheaval in France, Deléry compared events in Europe with his exalted view of contemporary realities in the United States. On the European continent, he complained, there are "only revolutions, slaughters, and calamities of every kind. Commerce is suffocated, industries are paralyzed, the earth rendered barren by the lava of the revolutionary volcano; literature is transformed into incendiary pamphlets in imitation of Hébert,"[38] while in the United States a "majestic and tranquil America spreads all the benefits of peace and harmony over its children." Europeans, "robbed in the ensuing convulsions of the great revolutions" emigrate to the United States to "work in the shade of the tree of liberty planted and blessed by Washington."[39] As events in the coming decade would show, Deléry spoke too soon.

Born on his family's plantation in St. Charles Parish in January 1815, Deléry was sent to Paris for his education at the age of fourteen. In 1842, he graduated from medical school and returned to New Orleans to begin his practice, just a few years ahead of Dr. Faget. According to Edward Larocque Tinker, he embarked upon his professional career with a "a pen in one hand and a thermometer in the other." While writing extensively on medicine, history, and politics, he authored poems, acrostics, fables, and a series of "Indian chronicles."[40] He was a prolific and disputatious author.

At the time of the 1848 French Revolution, the arrival in the city of Dr. Joseph Rouanet, a distinguished Parisian heart specialist, temporarily strengthened Faget's position. Rouanet, a friend and colleague, emigrated to New Orleans in 1847, where his reputation preceded him. Within months of his arrival, Rouanet's success in treating a number of patients won him several favorable references in Dr. Pierre Frédéric Thomas's 1848 edition of his *Traité pratique de la fièvre jaune* (Practical Treatise on Yellow Fever).

In early 1848, Rouanet firmly established his reputation in the city by accurately diagnosing the fatal illness of an esteemed medical professional, Dr. C. A. Luxemberg. The revered doctor's biographer noted, "Dr. Luxemberg's health began to fail suddenly. . . . The worst fears of his medical friends were now excited, and their diagnosis confirmed with an accuracy of the [Paris] school of Corvisart, by M. Rouanet from France, recently arrived in the city, who pointed out the precise location and character of the disease, which . . . was verified by the autopsy." At the Faculté de Médicine de Paris, meanwhile, Rouanet's study of heart sounds when applied by Dr. Jean-Baptiste Bouillaud and his students in their clinical studies yielded crucial practical information in the diagnosis of heart ailments. Notwithstanding Rouanet's reputation and professional accomplishments, however, he was no match for Deléry's treachery.[41]

In January 1852, the combative Deléry debuted a monthly medical journal, *l'Union Médicale de la Louisiane*. As the editor and manager of the publication, he authored many of its articles, including heated polemics on the subject of yellow fever. In the journal, he crossed swords with Dr. Rouanet. The French physician submitted an essay discussing what he rightly considered to be "the dangers of blood transfusion." Deléry's reply provoked a contentious exchange between the two doctors. Although there were more than enough Franco-phone physicians to sustain a medical journal, few were willing to subscribe to Deléry's journal, and he reluctantly suspended publication in December after only twelve issues.[42]

The angry debate between Deléry and Rouanet took a personal turn after a young doctor presented Rouanet with the diseased heart of a goose, passing the organ off as the heart of an infant. Rouanet, an authority on cardiac disease on both sides of the Atlantic, studied the organ with curiosity according to Faget, who later wrote, "I do not know to what extent Rouanet was deceived by it. What is certain is that he took it very poorly. This impropriety, or more this thoughtlessness, had wounded him in a sensitive spot!" When Deléry au-thored and circulated a viciously satirical verse, *Le Médecin et l'oie* (The Doc-tor and the Goose), ridiculing Rouanet, the infuriated French doctor sent his seconds to Deléry to arrange a duel. The two men met on the so-called field of honor, where they grazed each other with shots from their pistols. Over Rouanet's protests, their seconds called a halt to the confrontation.[43]

Within a year of Rouanet's arrival in the city, Faget's in-laws, Éléonore and Dr. Jacques Ligeret, disembarked in New Orleans. In the brewing medical-political storm, their professional and moral support temporarily eased the Faget family's burdens. Dr. Ligeret joined Faget's medical practice. On the occasion of Éléonore Ligeret's 1855 response to Grandfort's *l'Autre monde*, pro-slavery white supremacists like Dr. Deléry appear to have held their fire, de-spite the pamphlet's provocative references to slave mistresses who deplored slavery and Ligeret's description of women reading Félicité de Lamennais's books in the plantation parlor.[44]

By 1856, Faget had assembled a dedicated and talented New Orleans research team that included Doctors Allain and Henri-Charles d'Aquin. In their studies, Faget and his researchers collected data from previous yellow fever epidemics and set about gathering more information in their own carefully documented clinical observations. The close-knit research team had cause for celebration when d'Aquin's sister Hélène and Frédéric Allain announced their engagement.

The couple married on February 2, 1858, in St. Mary's Church, surrounded by family members and friends. The wedding party likely toasted the newly-weds at the nearby Daron compound, the d'Aquin family home on Chartres Street. After the wedding, Hélène returned to her position at the D'Aquin Institute, where her younger brother, Joseph-George d'Aquin, had joined the staff. Frédéric Allain resumed his work at the French Hospital. During the September outbreak of yellow fever, Faget, d'Aquin, Allain, and their fellow researchers continued to compile case studies.[45]

In the midst of the epidemic, however, Allain fell ill. He was himself admitted to the French Hospital, where he succumbed to yellow fever on September 4, 1858. Early the next morning, his widowed and pregnant wife, Hélène d'Aquin Allain, led the funeral procession from her family home, the Daron residence, to the cemetery. Escorted by members of the Société française de bienfaisance, she buried her twenty-seven-year-old husband. Eight months later, on May 2, 1859, Allain gave birth to their infant son Frédéric Marie François Joseph Allain. On May 12, the baby was baptized at St. Mary's Church, where his grandmother Marie Anne Elisabeth d'Aquin served in the ceremony as his *marraine* (godmother) and Frédéric Allain's brother, Albert-Louis Allain, acted as his *parrain* (godfather).[46]

At the time of Frédéric Allain's death, the Société française de bienfaisance expressed its condolences in a touching tribute published in the Francophone press: "We have lost a distinguished member of our medical corps and, what is sadder still, a good man. . . . Despite the danger that he saw with his own eyes, despite the numerous victims who, in spite of the most enlightened care, fell all around him—the young doctor remained unshaken, faithful to his post. . . . A loss to science, a loss to the community, [and] a loss to the young wife to whom M. Allain was united only months earlier."

La Société's president, Olivier Blineau, paid tribute to the doctor in his condolences, in an open letter to Hélène Allain in which he emphasized her husband's virtues and expressed the organization's sympathy: "In the nearly three years that Doctor Allain was called upon to take care of my members, never have we heard the slightest complaint raised against him. His pleasing and lively disposition, his modesty, his eminent knowledge won him the respect of his many patients."[47]

Amid the grief surrounding Allain's death and the ongoing yellow fever epidemic, malevolent attacks on La Société française and on Faget appeared in the city's Francophone newspapers. Alongside Allain's obituary and the letters of condolences in both *Le Courrier* and *l'Abeille*, the benevolent society defended the organization, insisting that La Société had "repeatedly proved itself. For one detractor," it continued, "a thousand admirers can be found. It keeps all of its promises. It is counted among the organizations that have done the most good. In the attack in question, [La Société] takes its revenge on the slander by the numbers [of clients and] by the eloquence with which those numbers speak." In fact, the hospital cared for hundreds of patients during the city's many epidemics.[48]

In August, at the outset of 1858 yellow fever epidemic, the proslavery French-born veterinarian Leon Raymond Delrieu published a series of pseudoscientific essays in which he repeatedly attacked Faget. Styling his own profession as a "sister and honored servant of human medicine," he titled his lengthy serial diatribes in *Le Courrier* "Reflexions sur la fièvre epidemique" (Thoughts on the Fever Epidemic). In a September 1 essay, Delrieu ridiculed Faget as the model of an "implacable observer, who, generalizing everything, defines nothing and only acknowledges as a principle what the facts have sanctioned through experiment." Faget, Delrieu continued, "is very assuredly this ideal type of the observer doctor isolated from the futilities of the earth here below," and "appears to direct all of his attention to tending the glorious aureole that already attaches to his name." In a subsequent entry on September 5, Delrieu disparaged Faget alongside Allain's obituary.[49]

The long-running fever debates between the Faget medical faction and Deléry, Delrieu, and their states' rights medicine allies culminated in 1859 with the July 15 publication of Faget's *Etude médicale de quelques questions importantes pour la Louisiane* (A Medical Study of Some Important Questions for Louisiana). In the study, Faget combined data from the 1839 yellow fever epidemic with information he and his researchers had gleaned from the 1853 and 1858 epidemics. His fourteen years of research cited international, national, and local sources and centered on young Francophone children and African-descended rural and urban populations.

On remote rural plantations between New Orleans and the pine forests north of the city, Faget found few instances of yellow fever among Creoles of either European or African descent. To his surprise, even newly arrived Europeans in the countryside appeared immune to the disease. His same findings held true for Afro-Creole New Orleanians, who demonstrated a notable resistance to yellow fever. Furthermore, patients of color were being mistakenly diagnosed with yellow fever when they actually suffered from a pernicious malarial fever. With the correct diagnosis, Faget concluded, most patients with a malarial fever could be effectively treated with dosages of quinine, "even during the reign of our most malicious autumnal fevers." As Faget's remarks indicate, his careful research yielded a number of key findings, including, most importantly, the first method of making an accurate diagnosis of the yellow fever virus.[50]

The doctor's discovery of the vital diagnostic tool involved a correlation between pulse rate and body temperature. Typically, as a patient's fever rises, their pulse rate increases. In yellow fever, however, the opposite occurs. As the fever rises, the pulse rate slows. Faget's finding became known as "Faget's sign," and it remains a leading diagnostic method for detecting yellow fever. His discovery became a lifesaving innovation and one of Louisiana's most significant contributions to medical science.[51]

In his team's study of Creole children, Faget likewise noted an apparent immunity to yellow fever in youngsters. In fact, the disease tends to be mild and virtually undetectable in young children of all ethnicities. In symptomatic children determined to be suffering from a malarial fever, Faget and his team administered quinine while documenting the medication's positive and negative effects. In an 1858 case study by d'Aquin, for instance, his three-year-old Afro-Creole patient appeared asymptomatic for yellow fever but died after a three-day regimen of quinine treatments.[52]

From the perspective of New Orleans doctors who practiced states' rights medicine, Faget's study violated all the rules. He breached the South's medical blockade by looking to science-based national and international sources to interrogate his local findings. His multiracial research population and his diagnostic innovations ignored the practice of segregated medicine. The publication ignited a firestorm of vicious attacks. With Deléry at the forefront of the storm, combatants began exchanging letters in the *Journal de la Société Médicale de la Nouvelle-Orléans*, *l'Abeille*, and other publications. Pamphlet after pamphlet followed as more and more physicians joined in the dispute. When the debate took a personal turn in 1859, Délery sent his seconds to Faget to a arrange a duel. The devout Catholic declined the challenge on the basis of his Christian faith. Louisiana's January 1861 secession from the United States and the ensuing Civil War temporarily interrupted the dispute. It would resume at the war's end and continue through Reconstruction.[53]

With the outbreak of hostilities on April 12, 1861, Faget remained in the city. In anticipation of the yellow fever season, he sent his wife and children to Mandeville, on the north shore of Lake Pontchartrain. In early September 1861, he fell ill in New Orleans. The severity of his condition persuaded his attendants to administer the last rites. By the end of the month, however, his condition had improved. By the time he returned to his work, his veterinarian critic, Dr. Delrieu, had enlisted in a Louisiana Confederate cavalry company with the rank of Veterinary Surgeon. Dr. Cartwright, the city's foremost advocate of states' rights medicine, joined Delrieu in enlisting in the army of the Confederate States of America, where he was assigned the responsibility for improving sanitary conditions in rebel encampments at Vicksburg and Port Hudson.[54]

After US Major General Benjamin F. Butler of Massachusetts occupied New Orleans on May 1, 1862, Deléry remained in the city, authoring violent attacks on occupying US forces that fearful local publishers refused to print. He sent a particularly venomous attack on General Butler, *Les Némésiennes confédérées* (The Confederate Avengers), to Mobile to be published at his own expense.[55] Butler likely learned of Deléry's planned publication through his extensive network of Black informants. When he did, he ordered Deléry's arrest. The doctor fled the city for Havana and made his way to France, where he continued his fierce attacks in satires such as *Confédérés et Fédéraux. Les Yankees, foundateurs de l'esclavage aux États-Unis et initiateurs de droit de Secession* (Confederates and Federals. The Yankees, Founders of Slavery in the United States and Initiators of the Right of Secession).[56]

General Butler dealt with the threat of yellow fever as decisively as he dealt with Deléry and his military occupation of the city. He imposed a strict quarantine on ships entering the Mississippi River below New Orleans. At Fort St. Philip, seventy miles downriver from the city, a duly appointed health officer inspected sanitary conditions aboard ships. If the passengers, crew, or cargo failed the inspection, a forty-day quarantine followed, after which another inspection would occur. A major cleanup of the city accompanied the quarantine. In the French Market, Butler observed, the "stall women were accustomed to drop on the floor around their stalls all the refuse made in cleaning their birds, meat, and fish . . . where it was trodden in and in. This had been going on for a century more or less." Appalled at the filth, Butler took action.[57]

The general directed the employment of two thousand men to clean the city's French Market, streets, squares, and unoccupied lands. Divided into squads, the men cleared away putrefying animal matter, swept out every ditch, and flushed the streets with clean water. He issued guidelines instructing the heads of households to clean the inside and outside of their residences, with military inspectors enforcing his instructions. Garbage collectors carried household refuse in mule-driven carts two or three times a week. Together, Butler's comprehensive quarantine and sanitary regulations proved successful. Under his regime and that of his successor, Major General Nathaniel P. Banks, the city suffered no yellow fever epidemics. With the postwar return of lax local conditions, Asiatic cholera claimed more than 1,200 fatalities in 1866, and yellow fever killed more than three thousand residents the following year.[58]

In 1864, General Banks appointed Dr. Faget as one of three members of a US Sanitary Commission to report on the contagious fevers of the South. When the committee completed its work, Faget drew up its findings in a study that was forwarded to Washington. The following year, Dr. Just Touatre, a French naval surgeon on a visit to the city, positively confirmed Faget's sign by using a large centigrade thermometer. At the time, the clinical thermometer had just come into use, and Dr. Faget immediately seized upon it as an indispensable diagnostic instrument in the treatment of his patients and in his research. While Dr. Touatre may have been the first to introduce the thermometer into the city, Faget was the first to demonstrate its efficacy in identifying malaria and yellow fever.[59]

In March 1865, ahead of the Confederacy's surrender at Appomattox Courthouse in April, Faget left for France. In Paris, the government decorated him with the Chevalier de la Légion d'honneur for his work in the yellow fever epidemics. Other distinguished honors included his election to Société Médicale d'Observation and the Société Anatomique de Paris. He returned to New Orleans in 1867, where Deléry, as disputatious, belligerent, and unrelenting as ever, used his poison pen to resume his attacks, using the same prewar arguments.[60]

During Reconstruction, Faget joined in discussions with his fellow physicians over the relative benefits of quarantine versus sanitation in the ongoing struggle to prevent yellow fever epidemics. After all of the studies and theories had been presented and discussed, Dr. Faget offered his conclusions. In the end, he grimly admitted, there were only two means of escaping the disease. The first, he said, "was to have it and recover; the second was to leave the city whenever yellow fever prevailed." He was right. The terrible outcome of the 1878 contagion dramatized the uphill battle in the struggle to combat the deadly viral infection.[61]

The Mississippi River valley yellow fever epidemic of 1878 resulted in 4,046 New Orleans fatalities and proved a devastating exception to the general rule regarding the relatively rare incidence of yellow fever among young children. On many days, youngsters under the age of ten made up half the number of recorded deaths. In response to the high rate of childhood fatalities in the city, the Société française's tomb in St. Louis Cemetery No. 1, the largest in the cemetery, built an entire wing for children.

In another deviation from the norm during the 1878 epidemic, African Americans, representing one-third of the city's population, suffered 183 fatalities. Their deaths offer further evidence of the exceptionally malignant strain of the virus that swept through nine states of the Mississippi River valley, resulting in as many as twenty thousand deaths. During the New Orleans disaster, Dr. d'Aquin remained at his post, working to mitigate the suffering of his French Hospital patients. La Société française praised him for his "service exceptionnel" during the crisis.[62]

Though Dr. Faget regretted his inability to defeat yellow fever, he struck a number of strategic blows against the disease, including the first method of diagnosing the viral infection. A physician's ability to distinguish the difference between yellow fever and malaria saved lives because malarial fever could be successfully treated with quinine, and Faget's sign is still used to detect yellow fever. In addition to his pivotal advances in the study of viral infections, Faget pioneered the use of chloroform during childbirth to relieve the suffering of women in the delivery room. Despite resistance from religious conservatives, his aggressive advocacy of anesthesia in childbirth, published in medical journals in New Orleans and Paris, contributed to a more humane approach to women's suffering. At the same time, he fought an equally aggressive information campaign in favor of science-based therapeutics and against states' rights medicine during a professional career that disregarded the barrier of segregated medicine.

As physician-activists, both Faget and Roudanez acted upon the Paris Medicale's revolutionary ethic by applying their healing skills to "human miseries that have no other origin but tyranny and slavery." During the Civil War and Reconstruction, Roudanez, like Faget, embarked upon a humanitarian mission as challenging and dangerous as his colleague's battle against yellow fever. For Roudanez, the task entailed a head-on assault on slavery and a visionary campaign to secure equal citizenship rights for African Americans throughout the nation. Roudanez's experience as a young Paris Médicale student at the 1848 barricades, when the revolutionary Second Republic abolished slavery and proclaimed universal male suffrage, convinced him that just such a revolution could be achieved in his homeland.

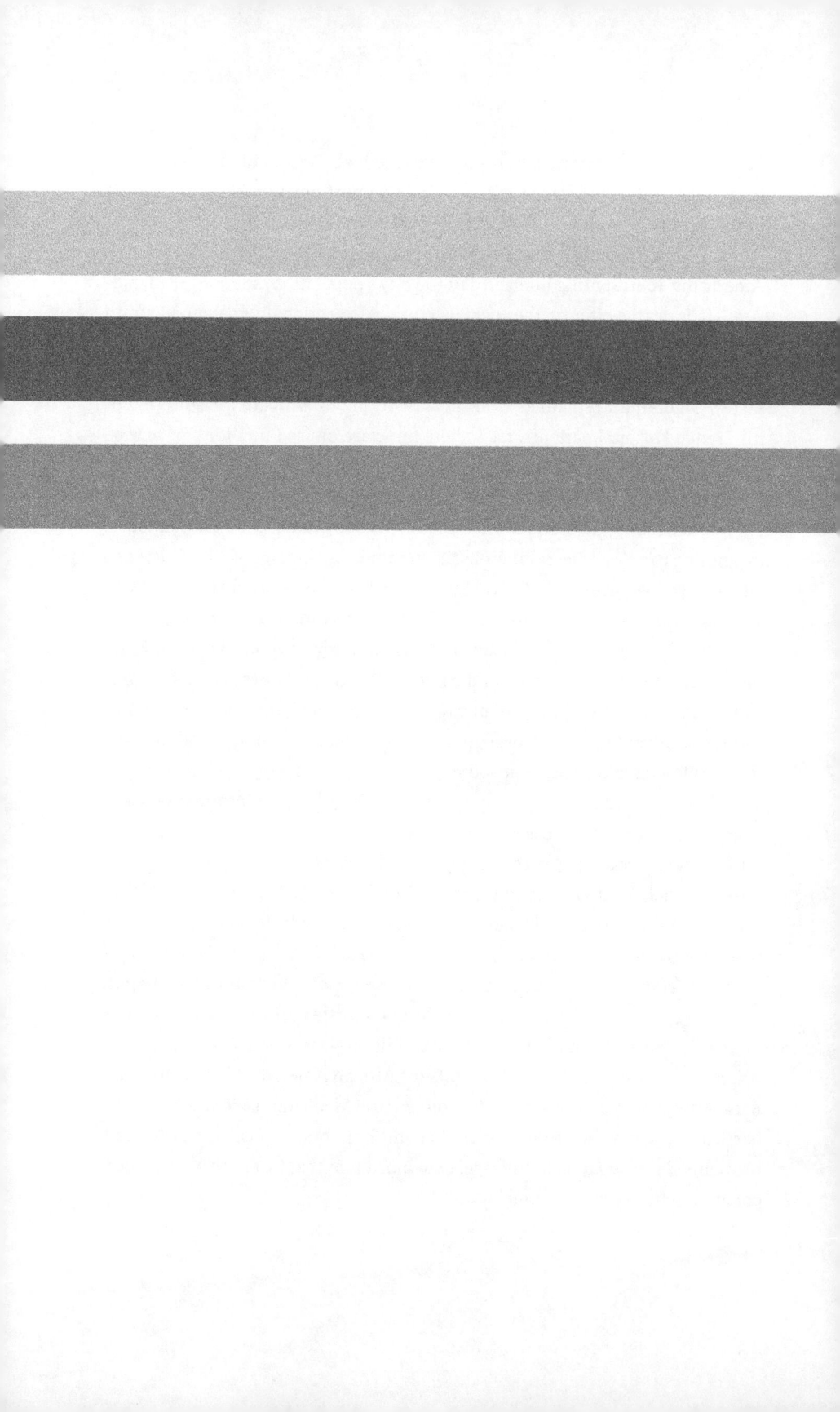

III.

CIVIL WAR AND

RECONSTRUCTION

> Of course revolutionary change was precisely what was necessary to advance
> authentic black freedom, and . . . nowhere in the South did black
> people speak more clearly . . . or insist more adamantly on the
> need for radical postwar change, than in New Orleans.
> —Vincent Harding, *There Is a River*, 255

During the Civil War and Reconstruction, the "Haitian influence" reemerged in Black New Orleans as a powerful force for change when the descendants of Haiti's diaspora mobilized. Union officer Henri-Louis Rey pointed to the courage of Vincent Ogé in the 1791 Haitian Revolution and urged his fellow Louisianians to join the struggle in "the cause of the rights of man."[1] In Paris during the 1848 French Revolution, New Orleanians Dr. Louis-Charles Roudanez and Joseph Tinchant witnessed slavery's abolition and the enactment of universal manhood suffrage. They, like Rey, welcomed the Civil War as a new phase in an Age of Revolution. The refugee descendants of the Rey, Roudanez, Tinchant, Desdunes, Estèves, Lafon, Mary, Boguille, and Plessy families joined with skilled and aggressive Anglophone allies like Oscar J. Dunn to transform the nation.

Upon the 1862 Union occupation of New Orleans the enslaved moved immediately to supply the US Army with intelligence. An elaborate network of informants emerged to support US General Benjamin F. Butler's effective management of the rebel city. From rural plantations, slave men literally fought their way into the occupied city, convincing the general to enlist them in the Union army. After they and their fellow soldiers prevailed against enemy forces in the Civil War, they looked to the reconstruction of the nation. As a spokesman for Black New Orleanians and the Friends of Universal Suffrage in July 1865, Dunn gave eloquent expression to their aspirations: "Let our republican government be upheld by all citizens and derive its just power from the expressed consent of ALL governed. Being just it will feel stronger; resting on the base of Universal Suffrage, it will be an example set to the world."[2]

SEVEN

Revolution and Counterrevolution

A fter April 12, 1861, when the opening shots at Fort Sumter signaled the onset of the Civil War, the city's Confederate leadership inaugurated a "reign of terror." This chapter documents that violence and the occupation of the city in May 1862 by the US Army under the command of General Benjamin F. Butler. Though the army was in New Orleans for less than nine months, the term *revolution* aptly applies to the dynamic resulting from the general's alliance with Black New Orleanians. From the outset, slave informants supplied Butler with valuable intelligence, while both free and enslaved men persuaded him to enlist Black soldiers in the US Army. The general also subsidized a radical Afro-Creole newspaper calling for an end to slavery and demanding equal rights for all African Americans.

In Washington, however, the Black civil rights campaign in south Louisiana ran counter to presidential politics and Butler was relieved of his command, with devastating consequences. This chapter ends in the fall of 1865, with the political takeover of Louisiana's state government by so many returning Confederate veterans that it became known as the Rebel Legislature.

* * *

Within two weeks of the opening shots of the Civil War on April 12, 1861, Louisiana's Confederate authorities issued an address in the *New Orleans Daily Crescent* to the "Defenders of the Native Land," calling upon free men of color to take up arms in defense of their homes and city. In the days that followed, free Black New Orleanians promptly organized a Native Guard regiment. On May 2, notwithstanding the 1834 state law restricting militia participation to "whites only," Confederate governor Thomas D. Moore authorized the addition of the new corps to the Louisiana state militia. Moore assigned a white rebel colonel, Henry D. Ogden, to command the thirty-three commissioned free Black line officers and the regiment's 731 soldiers. At the end of the month, the *Daily Crescent* assured its (white) readers that the men "will fight the Black Republican with as much determination and gallantry as any body of white men in the service of the Confederate States."[1]

Despite the expression of confidence in the new recruits, Louisiana's Confederate authorities withheld uniforms, arms, and other equipment from the Black regiment. In two grand reviews of the Louisiana militia, on November 23, 1861, and January 7, 1862, the Native Guard marched through the city boldly bearing their own arms, a sight that alarmed many white citizens. Their complaints prompted the governor to terminate the Afro-Creole regiment in February.

On March 24, after the US Navy under the command of David G. Farragut entered the Mississippi River, Governor Moore reinstated the Native Guard. With the city in a state of pandemonium, General John L. Lewis of the Louisiana militia issued the men obsolete weapons and commanded them to guard the east end of the French Quarter. Finally, Lewis ordered them to disband.

The bungling Confederate treatment of the militiamen supports scholar James G. Hollandsworth Jr.'s contention that rebel authorities created the Native Guard solely for propaganda purposes and never intended to use the Black troops for any serious assignment. The free Black regiment, Hollandsworth concluded, "was for public display; free blacks fighting for Southern rights made good copy for the newspapers."[2] With the approach of US naval forces, the Native Guard remained in New Orleans.

The expeditionary naval force commanded by Admiral David G. Farragut carried Major General Benjamin F. Butler, the new commanding officer of the Department of the Gulf. On April 25, 1862, he and his army of fifteen thousand soldiers arrived at New Orleans. As Union forces approached the Confederate South's largest city and principal port, they witnessed a shocking scene of violence. The flag-waving civilian Unionists on the city's levee who cheered the arrival of the US Navy were attacked by "a troop of horsemen [who] came riding up one of the streets and fired a volley into the men, women, and children."[3]

Pro-Confederate sources put the death toll at five, whereas a correspondent for the New York–based *Journal of Commerce* estimated that seventy-five people were killed and many more wounded. The victims were the casualties of New Orleans Mayor John T. Monroe's "reign of terror." After the opening shots of the Civil War, the *New York Daily Tribune* reported, "men who refused to take up arms for the 'Confederacy' were threatened with the direst penalties—imprisonment, confiscation, and even death!"[4]

On May 1, 1862, Butler and his advance guard marched to the customhouse, where the general proclaimed the national government's authority in his General Order 1, placing the city under martial law. The next day, when his negotiations with city officials at the St. Charles Hotel were interrupted by a roaring mob threatening to kill a Unionist sympathizer, Butler calmly ordered armaments to be brought forward. The sight of four artillery pieces rumbling up to the hotel cleared the city streets.[5]

At the outset of the Civil War in May 1861, Butler made history as the commanding officer at Fortress Monroe when three enslaved men—Frank Baker, Sheppard Mallory, and James Townsend—escaped to the Virginia fortification near the mouth of the Chesapeake Bay. When their Confederate owner demanded the return of the men, Butler refused. The question, the general replied, was whether the men would be used for or against the United States. Until the owner swore allegiance to the national government, Butler would hold the men as the "contraband of war."

By August, one thousand men, women, and children had arrived, with their numbers growing. By their actions Baker, Mallory, and Townsend, together with Butler's contraband policy, transformed Fortress Monroe, the 1619 landing site of the first captive Africans in the Virginia colony, into a "freedom fort."[6] News of events at Fortress Monroe spread like wildfire. Count Adam Gurowski, a Polish refugee and veteran of the revolutionary republican cause in Europe, proclaimed, the "emancipation of the slaves is virtually inaugurated."[7]

By the time of the Civil War, Senator Charles Sumner, the impressionable Massachusetts visitor to the Paris Médicale in 1838, was an abolitionist US senator belonging to the most aggressive radical faction of the Republican Party. He joined with Wendell Phillips and William Lloyd Garrison in openly attacking the government for its failure to set forth a clear-cut policy regarding the status of the fugitives. Under pressure from their demands, the Congress passed the first Confiscation Act on August 6, 1861, a measure that authorized the seizure of all property used in aid of the rebellion, including slaves.

The contraband-of-war strategy was not the well-defined policy Sumner and his abolitionist allies insisted upon. Nonetheless, as historian Adam Goodheart has pointed out, "it became hugely influential precisely *because* it was so impossible: it did not open the floodgates in theory, but it did so in practice." Events at Fortress Monroe were the first steps in a war that would end slavery.[8]

By the end of spring 1862, tens of thousands of self-emancipated men, women, and children were encamped in areas occupied by the Union army. As the war ground on, countless others looked to freedom in Union lines as US troops advanced into the South. From the beginning, their determination demonstrated the futility of half measures. Nothing short of freedom would suffice. Within two month of the shots fired at Fort Sumter, Baker, Mallory, and Townsend had achieved self-liberation and inspired Butler's contraband doctrine. In the wake of their actions, Goodheart writes, "slavery's iron curtain began falling, all across the South."[9]

As had happened in Virginia, enslaved Louisianians approached General Butler the day after his troops landed in the city and volunteered valuable information on enemy activities. At the outset of the war, Montgomery Blair, who was raised in a slaveholding Maryland family, emphasized to Butler the importance of formerly enslaved informants in intelligence gathering: "I have no doubt you will get your best spies from among them, because they are accustomed to travel in the night time and can go where no one not accustomed to the sly tricks they practice from infancy to old age could penetrate."[10]

Events in New Orleans validated Blair's advice. The men who first approached Butler represented the vanguard of an extensive network of informants whose support led Butler to order an open-door policy at his headquarters. According to James Parton, the general's "orders were, that whoever else might be excluded from head-quarters, no negro should ever be." As a consequence, "the general had a spy in every house, behind every rebel's chair as he sat at table." Effectively acting as Butler's eyes and ears, Black New Orleanians played a key role in Butler's remarkably efficient administration of the city.[11]

The general repaid their loyalty with access to the military justice system. After Butler dispatched the rebel mayor Monroe, his private secretary, his chief of police, and a city judge to Fort Jackson for treasonous activities, he appointed Major Joseph M. Bell, a Boston legal professional, to serve as a provost judge. With Judge Bell presiding, Black New Orleanians could seek legal redress in a court of law, with the freedom to testify against whites.

When Butler learned of a violation of his ban on contraband beatings, he dispatched Colonel Spencer H. Stafford, his provost marshal, to investigate the matter. Stafford learned that a jailer had ignored the general's edict by advertising that the "law of Louisiana for the correction of slaves would be enforced as heretofore." The colonel confirmed the accuracy of the charge by discovering the beating of a contraband on the morning of his visit. At that point, Parton observed, the "fell business stopped." In another mark of the US Army's civilizing influence, the city's domestic slave trade disintegrated after the federal occupation.[12]

The stealth and sophistication of Butler's Black informants is evident in the case of a discovery that created an international sensation. A few days after landing, one of the general's sources reported a large number of kegs filled with silver in the vault of a liquor merchant. The informer produced a Bible with "hieroglyphic" notations to validate his accusation. After the claim was verified by further investigation, Butler dispatched a troop of soldiers to search the business of the suspect, where the consular flag of the Netherlands hung over the door. The merchant was, in fact, the Dutch consul Amedée Couturié, and when he resisted a search of the building, the soldiers seized the premises and arrested the consul.

Couturié vehemently insisted that the vault in question contained nothing but his personal papers and consular materials. The soldiers opened the vault to discover 160 kegs containing $800,000 in Mexican silver coins and the silverware of private citizens. Further investigation uncovered bank bonds for the cities of New Orleans and Mobile as well as plates for Confederate treasury notes and the paper upon which the notes were printed. Soldiers loaded the kegs onto three wagons to be carried to the US Mint. Butler sent the Confederate plates to Washington.[13]

Butler's rows with foreign consuls began immediately after he landed. A "European brigade" had been organized to maintain an orderly interregnum after rebel forces fled the city. With the arrival of Union army, the organization voted to send their arms to Creole Louisianian P. G. T. Beauregard, the Confederacy's first brigadier general. When Butler learned of the group's actions, he demanded that they surrender their arms or leave the city.[14]

When the general was informed about the large numbers of slaves owned by French and British nationals on outlying plantations in Union-held parishes, he explored the legality of their ownership. His investigation confirmed that no French citizen could own slaves, due to France's 1848 abolition of slavery, and that the British government prohibited its subjects from owning slaves anywhere in the world, under threat of heavy penalties. Next, he ordered the registration of all residents in the city, indicating the nation to which they held allegiance. When French and British citizens affirmed their foreign nationality, Butler sprang his trap with the following mandate: "According to the law of the country to which you claim by the register to owe allegiance, all negroes claimed by you as slaves are free." The general thereby forced the French and British nationals and their consuls to accept the validity of his actions.[15]

According to historian Joe Gray Taylor, virtually all of the foreign consuls sympathized with the Confederacy, a circumstance that led to repeated confrontations with Butler. Until 1870, Europe's governing elite viewed republicanism as the most aggressive of revolutionary movements and disdained as militantly republican the founding principles of the United States. During the Civil War, the European upper classes favored the South and would hardly have regretted the new nation's collapse.[16]

The Confederacy's European support notwithstanding, a more powerful force pressed the democratic revolution forward. Even before federal forces landed in New Orleans, slave resistance on Louisiana's rural plantations escalated, with work slowdowns, insubordination among house servants, and a growing number of slave runaways. Between the outbreak of war in April 1861 and the end of January 1862, the state legislature's compensation to the owners of slaves convicted of crimes such as arson, revolt, or murder more than doubled. After the arrival of the Union army in south Louisiana, slave resistance and flight escalated dramatically, dealing a devastating blow to the region's slave regime and moving the matter of recruiting Black soldiers to the forefront of government policy.

During the spring and early summer of 1862, when freedom-seeking refugees sought sanctuary in areas of Union occupation, Butler imposed an emergency policy to bar from federal lines all those who could not be employed by the military. Within weeks of implementing the exclusion order, a Union officer reported a "large and constantly increasing number of blacks . . . congregated near the upper picket station." The number of men, women, and children doubled from 75 to 150 within hours. Some groups had traveled a hundred miles without food or shelter to reach the federal outpost. The officer, fearful that the refugees might starve, requested instructions. He was ordered to prevent them from entering the Union line of defense. Despite the exclusion order, fugitives intent on escaping slavery congregated at every Union post, camp, and fort, and their frustration sometimes gave way to anger, resulting in several instances of confrontation and revolt.[17]

On August 2, for instance, Union soldiers halted an insurrection a few miles upriver, after threatening the use of force. Two days later, a bloody en-counter arose when a large body of enslaved workers from downriver plan-tations approached the barracks of federal troops at the US Mint and the customhouse. Forty of the men carried cane knives and clubs and forced the retreat of the city's Third District police force. Union soldiers joined the strug-gle and helped to suppress the insurgents, but not before several of the en-slaved were killed and a number of policemen and enslaved men were badly injured. The city's US Treasury agent, George S. Denison, expressed the ines-capable logic of events when he wrote to Secretary of the Treasury Salmon P. Chase, "If untutored slaves fight thus for their liberty against the authorities, would they not do equally well when disciplined, encouraged, and upheld by the authorities?"[18]

Like enslaved New Orleanians, free men of color approached Butler soon after the general's occupation of the city. Four officers of Louisiana's Native Guard militia, brothers Octave and Henri-Louis Rey, Edgar Davis, and Eugène Rapp, volunteered their corps' services to the Union cause. The men made a favorable impression on Butler, who observed what "a very intelligent looking set of men they were."

In fact, the confident Afro-Creole officers who met with Butler were the heirs of a military history of service under France, Spain, and the United States. The 1834 state law restricting militia participation to "whites only" did not diminish their community's pride in their legacy of service. That leg-acy originated in 1729, when their enslaved forebears had won their freedom in exchange for their military service. Afro-Creole New Orleanians kept the memory of their historic contributions alive in a number of veterans' organi-zations, including La Société des Artisans and their Association of Colored Veterans of 1814 and 1815, incorporated in 1853.[19]

In view of Washington's opposition to arming African Americans and But-ler's awareness of the Native Guard's service in the city's Confederate militia, the general declined their offer. Still, on May 25, 1862, he transmitted his impression of the men to Secretary of War Edwin M. Stanton: "We have heard much in the newspapers of the free-negro corps of this city organized for the defense of the South. From this a very erroneous idea may have derived."[20]

Led by Rey, the Native Guard delegation remained determined to join the Union war effort. They next met with Brigadier General John W. Phelps, a fervent abolitionist from Vermont, who was bivouacked at Camp Parapet, guarding the river road near Carrollton, a few miles upriver from the city.[21]

Phelps was arming fugitive slaves, and in late July the New Orleans militia-men proposed raising a regiment of men of color under his authority. Phelps, having already run afoul of government authorities for arming slaves, declined and referred the men back to Butler.

The increasing strength of slave resistance and Butler's pressing need for reinforcements, however, forced a dramatic change in Union policy. On August 14, the general notified Secretary Stanton of his intention to arm free men of color. In August, as the general prepared for the official induction of free Black soldiers, he asked Native Guard officers why they had volunteered for the Confederate army. They replied that they "were ordered out and dared not refuse, for those who did so were killed and their property confiscated."[22]

When an authorization from Washington failed to materialize, Butler issued a general order on August 24, 1862, inviting all free Black men who had served in the Native Guard, a body of soldiers authorized by the state's Confederate governor, to enlist in the US Army. Agent Denison marveled at "the characteristic shrewdness with which General Butler has managed this affair. By accepting a regiment which had already been in Confederate Service, he left no room for complaint (by the Rebels) that the government was arming the negroes." In recruiting the soldiers, Butler likewise pointed to Andrew Jackson's 1815 precedent in enlisting Native Guard soldiers in the Battle of New Orleans.[23]

Within three weeks of the general's August 24 call to arms, African American Louisianians filled the First Louisiana Native Guard regiment, largely with fugitive recruits who had made their way into Union lines. "Nobody inquires whether the recruit is (or has been) a slave," Denison wrote to Chase. "As a consequence the boldest and finest fugitives have enlisted." On September 27, when Butler mustered the men into service, the First Native Guard became the first officially authorized Black regiment in the US Army.[24]

After the Second Regiment was mustered into service in mid-October, Butler informed General in Chief Henry W. Halleck that the "only drawback to two regiments of these Native Guards (colored) is the fear in their minds that the President will not sustain my action—a story, by the by, which is industriously circulated by the rebels here to prevent the enlistment of these loyal citizens." For both the Second and Third Regiments, Butler recruited soldiers from among those liberated from rebel sympathizers by the second Confiscation Act, in July 1862, and those freed from French and British nationals.[25] Men who had been slaves only months before now became soldiers in the US

Army. Three white officers with local ties were assigned to command each of the three regiments, which were brigaded under the overall command of Colonel Stafford, Butler's provost marshal.[26]

From September 27 to November 24, 1862, Butler enlisted approximately 1,800 Louisiana Native Guard soldiers. From the First Regiment's core of free Afro-Creoles, he created a corps of seventy-six commissioned line officers (captains and lieutenants) to command the soldiers in the three African American regiments. Butler promoted Captain François Ernest Dumas of the First Regiment to the rank of major, making the officer one of only two African American men in the US Army to reach that rank.[27]

Since 1792, the nation's state militias had barred African Americans from their ranks, even though men of color had served in the American Revolution and the War of 1812. Until the Civil War, the regular army never enrolled Black soldiers. By the time the Emancipation Proclamation went into effect on January 1, 1863, and provided for the enlistment of Black soldiers, African American soldiers filled the ranks of three Louisiana regiments.

Over the course of the entire Civil War, on the other hand, the regular army assigned only one hundred commissions to African American soldiers. Once again General Butler moved the revolution forward by issuing seventy-six of those commissions to Native Guard officers. None of the other US Army's fourteen commissioned officers held field command. They served as company-level officers, chaplains, surgeons, and recruiters. Thousands of Black soldiers served as noncommissioned officers, however, in their roles as sergeants major, quartermaster sergeants, commissary sergeants, and hospital stewards. Altogether, nearly 180,000 Black soldiers served in the US Army during the Civil War, with Louisiana enlisting more African American soldiers than any other state in the country—a total of twenty-four thousand men-at-arms.[28]

While Butler was reinforcing his army with Black recruits, he was also implementing a work program that W. E. B. Du Bois described as "perhaps the greatest and most systematic organizing of fugitives." Under the authority of the second Confiscation Act, which freed all the enslaved except those of loyal planters, and with the approval of the War Department, Butler issued General Order 91 to bring order, productivity, and a free labor system to south Louisiana plantations. Beginning in Plaquemines, St. Bernard, and Lafourche Parishes, the project demonstrated that plantations could be run by free Black workers. The US Army-regulated program created colonies of Black laborers who worked for wages on sequestered plantations as well as those of loyal planters. The contracts protected workers' wages while the US government profited from the harvest.[29]

Black Louisianians, Du Bois wrote, stood at "Butler's right hand during the trying time of his administration," and the Yankee general reciprocated. At one of their early meetings, for instance, they asked him to desegregate the city's public transportation system. The omnibus lines relegated Black New Orleanians to overcrowded streetcars—so-called star cars, marked with a large star. Even if a white streetcar was only half full, official policy prohibited African Americans from boarding the carriage.

Butler ordered the streetcars desegregated in a decree that the omnibus companies challenged. When Butler's provost marshal, Colonel Stafford, tried to persuade streetcar officials to increase the number of cars, they refused. Eventually, an uneasy, short-lived peace was achieved when the car companies allowed the Native Guard's Black officers to ride on streetcars reserved for whites.[30]

At the same time, free families of color defied the exclusion of their children from the city's educational system. Although the property taxes of the population of color contributed in 1841 to the funding of the city's public schools, their children were barred from enrolling in the free, all-white school system. In September 1862, the discovery that a student of color had enrolled in the Fourth District's Barracks School set off an investigation of birth certificates. The school board dismissed three children and fired a teacher when their records revealed their African American ethnicity.

After the mother of one of the children raised the issue with Butler, he immediately ordered the girl reinstated. When the school board resisted his order, he summoned its members to a hearing at which the board proposed organizing a committee to investigate the matter. An impasse resulted when the committee members resigned rather than advocate school integration. The struggle for equal access to the city's public schools would resume with renewed vigor in postwar New Orleans.[31]

Throughout his presence in the city, the general enjoyed the company and confidence of the city's affluent Afro-Creole leadership at whose tables he dined. In September 1862, white officer John W. De Forest described one of these interracial dinner parties, where eight Union officers gathered in the home of wealthy businessman P. A. Dumas. De Forest observed that the host and his brother, François Dumas, "did not differ in air and manners from the young Frenchmen whom I used to know abroad." He was especially impressed by François, who "has the complexion of an Italian and features which remind one of the first Napoleon."[32]

Officer Dumas, one of the South's wealthiest African Americans, was said to be a distant cousin of Alexandre Dumas, the larger-than-life Afro-French author whose dedication to republican ideals François Dumas clearly shared. Like Alexandre Dumas, who played an active role in the 1830 and 1848 French Revolutions and helped procure arms for Italian revolutionary Giuseppe Garibaldi, François Dumas embraced the republican cause. In France, where he was born, raised, and educated, he "imbibed his Republicanism and principles of the equality of men."[33]

Upon his arrival in antebellum Louisiana, Dumas treated the slaves he inherited from his father "as freemen, and . . . he would not sell them at any price, because he would not give them a master." He conceived of the struggle against slavery and racial oppression in the South as another chapter in "the great universal fight of the oppressed of all colors and nations." In Civil War and Reconstruction Louisiana, he became an active agent of liberation and democracy, and though he did not achieve Alexandre Dumas's fame, his accomplishments are equally compelling.

As a newly commissioned officer, Dumas disregarded the military's restriction against slave recruits, instead freeing and arming his bondsmen at his own expense in the tradition of the Haitian Revolution's free Black slaveholders. He was reported to have called them together and asked them if they were willing to "break the bonds of their fellow men." When they said yes, the US Army's first African American major organized them into an entire company of approximately a hundred men.[34]

Like Dumas, eighteen-year-old free man of color Pierre-Aristide Desdunes was among the first Afro-Creole New Orleanians to enlist in the First Native Guard regiment, signing on as a private on September 1, 1862. The army official who documented his enrollment listed his occupation as a carpenter and described him as five feet four inches tall with a light complexion, black hair and eyes, and "no permanent marks or scars." On September 27, Desdunes's regiment, one thousand strong, was mustered into military service for three years.[35]

Like Dumas, Desdunes also possessed ancestral ties to the broader Francophone Atlantic. During the 1850s, he had traveled with his father to Haiti, where his Caribbean relatives possessed considerable wealth and influence, with one family member, Alcibiade Desdunes, serving in the Haitian senate for several years. During his sojourn, Jean-Baptiste, a vaudoux *papalwa* (high priest) and veteran grenadier in Alexandre Pétion's revolutionary army, initiated Desdunes into the religious sect as an honorary member. Pierre-Aristide's friendship with the veteran Haitian soldier and his initiation into Haitian vaudoux exposed the youth to influences that Louisiana's slaveholding elite most feared.[36]

Upon his return to New Orleans, those radicalizing influences were reinforced at the Couvent School, an incubator of republican idealism, where Desdunes acquired a lifelong admiration for Lamartine and Haitian poet Coriolan Ardouin. He revered Lamartine's work for having "paved the way for *La République* de 1848" by defending the 1789 French Revolution and France's First Republic. At an early age, Desdunes developed an equally high regard for Ardouin, who is credited with authoring Haiti's first Romantic literary work. Desdunes considered Ardouin "the Haitian Lamartine" and found his tribute to Alexandre Pétion in the poem "Pétion," with its stirring commemoration of Haiti's revolutionary heritage, especially moving. Schooled in the empowering ethics of the Romantic art form and fully aware of advances in freedom and equality in the Atlantic world, Desdunes was well prepared for his new role as a soldier in the army of the United States republic.[37]

For Desdunes, military service alongside contraband soldiers made a deep and lasting impression. During the postwar era, he transcribed an 1883 poem by Tertulien Guilbaud, one of Haiti's seminal Romantic literary artists, entitled "Toussaint Louverture à l'aspect de la flotte française, 1802" (Toussaint Louverture Upon Sighting the French Navy, 1802). Guilbaud's Louverture, a composite of the real and the mythical heroes of the Haitian Revolution, issues a call to arms: "Array yourselves beside me, noble sons of Africa!" In his far-reaching plans, Louverture continues, "I have God on my side! And I feel boiling in my veins of iron / The creative power which brings forth worlds!" In his transcription, Desdunes introduces Guilbaud's poem with the title "Les pensées d'un esclave soldat" (The Thoughts of a Slave Soldier), a heading that recalls his own perceptions of his fellow Civil War soldiers. Desdunes, like Guilbaud, viewed the hemispheric struggle for freedom through the prism of the Haitian Revolution. In Desdunes's experience, however, the "esclave soldat" wore the uniform of the US Army.[38]

Southern slaveholders in Louisiana and elsewhere in the South likewise viewed the Civil War through Haiti's revolutionary prism. For them, recruits like Desdunes, Dumas, and their fellow African American soldiers represented a profoundly dangerous presence. North Carolina's state representative Lewis Hanes warned that Black soldiers would reproduce "among us all the inexpressible horrors of the massacre of Saint Domingo." One of Hanes's colleagues echoed his belief that arming Black soldiers meant that "society is to be not merely upset, but destroyed."[39]

Armed Blacks, according to James M. McPherson, "were truly the bête noire of southern nightmares." As Confederates recognized, the creation of Black regiments transformed the Civil War into a revolution to destroy the South's slave-based regime. On August 21, after receiving word of plans to enlist Black soldiers in Louisiana and South Carolina, the Confederate military high command responded ferociously with an order that such "crimes and outrages" required the "execution as a felon" of captured officers of Black soldiers.

In November 1862, when rebel raiders captured four Blacks in Union uniforms on a South Carolina island, Confederate president Jefferson Davis had approved their "summary execution" as an "example" to discourage arming slaves. On Christmas Eve of that year, Davis issued a general order requiring that all captured former slaves and their officers be turned over to state officials to be tried and punished. In the end, the refusal of the Confederates to treat Black soldiers as legitimate prisoners of war led to a breakdown in prisoner exchanges, with tragic consequences for both the South and the North.[40]

New Orleans' contraband, fugitive, free, Francophone, and Anglophone African Americans continued to enlist in the Native Guard regiments despite the horrific threats. The white abolitionist colonel of the Second Native Guard regiment, Nathan W. Daniels, wrote in 1863 that the soldiers of his regiment would "never surrender. Defeat in our case is worse than Death. Victory the only alternative—my men are well aware of this and will vent themselves accordingly." Daniels's remarks capture the esprit de corps that developed between Black soldiers and their officers, which as scholar Dudley Taylor Cornish has observed, "is rare in military annals."[41]

On September 27, 1862, the same day that Pierre-Aristide Desdunes's First Native Guard made history as the US Army's first officially recognized Black regiment, New Orleans activists embarked upon another history-making event, the establishment of the South's first African American newspaper, *l'Union: memorial politique, littéraire et progressiste*. Founded by Dr. Louis-Charles Roudanez, his brother Jean-Baptiste Roudanez, and Paul Trévigne, the militant republican journal set out to direct the energies of Black Louisianians into an effective political force.

Though initially published as a one-page, front and back, French-language journal, the diminutive new biweekly hurled well-aimed editorial stones at the South's slaveholding behemoth. A front-page essay condemned slavery and predicted its destruction. It appeared alongside an exchange between Haiti's republican journalist Eugène Heurtelou and French Romantic author Victor Hugo. In their letters, Heurtelou and Hugo deplored John Brown's death, with Hugo predicting a future in which "servitude in every form will disappear." Heurtelou envisioned the dawning of a new age when "liberté, egalité, fraternité" would open the way for the "fusion of peoples and of races through fraternity, their union in a great and universal republic." With the publication of the dramatic exchange, l'Union's staff set the newspaper's narrative within a global struggle for freedom and equality.[42]

In another one of l'Union's earliest issues, renowned Afro-Creole orator François Boisdoré drew attention to events in France and the French Caribbean at the outset of the 1848 French Revolution, when the French Second Republic abolished slavery and provided for universal male suffrage. Boisdoré immortalized the watershed event in an inspiring essay entitled "Liberty." Accorded direct representation in the parliament, the new voters in each West Indian island sent three representatives to France's National Assembly. In his indelible literary portrait, Boisdoré featured Félicité de Lamennais, Victor Hugo, and Alphonse de Lamartine seated on the same bench in the National Assembly alongside African-descended representatives François-Auguste Pérrinon, Charles Dain, and Louisy Mathieu, a former slave, representing Guadeloupe, with Pierre-Marie Pory-Papy and Victor Mazuline representing Martinique.[43]

The political landscape of the fledgling newspaper's founders and supporters encompassed the American, French, and Haitian Revolutions as well as the February phase of France's 1848 Revolution. l'Union's founders viewed the Civil War within the context of an ongoing Age of Democratic Revolutions and they moved aggressively to strike a blow for freedom and equal citizenship. They combined their formidable talents to make their shared vision of a social, political, and economic revolution a reality. General Butler's army of occupation supported their cause with a newspaper subsidy.

Dr. Roudanez, a fearless humanitarian like his colleague and friend Dr. Faget, shared his awareness of the Civil War's revolutionary possibilities with his fiery ally Joseph Tinchant, one of the bold men of color who rallied to l'Union's support. The two Louisiana-born men traced their ancestral roots to

Haiti and both were educated in France. As a twelve-year-old, Tinchant emigrated to the French city of Pau with his family and attended the elite *collège royal*, where he acquired a classical education from one of the best schools in the region. In 1846, the eighteen-year-old Tinchant struck out for Paris, where he, like Roudanez, learned real-time republican lessons in the 1848 Revolution. For Roudanez and Tinchant, the lightning-like collapse of the monarchy and the overnight arrival of the Second Republic with its abolition of slavery and declaration of "social equality" raised the prospects for change in their own country. When the republican euphoria of February gave way to the ferocious violence of the June Days, Tinchant the "Forty-Eighter" sailed for New Orleans.[44]

Jean-Baptiste Roudanez, a cofounder of *l'Union* with his brother, was also educated in Paris, where he studied mechanical engineering. He returned to Louisiana to work on sugar plantations where planters valued his mechanical skills. To the task of setting forth *l'Union*'s political and humanitarian objectives, Roudanez brought his eyewitness accounts of slave life on sugar plantations. He was interviewed by Commissioner James M. McKaye of the three-man American Freedmen's Inquiry Commission, created by the administration in early 1863. At the urging of Senator Sumner of Massachusetts, McKaye was investigating the labor system in south Louisiana. The commissioner described Roudanez as "a man of great intelligence and probity" and commented on his expertise and character: "No man could have had a more thorough acquaintance with plantation life than he, and no man in the city of his residence bears a higher reputation for truth and sobriety."

In his testimony, Roudanez described a world in which enslaved laborers arose between three and four in the morning to work fifteen to eighteen hours a day or longer during certain seasons. On some plantations, "the women were worked as hard as the men, and in some instances were kept at labor in every stage of pregnancy, even up to the moment of delivery." Enslaved women and girls suffered pervasive sexual predation, since the "overseers had the run of all the field women, and if one of them refused, an occasion was soon found for subjecting her to a severe punishment." In 1864, Roudanez's damning account of south Louisiana slavery was published in McKaye's report to Stanton. Altogether, the commission report would form the basis for the Freedmen's Bureau, the nation's first social welfare agency. Roudanez's testimony was another step in a campaign for social and political justice that he would pursue to the nation's highest political office.[45]

Paul Trévigne, *l'Union*'s editor, was an author, activist, and instructor at the Couvent School. He was born in 1825 into a New Orleans social system in which unions between white men and African-descended women (both enslaved and free) were common. Those interracial liaisons led to considerable transfers of wealth from white men to their Black partners and their biracial children. In Trévigne's case, his eighteenth-century African ancestor Nanette Dubreuil was a slave from Senegambia who had five children with Frenchman Claude Joseph Dubreuil, one of the 1718 founders of the city with Jean-Baptiste de Bienville. By the time of his death in 1757, Dubreuil was the wealthiest man in New Orleans, with more than five hundred enslaved laborers, and had provided the city with its first system of levees and canals.

When Nanette Dubreuil's grandson Charles Decoudreau married in 1798, his sister Françoise Decoudreau's quasi-husband, Louis Dauquemenil de Morand, stood as one of the couple's witnesses. De Morand's father owned most of the land north of the city, including what was to become the Faubourg Tremé. Joséphine Decoudreau, Charles Decoudreau's daughter, married José Antonio de Paula de Trebiño, a veteran of the Battle of New Orleans, and Paul Trévigne's Spanish grandfather. When his wealthy white grandfather died in 1828, he bequeathed his entire fortune to Trévigne's father, Francisco de Paula de Trebiño. Trévigne's complex web of interracial family ties linked him to some of the most powerful families in New Orleans. Though most of his ancestors were European, the urbane and cosmopolitan Trévigne wholly identified as African American, condemned slavery, and campaigned relentlessly for Black equal rights until his death in 1908.[46]

In late October 1862, Butler launched an expedition west of the city to clear the region of Confederate forces and restore transportation links on the Mississippi River's west bank. The mission involved opening, repairing, and guarding the seventy-mile Opelousas Railroad connecting Algiers, across the river from New Orleans, to Brashear (present-day Morgan City) at Berwick Bay and Bayou Teche. He assigned the mission to Pierre-Aristides Desdunes's First Native Guard regiment commanded by Colonel Spencer H. Stafford, Colonel Nathan W. Daniels's Second Native Guard, and Colonel Stephen Thomas's Eighth Vermont Volunteers. Given the diversity of skilled tradesmen and professionals in Desdunes's regiment, Colonel Stafford bragged that his unit could construct a whole town within sixty days.

After the Union capture of New Orleans, Confederate smugglers shifted their commerce from the city to the smaller rivers, bayous, and inlets to carry materials to the Gulf of Mexico, where rebel blockade runners awaited their cargoes. The region west of the city, surrounding Berwick Bay, Bayou Teche, and Bayou Lafourche, became a hotbed of Confederate smuggling and troop movements. By December, the two Native Guard regiments and the Eighth Vermont Volunteers had taken Donaldsonville, Thibodaux, and Berwick Station, forcing the Confederates to retreat from Des Allemands while restoring fifty-two miles of railroad track and rebuilding two large bridges. The expedition achieved all of Butler's objectives.[47]

In Washington, Butler elated Radical Republicans like Charles Sumner with his successful deployment of one of the nation's first African American regiments. They delighted in his strict enforcement of martial law, his rough treatment of Confederate sympathizers, and his crackdown on foreign consuls and their nationals. While Sumner and his allies applauded Butler's actions, President Lincoln insisted that foreigners be appeased. In keeping with that objective, the administration dispatched a commissioner hostile to Butler, Baltimore attorney Reverdy Johnson, to investigate the matter of the seized Dutch funds. After completing his assignment, Johnson attacked Butler for a state of corruption and fraud "without parallel in the past history of the country." Butler's enemies piled on, though charges of impropriety were never proven.[48]

Looming at least as large as the accusations of corruption and the general's rigorous command of the Department of the Gulf was the radical agenda advanced by Butler in coordination with Black New Orleanians. The president countenanced the rapid return of Louisiana to the Union under a mild plan of reconstruction designed to cultivate Unionist sentiment in the state. The general and his Black allies clearly stood in the way of those plans. Without informing Butler, Lincoln ordered Major General Nathaniel P. Banks to take command of the Department of the Gulf. On his return to Washington, Butler demanded to know how Jefferson Davis knew of his removal before he knew himself. No one gave him an answer. Lincoln tried to mollify the general, but Butler insisted on returning to his command in New Orleans. The president refused.[49]

On the day of Butler's departure from the city, Banks embarked upon his conciliatory policy of winning the allegiance of white Louisianians by bowing to the wishes of St. Charles Parish slaveholders who feared the presence of Black soldiers among their slaves. He ordered companies of the Second Native Guard regiment dispersed to the region's remote shoreline defenses at Ship Island in the Gulf of Mexico and Fort Pike on the Rigolets strait near Lake

Pontchartrain. In January, Banks scattered companies of the First Regiment to outlying posts on the west bank of the Mississippi, fifteen miles below the city at Fort St. Leon, and on the east bank at Fort McComb, guarding Chef Menteur Pass at Lake Ponchartrain. The Third Regiment remained in Bayou Lafourche, harvesting sugar.[50]

Banks also took pains to stress the conservatism of President Lincoln's September 1862 preliminary Emancipation Proclamation. The proclamation, Banks emphasized, did not provide for emancipation in areas under Union control: "It is manifest that the changes suggested therein and which may hereafter be established do not take effect within this State on the 1st of January proximo nor at any precise period which can now be designated, and I call upon all persons—soldiers, citizens, or slaves—to observe this material and important fact, and to govern themselves accordingly." The president made his desire to placate south Louisiana slaveholders explicit in the final text of the proclamation, when he exempted thirteen Union-occupied Louisiana parishes in the final version of the January 31 emancipation decree.[51]

When Butler left the city on Christmas Eve 1862, Admiral Farragut's flagship and a shore battery saluted his departure. Farragut would later observe, "They may say what they please about General Butler, but he was the right man in the right place in New Orleans." Butler's experiences in Virginia and Louisiana transformed him from a Democrat into an uncompromising Republican. In political office, he would become one of the nation's leading Radical Republicans, and he would remain loyal to Black New Orleanians and all African Americans until his death in 1893.[52]

Within approximately two months of assuming command on December 9, 1862, Banks began a purge of the seventy-six Black officers commissioned by Butler. By the end of 1863, he had replaced sixty-three of the men with white officers. Only two commissioned Black officers remained at the end of the war. In Massachusetts, Butler reacted angrily to the decommissioning of the officers. How, he asked, "can we expect the Black man to stand up against the White rebel when we allow him to be insulted by our own soldier because he [the Union soldier] is White?"

In May 1863, the Native Guard officers and soldiers of the First and Third Regiments distinguished themselves in fierce fighting at Port Hudson. Their courage under fire was decisive in winning northern public opinion over to the US Army's enlistment of Black soldiers. In their assault on Confederate defenses, Banks wrote, "They fought splendidly! . . . Their charges upon the rebel works, of which they made three, exhibited the greatest bravery and caused them to suffer great losses." Still, the general continued his policy of purging Black commissioned officers in dismissals that Butler would refer to as "unmanly."[53]

In his ongoing efforts to appease white conservatives, Banks slowed the recruitment of Black soldiers and purged at least two white officers assigned by Butler and favored by Black soldiers. In the midst of the Port Hudson campaign in May 1863, the general ordered the arrest of Colonel Stafford of the First Native Guard for "conduct to the prejudice of good order and military discipline." In the incident, Stafford was accused of cursing Captain J. P. Garland of the Twenty-First Maine for calling one of his officers a "black son of a bitch." Stafford, a trusted and disciplined provost marshal under Butler, had coordinated the initial organization of the three Native Guard regiments and remained a forceful spokesman for the Black soldiers. He was tried, found guilty, and dismissed. He appealed the case after the war and won an honorable discharge retroactive to the date of his dismissal.[54]

Colonel Nathan W. Daniels, a white native of Syracuse, New York, resided in Pointe Coupée Parish, Louisiana, when the war began, and he assisted Butler in choosing local officers for staff positions. In that capacity, Daniels recommended officer François Dumas for major. The promotion made Dumas the first Black commissioned staff officer in the entire US Army and the only nonwhite at the rank of major to engage in battlefield combat. An abolitionist and Spiritualist, Daniels attended séances with his comrade in arms Captain Henri-Louis, a commissioned officer in the First Native Guard, and J. B. Valmour Averin. Both Rey and Valmour were revered Afro-Creole mediums in the city's Spiritualist movement.

On May 4, 1863, General Banks ordered Daniels's arrest on a number of trivial charges that baffled the colonel. While Black officers resigned in waves, Daniels waited five months in New Orleans for a trial that never occurred. According to the Afro-Creole *New Orleans Tribune*, Daniels "incurred the ill-will of Gen. Banks for his having taken part in behalf of his colored officers." Daniels finally negotiated an agreement with Banks whereby he resigned his commission and left the military. His resignation was designated a "dishonorable dismissal," a damaging slight that did not prevent him from becoming actively involved in Republican politics. Dumas maintained his rank as major in the Second Regiment for two months after Daniels's ouster. On July 7, 1863, he resigned in the face of Banks's ongoing purge of Black officers.[55]

The day after General Butler's 1862 Christmas Eve departure, an editorial in *l'Union* entitled "A Step into the Future" insisted on the necessity of converting the South to a land of free labor as one of the steps toward ensuring the nation's prospects for the future. General Banks, on the other hand, took a decidedly backward step by applying the same conciliatory policy toward conservative white planters that had guided his treatment of Black officers and soldiers. On January 30, 1863, Banks issued General Order 12 for regulating labor in occupied Louisiana. According to Virginia officer David H. Strother, who accompanied Banks to the region, the policies "gave great satisfaction to the planters." Workers were paid less than half the wages provided under Butler's system, the seizure of Confederate-owned plantations came to a virtual halt, planter security forces exercised increased autonomy, and workers who left their place of employment were threatened with arrest on the charge of vagrancy.[56]

Initially, the city's Black leadership centered at *l'Union* accepted General Banks's labor system as a temporary, military necessity. Regarding vagrancy policy, they urged the avoidance of "cruel regulations" and looked forward to the day when freedmen would "become proprietors themselves." Like abolitionists and congressional radicals in the North, they viewed land ownership as an essential prerequisite to freedom and they insisted on a government policy of land distribution. Their insistence on the proprietary rights of the freedmen together with their calls for political equality ran entirely counter to the speedy "reunionizing of Louisiana" envisioned by Banks and the president.[57]

In inaugural issues of *l'Union*, the Roudanez brothers, editor Trévigne, and their allies had announced their intention to revolutionize race relations. After white radicals founded the Union Association of New Orleans the following summer, free Black leaders began attending their meetings. Owing to their close ties to the organization's leadership, *l'Union*'s staff published its public notices and accounts of its activities. In June 1863, the association acknowledged the paper's support by naming it the French-language publisher of its official announcements. By that time, *l'Union* had expanded into a triweekly newspaper, and in July it began appearing in both French and English.[58]

In the spring of 1863, when the Union Association won approval for a constitutional convention as a step toward reestablishing a state government, the Lincoln administration approved the registration of voters for the election of its delegates. With calls for "liberté, égalité, fraternité," *l'Union* and its allies demanded suffrage and seized upon the election of delegates to call for immediate enfranchisement. At a November interracial rally, Afro-Creole activist Boisdoré asserted that voting rights were long overdue: "When our fathers fought in 1815 they were told that they should be compensated. . . . We have waited long enough. . . . If the United States has the right to arm us, it certainly has the right to allow us the rights of suffrage." If local authorities denied them their hard-fought rights, they would take their appeal "to a higher power. We will go to President Lincoln, and then we shall know who we are dealing with." At the end of the month, the Union Association approved free Black demands for voting rights.[59]

By that time, Banks had effectively stymied the convention movement by withholding military support. The slow pace of the Union Association's progress and Banks's misrepresentations of Unionist activities persuaded the impatient president to abandon Louisiana's free state movement. On December 8, 1863, Lincoln issued his Proclamation of Amnesty and Reconstruction and its Ten-Percent Plan, offering a full pardon to antebellum voters, with the exception of high-ranking Confederates, who took an oath of loyalty and accepted slavery's abolition. When 10 percent of those who voted in 1860 took the oath, a new government could be organized.

On Christmas Eve, Lincoln wrote a letter to Banks making him "master of all" and urging him to "give us a free-state reorganization of Louisiana in the shortest possible time." The president's Reconstruction plan and his designation of Banks as the master of the state's political reorganization delivered the coup de grâce to the Unionist movement. According to historian Peyton McCrary, Lincoln's motivation in surrendering control of Reconstruction to the hands of the ambitious Banks is unclear. He speculates, however, that Lincoln shared the general's opposition to Black suffrage out of fear of antagonizing white conservatives.[60]

With the sabotage of the free state movement, Afro-Creole leaders moved quickly to make good on Boisdoré's threat to take the suffrage issue to Washington. In their December 1863 petition campaign, they collected the signatures of a thousand free Black property holders, twenty-seven veterans of the War of 1812, and twenty-two white radicals. In mid-February, they dispatched two emissaries, l'Union cofounder Jean-Baptiste Roudanez and E. Arnold Bertonneau, to Washington to present their petition to the president and Congress. Bertonneau was a former officer in the Union army whose light complexion would later save his life.

Like his close allies at l'Union, Bertonneau was wholly committed to the shared vision of freedom and republican egalitarianism. Born in the city in 1834 to Marie Estella, a Cuban, and Louis Bertonneau, a French-born coffee shop owner on Royal Street, he was a prosperous wine merchant and coffee-house operator by the time of the Civil War. When he enlisted in the US Army, Butler assigned him to his corps of commissioned officers. On March 5, 1863, after Banks replaced Butler, Captain Bertonneau resigned from the Second Native Guard regiment. In his letter of resignation at his post on Rigolets at Fort Pike, he wrote, "When I joined the army I thought that I was fighting for the same cause, wishing only the success of my country would suffice to alter a prejudice which had long existed. . . . But I regret to say that five months experience has proved the contrary." In New Orleans, he joined disillusioned former officers like himself, and civilian activists, in organizing the city's burgeoning civil rights movement.[61]

Just ahead of Bertonneau's and Roudanez's departure for Washington, Black New Orleanians held a mass meeting for the first time, in the Lyceum Hall, the largest such meeting room in the city. Although municipal officials had never authorized the use of the facility by African Americans, Colonel McKaye of the American Freedmen's Inquiry Commission prevailed upon George F. Shepley, the state's military governor, to order access to the hall. Commissioner McKaye's fact-finding mission in Louisiana had already led him to interview Jean-Baptiste Roudanez.

As McKaye continued his work, he kept Senator Sumner, a close observer of the occupied South's freedmen, informed of his Louisiana findings. McKaye confirmed Sumner's mounting concerns over Banks's willingness to accommodate white planters and political conservatives. After only a few days in New Orleans, McKaye expressed his utter dismay at the raging dispute between the free state movement and the Banks faction. While the rural freedmen and the free New Orleanians of color constituted a reliable body of loyal Unionists, he observed, "here, as so often before, the government seems to have repudiated the support of its only earnest and true friends." Amid "the trials of the great revolution," McKaye confided to Sumner, "only the colored people seem entirely sane."[62]

In Washington on March 10, 1864, Roudanez and Bertonneau met with Senator Sumner and Congressman William D. Kelley of Pennsylvania. Sumner had taken a keen interest in the suffrage petition, and the men joined together to revise the document to create a more comprehensive memorandum extending suffrage to all African American males in all regions of the South. Both justice and political expediency, it declared, required that "full effect should be given to all the Union feeling in the rebel States, in order to secure the permanence of the free institutions and loyal governments now organized therein."[63]

Two days later, Roudanez and Bertonneau presented the document to the president. Reportedly, Lincoln listened attentively to the two men, who apparently made a considerable impression on him. The next day, he wrote a letter to Michael Hahn, Louisiana's newly elected governor, to "barely suggest" extending voting rights to "the very intelligent, and especially those who have fought in our ranks." In the February election, Governor Hahn, General Banks's candidate and close friend, won by a wide margin of votes with his opposition to Black suffrage and his assurances to planters of more "stringent and effective vagrant laws" to secure the freedmen's labor. Given his agenda, Hahn "barely" gave serious consideration to Lincoln's suggestion.[64]

After presenting their petition to the president, Roudanez and Bertonneau left the document with Sumner, who presented it to the Senate on March 15. Thereafter, the New Orleanians kept the senator fully informed of the provisional government's treatment of Black Louisianians. Sumner's pioneering commitment to racial equality envisioned equal access to public accommodations, land redistribution to the freedmen, and equal voting rights as a prerequisite for reconstruction. He, like petitioners Roudanez and Bertonneau, looked for a revolutionary change in race relations.

Acting upon an invitation to visit Massachusetts after their meeting with Lincoln, Roudanez and Bertonneau traveled from the nation's capital to the cradle of the American Revolution, where they were greeted with a heroic welcome at Boston's Parker House Hotel. Massachusetts governor John A. Andrew acted as the master of ceremonies at a dinner in their honor attended by abolitionists Frederick Douglass, William Lloyd Garrison, and Wendell Phillips. Roudanez described their meeting with Lincoln and noted that their petition had been laid before the House of Representatives as well as the Senate.

Bertonneau began his remarks with a tribute to General Butler, under whose regime "we had a foretaste of freedom. The colored people of Louisiana venerate his name; with us it is a household word." Under Butler, he continued, "we felt that we were men and citizens, and were to be treated as such; we were animated by new hopes and new desires; we felt that there was a new life opened before us." The Louisianian assured his hosts that when he and Roudanez returned to New Orleans, they would describe to their friends that "in Massachusetts we could ride in every public vehicle; that the colored children not only were allowed to attend public schools with white children, but they were compelled by law to attend such schools; that we visited your courts of justice and saw colored lawyers defending their clients; and we shall tell them, too, of this most generous welcome extended to us by you." Toasts and applause accompanied Bertonneau's speech, and after Garrison stood to praise both visitors, the entire party broke into a loud rendition of "John Brown's Song."[65]

In New Orleans, *l'Union* incurred the wrath of General Banks for its advocacy of suffrage for all Black men regardless of their previous condition. During the summer, Banks retaliated by ordering the army of occupation to halt its subsidy to the South's first African American newspaper. With threats on editor Trévigne's life and white extremists talking openly of destroying *l'Union*'s printing press, Dr. Roudanez bought out his nervous associates and closed down the newspaper. Its final issue appeared on July 19, 1864.

Two days later, another bilingual newspaper, *La Tribune de la Nouvelle-Orléans/New Orleans Tribune* appeared, with Trévigne as its editor and Roudanez as its founder and driving force. Having invested more than $30,000 in the new journal, Roudanez was the *Tribune*'s principal financier. After a new printing press arrived from New York on October 4, the newspaper became the nation's first African American daily and the first in the South to advocate enfranchising the freedmen. Staking everything on universal Black suffrage, the paper looked to congressional intervention.[66]

By the fall of 1864, the suppression of personal liberties, the exploitative nature of the labor regulations, and the realization that strict worker controls were not temporary convinced the *New Orleans Tribune* to repudiate Banks's labor system. With the lapse of the yearly contracts in December, the newspaper warned Black workers against entering into new labor agreements. Banks's "bastard regime" paid freedmen "scarcely enough to put an extra pair of boots on their feet." Comparing the general's contract system with the labor regime on an antebellum plantation, the paper found that if "we except the lash . . . one is unable to perceive any material difference between the two sets of regulations."[67]

Commissioner McKaye's report to Secretary Stanton, *The Mastership and its Fruits*, substantiated the *Tribune*'s charges and validated its political stance. The federal government, he concluded, must ensure the right of the freedman to negotiate his own contracts, possess the power to sue and testify in court, acquire property, bear arms, and enjoy freedom of movement, rights severely curtailed by Banks's provost marshals. The government must also guarantee African Americans "the right to the elective franchise." Otherwise, they would be defenseless with the reestablishment of the civil government. "No such thing," McKaye continued, "as free, democratic society can exist in any country where all the lands are owned by one class of men and are cultivated by another. . . . Upon this foundation stood for a thousand years the feudal aristocracy of France." A successful plan of reconstruction, he concluded, must be founded upon "the ultimate division of the great plantations into moderate-sized farms, to be held and cultivated by the labor of their owners." He considered this "of the utmost importance."[68]

Afro-Creole New Orleanians with ancestral roots in Haiti were wholly familiar with McKaye's line of argument. Haitian president Alexandre Pétion enjoyed a reputation as "the founder of rural democracy" for his dismantling of the colonial plantation system. During his presidency, laws enacted in 1809 and 1814 codified his distribution of the confiscated estates as "national gifts" to the officers, citizen-soldiers, and laborers of the Haitian republic.

In the project, nearly 250,000 acres of confiscated plantations were divided into mostly sixty- to one hundred–acre plots. By the 1830s, not one plantation remained intact, with nineteenth-century Haiti possessing the lowest percentage of landless workers of any island nation in the Caribbean. Like Pétion, the *Tribune's* Afro-Creole leadership staked their claim to political stability and economic equity on the democratization of land ownership through the distribution of confiscated plantation lands to the freedmen. Their insistence began with the military occupation of the city in 1862 and persisted even after the *Tribune's* demise in 1870.[69]

The provisional government's contract labor system, as well as its refusal to extend even limited voting rights to Black Louisianians, doomed the new regime's prospects for congressional approval. Despite Lincoln's strenuous efforts to achieve recognition of the Louisiana delegation in the winter of 1864–1865, he could not overcome his opponents. Senator Sumner's unyielding opposition to the Banks government's labor policies and suffrage position led him to filibuster against congressional acceptance. Almost single-handedly, Sumner prevented the Senate from approving the president's Reconstruction policy in Louisiana.

After Congress voted on January 31, 1865, to pass the Thirteenth Amendment abolishing slavery, the Black community bustled with activity. The Third African Church of New Orleans began organizing and sponsoring farmer co-operatives. At the same time, the interracial Freedmen's Aid Association set out to supply the freedmen with the necessary capital on an interest-free basis. Determined to make emancipation a reality for Black Louisianians, the members of the benevolent organization proposed to buy land from the government and lease it to voluntary associations of farmworkers. The formerly enslaved, the *Tribune* insisted, "are entitled by a paramount right to the possession of the soil they have so long cultivated. . . . If the Government will not give them the land, let it be rented to them."

On March 3, 1865, in the midst of the drive for a cooperative economic model, President Lincoln signed legislation creating the Bureau of Refugees, Freedmen, and Abandoned Lands. In addition to distributing life-sustaining necessities to the war's refugees, the legislation directed the new bureau's director to assign every male freedman and white refugee a tract of up to forty acres of confiscated land. The tracts were to be rented for three years on favorable terms with an option to purchase the land within the three-year period.[70]

On April 14, a little over a month after he had approved the Freedmen's Bureau, President Lincoln was assassinated and Andrew Johnson assumed the office of the presidency. Johnson's political ambitions centered on his determination to win the 1868 presidential election. He courted northern Democrats and moved to reconstitute the South's Democratic Party by restoring the planter elite to political and economic dominance. The Freedmen's Bureau became a key instrument of his electoral ambitions.

In his May 29 Amnesty Proclamation, Johnson offered full pardons to all former Confederates who would pledge their allegiance to the national government. By the fall, Johnson had pardoned all but a handful of ex-Confederates. Confiscated lands slated for agrarian reform—lands designated to fund the Freedmen's Bureau—were returned to their former owners. Finally, the president directed bureau officials to help planters round up freedmen to work on their restored estates. Whereas the *Tribune* had envisioned "both banks of the Mississippi River peopled by . . . well-armed and well-drilled cultivators, from the Gulf of Mexico to Cairo [Illinois]; men of unquestioned and unquestionable loyalty to the 'old flag,'" Johnson looked to the status quo ante.

The new president's political strategy produced overwhelming Democratic victories in November elections throughout the South. In Louisiana's fall balloting, so many Confederate veterans won legislative seats that the state assembly in New Orleans, Louisiana's capital from 1862 to 1879, became known as the Rebel Legislature. The doorkeeper wore a Confederate uniform and state legislators passed Black Codes that reduced the freedmen to a condition of near slavery. The city government was as overwhelmingly Confederate as the state legislature. The newly elected mayor, John T. Monroe, had been removed from the same office under General Butler when he refused to swear allegiance to the Union. The mayor's new police chief, former Confederate colonel Thomas E. Adams, later testified under oath that two-thirds of his 550 officers were Confederate veterans.[71]

With encouragement from President Johnson, the large population of Confederate veterans who returned to the state looked to the restoration of the antebellum society they had left behind. Decommissioned Black soldiers, on the other hand, aspired to enfranchisement as a reward for putting their lives on the line in the service of their country. Upon their return to Louisiana, they joined the largest population of African American veterans in the South, in a state where the 1860 Black population approximated the number of whites. Black suffrage raised the prospects for revolutionary political change. In New Orleans, however, when African Americans and their allies rallied in anticipation of a biracial democracy, ex-Confederate policemen and firemen stopped them dead in their tracks.[72]

EIGHT

Reconstruction and Coup d'État

As to myself and my people . . . we simply ask to be allowed an equal chance in the race of life; an equal opportunity of supporting our families, of educating our children, and of becoming worthy citizens of this government.
—Lieutenant Governor Oscar J. Dunn, July 13, 1868

This chapter begins with the 1866 New Orleans Massacre, when scores of Black New Orleanians petitioning for voting rights suffered a deadly attack by ex-Confederate city police and firemen. The bloody assault and violence throughout the South prompted military occupation and the ratification of the Fourteenth Amendment providing for Black suffrage. Under congressional Reconstruction, African American Louisianians moved aggressively to secure equal access to political office, the jury box, the school room, and all places of public accommodation. Driven by aspirations for freedom and a protest tradition with deep roots in the revolutionary Atlantic, their civil rights campaign proved remarkably successful.

Betrayed by unscrupulous Republicans, an unrelenting campaign of white supremacist terror, and the US Supreme Court, Black southerners saw their aspirations for equal citizenship dashed in the contested presidential election of 1876. The following spring, a coup d'état in New Orleans ended prospects for a representative democracy.

In the 1880s, the city's veteran and fledgling civil rights activists fought back. When their legal challenge to state-enforced segregation failed in Louisiana, they advanced their case to the US Supreme Court, where they suffered a devastating defeat in the 1896 *Plessy v. Ferguson* decision. Led by the determined twentieth-century Afro-Creole heirs of the Civil War and Reconstruction civil rights movement, Black New Orleanians would resume their campaign to achieve a truly democratic republic in the twentieth century.

* * *

On the morning of July 30, 1866, hundreds of enthusiastic "black men, women, and children dressed in their Sunday best" gathered outside the New Orleans Mechanics' Institute, the Louisiana statehouse at the time, to show their support for Black suffrage. Inside the hall, white Unionists prepared to reconvene the 1864 constitutional convention to petition for Black suffrage in a challenge to ex-Confederate control of state government, the Rebel Legislature. At the same time, approximately two hundred Black veterans of the Union army, members of the Native Guard regiments, formed into marching columns in the city's downriver Third District, where free Black New Orleanians were concentrated. Led by a flag bearer, a drummer, and a fife player, they marched through the French Quarter and across Canal Street to the convention hall. As they advanced, they gathered followers along the way.

By the time, they reached the Mechanics' Institute at noon, a crowd of 1,500 white civilians and police lined the streets. When the procession reached the front doors of the Institute, infuriated whites threw bricks at the men, who threw them back. Upon entering the hall, where as many as forty white participants and nearly 150 Black had spectators gathered, the marchers barricaded the entranceway. Police broke through and targeted well-known white and Black leaders. Ex-Confederate policemen and firemen continued the cold-blooded murder of defenseless civilians both inside and outside the hall for two hours. According to a conservative estimate, thirty-eight were killed and 184 were wounded. Of the white attackers, twenty-two were injured and one died of sunstroke.[1]

Arnold Bertonneau escaped the Institute and hid in an adjacent lot, where the mob discovered him. Mistaking him for a white man, a policeman defended him, saving his life. Another member of the *Tribune* faction, Jean-Charles Houzeau, the newspaper's editor at the time and a Belgian Forty-Eighter, also survived the attack. He escaped to the street, where a Black New Orleanian in a nearby residence recognized him and sheltered him in his home. From his hiding place, Houzeau heard the shout, "To the *Tribune!*"

At the newspaper's offices, however, a company of Black soldiers guarded the journal's office. In the immediate aftermath of the attack, Houzeau and his colleagues kept the newspaper's press running, publishing their eyewitness accounts of the assault. One victim of the violence, a former slave, expressed outrage that police and the white mob had "murdered our friends in their own yards, in the presence of their own family, and yet our civil government is still running, and the murderers are still allowed to roam our streets undisturbed. We submit to it, and [are] ruled by a man [Mayor John T. Monroe] that was a rebel when Gen. Butler came here, and is a rebel yet." At the time of the attack, the *Tribune* was the only newspaper recording events from the perspective of the convention's victims. To ensure that northerners heard those voices, "Thousands of *Tribunes*," the newspaper reported, "have been taken by our Unionists to be sent at the North."[2]

Two months earlier, in May, a quarrel between two hack drivers, one Black and the other white, exploded into three days of racial violence in Memphis when demobilized Black soldiers and local whites took sides in the dispute. Rioting Irish policemen and firemen invaded the city's Black neighborhoods, burning hundreds of homes, schools, and churches. When the rampage ended, forty-eight Blacks and two whites lay dead. Both riots shocked northerners, but events in New Orleans, the South's largest city, convinced voters that Johnson's restoration plan was a tragic failure. The bloodshed, together with the president's appalling response to the disasters, resulted in landslide victories in midterm November elections. Republicans retained their two-thirds majorities in both houses of Congress. Led by Pennsylvanian Thaddeus Stevens in the House of Representatives and Massachusetts Senator Charles Sumner, congressional Republicans set a course for Reconstruction by constitutional amendment.

In the 1867 Reconstruction Acts, the Congress nullified the existing southern governments in the ten unreconstructed states and divided them into five militarily occupied districts. Under congressional Reconstruction, federal troops returned South to oversee new state constitutional conventions elected by all adult males, Black and white, excluding those ex-Confederates disqualified by the Fourteenth Amendment. Convention delegates were to adopt new constitutions providing for Black suffrage and to ratify the Fourteenth Amendment defining African Americans and all other native-born or naturalized people as citizens. Upon states' achievement of these requirements, their state representatives would be readmitted to Congress. After Grant's election to the presidency in 1868, Congress would undertake to ensure the future of Black suffrage throughout the nation in a Fifteenth Amendment forbidding states from denying the right to vote on the grounds of race, color, or previous condition. The Fourteenth and Fifteenth Amendments were ratified in July 1868 and March 1870, respectively.[3]

With the return of the US Army to Louisiana in March, community activists accelerated their civil rights campaign. In April, Dr. Roudanez's *Tribune* inaugurated the new movement by insisting on equal access to political office, the franchise, the jury box, the schoolroom, and public conveyances. An editorial demanded action from their purported allies: "All these discriminations that had slavery at the bottom, have become nonsense. It behooves those who understand the new era, and who feel bold enough to shake off the old prejudice and to confront their prejudiced associates, to show their hands, and gain the friendship of the colored population of this State."[4]

Within two weeks of the commentary, the city's Black community launched a full-scale assault on segregated streetcars. Racial tensions approached a flash point as Black passengers forced their way onto cars set aside for whites. On May 7, a massive crowd of Black New Orleanians gathered at Congo Square and "liberated" a white streetcar. They forced the driver to chauffeur them back and forth in front of the cheering crowd. After meeting with federal authorities, railroad executives agreed to dispense with the segregated rail coaches and instructed drivers to permit riders of all colors to ride the cars. Mass resistance had produced a victory on the city's public conveyances that endured until the Louisiana legislature segregated the streetcars once again after the 1896 *Plessy v. Ferguson* Supreme Court decision.

By the time of the Congo Square triumph, the *Tribune* was at the height of its influence. After its 1864 debut, the newspaper attracted national and international attention, with excerpts and references from its pages appearing in newspapers across the North, including the *New York Times*, the *Liberator*, the *Chicago Tribune*, the *Philadelphia Inquirer*, and many others. Internationally, it was particularly popular in French-speaking Europe and the Caribbean. In 1867, when Congress proposed to assign contracts to two newspapers in each southern state to print official government documents, a competition ensued.

The lucrative designations brought increased circulation, influence, and revenue. In Congress, an intense debate challenged the *Tribune*'s application, until Representative Benjamin Butler intervened: "Select whatever other newspaper you want provided that you give me my Black newspaper." An exception was made by allowing Louisiana three contracts, with two assigned to white newspapers and one to the *Tribune*. In an April 11 letter, the newspaper received notification of its recognition as an "Official Journal of the United States Government."[5]

A few months later, on July 30, the *Tribune* organized a memorial at the

Mechanics' Institute for the victims of the attack the year before, with a program attuned to the sensibilities of Spiritualists and Catholics. Claude Paschal Maistre, a French priest and high-profile advocate of equal rights, began the solemn ceremony with a Requiem Mass, after which Rufus Waples, an attorney injured in the assault, addressed the audience. Next, Cora L. V. Hatch, a literary artist and celebrated Spiritualist lecturer, read a poem she authored for the occasion, "In Memoriam—July 30," commemorating those who lost their lives in the massacre.

Hatch's husband, Nathan W. Daniels, a close ally of the city's Afro-Creole leadership, accompanied his wife to the service. After Banks had ousted him from the army, Daniels moved to the nation's capital, where he met with President Lincoln, General Butler, Colonel Stafford, and Robert Dale Owen, a member with James McKaye of the American Freedmen's Inquiry Commission. As committed abolitionists and reformers, Daniels and his wife campaigned for the Freedmen's Bureau and equal rights for African Americans. At the same time, Daniels wrote articles for the *National Anti-Slavery Standard* and the *Tribune*, keeping New Orleanians abreast of Reconstruction politics in the House of Representatives and the Senate.

In Washington, Daniels and Hatch were frequent and popular speakers at Black churches and meetinghouses. Hatch expressed her pride in Daniels's presentation at Asbury Methodist Church on February 23, 1866: "My darling husband addressed them [the Black congregants] on the 'Rights, Qualifications and Injustices of the Color'd Freemen of America' relating his personal experience among them as citizen and soldier—declaring that their rights were the same as our own and their qualifications equal."[6]

As devout Spiritualists, the couple remained active in the movement, reaching out to believers in Washington and attending séances. In March 1865, Daniels accepted an invitation to attend a séance in the Green Room of the White House with Mary Todd Lincoln for the purpose of communicating with her son, William "Willie" Lincoln, who died in 1862 at the age of eleven. Both Daniels and Hatch were born in upstate New York. While Hatch's father, David W. Scott, acted upon his dream of building a utopian community, his eleven-year-old daughter refined her skills as a Spiritualist trance lecturer, and by the age of fourteen she had developed into a celebrity medium. She was in her twenties when she met Daniels. On May 29, 1867, after Daniels was assigned a government post in Reconstruction Louisiana, he, his wife, and their one-year-old daughter, Henrietta "Etta" Daniels, arrived in the city.

In the fall, yellow fever struck with a vengeance, claiming 3,320 lives and taking an unknown toll in rural areas. After General Butler's departure from the city, his successful cleanup program was allowed to lapse, and Daniels perished in the ensuing disaster, on October 1. Two weeks later, Louis A. Snaër, a veteran officer of the First Native Guard, reported the death of Daniels's toddler, Henrietta, to the authorities. Etta's grief-stricken mother contracted the disease but survived. Cora Hatch returned North to become one of the nineteenth century's most famous mediums and trance lecturers.

A *Tribune* obituary on October 3 expressed its profound regret at the loss of Daniels's leadership, emphasizing his role as a US Army officer, when "hundreds of our friends served with him under his command" and were acquainted with "his noble character and his perfect sense of the equality and rights of men." Politically, the essay continued, his death was a devastating blow: "Scarcely a greater loss could befall the liberal party at this time." After his arrival in Louisiana, Daniels had immersed himself in Republican politics and the *Tribune* had looked to him as an important ally in November's 1867 constitutional convention.[7]

Throughout the summer, Louisiana's military commander, General Philip H. Sheridan, had enrolled Black and white voters in anticipation of elections for delegates to the convention. The September balloting resulted in the fifty Black delegates and forty-eight whites who met the following month at the Mechanics' Institute to write a new Louisiana state constitution. With its first meeting in November, the Louisiana convention was the first major elective body in the history of the South to be dominated by a Black majority.

Within the Republican Party, politically sophisticated and aggressive African Americans constituted the most radical faction, with a leadership that included Dr. Roudanez, Oscar J. Dunn, Paul Trévigne, P. B. S. Pinchback, and James H. Ingraham, among others. Four months ahead of the convention, Roudanez's *Tribune* proclaimed voting rights and education the two paramount objectives for Black Louisianians. The resulting charter exceeded the newspaper's demands. Article 100 required every state official to take an oath to "accept the civil and political equality of all men, and agree not to attempt to deprive any person or persons, on account of race, color, or previous condition, of any political or civil right, privilege, or immunity enjoyed by any other class of men."[8]

James H. Ingraham, a former lieutenant in the First Native Guard who was promoted for bravery at the battle of Port Hudson, led his fellow delegates in drafting a constitutional Bill of Rights, the first in Louisiana's history. It declared the equality of all men, and Article 13 guaranteed all citizens "equal rights and privileges upon any conveyance of a public character; and all places of business or of public resort." A rider defined "places of a public character" as all businesses requiring a state, parish, or city license to operate. P. B. S. Pinchback, an officer in the Second Native Guard regiment who had resigned in 1863 with other Black officers under pressure from Banks, drafted the final version of Article 13. The proposed public education resolutions resulted in Article 135 in the final constitution. The measure represented the most ambitious effort to desegregate schools attempted anywhere in any southern state during Reconstruction. It prohibited "separate schools or institutions of learning established exclusively for any race by the State of Louisiana." The provision directed the state legislature to provide for the establishment in each parish of at least one free public school open to all people between the ages of six and twenty-one, regardless of their race.

Owing to the aggressive stance, republican idealism, and tough-minded determination of Black delegates, the new constitution exceeded the *Tribune*'s expectations and represented a monumental victory for Black Louisianians. With its Bill of Rights requiring public officials to swear to their belief in racial equality, and its prohibition of segregation in all places of public accommodation, Louisiana's state constitution represented the South's most visionary blueprint for change.[9]

The subsequent 1868 Reconstruction legislature would strike another blow for freedom and justice by repealing laws prohibiting interracial marriage. Louisiana's 1808 civil code had prohibited such unions, and a subsequent 1831 statute barred the legitimation of a mixed-race child under any circumstances. Categorized as bastards, such children could not inherit from either parent. In antebellum Louisiana, the anti-miscegenation laws and the legal ostracism of racially mixed children signified the imposition of a two-category pattern of racial classification that reduced all free people of African descent to a degraded status. The reconstructed Louisiana legislature overturned those egregious social, economic, and legal disabilities.[10]

On January 4, 1868, when Republicans convened to nominate candidates for an April election, the Radical Republican faction led by Roudanez insisted on a Black nominee for governor. Their choice, Major François Dumas, prevailed on the first ballot by four votes. After the lowest three candidates were eliminated, the second ballot pitted Dumas against Henry Clay Warmoth, an

Illinois-born regimental commander during the war and an heir to the Banks faction. Dumas lost by only two votes, 45 to 43. But even before the balloting began, Dumas's nomination was doomed.

The white Republican operatives who controlled the levers of power within the party had already assured Warmoth's victory. When the triumphant Warmoth offered Dumas the nomination for lieutenant governor, Dumas declined and ran instead for the office on a rival ticket. When the *Tribune* refused to support the Republican ticket, the party's executive committee expelled nine Roudanez loyalists and replaced the *Tribune* with the pro-Warmoth *Republican* as the government's official journal. Once again, Republican conservatives silenced the Black newspaper. Lacking financial support, the *Tribune* temporarily ceased regular publication on April 25.

Largely owing to the huge majority of Black Louisianians who registered to vote, the constitution was ratified in elections on April 17 and 18, 1868. In balloting for state officials, voters elected Warmoth governor for his advocacy of civil and political equality for Louisiania freedmen and his denunciation of their former enslavers. The popular and influential New Orleanian Oscar J. Dunn, a US officer during the war, won election to the post of lieutenant governor. Dunn, like Dumas, Pinchback, and other Black officers, had resigned from the US military owing to discrimination. His victory in the spring 1868 election made Dunn the first Black in the nation's history to hold that office. Republicans also won control of both houses of the state legislature.[11]

From the beginning of congressional Reconstruction, Louisiania was the only state where African Americans held more than one major office at the highest levels of state government. Lieutenant Governor Dunn would go on to become the first African American to serve as acting governor of a state. Both Pinchback and C. C. Antoine served as lieutenant governors, with Pinchback, like Dunn, later serving as acting governor. New Jersey–born and Jamaican-educated William G. Brown served as the superintendent of education from 1873 to 1877. Afro-Creole Louisianian Antoine Dubuclet, a wealthy planter and skilled financier, was one of only two Blacks to serve as state treasurer. Remarkably, both Republicans and Democrats respected him for his honesty throughout the ten-year period of Reconstruction. Dubuclet's two Paris-educated sons, influential Spiritualist medium François Louis "Petit" Dubuclet and Auguste Dubuclet, held the state treasury offices of chief clerk and assistant clerk, respectively, during their father's entire tenure.

Henri-Louis Rey, François Dubuclet's fellow medium in the Spiritualist

Cercle Harmonique and a veteran officer of the Native Guard regiment, was elected by New Orleanians to represent them in Louisiana's house of representatives. He was among the ninety-five legislators and thirty-two African American senators who served in state government between 1868 and 1896. Like Dubuclet, Rey assumed a key post in the new government. In Louisiana as in Mississippi and Alabama, African American representatives constituted a larger portion of the first Reconstruction legislatures, and those numbers grew over time. For ardent Spiritualists Rey and Dubuclet, slavery's abolition and Reconstruction's Black male suffrage betokened the arrival of the spirit world's egalitarian republic. For white supremacist Democrats, congressional Reconstruction was an abomination. They resolved to destroy it.[12]

They organized covertly and massively in paramilitary societies like the Ku Klux Klan and embarked upon a reign of terror in the run-up to the November 1868 presidential election. Louisiana became an epicenter of violence as a tidal wave of lawlessness swept the state. Armed marauders intent upon restoring white supremacy by any means terrorized mostly Black Republicans in a series of horrendous massacres beginning in May.

During the summer months in Franklin Parish, sources reported that white supremacist vigilantes killed somewhere between 150 and 300 of the Republican regime's supporters. In St. Landry Parish, a white mob invaded the plantations and killed as many as two hundred Black workers. In October, white mobs roamed the streets of New Orleans, breaking up Republican gatherings and attacking participants. From Orleans Parish, the violence spread to neighboring St. Bernard and Jefferson Parishes. Between September 22 and election day, at least sixty people, mostly Black, were killed in the three parishes.

The terrorist attacks succeeded. Fearing that attempts to encourage Black voting would result in further bloodshed, Louisiana Republicans abandoned the presidential campaign. Lieutenant Governor Dunn later testified in a congressional hearing that he was threatened with violence and didn't venture outdoors at night. He didn't vote himself and remained at a loss as to how he should counsel his fearful supporters. Major General Philip H. Sheridan, who had commanded forces in Louisiana and Texas during Reconstruction, later estimated that 1,880 Louisianians were killed or wounded in 1868. For his active assistance to the fledgling Reconstruction governments, President Andrew Johnson removed Sheridan from his command in 1867, thereby contributing to the carnage.[13]

Within three months of taking office, in June 1868, Governor Warmoth vetoed a bill designed to enforce Article 13 of the constitution providing for equal access to public accommodations. When the state legislature passed another bill, in 1870, providing for criminal prosecution of civil rights violations, Warmoth vetoed that measure as well. The governor and his superintendent of education, Thomas W. Conway, resisted the desegregation of New Orleans public schools and succeeded in maintaining segregated rural schools. At the same time, Warmoth curried favor with white conservatives by appointing white supremacist Democrats to political offices and set about amassing a personal fortune by "exacting tribute" from railroad companies. Though brief, Warmoth's tenure in office would amount to one of the most corrupt administrations in Louisiana history.[14]

In an effort to fortify Louisiana Republicans by appointing reliable loyalists to federal posts, President Grant reached out to Lieutenant Governor Dunn for guidance. In the nation's capital, Dunn met with Grant on April 2, 1869, in a private half-hour exchange in which the two men discussed federal appointments in New Orleans. Dunn's visit marked the first time that an elective African American official had visited the White House. Afterwards, Dunn met with Charles Sumner, who invited him onto the Senate floor. From Washington, the lieutenant governor continued his political junket to Boston, Philadelphia, and New York City.

Back in Louisiana, Governor Warmoth's actions convinced Louis-Charles Roudanez, Jean-Baptiste Roudanez, and Paul Trévigne to briefly revive the *Tribune* in late 1868. The newspaper promptly attacked the governor as "unfaithful to the principles upon which he was elected." The "odious and unjust restrictions" of segregation "were un-American, un-republican, un-democratic, un-reasonable, and un-Christian." The newspaper urged all Black Louisianians to unite to "throw off a tremendous load which has been our inheritance for centuries." After the state legislature passed enabling legislation in February, the Civil Rights Act of 1869, Warmoth reluctantly signed the measure into law.

Still, obstructionist white supremacists on the New Orleans school board barred the desegregation of the city's public schools. In response, Republican legislators passed an act to reform both the state and city school systems. Under the new authority, education officials disbanded the recalcitrant city school board and the desegregation of the city's public schools began during the 1870–1871 school year. The legislature's extraordinary action made New Orleans the only southern city to desegregate public schools during Reconstruction.[15]

Between 1870 and 1877, according to the best estimates, approximately one-third of the schools remained overwhelmingly white, a third were all-Black, and a third were integrated. Still, the gains made in the desegregation of the urban schools over nearly seven years were truly remarkable by any measure. At a time when few desegregated public schools existed in the North, and virtually none in the South, the city's interracial public school system represented a major triumph in the struggle to revolutionize race relations in Reconstruction Louisiana. In an outstanding example of interracial coexistence, five hundred to one thousand Black children and several thousand white children attended at least nineteen desegregated schools in the spring of 1874.

Despite the resistance of Governor Warmoth and Superintendent Conway, the schools prospered with successful fund-raising, good management, and a substantial group of white businessmen who joined leading Black spokesmen in advocating for school desegregation. The presence of several prominent white southerners on the local school board helped, as in the case of renowned former Confederate general James Longstreet, a close personal friend of President Grant. Longstreet urged the white South to accept emancipation and enfranchisement in a series of widely discussed letters in 1867 in the *New Orleans Times*.[16]

On the school board, Longstreet worked well and conscientiously with fellow Black board members like Henry-Louis Rey, who was appointed in 1873 to a two-year term as the director of the board. Both Longstreet and Rey attended the board's monthly meetings and served together on some of the same visiting and standing committees. According to historian Melissa Daggett, a reading of the school board's minutes reveals Longstreet's genuine interest in the progressive agenda of Afro-Creole leaders like Rey.

The 1872 election of African American William G. Brown to the office of state superintendent of education added to the luster of Louisiana's educational system. The cosmopolitan and well-educated Brown was born in New Jersey and resided in Washington, DC, and Jamaica. He arrived in New Orleans after the war and worked as a teacher and editor of the *New Orleans Louisianian*. In his role as state superintendent, he advocated aggressively for universal education, an effort that culminated in the creation of the Agricultural and Mechanical College supported with federal land grant funds. Before it was moved after 1877 to Baton Rouge and incorporated into all-white Louisiana State University, the college graduated both Black and white students.[17]

Its universalist ethic notwithstanding, the completely segregated New Orleans Catholic school system benefited enormously from the desegregation of the city's public schools. With the onset of school integration in 1870, scores of white parents moved their children to segregated Catholic parochial schools in a dynamic that resulted in an enormous expansion of the Catholic educational system. The number of Catholic schools increased from eleven in 1869 to forty-nine in 1874. In rural Louisiana, public education advanced during Reconstruction, but only when accompanied by segregation.[18]

Warmoth's resistance to school desegregation and civil rights legislation irreversibly damaged his political ties to Lieutenant Governor Dunn, a man widely respected for his integrity and one of the South's most influential Black leaders. Dunn and his Republican allies were likewise alarmed by Warmoth's penchant for appointing white supremacist Democrats to judgeships and other state and local offices. One angry Republican asked Warmoth's ally Superintendent Conway, if the governor "is the staunch Republican you take him to be, why is it that he invariably appoints the most ultra democrats to offices of trust & emolument?" By 1871, Warmoth was estranged from Dunn, President Grant, and nearly every federal officeholder in Louisiana.[19]

In an August 31 letter to Horace Greeley, written less than three months before his death, Dunn didn't mince words in attacking Warmoth's racist policies. In the widely published letter, Dunn complained that the governor "has shown an itching desire . . . to secure the personal support of the Democracy at the expense of his own party, and an equally manifest craving to obtain a cheap and ignoble white respectability by the sacrifice of . . . the masses of that race who elected him." Warmoth was, Dunn continued, "the first Ku Klux Governor" of the Republican Party.

Dunn's message dramatized the split between Warmoth and his Republican opposition centered at the US customhouse. The so-called Custom House faction laid plans to impeach the governor after their August Republican Party convention. The project temporarily stalled when Lieutenant Governor Dunn died unexpectedly on November 22, 1871, dealing a devastating blow to his party and his African American constituents. A number of prominent Black legislators claimed foul play, and an autopsy revealed arsenic in his stomach, but no one was charged. With rumors of Dunn's poisoning gaining momentum and a Black revolt threatening, four of the lieutenant governor's seven doctors published a statement declaring that he died of natural causes. Significantly, Dunn's ally Dr. Roudanez refused to sign the document.[20]

In Warmoth's calculations, Dunn's death served as an opportunity to safe-guard his political position. He acted quickly to fill the lieutenant governor's seat with an ally who could be expected to sidetrack the Custom House faction's effort to impeach him. Thus, the governor orchestrated the election of Pinchback, who was, after Dunn, the most influential Black leader in the state. In his escalating rivalry with the Custom House faction, Warmoth maintained control of the Republican machinery even as his unpopularity mounted. Ultimately recognizing the impossibility of his position, he led his remaining Republican allies into an outlandish alliance with Democrats, an alliance referred to as the Fusionists, to prevent the Custom House faction from gaining control of the state government in the November 4, 1872, election.[21]

In the gubernatorial contest, the Fusionist Democrats nominated Confederate veteran John McEnery, who had commanded troops at Vicksburg. At the war's end, he was elected to Louisiana's Rebel Legislature, where he earned a reputation as a fiery racist who backed the Louisiana's Black Codes. Consistent with his support for state laws designed to reduce freedmen to a condition of virtual slavery, McEnery opposed the Fourteenth Amendment. Warmoth's allies expressed dismay at their colleagues' support for the McEnery ticket, with the New Orleans Republican announcing its opposition in the following terms: "We regard the McEnery ticket as representing the negro-hating, schoolhouse burning, fire-eating Bourbonists. . . . Good these last ditchers cannot learn, and bad they will not forget."[22]

For the November election, Republicans nominated William Pitt Kellogg for governor and C. C. Antoine for lieutenant governor. Kellogg was a Vermont-born veteran of the Civil War who rose to the rank of brigadier general while developing close ties to General Grant. In 1868, he was elected Louisiana's US Senator after being appointed collector of the New Orleans port by President Lincoln. He did not share Warmoth's contempt for Black Louisianians, and his platform endorsed desegregated public schools and accommodations. Candidate Antoine, whose father fought in the Battle of New Orleans, was educated in the city's private schools for Black children. He was an officer in the Civil War in a unit he raised himself, Company I, Seventh Louisiana Infantry. He was a delegate to Louisiana's 1868 constitutional convention and developed close political and business ties to Pinchback. Until the 1872 election, he served in the state senate.[23]

In the November 4 election, both the Republicans and the Democrats claimed victory in a political showdown that lasted for months, with Governor Warmoth exacerbating the crisis at every opportunity. Since Warmoth's term of office didn't end until mid-January 1873, governor-elect Kellogg undertook to remove him from his post. Pinchback, Warmoth's lieutenant governor, proved decisive in unseating the governor by disclosing that Warmoth had offered him a $50,000 bribe to manipulate the legislature. Kellogg included Pinchback's accusation on a list of impeachment charges that resulted in Warmoth's suspension from office on December 9. With Warmoth's removal, Pinchback briefly assumed the office of governor.[24]

On January 14, 1873, William Pitt Kellogg took the oath of office as governor of Louisiana after receiving word of President Grant's de facto recognition. McEnery, however, insisted on the legitimacy of his rival government and attempted a March 5 coup with two hundred white militiamen. General Longstreet, commanding the Louisiana state militia, together with the city's Metropolitan Police and a unit of US Army soldiers, completely routed McEnery's demoralized and wounded mutineers. The Republicans had overcome their internal divisions, dealt their Democratic opponents a humiliating defeat, and won four more years for Louisiana's fledgling multiracial government. The fragility of their achievements soon became apparent, however, as white rage over McEnery's defeat in New Orleans raced through the Louisiana countryside, where the rivalry between Republicans and Democrats played out with deadly consequences.

The fury erupted first in mid-April 1873, in Colfax, the seat of government for Grant Parish on the Red River between Alexandria and Shreveport. After the 1872 election, McEnery's rival government recognized Alphonse Cazabat as Grant Parish judge and Christopher C. Nash as sheriff. In March 1873, after his inauguration, Governor Kellogg named his own appointees to head the Grant Parish government: R. C. Register as judge and Daniel Shaw as sheriff. As in Colfax, rival Kellogg and McEneryite governments faced off against each other throughout the Red River region in the spring of 1873. The powder keg exploded in Colfax after the Kellogg-appointed officials took possession of the Colfax courthouse and refused to yield their authority.

Anticipating an armed coup by the McEnery Democrats, approximately 150 Black Union veterans and militiamen guarded the Kellogg officials in the courthouse. Nash, an ex-rebel officer in General Thomas J. "Stonewall" Jackson's brigade and organizer of the white paramilitary forces at Colfax, was known to US authorities. After the passage of the 1871 Enforcement Act—legislation guided through the US House by Representative Butler and popularly referred to as the Ku Klux Act—General Philip Sheridan arrested Nash during a crackdown on the Klan. In 1872, the roundup of thousands of Klansmen like Nash resulted in the South's most democratic election until 1968. President Grant would later approve Nash's indictment on federal charges of murder and conspiracy for his part in the 1873 Colfax massacre.

In early April 1873, in Colfax, negotiations between the two sides ended when an unarmed Black farmer, Jesse McKinney, working on his fence near Colfax, was shot and killed by a group of white men. Fearful Black families from the surrounding countryside gathered at Colfax for protection. On Easter Sunday, April 13, Nash's well-armed white supremacist force of an estimated three hundred men stormed the courthouse, massacring somewhere between 70 and 165 victims. Either way, the number of those killed was larger than in any other instance of racial violence in US history. Among the victims were twenty-eight to forty-eight unarmed men who were executed after they surrendered. Two whites were killed, probably by friendly fire.

White residents shielded Nash from the ensuing federal dragnet, and in mid-1874 he resurfaced in Natchitoches, Louisiana, at the head of an armed force of approximately one thousand men. The three convictions of massacre participants that the government managed to obtain were overturned in the Supreme Court's 1876 *US v. Cruikshank* decision. Emboldened by the Colfax massacre and enraged by McEnery's failed 1873 coup attempt in New Orleans, in 1874 more than ten thousand white Louisianians joined white supremacist paramilitary companies that came to be called White Leagues.[25]

In the state capital, fire-eating extremists like New Orleanian Dr. Charles Deléry fanned the flames of race hatred and political division in an outpouring of hate-filled verse, pamphlets, and newspaper commentary. After escaping General Butler's wrath at the outset of the city's 1862 military occupation, Deléry, a fierce proponent of states' rights medicine, settled in Paris, where he continued his attacks on the North without fear of censorship or arrest. Upon returning to New Orleans in 1865, he resumed his feud with Dr. Faget, rehashing his prewar yellow fever arguments. Faget's rebuttal set off a continuation of their dispute that would, according to Edward Larocque Tinker, "last as long as the two combatants."[26]

Deléry's homecoming prompted Louisiana's reconstituted Confederate government to designate him the coroner of Orleans Parish. With the onset of congressional Reconstruction, he embarked on a vicious propaganda campaign aimed at destroying Louisiana's Reconstruction state government.

His attacks on the US military once again led to an expulsion order, though a reputed typographical error waylaid its enforcement. Emboldened, Deléry continued to excoriate the federal government and Louisiana's Black political leaders in newspapers and pamphlets.

In his 1877 one-act play, *l'École du Peuple* (The People's School), Deléry singled out C. C. Antoine and P. B. S. Pinchback, two of Louisiana's most influential Black political leaders, for a particularly vile attack. During Reconstruction, both men had served in the offices of lieutenant governor and state senator, with Pinchback also serving as governor. *l'École du Peuple*, written to portray "the most hideous" Reconstruction leaders, was barred from being staged in New Orleans.[27]

Of one mind with his Creole colleague Dr. J. M. Durel, a Confederate surgeon during the Civil War, Deléry submitted his racist diatribes to Durel's *Le Carillon*, a weekly French-language journal founded in 1869 and wholly dedicated to the restoration of white rule. Suffering serious financial losses during the war, Durel staked his remaining financial assets, including his wife's family heirlooms, on launching the journal. In its vile pages, Deléry pilloried President Grant, Governor Henry Clay Warmoth, and Louisiana's first democratically elected biracial legislature. By the time *Le Carillon* ceased publication upon Durel's death in 1875, the doctor had largely achieved his objective. Writing in 1934, Tinker, an admirer of Durel, praised the hate-filled *Le Carillon* for "the important part it played in restoring white supremacy to Louisiana." The journal's success, Tinker continued, "justified the many sacrifices made by the doctor and his wife to keep it alive." In Reconstruction New Orleans, Deléry, Durel, and their white supremacist, fourth estate colleagues fueled the gathering momentum of counterrevolutionary forces.[28]

With the state on the verge of anarchy and economic collapse after the tumultuous election of 1872, the city's white business elite organized the Louisiana Unification Movement and invited Black Louisianians to join them in a political coalition. In a move to discourage white backlash, the leadership chose ex-Confederate general P. T. G. Beauregard, the president of the New Orleans and Carrollton Railroad, as the nominal head of the movement. In June 1873, a committee of one hundred New Orleanians, equally divided between whites and Blacks, met and designated a committee of five whites and five Blacks to formulate an agenda setting forth the reform group's objectives.

The five African American leaders included Dr. Roudanez, Lieutenant Governor C. C. Antoine, and political activist Aristide Mary, a wealthy philanthropist. Judge William Randolph; Auguste Bohn, a bank president and director of the New Orleans Cotton Exchange; and Isaac Marks, the president of one insurance company and the director of another, were among the five white committee members. The motives of the white sponsors were decidedly mixed, though Marks, the ideological creator of the movement, publicly expressed a genuine commitment to racial egalitarianism. "It is my determination, he insisted, "to continue to battle against these abstract, absurd and stupid prejudices, and to bring to bear the whole force of my character . . . to break them down. They must disappear; *they will disappear.*"[29]

In return for their support, Black committee members negotiated remarkable concessions. The unifiers approved a report published in New Orleans newspapers on June 17 pledging to guarantee Black civil and political rights. It accepted an equal distribution of political offices between the races, and it sanctioned the desegregation of all places of public accommodation, including schools, factories, and transit carriers. The agreement even promised to consider the breakup of large landholdings into small farms so that "our colored citizens and white emigrants may become practical farmers and cultivators of the soil." Roudanez's newspapers had been pressing for just such a land distribution policy for the freedmen since the 1863 Emancipation Proclamation.[30]

The unifiers urged "the rapid removal of all prejudices heretofore existing against the colored citizens of Louisiana" and called upon all Louisianians to "join and cooperate with us in erecting this monument to unity, concord & justice and like ourselves forever bury beneath it all past prejudices on the subject of race or color." The unification platform won significant support from white New Orleanians until Roudanez, Mary, Antoine, and other Black leaders publicly withheld their backing of home rule until "the existing opposition against the enjoyment of our rights . . . shall have ceased." The July statement formally ended the short-lived Unification Movement.[31]

In the state's rural districts, the mounting white supremacist insurgency ruled out any real chance of an interracial coalition. In New Orleans, Dr. Durel's hate-filled *Le Carillon* with contributors like Dr. Deléry did its part to encourage the city's racist insurgents. In a July 13 editorial entitled "On One Side or the Other," the Francophone newspaper delivered an ominous ultimatum demanding allegiance to a whites-only Louisiana:

The moment has come to say what the sons of Louisiana desire: One must be WHITE OR BLACK, each person must decide. Two races are present: one superior, the other inferior . . . their separation is *absolutely* necessary. Let us separate, from today on, into two well distinct Parties: the WHITE PARTY and the BLACK PARTY. The stance will then be clear: the white Louisiana or the black Louisiana. . . . It is only under the folds of the white men's flag that Louisiana can be saved.[32]

The news from the nation's capital was equally alarming. On April 14, 1873, the day after the Colfax massacre, the US Supreme Court issued a Fourteenth Amendment ruling in the *Slaughterhouse Cases*. The case originated in New Orleans, where butchers opposed health regulations detrimental to their economic interests. In the ruling, the court rejected the butchers' plea but went on to make a sharp distinction between national and state citizenship. The Fourteenth Amendment, the court maintained, protected only those rights that originated in the federal government, namely, the ability to run for federal office, protection on the high seas, and other activities remote from the interests of most freedmen. The amendment, Justice Samuel F. Miller maintained, had "nothing to do" with most of the rights of citizens.

The fundamental authority over citizens' rights rested with the states. The court's reasoning called into question the constitutionality of the federal government's ability to protect Black civil rights. After *Slaughterhouse*, the prospects for legal proceedings under the Enforcement Acts of 1870 and 1871 were so grim that Grant's Justice Department ordered a halt to Ku Klux Klan prosecutions for much of 1872 and 1873.[33]

In New Orleans in the ensuing months, white supremacist excitement surged at news of the *Slaughterhouse* decision. Attorneys for the nine white Colfax defendants immediately seized upon the Supreme Court's decision to build a case for their clients. In the first Colfax trial, held in the city in February 1874, the defendants' attorneys denied the constitutionality of the Ku Klux Klan Act under which the men had been charged. When federal prosecutor J. R. Beckwith won conviction of William Cruikshank and the other two men, their attorney appealed in the federal courts, citing the *Slaughterhouse* verdict.

On June 27, Justice Joseph P. Bradley voided the indictments of the three men in an action that would lead to the 1876 *United States v. Cruikshank* Supreme Court decision. Observing white reaction to the unfolding events in the city, Governor Kellogg observed that the "opinion of Judge [Joseph] Bradley was hailed with the wildest demonstrations of approval; it was regarded as establishing the principle that hereafter no white man could be punished for killing a negro, and as virtually wiping the Ku-Klux laws off the statute books." Building on the logic of *Slaughterhouse*, the *Cruikshank* decision did just that by gutting the Fourteenth Amendment of protections. According to scholar Eric Foner, the decision "gave a green light to acts of terror where local officials either could not or would not enforce the law."[34]

Across Louisiana, white supremacists readily grasped the "green light" implications of the *Slaughterhouse* decision. Paramilitary White League companies mushroomed across the state, under the leadership of a phalanx of Confederate veterans. By August 1874, active White Leagues with as many as fourteen thousand men embarked upon a campaign of terror to force the resignations of local Republican officeholders. In New Orleans, Frederick N. Ogden created the Crescent City White League. Ogden was an ex-Confederate officer who fought during the war under Nathan Bedford Forrest, infamous for the massacre of several dozen Black prisoners at Fort Pillow, Tennessee. By the fall, Ogden commanded a force of more than 1,500 men who drilled openly in the state capital's streets in New Orleans. Eighty-eight percent of the 111 White League officers in the city's 1874 coup attempt, the so-called Battle of New Orleans, were Confederate veterans with extensive combat experience.[35]

On Monday, September 14, on the steps of the Clay statue on Canal Street, attorney R. H. Marr, the lead defense lawyer for the Colfax defendants, harangued a mass gathering of an estimated two thousand to five thousand angry white men demanding Governor Kellogg's immediate resignation. Before leaving the podium, Marr directed his frenzied audience to retrieve their arms and assert the will of Louisiana whites. For some observers, the scene in New Orleans recalled Paris in 1870, under siege during the Franco-Prussian War.

At the French Quarter statehouse (the St. Louis Hotel), General Longstreet ordered the interracial Metropolitan Police of five hundred men to march from Jackson Square to Canal Street with the objective of dispersing the rally and securing control of the city. At the same time, he assigned a defensive force of approximately 475 Black militiamen to guard the governor in the statehouse. As Longstreet's Metropolitans advanced, Governor Kellogg abandoned his office and retreated to the safety of the impregnable customhouse and a contingent of US troops.

When Longstreet's forces reached Canal Street with the objective of dispersing the crowd, White League companies concentrated at both ends of the boulevard (near the Clay statue at one end and the river levee at the other) opened fire. When the insurgents seriously injured commanding officers

Longstreet and General Algernon S. Badger, the Metropolitans faltered and then retreated to the St. Louis Hotel and the state arsenal adjacent to the Cabildo. The triumphant White League installed ex-Confederate officer D. B. Penn, a McEnery ally, as governor. By that time, the insurrectionary forces occupied most of the city, after a battle that left scores of men dead or wounded.

The next day, when state treasurer Dubuclet was denied entry to his office by a White League sentry, he returned home. When insurgent governor Penn learned of the incident, he "ordered one of his aides to go to Dubuclet's residence in his, the Governor's carriage, and apologize to Mr. Dubuclet for the unintentional rudeness of the sentinel." In the coup, Dubuclet and his two clerks, his sons François and Auguste, were the only top officials allowed to return to their duties without interruption. One of Penn's first three proclamations as "acting governor" addressed "the colored people of Louisiana," assuring them of their safety and their rights. Penn's proclamation and his courteous treatment of Dubuclet were intended to maintain calm among Black Louisianians.[36]

The day after the Canal Street battle, President Grant issued a proclamation ordering all "turbulent and disorderly persons" to disperse. On September 17, federal troops arrived in the city to enforce the president's decree. Two days later, Governor Kellogg returned to his office in the St. Louis Hotel. Over the next few weeks, three federal infantry regiments, a battery of artillery, a naval flotilla, and detachments of marines under the overall command of Lieutenant General Philip Sheridan swept aside the rebel government. The White League's bloody coup attempt, though only temporarily successful, emboldened opponents of the multiracial government. The city's white supremacists took aim at a more vulnerable target, the city's public schools.[37]

In December, so-called boy regulators took to the streets in a campaign to force the resegregation of the city schools. The gangs of white youth, "boys" whom observers described as not so young, invaded school classrooms and demanded the expulsion of all students they identified as Black. The New Orleans Bulletin, a staunch supporter of the White League, goaded the invaders on with editorials demanding a return to segregated schools and streetcars.

Intimidation, threats, and physical assaults notwithstanding, Black students remained in predominantly white schools in relatively large numbers. From five hundred to a thousand Black children were enrolled in desegregated schools before the attempted 1874 coup. After the violent clash, more than three hundred children remained in the city's schools until the end of

Reconstruction. Calculated on a yearly average, approximately five hundred African American boys and girls attended school with white classmates for nearly seven years.[38]

Yet the gains in interracial education in New Orleans lasted only so long as federal troops remained in the city. The collapse of Reconstruction and the Democratic takeover of state government resulted in disastrous changes in education. In April, the new governor, white supremacist Francis T. Nicholls, immediately created a Democrat-dominated school board intent on resegregating the public schools. Their actions ended the "only serious experiment with public school integration in the postwar South." However, by the time the city's interracial school system collapsed in 1877, the handwriting had already been written large on the walls of Congress.[39]

In Washington on February 3, 1875, US Representative Benjamin Butler took to the floor to champion Charles Sumner's Civil Rights Act, a measure the Massachusetts senator had advocated up the time of his death in 1874. Sumner conceived the legislation as completing the work of Reconstruction by expanding civil rights from the ballot box to the public domain where Americans lived their daily lives. Initially, Sumner's supplementary Civil Rights Act of May 1870 guaranteed citizens throughout the nation equal access to public accommodations. The bill, historian Philip Dray explains, provided that "no public inns or places of public amusement for which a license was needed, no railroads or stage lines, charities or cemeteries, no churches or jury boxes, and no schools supported at public expense should make any distinction as to admission on account of race, color, or previous condition of servitude."[40]

At the 1870 debut of the Civil Rights Act, Paul Trévigne and the Roudanez brothers applauded the senator's bill, immediately assuring him that his initiative "has been gratefully received by the whole colored population here and deserves the thanks of all friends of human rights through the world for it is the very thing which is needed to ensure the triumph of Republicanism over the narrow tyranny of prejudice. Our only hope now is in National legislation[;] we therefore thank you for your noble initiative." Their hopes were dashed.[41]

After Congress had shorn the act of its provisions for equal rights in schools, churches, and cemeteries, President Grant signed "Sumner's law" on March 1, 1875. By then, the Republican Party had lost the House of Representatives in the 1874 congressional elections and Louisiana Republicans had lost a crucial ally in Washington, Benjamin Butler. The Civil Rights Act wasn't enforced in the South and the Supreme Court ruled it unconstitutional in 1883. Its provisions did not become federal law until the civil rights legislation of the 1960s.[42]

In the face of an unrelenting campaign of terror, northern resolve faltered. Frustrated by its inability to subdue an unrepentant and hostile South, the North turned its attention from the plight of southern Blacks to national reconciliation and economic expansion. In the contested presidential election of 1876, outgoing Republican president Grant urged an end to the crisis, with a call for "peace at any price." During the crisis, Democrats agreed to halt their opposition to the presidency of Republican Rutherford B. Hayes in return for the withdrawal of federal troops from the South. Hayes agreed, signaling Reconstruction's demise. The white-ruled South immediately undertook to inaugurate and fortify a caste system of racial repression based on segregation, exclusion, disfranchisement, economic servility, and the ever-present threat of violence.

On April 24, 1877, Rutherford B. Hayes, the newly inaugurated Republican president, ordered the withdrawal of the last remaining federal troops from New Orleans, the capital of the South's last Republican state government. Confronted in the city by nearly four thousand white supremacist militiamen commanded by former Confederate general Francis T. Nicholls, Stephen B. Packard, the Republican state governor, fled in the 1877 coup d'état. In the last of the major street battles waged during the "uncivil war" in New Orleans from 1866 to 1877, counterrevolutionary forces finally prevailed. On April 25, 1877, General Nicholls's takeover of the statehouse in New Orleans marked the end of Reconstruction in the city, the state, and the nation.[43]

In the end, the national government's support for biracial, representative governments in Louisiana and elsewhere in the South collapsed. In New Orleans, the horrendous 1866 Mechanics' Institute attack marked the beginning of a series of major street battles in which white supremacist militia forces mounted repeated assaults on efforts to build a multiracial state government. Between 1866 and 1877 statewide, Louisiana became an epicenter of political violence in which more than 3,500 Louisianians, mostly Black, were killed. None of the more than 1,200 politically motivated murders up to 1875 resulted in a successful prosecution.[44]

Instead of fleeing New Orleans like Governor Packard, however, Black civil rights activists remained in their dangerous city and continued their campaign for racial justice. At the start of the 1877 school year, Paul Trévigne and E. Arnold Bertonneau undertook legal challenges to the resegregation of the city's public schools. In two separate cases, the men filed suit against restoring the color line on the grounds that it violated the 1868 Louisiana constitution's Article 135 prohibiting segregated schools and the US Constitution's Fourteenth Amendment. When Trévigne's suit was dismissed on the basis of technicalities, Bertonneau immediately filed the second suit.

In the 1879 case of *Bertonneau v. New Orleans Board of School Directors et al.*, US Circuit Court judge W. B. Woods dismissed the suit in a decision that foreshadowed the US Supreme Court's "separate but equal" doctrine in the 1896 *Plessy v. Ferguson* case. Woods wrote, "Both races are treated precisely alike. White children and colored children are compelled to attend different schools. That is all. The State, while conceding equal privileges and advantages to both races, has the right to manage its schools in the manner which in its judgement will best promote the interests of all."[45]

In October 1883, the US Supreme Court assisted Louisiana segregationists by invalidating the remnants of Charles Sumner's 1875 Civil Rights Act in the *Civil Rights Cases*, a collective ruling on five individual cases. With yet another discriminatory green light from the nation's highest court, Louisiana Democrats segregated the races in facilities under their direct control, such as public schools, institutions of higher learning, hospitals, and theaters, where, as one angry patron complained, they were required to "sit in the cockloft of a theatre or stay at home." Even the 1883 Louisiana chapter of the Grand Army of the Republic fell in line, steadfastly excluding Black veterans from its ranks. When the national leadership insisted on the chapter's recognition of Black veterans, whites abandoned the organization.[46]

Other equally immediate dangers confronted freedmen in New Orleans and its environs, where overcrowding, unsanitary conditions, and inadequate nutrition resulted in a health crisis. The port city's vulnerability to contagious diseases exposed Black families to a variety of health hazards, with cholera and smallpox taking the greatest deadly toll. Between 1860 and 1880, the catastrophic annual death rate for Blacks fluctuated between two to six times the death rate for whites. As late as 1880, Black infants perished at a rate of 450 per 1,000, with only one Black physician for every 5,094 African Americans.

In a step toward addressing the crisis, Louisiana's Reconstruction state legislature chartered Straight University (present-day Dillard University) in 1869, with authorization to establish a medical school. The university enjoyed the overwhelming support of Louisiana's most influential Black leaders, including Lieutenant Governor Dunn, Dr. Roudanez, Aristide Mary, and other distinguished leaders. Unlike Louisiana State University in Baton Rouge, where Black students were excluded, Straight admitted applicants of both races, a feature of its charter that prompted Governor Warmoth to undertake repeated attempts to sabotage the new institution.

Soon after its opening, Straight's medical department admitted Louis André Martinet, a wunderkind in his early twenties determined to address the health care needs of his fellow Louisianians. In 1870, he was assigned to the three-member Collegiate Division, which included faculty members Reverend C. H. Thompson, a graduate of Oberlin, and P. M. Williams, a Dartmouth graduate. Interestingly, though he was a student and a linguist, Martinet was the third member of the triumvirate. Apparently, he had made a considerable impression on administrators, whose numbers included Roudanez, an enthusiastic supporter of Straight and a member of the university's examining committee. Little in Martinet's early biography offers insight into his extraordinary talents.[47]

He was born in 1849, the eldest of five children, in St. Martinsville on Bayou Teche in southwest Louisiana. His parents were Hippolite Martinet, a white Belgian carpenter, and Marie Louise Benoit, a woman of color and native Louisianian. He was educated in New Orleans, and while he was attending Straight's medical school, in 1872, he was elected to Louisiana's House of Representatives, representing St. Martin Parish, though his term of office was short-lived. In the fiercely disputed 1874 election, he was stripped of his legislative seat. Still, his medical education at Straight University, under the influence of Dr. Roudanez, combined with his political ambitions to produce yet another enormously influential physician-politician.

Still determined to practice medicine, Martinet entered Straight's law school, where two years of study led to an 1876 bachelor of laws degree. By the terms of an act of the state legislature, graduates of the university's law department were automatically admitted to the bar. Between 1876 and 1886, the law school proved to be the university's most successful department, with eighty-one graduates and 115 students. After the collapse of Reconstruction in the April 1877 coup d'état, however, the presence of an integrated university attended by the city's Black political elite posed an intolerable presence. In the fall, an arsonist's bomb ignited a fire that destroyed the university's main campus building and library. Though Straight survived, the terrorist attack persuaded the president and several staff members to resign.[48]

In 1877, P. B. S. Pinchback negotiated Martinet's appointment to the New Orleans school board, where he voted, to no avail, against a measure to re-segregate the city's public schools. He remained on the school board until 1881, when all of the African American board members were removed. After Pinchback won a concession in the 1879 constitutional convention for a Black college in New Orleans, Martinet was appointed to the new Southern University's board of trustees when the school opened in 1881. In addition to serving on the board, he taught classes as a member of the faculty.[49]

During the 1880s, the incredibly industrious Martinet also actively lobbied Catholic Church clerics and political officials to maintain the legality of in-terracial marriages. The attorney had a personal stake in the legislation since he had grown to adulthood as the illegitimate son of a white immigrant and a woman of color. His parents married in 1869, when Martinet was in his early twenties, after the Reconstruction repeal of legislation barring interracial cou-ples from marrying. In the end, however, his efforts failed, and the state legis-lature reimposed the ban in 1894. The ban would remain in effect until 1972.

In the early 1880s, Martinet also joined the Desdunes brothers, Rodolphe Lucien and Pierre-Aristide, in l'Union Louisianaise (the Louisiana Union), an Afro-Creole organization whose membership included newspaper civil rights veteran Paul Trévigne. They united to restore the antebellum Couvent school, where Trévigne had taught and where the Desdunes brothers had attended classes in an academic setting that has been accurately described as the city's incubator for revolutionary change. By 1880, the school had fallen into almost complete ruin as a result of the desegregation of the city's tuition-free public schools during Reconstruction.

In 1884, l'Union Louisianaise acquired the authority to restore the facil-ity to its prewar role as a tuition-free school for indigent orphans. The men chose Arthur Estèves, a prosperous Haitian-born sail manufacturer, as presi-dent of the Couvent's board of directors, and Martinet served as the school's legal advisor. Rodolphe Desdunes, also an alumnus of Straight law school, played a key role in the restoration project as a member of the board of direc-tors. He remained at his alma mater as an instructor upon the renovation's completion.

Before long, l'Union Louisianaise was soliciting contributions for the publi-cation of a French-language journal reflecting the priorities of its membership and bearing the name of the organization. The publication's 1887 prospectus assured its readers of its "républicain" credentials and explained that its "efforts will always be directed toward reclaiming the privileges which follow from our participation as members of the great human family in the moral and intellectual development of all classes of society."[50]

Soon after announcing their publication's debut, however, a mounting white supremacist campaign to legally nullify the intent of the Fourteenth and Fifteenth Amendments persuaded l'Union Louisianaise's members to redraw their plans. They resolved to confront the Democrats' violent campaign to suppress voting rights, extend forced segregation, and subjugate Black workers. In November 1887, white vigilantes had ended a sugar strike in south Louisiana's bayou parishes with a massacre of Black workers in Thibodaux. When White Leagues from St. Martin Parish broke up the 1889 election in Lafayette Parish, their actions led to the murder of a Black family.

In early March 1889, Martinet launched the New Orleans Crusader, a bilingual weekly newspaper, to serve as a public platform for a powerful new civil rights movement. The paper's banner pledged to advocate for "A Free Vote and Fair Count, Free Schools, Fair Wages, Justice and Equal Rights."[51] The newspaper emphasized its solidarity with laborers and their rights: "We shall pay much attention to industrial and economic questions . . . and particularly shall we devote space to questions of labor. Our special aim, in fact, shall be to make a great Republican-Labor organ through which the working classes can at all times be heard and have their grievances made known and their wrongs righted."[52]

A community corporation, the Crusader Publishing Company, assumed control of the newspaper on March 29, and in 1890 it became a daily. Paul Trévigne, a veteran editor of Roudanez's l'Union and Tribune, assisted in the founding of the Crusader and became one of its regular contributors. By the end of its first year, the paper boasted an office in the heart of the French Quarter and an electric-powered printing press. With the support of Black New Orleanians, the paper would evolve into the only African American daily newspaper in the nation in 1895.[53]

Attorney Martinet, still determined to provide health care to Black New Orleanians after launching the Crusader, resumed his studies in 1889 when New Orleans University opened a medical department. Just as he had been among the first class of law school students to graduate from Straight University, in 1892 he was among the first five students to graduate from New Orleans University's three-year course. Throughout his studies, he maintained his presence at the Crusader, where his activism accelerated after Governor

Francis T. Nicholls signed the Separate Car Act on July 10, 1890. The legislation mandated the segregation of Louisiana's interstate railway cars.

With the financial support of Aristide Mary and at his suggestion, Martinet, Rodolphe Desdunes, Arthur Estèves, and C. C. Antoine organized an eighteen-member Comité des Citoyens (Citizens' Committee) on September 1, 1891, to formulate legal strategy and build a broader base of support. As the committee recognized, the Separate Car Act represented caste legislation with far-reaching and disastrous consequences. After all, legally mandated caste distinctions were the building blocks of slavery. If allowed to stand, other laws with the same intent were sure to follow. Within a week of its creation, the committee issued an appeal "to the citizens of New Orleans, of Louisiana, and of the whole Union to give us their moral sanction and financial aid in our endeavors to have that oppressive [separate car] law annulled by the courts."[54]

In 1892, the Citizens' Committee recruited thirty-year-old Daniel Desdunes, Rodolphe's son, to test the segregation statute by purchasing a first-class ticket on February 24 and taking a seat in the whites-only car bound for Mobile, Alabama. When he tried, he was arrested for violating the segregation law. However, in a set of judicial opinions, the Separate Car Act was determined to be in violation of the US Constitution insofar as it imposed restrictions on interstate travel. The charges against Desdunes were dropped.

To effectively challenge state-enforced segregation, the committee proceeded to test the law on travel within state boundaries. For the next step in their legal project, the committee recruited Homer Adolphe Plessy, a Creole descendant of the Haitian refugee community. They arranged for him to board the East Louisiana Railroad train for an intrastate journey from New Orleans to Covington, Louisiana. On June 7, 1892, as they anticipated, Plessy was arrested when he took a seat in the white railway car and refused to move to the segregated coach. He was arrested and Judge John H. Ferguson of the New Orleans criminal court found him guilty of violating the Separate Car Act. When the Louisiana Supreme Court upheld his conviction, Plessy's attorneys proceeded to their ultimate objective, a ruling from the US Supreme Court.[55]

The committee's 1892 challenge coincided with attorney/physician Martinet's graduation from medical school at the University of New Orleans. While studying for his degree, Martinet once again crossed paths with Dr. Louis-Charles Roudanez. The distinguished doctor's involvement in the medical schools at both Straight and the University of New Orleans reflected his dedication to the urgent health care needs of Black New Orleanians—a humanitarian dedication rooted in his medical education in Paris.

At the Paris Médicale, Roudanez had fully absorbed the philosophy of doctors as political activists. In a profession reimagined under the 1792 French Republic, doctors were seen as being especially well equipped to address the ills of society—ills originating in despotism and human bondage. As Roudanez's wartime activism demonstrated, he had fully embraced the Médicale's political lessons. It is equally clear that Roudanez succeeded in passing his medical-political idealism on to his protégés Doctors Martinet and George Alexandré Roudanez.[56]

Like his father, Dr. George Roudanez graduated from the Geisel School of Medicine at Darmouth College in Hanover, New Hampshire, which had been conferring degrees on Black candidates since 1821. George's two brothers, Louis-Charles Roudanez II and Albert Francis Roudanez, also graduated from Geisel, in 1890 and 1893, respectively. George Roudanez completed his medical training in 1890, the year of his father's death, and returned to New Orleans, where he joined the civil rights movement. In July 1893, while Martinet was continuing his medical studies at the Chicago Polyclinic, Roudanez presided over a mass protest meeting as the president of the Citizens' Committee. Both he and Martinet would later join the teaching staff at the University of New Orleans Department of Medicine and Surgery.[57]

Between 1892 and 1896, as the committee's challenge to segregation made its way through the courts, the organization took legal action against the practice of barring African Americans from sitting on criminal juries. They fought efforts to disfranchise Black voters and advocated workers' rights to unionize, with the *Crusader* reporting instances of police brutality, forced labor, and lynching.

Their hard-fought civil rights campaign notwithstanding, the US Supreme Court upheld Louisiana's separate car law in the *Plessy v. Ferguson* decision on the basis of the "separate but equal" doctrine. In yet another disastrous ruling, the Supreme Court put its stamp of approval on Jim Crow, a system of state-enforced segregation that endured for more than fifty additional years and extended to nearly every facet of southern life. In compliance with the court's decision, Plessy pleaded guilty and paid a fine of twenty-five dollars. Soon afterwards, the Citizens' Committee disbanded and the *Crusader* ceased publication. As Rodolphe Desdunes later wrote, most of the leaders "believed that the continuation of the *Crusader* would not only be fruitless but decidedly dangererous."[58]

Another ruinous blow came soon afterwards, when Louisiana's 1898 constitution legislated a "grandfather clause" permitting illiterate whites to vote while barring the descendants of slaves from the franchise. A poll tax and a literacy test fortified the barrier to Black voting rights. In Jim Crow Louisiana, the number of registered African American voters plummeted from 130,000 in 1896 to 1,342 in 1904. The same pattern of voter repression accompanied by segregation, exclusion, and debt peonage spread throughout the South.

In their violent campaign to restore the South's status quo ante, white supremacists refashioned the region's unique brand of Romanticism to suit their new objectives. The antebellum South's code of chivalry, having survived the destruction of slavery and the plantation system, reemerged after 1865 as the cult of the Lost Cause. In its postwar reincarnation, southern Romanticism sustained the white South's nostalgia for its heroic Confederate "knights" who had battled to defend the South's honor, preserve slavery, and achieve southern nationhood.

In the post–Civil War era, the white supremacist Lost Cause mythology served as a key building block of Jim Crow. Its legacy can be seen in the thousands of Confederate monuments and place names in public spaces throughout the South, and even in some instances in the North. Their ubiquity testifies to the power of the South's cult of the Lost Cause.[59]

T hroughout the revolutionary era, Black New Orleanians fought for freedom and citizenship at home and abroad. Reinforced by a huge influx of Haitian refugees and abetted by their interracial military alliances and kinship ties, they reshaped the city's culture, politics, and race relations. The "Haitian influence" growing out of the diasporic community would exert a potent influence in the city for generations. Nowhere else in the United States did the French and Haitian Revolutions exert as enduring an influence as in New Orleans and south Louisiana.

In a sign of the perilous times to come, however, reactionary forces gathered momentum on both sides of the Atlantic. In the postwar South, white supremacists refashioned their feudal brand of Romanticism into the cult of the Lost Cause as a means of restoring the status quo ante. At the same time, Romanticism in France suffered a fatal blow when the nation's political right blamed the movement's influence for the nation's defeat in the 1870 Franco-Prussian War.

Undaunted, Afro-Creole Romantics in New Orleans and Haiti nurtured the movement as a means of advancing their republican vision—a vision rooted in their singular experiences in the Age of Revolution. Pierre-Aristide Desdunes and his younger brother Rodolphe, descendants of the diaspora who maintained their links to their Haitian family, offer compelling evidence of Romanticism's ongoing influence. Both men had taken up arms to fulfill the promise of the revolutionary age. Pierre-Aristide fought in the US Army and Rodolphe served in the city's Metropolitan Police, where he was seriously injured during the White League's 1874 attempt to overthrow Louisiana's interracial government.

Like Romantic writers in the Francophone Atlantic, they considered their work a means of preserving the spirit of the revolutionary age. Their resources would serve their community and their country in the future. A knowledge of past events, they believed, would lead individuals to make decisions that would contribute to everyone's well-being. In this view, according to Haitian writer Beaubrun Ardouin, "the past is the regulator of the present as of the future." The writer's object was to inspire future generations by educating them on the deeds of their predecessors.[1]

It is in this Romantic spirit that Pierre-Aristide transcribed Les Cenelles, his own works, and those of his fellow artists. The same logic led his brother Rodolphe to translate excerpts of Joseph Saint-Rémy's five-volume work Pétion et Haïti (1854–1857) for serial publication in the New Orleans Daily Crusader from July through October 1895. During the 1890s struggle against forced segregation in the Plessy v. Ferguson Supreme Court proceedings, Rodolphe sought to inspire his fellow Louisianians by educating them about the deeds of champions of freedom and equality like Haiti's President Pétion. Like Haitian Romantics, Rodolphe and Pierre-Aristide Desdunes revered Pétion for his military prowess in the Haitian Revolution, his popular republican presidency, his abolition of forced labor, his transfer of confiscated plantations to Haitian citizens, and his active support of international abolitionism.[2]

In the tradition of highly politicized Romantic historians like Haiti's Saint-Rémy and France's Jules Michelet, Rodolphe Desdunes later authored his own historical tribute. His book, Our People and Our History, documented the history of the city's French-speaking Creoles of color and their civil rights struggles. At the time of its publication, it was the only historical study of the city's Afro-Creoles. It remains a starting point for studies of the nineteenth-century Creole population of color.

As their work indicates, Pierre-Aristide and Rodolphe Desdunes, like French historian Michelet, recognized the power of history in the struggle for freedom and equality. In discussing his passion for re-creating the past, Michelet, an ardent republican, explained that history writing sustained the living as well as the dead: "I have exhumed them [the dead] for a second life . . . Thus a family is formed, a common city between the living and the dead." In New Orleans, Romantic activists and their allies gave this idea powerful expression.[3]

In their histories, their literary art, their newspapers, and their Spiritualist communications, Creole New Orleanians documented the links that bound them to the revolutionary Atlantic's Francophone world. They understood the importance of those ideological ties—ties that would be central to the formulation of Louisiana's twentieth-century civil rights movement.

The French Hospital, founded by the benevolent La Société française, sustained the spirit of the revolutionary age into the twentieth century. One of the organization's most influential members, Pierre Soulé, had incorporated his revolutionary republican views into the benevolent society's 1843 founding charter. Among the primary obligations of its members was "to mutually encourage the acquisition of rights which assure the liberty of man in every country." While the ambitious Soulé eventually chose political expediency over his humanitarian and political ideals, La Société did not. The organization became the target of proslavery attacks in the 1850s. Their detractors were undoubtedly aware of its revolutionary genesis.

Dr. Faget continued his public service, serving as the chairman of the Committee on Contagious Disease at the Louisiana State Board of Health until his failing health forced his resignation four months prior to his death. Having lived a life of remarkable accomplishments, the devout Catholic doctor died poor in New Orleans on December 9, 1884, at the age of sixty-six. From his home on North Rampart near Hospital Street (present-day Governor Nicholls), the monolingual Faget attended Catholic services at nearby St. Augustine Church, where the similarly monolingual French priest, Joseph Subileau, served the surrounding community. Subileau officiated at Faget's funeral service, and a procession of relatives and friends followed the hearse to St. Louis Cemetery No. 1, where the doctor was laid to rest.[4]

After the failure of the 1873 Unification Movement, Dr. Faget's ally Dr. Louis-Charles Roudanez returned to his medical practice. In January 1879, he attended a Republican Union Club banquet, where, according to the *Weekly Louisianian*, he emphasized his Reconstruction aims as having been "to elevate the oppressed, and to educate and advance the interest of his down-trodden people." At the same time, Roudanez permanently relocated his wife, daughters, and youngest son to Paris owing to mounting racial oppression. The doctor remained in New Orleans with his eldest sons for the rest of his life. He died in the city on March 11, 1890, at the age of sixty-seven and was buried, like Dr. Faget, in St. Louis Cemetery No. 1. Dr. George A. Roudanez continued his father's legacy in the 1890s as the president of the Citizens' Committee organized to fight state-imposed segregation, a struggle that culminated in the 1896 *Plessy v. Ferguson* Supreme Court decision.[5]

Their Civil War ally General Benjamin Butler also remained true to the nation's founding republican ideals, doing his part to advance the military and political interests of African Americans. After leaving New Orleans in 1863, Benjamin Butler fought unsuccessfully for equal treatment of Black soldiers, including equal pay and protections from the Confederacy's prisoner of war policy of reenslaving captured men. After his Black regiments conquered a heavily fortified enemy position at New Market Heights in a diversionary movement against Richmond on September 29, 1864, the general proposed to honor the men for their courage. When army policy prohibited him from promoting the Black soldiers to officer rank or awarding them medals for outstanding service, he personally commissioned Tiffany and Company of New York City to manufacture two hundred medals portraying two Black soldiers under a Latin inscription, "Freedom Comes Through the Sword."

After the war, Butler entered politics as a Radical Republican, championing labor reforms such as the eight-hour day, women's suffrage, and Irish nationalism. In the 1871 French Revolution, he praised the Paris Commune. Outraged by the ongoing violence against Black southerners, Butler wrote the initial version of the Civil Rights Act of 1871 (the Ku Klux Klan Act). In the debates surrounding passage of the legislation, Butler reportedly displayed the bloodied shirt of a Mississippi school superintendent who had been flogged by the Klan. His advocacy in the Congress and President Grant's enforcement of the legislation resulted, in 1872, in the most democratic election in the South until 1968. During his several terms of office in the US Congress, representing Massachusetts from 1867 to 1875 and from 1877 to 1879, Butler remained the most steadfast defender of African Americans in the US House of Representatives.[6]

The French Hospital in the Faubourg Tremé on Orleans Avenue closed in 1949. However, its humanitarian mission continued after La Société française sold the property in 1951 to the Knights of Peter Claver, the nation's largest and oldest fraternal society of African American Catholics. Founded for "fraternal, benevolent, and charitable purposes," the society used the property's buildings as its national headquarters. Celebrated civil rights attorney A. P. Tureaud was the general counsel to the Knights and moved his law practice as well as the offices of the local chapter of the National Association for the Advancement of Colored People onto the site shortly after the purchase.

Born soon after the *Plessy* decision in 1899, A. P. Tureaud embraced his Creole heritage. With ancestral roots in France, Haiti, and rural south Louisiana, he revered the literary works and political commentary that belied the notion of white supremacy. He studied the experiences of his nineteenth-century predecessors who aspired to revolutionize race relations in the Civil War and Reconstruction. After graduating from Howard University School of Law, he set a course to give full meaning to the promise of the Thirteenth, Fourteenth, and Fifteenth Amendments.

Beginning in the 1920s, he worked with Thurgood Marshall and other members of the NAACP for nearly fifty years, arguing more than one hundred cases in state and federal courts. Those cases represented all of the significant civil rights litigation in Louisiana—litigation that produced salary equalization for teachers, expanded voting rights, and desegregated public education, public buildings, buses, parks, and housing. In *Alexander P. Tureaud, Jr. v. Board of Supervisors of Louisiana State University* (1953), Tureaud's young son desegregated the state's premier public university. Finally, in 1954, in his work with Marshall and the other members of the NAACP Legal Defense Fund to end racial segregation in *Brown v. the Board of Education,* Tureaud and his colleagues overturned the *Plessy* decision.

Tureaud recognized the power of history to breathe a "second life" into the extraordinary lives of his civil rights predecessors. Like them, he understood that in this way "a family is formed, a common city between the living and the dead." In their lives and in their legacies, they helped build a "common city" with a history and a collective memory that moved the nation closer to a multiracial democracy of freedom and equal citizenship.[7]

Growing up with the New Orleans civil rights movement, community activist Jacques Morial recalled roaming through the deserted upper floors of the French Hospital while his father Ernest Nathan "Dutch" Morial strategized with A. P. Tureaud and other civil rights luminaries in the NAACP offices below. Bearing witness to history-making events in the building, Jacques explored the remnants of the former hospital in the upper floors where Dr. Faget treated his yellow fever patients. As a young boy, his discovery of the "old hospital beds, ancient wheel chairs and a skeleton" made a lasting impression. In 1967, Jacques's father Dutch Morial made history when he became the first African American since Reconstruction to win a seat in the Louisiana state legislature. In 1977, he won election as New Orleans' first Black mayor and was reelected in 1982.[8]

Another property owned and developed by La Société, the present-day Christian Mission Baptist Church at 1477 North Robertson Street, also became an important site of African American history. As an early twentieth-century music hall, the site attracted artists who played an important role in the development of jazz, a uniquely New Orleans African American art form.[9]

In the twenty-first century, the city's civil rights activists took another step toward memorializing their history. Keith M. Plessy, a descendant of Homer A. Plessy, and Phoebe Ferguson, the great-great-granddaughter of Judge John H. Ferguson, first met at a 2004 book signing for Keith Weldon Medley's *We as Freemen: Plessy v. Ferguson.* When Phoebe Ferguson began apologizing for Judge Ferguson's 1892 ruling against Homer Plessy's challenge to segregation, Keith Plessy stopped her. "I told her," he later explained, "it's no longer Plessy *versus* Ferguson; it's now Plessy *and* Ferguson. And we became great friends."

In 2009, they founded the Plessy & Ferguson Foundation to honor and preserve Homer Plessy's legacy. Together, they worked to place five historical markers throughout the city commemorating major turning points in African American history. With the assistance of New Orleans district attorney Jason Williams, they worked with the Louisiana Board of Pardons to approve a pardon for Homer Plessy. The board issued its unanimous decision in 2021, with Louisiana governor John Bel Edwards welcoming the opportunity to sign the historic document.

At the Posthumous Pardoning Ceremony for Mr. Homer A. Plessy on January 5, 2022, Kate Dillingham, a cellist and the great-great-granddaughter of Supreme Court Justice John Marshall Harlan, performed James Weldon Johnson's "Lift Every Voice and Sing," accompanied in song by an entranced audience. Her presence recalled Justice Harlan's lone dissenting voice in the US Supreme Court's 8–1 *Plessy* decision. He rightly predicted that the ruling would open the gates to a flood of laws segregating every aspect of southern life.

In his dissenting opinion read from the bench, Harlan observed, "Our Constitution is color-blind, and neither knows nor tolerates classes among citizens. In respect of civil rights, all citizens are equal before the law. The humblest is the peer of the most powerful. . . . In my opinion, the judgment this day rendered will, in time, prove to be quite as pernicious as the Dred Scott case." Harlan concluded his remarkable dissent by emphasizing that the "thin disguise of 'equal' accommodations for passengers in railroad coaches will not mislead anyone, nor atone for the wrong this day done."

At the pardoning ceremony, Governor John Bel Edwards emphasized that the Plessy ruling "left a stain on the fabric of our country and on this state and on this city, . . . And, quite frankly, those consequences are still felt today." And, he added, "Homer Plessy more than did his part to prevent this stain." Next, the governor erased the record of Homer Plessy's purported crime with the stroke of his pen. Keith Plessy's joy overflowed: "I feel like my feet are not touching the ground today because the ancestors are carrying me. This is truly a blessed day!" Both Keith Plessy and Phoebe Ferguson understood the power of history to build a future of equal rights before the law. In achieving a pardon for Homer A. Plessy, they and their allies gave powerful twenty-first-century expression to their shared vision of justice.[10]

During the Civil War, Hélène d'Aquin Allain remained in New Orleans with her young son, her mother, and other members of her family. From her French Quarter residence on Chartres Street, she experienced the war's toll. Twenty years later, she described an overwhelming sense of melancholy "at the mere mention of Atlanta, Manassas, and Shiloh." At such moments, she recalled "the brokenhearted mothers, the inconsolable widows, the orphaned children! Dismal images pass again before my eyes one after another: a man dressed in black, seated on a hearse, followed on foot by a woman in mourning; someone says, 'That is his mother!' and from our windows we bear witness, brokenhearted, to the passage of the funeral cortège."[1]

Before her departure from Louisiana in 1869, Allain traveled to the summer residence of her two aunts, Lilia and Adèle d'Aquin, in Biloxi, Mississippi. It was her last visit with Suzanne, who was gravely ill, and it had come "to little Adèle, who had been in Suzanne's care during her childhood, to serve her as a daughter would."[2]

From New Orleans, Allain moved to Toulouse in the south of France, where she was struck by the French city's resemblance to her former home. In Toulouse, as in New Orleans, she encountered "people on the streets speaking different languages, representing various national types, and varying as much in color as in language." The river running through the heart of the city likewise recalled her Louisiana home: "The yellowish and muddy water of the Garonne at the time reminded me a lot of our wide Mississippi." On her first morning in Toulouse, the music of a peasant goatherd driving his animals through the city streets with his panpipe brought the "banjo des nègres" to mind. Similarly, the aphorisms she learned in Toulouse struck her as being "as fine as our *nègre* proverbs."[3]

Allain arrived in Toulouse just ahead of the outbreak of the Franco-Prussian War on July 19, 1870. Within two months of the war's opening shots, France's Second Empire collapsed when the Prussians took Emperor Napoleon III prisoner. In Paris on September 2, republican insurgents proclaimed France's Third Republic and refused to capitulate. On September 19, Prussian forces surrounded the city in a four-month siege that ended when the National Assembly in Versailles agreed to Prussia's harsh armistice terms.

When Parisians rejected the settlement, a civil war ensued, with the Communards in Paris fighting the French Assembly's army of Versailles. The savage fratricidal conflict ignited fires that destroyed the Tuileries, the Palais-Royal, the Hôtel de Ville (city hall), the Légion d'honneur building, the Cour des Comptes (Revenue Court), and much else.

In the bloodiest urban conflict in Parisian history, the army of Versailles finally crushed the Communards in what has come to be known as the Bloody Week, which began on May 22, 1871. By June 13, between twelve thousand and fifteen thousand Communards were summarily executed by the Versaillais military. The Third Republic survived but the Communards did not. Auguste Reynaud de Barbarin, a favorite first cousin of Allain's father, was a senior officer in the burned-out Cour des Comptes. He never recovered from the shock of its destruction, with its centuries of France's recorded history.[4]

After the war, Allain moved to Paris, where her son Frédéric Allain earned his law degree and practiced in the Paris Court of Appeals. After the United States entered World War I in 1917, Frédéric Allain moved to Washington, DC, where he represented France's Third Republic until the war's end. In 1919, he was awarded the Chevalier de la Légion d'honneur for his distinguished service.

In 1879, Hélène Allain crossed the Atlantic once more for visits to New York and Jamaica. Upon her return to France, she settled in affluent Saint-Germain-en-Laye, a historic city approximately fifteen miles west of Paris. The city's fourteenth-century Château de Saint-Germain was the birthplace of Louis XIV and his royal residence from 1661 until 1682, when he moved to Versailles. Allain's arrival in the city brought the d'Aquins' Atlantic odyssey full circle; she had returned to the site of her ancestors' fateful presence in Louis XIV's court during his residence in Saint-Germain.

Allain's ancestral roots in Saint-Germain also intersected with those of Alexandre Dumas. The famed novelist's father, Thomas-Alexandre Dumas, was born into slavery in Saint-Domingue's South Province in the parish of Jérémie, approximately sixty miles from Aquin, a town founded by Allain's forebears. Emancipated at the age of fourteen upon his arrival in France in 1776, Thomas-Alexandre Dumas grew up in opulence in Saint-Germain. His sparring with his fellow fencing students at the urban enclave's elite La Boëssière academy paved the way for his meteoric ascent in the military during the French Revolution and the Napoleonic wars. His gains would set his son, Alexandre Dumas, on his own meteoric ascent in France's nineteenth-century literary revolution. In tribute, Dumas immortalized his father in his masterpiece *The Count of Monte Cristo* (1844–1845).[5]

On January 31, 1925, at the age of ninety-two, Allain died in an elegant multistoried residence with a commanding view of the surrounding French countryside. At the time of her death, according to Edward Larocque Tinker, she possessed "a mind as lucid and active as ever." Her son, Frédéric Allain, died at his home in Cannes on September 17, 1937, at the age of seventy-eight.[6]

NOTES

INTRODUCTION

1. Charles Barthelemy Rousséve, *The Negro in Louisiana: Aspects of His History and His Literature* (New Orleans: Xavier University Press, 1937), 170–171. In the present work, the terms *Afro-Creole* and *Creole* refer to all Standard or Creole French speakers born in the Francophone Caribbean and south Louisiana.

2. Rodolphe Lucien Desdunes, *Our People and Our History*, trans. and ed. Sister Dorothea Olga McCants (Baton Rouge: Lousiana State University Press, 1973); Charles Testut, *Le Vieux Salomon, ou une famille d'esclaves au XIXème siècle* (New Orleans, 1872).

3. Sheri Lyn Abel, *Charles Testut's "Le Vieux Salomon": Race, Religion, Socialism, and Freemasonry* (Lanham, MD: Rowman & Littlefield, 2009).

4. Hélène d'Aquin Allain [une Créole, pseud.], *Souvenirs d'Amérique et de France* (Paris, 1883), i, vi. The French-language quotations here and all other quotations from Allain's *Souvenirs*, including the Louisiana Creole aphorisms, were translated by Dr. Anne Malena, Emerita Professor of French and Translation Studies at the University of Alberta, Canada. All other translations from the French are my own, unless otherwise noted.

5. Lynn Hunt, *Inventing Human Rights: A History* (New York: W. W. Norton, 2007), 160.

6. Warren Breckman, *European Romanticism: A Brief History with Documents* (Boston: Bedford/St. Martins, 2008), 1, 26–28; Andrea Ciccarelli, "Introduction," in *The People's Voice: Essays on European Romanticism*, ed. Andrea Ciccarelli, John C. Isbell, and Brian Nelson (Melbourne: Monash Romance Studies, 1999), 1, 4; Frank Paul Bowman, "The Specificity of French Romanticism," in Ciccarelli, Isbell, and Nelson, *People's Voice*, 78–80; Stephen G. Hall, *A Faithful Account of the Race: African American Historical Writing in Nineteenth-Century America* (Chapel Hill: University of North Carolina Press, 2009), 77–85; James M. McPherson and James K. Hogue, *Ordeal by Fire: The Civil War and Reconstruction*, 4th ed. (New York: McGraw-Hill, 2009), 21.

7. Hélène d'Aquin Allain [Nihila, pseud.], *New-York et Paris* (Paris, 1884), 81–115, includes two chapters on the subject of Native Americans, with one chapter on Choctaw Louisianians authored by Abbé Adrien Rouquette. Allain donated the proceeds of this, her second book, to the Catholic Auteuil Orphanage in France.

8. Rousséve, *Negro in Louisiana*, 53–54; John W. Blassingame, *The Slave Community: Plantation Life in the Antebellum South* (1972), revised and enlarged (New York: Oxford University Press, 1979), 36–38; Gwendolyn Midlo Hall, "The Formation of Afro-Creole Culture," in *Creole New Orleans: Race and Americanization*, ed. Arnold R. Hirsch and Joseph Logsdon (Baton Rouge: Louisiana State University Press, 1992), 59; Hall, *Africans in Colonial Louisiana: The Development of Afro-Creole Culture in the Eighteenth Century* (Baton Rouge: Louisiana State University Press, 1992).

9. On Thomas Fiehrer's leading role in conceptualizing Louisiana's circum-Caribbean iden-

tity, see Jerah Johnson, "Colonial New Orleans," in Hirsch and Logsdon, *Creole New Orleans*, 19 note 9; Fiehrer, "From La Tortue to La Louisiane: An Unfathomed Legacy," in *The Road to Louisiana: The Saint-Domingue Refugees, 1792–1809*, ed. Carl A. Brasseaux and Glenn R. Conrad (Lafayette: Center for Louisiana Studies, University of Southwestern Louisiana, 1992), 28–30; Médéric-Louis-Élie Moreau de Saint-Méry, *Description topographique, physique, civile, politique et historique de la partie française de l'isle Saint-Domingue*, 3 vols. (1796; reprint, Paris: Librairie Larose, 1958). See Allain, *Souvenirs*, 132–170, for the Moreau transcription.

10. Ruby Van Allen Caulfeild, *The French Literature of Louisiana* (New York: Institute of French Studies, Columbia University, 1929), 185–186; Armand Lanusse, ed., *Les Cenelles: choix de poésies indigènes* (New Orleans, 1845). Caulfeild's flawed judgment is clear in her omission of Louisiana's most celebrated Francophone literary artist, Afro-Creole New Orleanian Victor Séjour. Though Séjour was the South's greatest antebellum dramatist, Caulfeild makes no mention of his remarkable body of work apart from his contribution to *Les Cenelles*.

11. Edward Larocque Tinker, *Les Écrits de langue française en Louisiane au XIXe siècle* (Paris: Librairie Ancienne Honoré Champion, 1932), 14.

12. Robert C. Reinders, *End of an Era: New Orleans, 1850–1860* (New Orleans: Pelican Publishing, 1964), 224.

13. Catherine Clinton, review, *Journal of American History*, 68 (March 1982), 939, 941; Mary Boykin Chesnut, *Mary Chesnut's Civil War*, ed. C. Vann Woodward (New Haven, CT: Yale University Press, 1981).

1. ROOTS: *From the Sun King to the Haitian Revolution*

1. Allain, *Souvenirs*, 3–4.

2. Tinker, *Les Écrits*, 83. On the formation of transatlantic familial links, see Darrell R. Meadows, "The Planters of Saint-Domingue, 1750–1804: Migration and Exile in the French Revolutionary Atlantic" (PhD diss., Carnegie Mellon University, 2004).

3. Allain, *Souvenirs*, 4.

4. Meadows, "Planters of Saint-Domingue," vii.

5. Allain, *Souvenirs*, 3. She is referring here to the presumed Irish ancestry of her mother, Marie Anne Elisabeth Daron.

6. Ibid., 7. For an excellent discussion of the complexity and ambiguity of Creole linguistics and identity, see Albert Valdman et al., eds., *Dictionary of Louisiana French: As Spoken in Cajun, Creole, and American Indian Communities* (Jackson: University of Mississippi Press, 2010), xi–xii.

7. *Nouveau Dictionnaire de Biographies françaises et étrangères* (Paris, 1964), 662–664; Count François d'Aquin et al., "The Antiquity of the D'Aquin Family," *New Orleans Genesis*, part 1, 18 (March 1979), 129, 133–134; d'Aquin et al., "Antiquity," *New Orleans Genesis*, part 2, 18 (June 1979), 261; Alcée Fortier, ed., *Louisiana: Comprising Sketches of Parishes, Towns, Events, Institutions, and Persons* (Madison, WI: Century Historical Association, 1914), 3:752–753.

8. Aramaic, a Semitic language spoken in Palestine, Syria, and Mesopotamia, was the lingua franca in the region from about 300 BCE to 650 CE, when it was supplanted by Arabic.

9. "Aquin, Philippe D." and "Aquin, Antoine D.," in *Dictionnaire de Biographie Française* (Paris, 1939); D. Labarre de Raillicourt, *Filiations et notices généalogiques de Familles Notables Françaises*

(Paris, 1965), tables 1 and 2. Louis de Rouvroy duc de Saint-Simon, *Saint-Simon at Versailles*, ed. and trans. Lucy Norton (New York: Hamish Hamilton, 1980), 57–58, 248. For an intriguing study of Françoise de Maintenon's rise to power, see Veronica Buckley, *The Secret Wife of Louis XIV: Françoise d'Augigne Madame de Maintenon* (New York: Farrar, Straus and Giroux, 2008). See also R. R. Palmer, Joel Colton, and Lloyd Kramer, *A History of the Modern World*, 9th ed. (New York: Alfred A. Knopf, 2003), 1:144; Robin Blackburn, *The Making of New World Slavery: From the Baroque to the Modern, 1492–1800* (London: Verso, 1997), 282, 292–294.

10. Fiehrer, "From La Tortue," 6–7; d'Aquin et al., "Antiquity," part 2, 263; Charles R. Maduell Jr., "d'Aquin Family," *New Orleans Genesis*, 10 (June 1971): 256–257; Daniel H. Usner Jr., *Indians, Settlers & Slaves in a Frontier Exchange Economy: The Lower Mississippi Valley before 1783* (Chapel Hill: University of North Carolina Press, 1992), 65–87; Moreau de Saint-Méry, *Description*, 3:1444; Allain, *Souvenirs*, 7.

11. Stewart R. King, *Blue Coat or Powdered Wig: Free People of Color in Pre-Revolutionary Saint Domingue* (Athens: University of Georgia Press, 2001), xiv, quote at 52; Fortier, *Louisiana*, 3:753; d'Aquin et al., "Antiquity," part 2, 263; Maduell, "d'Aquin Family," 257; Elizabeth Sullivan-Holleman and Isabel Hillery Cobb, *The Saint Domingue Epic: The de Rossignol des Dunes and Family Alliances* (Bay St. Louis, MS: Nightingale Press, 1995), 228, 383–384.

12. King, *Blue Coat*, xiii–iv, 72, 76–77.

13. Fortier, *Louisiana*, 3:753; John D. Garrigus, *Before Haiti: Race and Citizenship in French Saint-Domingue* (New York: Palgrave Macmillan, 2006), 1, 53–54; Carolyn E. Fick, *The Making of Haiti: The Saint Domingue Revolution from Below* (Knoxville: University of Tennessee Press, 1990), 16, 22, 25–27.

14. Garrigus, *Before Haiti*, 21–22, 28–31, 52–53, 80–81, 110–132, at 123, 131; Jacques de Cauna, *L'Eldorado des Aquitains: Gascons, Basques et Béarnais aux Iles d'Amérique* (Biarritz: Atlantica, 1998), 178–179; Maduell, "d'Aquin Family," 256–257, 261; Francis X. Delany, *A History of the Catholic Church in Jamaica* (New York: Jesuit Mission Press, 1930), 66.

15. Allain, *Souvenirs*, 375–376.

16. Though the text is unclear, Allain appears to be referring to either "Mme Gabriel du Bourg" or the "vicomtesse de Saintegème" in her reference to "Mme la Présidente du Bourg." Alcée Fortier, *A History of Louisiana* (New York: Manzi, Joyant, 1904), 3:753; Sullivan-Holleman and Cobb, *Saint Domingue*, 384; d'Aquin et al., "Antiquity," part 2, 263; Delany, *History of the Catholic Church*, 66–67. During Allain's lifetime, the d'Aquin–Dubourg alliance would be further strengthened by the 1834 marriage of Charles-Pierre's son Henri-Philippe to Louis William DuBourg's niece, Louise Adele de Sainte Marie. Annabelle M. Melville, *Louis William DuBourg: Bishop of Louisiana and the Floridas, Bishop of Montauban, and Archbishop of Besançon, 1766–1833* (Chicago: Loyola University Press, 1986), 1:4.

17. Usner, *Indians*, 254–255; Sue Eakin, *Rapides Parish History* (Alexandria: Historical Association of Central Louisiana, 1976), 6–8; Allain *Souvenirs*, 9. Lessard is also spelled Leyssard and Laysard.

18. Allain, *Souvenirs*, 9; Sullivan-Holleman and Cobb, *Saint Domingue*, 390; *État détaillé des liquidations opérées à l'époque du 1er janvier, 1832*, 174–175, and 1834, section 1, 124–125, Earl K. Long Library, University of New Orleans, Louisiana; Laurent Dubois, *Avengers of the New World: The Story of the Haitian Revolution* (Cambridge, MA: Belknap Press of Harvard University Press, 2004), 21–24.

19. Palmer, *Intimate Bonds*, 11; Franklin W. Knight, "The Haitian Revolution," *American Historical Review*, 105 (February 2000), 103–115.

20. Dubois, *Avengers*, 19, 42, quote on 94; Fick, *Making of Haiti*, 9, 92, 105, 137, map on 101 for the proximity of the Plaisance and Grande Rivière Parishes to the center of the slave revolt. The spelling of *vaudoux* follows the term's usage in Moreau de Saint-Méry's *Description* and Allain's *Souvenirs*.

21. Allain, *Souvenirs*, 16. *Dédé* is a Creole designation notable as a prefix in enslaved women's names. It appears to derive from the verb *dédier*, which means "to devote"; hence, "Devoted Sophie." See Valdman et al., *Dictionary of Louisiana French*, 190. The racial term *nègre* in its various forms is untranslated in the text because no Anglophone term expresses its exact meaning. Depending upon the political and social context in which it was used, it could mean "Negro," "Black," or "slave." See Laurent Dubois and John D. Garrigus, eds., *Slave Revolution in the Caribbean, 1789–1804: A Brief History with Documents* (Boston: Bedford/St. Martin's, 2006), vi–vii.

22. Allain, *Souvenirs*, 16. The "coast" Allain refers to appears to be the bank of the Grande Rivière, a waterway that flows through the Haitian parish of the same name. Allain does not name the river, but this appears to be the most likely path of escape.

23. Ibid., 16–17. Professor Clint Bruce from Université Saint-Anne, Nova Scotia, graciously translated Dédé-Sophie's Louisiana Creole phrases.

24. Ibid., 19.

25. Ibid., 15.

26. Allain, *Souvenirs*, 11, 14, 15; Sullivan-Holleman and Cobb, *Saint Domingue*, 228, 374–375. The genealogical records cited here indicate that Marguerite-Charlotte Bizoton d'Aquin had eight children rather than the seventeen referred to by Allain. One of the eight, Charles-Antoine, died at the age of eight, and eighteen-year-old Pierre-François was killed in the revolution. Marguerite-Charlotte died in New Orleans in 1821. She is buried in St. Louis Cemetery No. 1. Also see d'Aquin et al., "Antiquity," part 2, 263; Charles E. Nolan, ed., *Sacramental Records of the Roman Catholic Church of the Archdiocese of New Orleans* (New Orleans: Archdiocese of New Orleans, 1999), 14:39.

27. Garrigus, *Before Haiti*, 45; Sullivan-Holleman and Cobb, *Saint Domingue*, 386, 390–391; Allain, *Souvenirs*, 9–13; David P. Geggus, ed., *The Impact of the Haitian Revolution in the Atlantic World* (Columbia: University of South Carolina Press, 2001), x; Fick, *Making of Haiti*, 66–67; Michael Craton, "Forms of Resistance to Slavery," in *General History of the Caribbean*, ed. Franklin W. Knight (London: UNESCO Publishing, 1997), 231. Colonial censuses regularly described girls over the age of twelve as "of marrying age."

28. Raillicourt, *Filiations*, table 2; Garrigus, *Before Haiti*, 21–22, 260; David Patrick Geggus, *Slavery, War, and Revolution: The British Occupation of Saint-Domingue, 1793–1798* (Oxford: Oxford University Press, 1982), 71; Robert Louis Stein, *Léger Félicité Sonthonax: The Lost Sentinel of the Republic* (Rutherford, NJ: Fairleigh Dickinson University Press; London: Associated University Presses, c1985), 27–28, 65; Palmer, *Intimate Bonds*, 11, 185–186.

29. Dubois, *Avengers*, 131–134, at 134. Bowing to slave resistance in all its forms in spring 1793, French revolutionary commissaire Léger Félicité Sonthonax relaxed plantation discipline, permitted the enslaved to denounce their enslavers, and began recruiting armed slaves into

Légions de l'Egalité. See also Fick, *Making of Haiti*, 27–28, 36, 91; Fiehrer, "From La Tortue," in Brasseaux and Conrad, *Road to Louisiana*, 19–20; Nolan, *Sacramental Records*, 10:111; Sullivan-Holleman and Cobb, *Saint Domingue*, 259–260; Geggus, *Slavery, War, and Revolution*, 22, 42, 64, 101.

30. Dubois, *Avengers*, 120–121, at 121; Fick, *Making of Haiti*, 118–124; *Traité de Paix, Entre les Citoyens Blancs & les Citoyens De Couleur, des quatorze paroisses de la province de l'Ouest, de la partie française de Saint-Domingue*, October 23, 1791, John Carter Brown Library, Brown University, https://archive.org/details/traitedepaixentreoounkn. For a translated excerpt of the *Traité*, see David Geggus, ed. and trans., *The Haitian Revolution: A Documentary History* (Indianapolis, IN: Hackett, 2014), 68–70.

31. Prior to his emigration to Louisiana, where he died in 1830 at the age of seventy-five, Charles Savary *aîné* is referred to in primary and secondary sources as Savary *aîné* and/or Savary, with no given name. Jean Savary and Savary *aîné* both appear among the Saint-Marc signers of the 1791 Concordat. It appears that Jean, probably Charles's brother, was killed in the village of Sibert during the ensuing white resistance, a struggle that led to Port-au-Prince's November 1791 devastation. See Fick, *Making of Haiti*, 123–126. Beaubrun Ardouin uses both versions of Savary's surname. See Ardouin, *Études sur l'Histoire d'Haiti* (Paris: Dezobry et E. Magdeleine, 1853), 2:45, 47, 301. Jean Phillippe Garran de Coulon, *Rapport sur les Troubles de Saint-Domingue* (Paris, 1797–1799), 2:146, 424, follows the same naming pattern as Ardouin. In New Orleans, Savary's given name, Charles, appears in primary and secondary sources. See, for instance, his New Orleans death certificate, Vital Records, Louisiana State Archives (August 30, 1862). Also see Gabriel Debien and René Le Gardeur, "The Saint-Domingue Refugees in Louisiana, 1792–1804," trans. David Cheramie, in Brasseaux and Conrad, *Road to Louisiana*, 174, where the authors report his given name as Charles, together with references to his actions as a signatory to the 1791 Concordat and his position as mayor of Saint-Marc. One of the Savary brothers, though it is not clear which one, fought in the American Revolution. See Geggus, *Slavery, War, and Revolution*, 22; and reference to "Savary and his brothers," in Ardouin, *Études*, 2:301.

32. *Traité de Paix*, 4; Ardouin, *Études*, 2:45–46, 51, 301; Fick, *Making of Haiti*, 121–122, 166; Stein, *Sonthonax*, 38, 64; Geggus, *Slavery, War, and Revolution*, 66; "Savary, Charles-Joseph," in *African American National Biography*.

33. For Savary's rank, see his letter to Andrew Jackson, March 31, 1815, Edward Livingston Papers, Firestone Library, Princeton University, box 23, folder 41; Geggus, *Slavery, War, and Revolution*, 64, 328; Stein, *Sonthonax*, 24, 64–66. On d'Aquin's nativity, see Nolan, *Sacramental Records*, 10:111. For the date of his death, see Maduell, "d'Aquin Family," 262; Dubois, *Avengers*, 130–131; King, *Blue Coat*, xiii, 265; Garran, *Rapport sur les Troubles*, 4:157–158.

34. Stein, *Sonthonax*, 88, 92–94; Fick, *Making of Haiti*, 160–168, 186–189; Garrigus, *Before Haiti*, 270–273. Rigaud introduced profit sharing, abolished the whip, freed prisoners on slave ships, and garnered government revenues that spared South Province residents from the famine that plagued Saint-Dominguans elsewhere in the colony. For Napoleon Bonaparte's reversal of revolutionary France's emancipation decree, on May 20, 1802, and his discriminatory legislation targeting free people of color, see Palmer, *Intimate Bonds*, 197.

35. Ashli White, *Encountering Revolution: Haiti and the Making of the Early Republic* (Bal-

timore: Johns Hopkins University Press, 2010), 104–106, at 105; Rashauna Johnson, *Slavery's Metropolis: Unfree Labor in New Orleans during the Age of Revolutions* (New York: Cambridge University Press, 2016), 37–38 note 25, quote on 38. Initially disbarred for nearly twenty years, Dormenon became a planter and judge in Pointe Coupée Parish.

36. Geggus, *Slavery, War, and Revolution*, 66–70, at 66; also 105–108, 423 note 175; Stein, *Sonthonax*, 63–65, 78–79, 93, 99–101; Dubois, *Avengers*, 166. For a thorough description of Étiénne Polvérel's plan for gradual emancipation and France's critical military situation, see Fick, *Making of Haiti*, 166–183.

37. Geggus, *Slavery, War, and Revolution*, 118, 179, 234; Garrigus, *Before Haiti*, 274; Fick, *Making of Haiti*, 199–201, 210–212; Cauna, *L'Eldorado*, 43–44. For d'Aquin's military rank, see Archives nationales d'outre-mer, Inventaires détaillés, Personnel colonial modern, 2018, http://www.archivesnationales.culture.gouv.fr/anom.

38. Geggus, *Slavery, War, and Revolution*, 68, 95, 112, 124, 153; Garrigus, *Before Haiti*, 260, 273; Sullivan-Holleman and Cobb, *Saint Domingue*, 377; Gwendolyn Midlo Hall, *Afro-Louisiana History and Genealogy, 1719–1820*, http://www.ibiblio.org/laslave; Nathalie Dessens, *From Saint-Domingue to New Orleans: Migration and Influences* (Gainesville: University Press of Florida, 2007), 24.

39. Debien and Le Gardeur, "Saint-Domingue Refugees," 225–227; Nolan, *Sacramental Records*, 10:111; Raillicourt, *Filiations*, table 2; Allain, *Souvenirs*, 11; Sullivan-Holleman and Cobb, *Saint Domingue*, 374–377.

40. Dubois, *Avengers*, 303–304, at 303; Meadows, "Planters of Saint-Domingue," vii–viii; *État détaillé des liquidations* (1832), 174–175, 256–257, and (1834), section 1, 124–125, section 2, 126–127, 200–201, 206–207, 210–211, 216–217, 226–227, 274–275, section 3, 562–563; "Pouyat and Daron," in the Jamaican Family Search Genealogy Research Library; David Nicholls, *From Dessalines to Duvalier: Race, Colour and National Independence in Haiti* (1979; reprint, New Brunswick, NJ: Rutgers University Press, 1996), 65; Stein, *Sonthonax*, 170–171. Like France and other major powers, the United States withheld diplomatic recognition. Finally, after the slaveholding South's secession in the US Civil War, Massachusetts senator Charles Sumner won passage of legislation acknowledging Haiti's independence. President Abraham Lincoln signed the measure into law on June 5, 1862. See Fritz Daguillard, *A Jewel in the Crown: Charles Sumner and the Struggle for Haiti's Recognition* (Washington, DC: Haitian Embassy, 1999), ix, 34.

41. Thomas Marc Fiehrer, "Baron de Carondelet as Agent of Bourbon Reforms: A Study of Spanish Colonial Administration in the Years of the French Revolution" (PhD diss., Tulane University, 1977), 473; Hunt, *Haiti's Influence on Antebellum America*, 25.

42. Kimberly S. Hanger, *Bounded Lives, Bounded Places: Free Black Society in Colonial New Orleans, 1769–1803* (Durham, NC: Duke University Press, 1997), 152–157; Caryn Cossé Bell, *Revolution, Romanticism, and the Afro-Creole Protest Tradition in Louisiana, 1718–1868* (Baton Rouge: Louisiana State University Press, 1997), 24–27.

43. Paul F. Lachance, "Repercussions of the Haitian Revolution," in Geggus, *Impact of the Haitian Revolution*, 211–212, at 212. For a depiction of the German Coast, a region extending roughly from Orleans Parish through St. Charles and St. John the Baptist Parishes on both sides of the Mississippi river, see Charles Robert Goins and John Michael Caldwell, *Historical Atlas of Louisiana* (Norman: University of Oklahoma Press, 1995), 27.

44. David Patrick Geggus, "Slavery, War, and Revolution in the Greater Caribbean, 1789–

1815," in *A Turbulent Time: The French Revolution and the Greater Caribbean*, ed. David Barry Gaspar and David Patrick Geggus (Bloomington: Indiana University Press, 1997), 13–14, at 14; Paul Lachance, "The Politics of Fear: French Louisianians and the Slave Trade, 1786–1809," *Plantation Society*, 1 (June 1979), 183;

45. For quote and discussion of DuBourg's participation in the slave trade, see Claiborne to James Madison, October 28, 1804, in Dunbar Rowland, ed., *Official Letter Books of W. C. C. Claiborne, 1801–1816* (Jackson: Mississippi Department of Archives and History, 1917), 2:346–347. Théodat Camille Bruslé's sister, Joséphine-Charlotte Benigne Bruslé, married Pierre-François DuBourg's brother, Joseph Patrice DuBourg. See "DuBourg" in Jamaican Family Search; Melville, *William DuBourg*, 1:8–10; Debien and Le Gardeur, "Saint-Domingue Refugees," 190; Powell A. Casey, *Louisiana in the War of 1812* (Baton Rouge: Self-published, 1963), 30, 32 note 4. On January 1, 1808, the US Congress abolished the foreign slave trade, though it left the statute's enforcement in the hands of the individual states. See White, *Encountering Revolution*, 168.

46. "Bringier, Marius Pons," in *Dictionary of Louisiana Biography*; Craig A. Bauer, *Creole Genesis: The Bringier Family and Antebellum Plantation Life in Louisiana* (Lafayette: University of Louisiana at Lafayette Press, 2011), x 1–29, 151. For marriage patterns and godparentage among the Francophone refugees, see Patrick Bryan, "Émigrés, Conflict and Reconciliation. The French Émigrés in Nineteenth Century Jamaica," *Jamaica Journal*, 7 (September 1973): 18; Rafe Blaufarb, *Bonapartists in the Borderlands: French Exiles and Refugees on the Gulf Coast, 1815–1835* (Tuscaloosa: University of Alabama Press, 2005), 39, 162–163.

47. Nolan, *Sacramental Records*, 15:111; Hanger, *Bounded Lives*, 106.

48. For d'Aquin's real estate purchases, see "Louis Daquin," in Collins C. Diboll Vieux Carré Digital Survey, Historic New Orleans Collection, http://www.hnoc.org/vcs. For the quote and reference to d'Aquin's financial instability, see the transaction between Augustin Griffony and Louis Daquin, March 1, 1804; C. C. Robin, *Voyages dans l'intérieur de la Louisiane* (Paris, 1807), 2:78; John W. Blassingame, *Black New Orleans, 1860–1880* (Chicago: University of Chicago Press, 1973), 74–77.

49. A nabot, used in the West Indies to prevent the enslaved from running away, was an iron ring of varying size, weighted in proportion to the age and strength of the individual and worn with a chain. See J. Clancy Clements et al., eds., *History, Society, and Variation: In Honor of Albert Valdman* (Amsterdam: John Benjamins, 2006), 66; Lachance, "Repercussions," 213; Dessens, *From Saint-Domingue to New Orleans*, 74.

50. Albert Thrasher, *"On to New Orleans!": Louisiana's Heroic 1811 Slave Revolt* (New Orleans: Cypress Press, 1996), 43–46; Thrasher's book is extremely valuable for its voluminous copies of primary documents. Debien and Le Gardeur, "Saint-Domingue Refugees," 225; *Le Moniteur de la Louisiane*, May 17, July 1, and December 9, 1807.

51. Lacy K. Ford, *Deliver Us from Evil: The Slavery Question in the Old South* (New York: Oxford University Press, 2009), 134–135; Virginia Guedea, "The Process of Mexican Independence," *American Historical Review*, 105 (February 2000): 116–122; Blackburn, *Making of New World Slavery*, 369.

52. In the first authoritative study of the revolt, James H. Dorman concluded that Charles was "probably of Santo Domingan origins." Dorman, "The Persistent Specter: Slave Rebellion in Territorial Louisiana," *Louisiana History*, 18 (Fall 1977): 394. More recently, Robert L. Paquette

wrote that the rebel leader was "most likely born in Spanish Louisiana." See Paquette, "German Coast Slave Insurrection of 1811," *64 Parishes,* January 10, 2011, https://64parishes.org/entry/slave-insurrection-of-1811.

Though Governor Claiborne expressed no opinion regarding Charles's background, he nonetheless believed that the revolutionary ideology of the rebels had originated in the Caribbean. See Junius Rodriguez, "Rebellion on the River Road: The Ideology and Influence of Louisiana's German Coast Slave Insurrection of 1811," in *Antislavery Violence: Sectional, Racial, and Cultural Conflict in Antebellum America,* ed. John R. McKivigan and Stanley Harrold (Knoxville: University of Tennessee Press, 1999), 78.

Notwithstanding the uncertainty, the prevailing scholarly consensus agrees on the Saint-Domingue background of Charles. See Thomas Marshall Thompson, "National Newspaper and Legislative Reactions to Louisiana's Deslondes Slave Revolt of 1811," *Louisiana History,* 33 (Winter 1992): 21 note 38; Geggus, "Preface," in *Impact of the Haitian Revolution,* xii; Geggus, "Slavery, War, and Revolution," 14; Rodriguez, "Rebellion on the River Road," 69–70; Jean-Pierre Le Glaunec, "German Coast (Louisiana) Insurrection of 1811," in *Encyclopedia of Antislavery and Abolition,* vol. 1, *A–I,* ed. Peter Hinks, John McKividgan, and R. Owens Williams (Westport, CT: Greenwood Press, 2007), 300; Thrasher, *"On to New Orleans!,"* 70.

53. Robert L. Paquette, "'A Horde of Brigands?' The Great Louisiana Slave Revolt of 1811 Reconsidered," *Historical Reflections/Réflexions Historiques,* 35 (Spring 2009): 74, 81–82, 86; Thompson, "National Newspaper," 7 note 3, 21; Rodriguez, "Rebellion on the River Road," 76; Dorman, "Persistent Specter," 397–398; Thrasher, *"On to New Orleans!,"* 51.

54. Rodriguez, "Rebellion on the River Road," 71–72, 78; Claiborne to Secretary of State James Madison, January 14, 1811, in Rowland, *Official Letter Books,* 5:100; Roland C. McConnell, *Negro Troops of Antebellum Louisiana: A History of the Battalion of Free Men of Color* (Baton Rouge: Louisiana State University Press, 1968), 49. For reference to DuBourg's military service, see Winston De Ville, *The Territory of Orleans, 1803–1812* (Ville Platte, LA: W. De Ville, 1987), 631–632, 639; Kenneth R. Aslakson, *Making Race in the Courtroom: The Legal Construction of Three Races in Early New Orleans* (New York: New York University Press, 2014), 93.

55. Dorman, "Persistent Specter," 396–398, at 397; Paquette, "A Horde of Brigands?," 74, 76 note 26, 77–78, 82; Ford, *Deliver Us from Evil,* 132; Destrehan Plantation, *The 1811 Slave Revolt and Trial at Destrehan Plantation* (Destrehan, LA: Author, 1999), 2:4.

56. Rodriguez, "Rebellion on the River Road," 80; Herbert Aptheker, *American Negro Slave Revolts,* 6th ed. (New York: International Publishers, 1993), 251.

57. Dubois and Garrigus, *Slave Revolution,* 75; Geggus, *Haitian Revolution,* 48, 57. Ogé was the light-complexioned son of a French colonial merchant in Cap-Français with three white grandparents and a white brother-in-law. For their failed 1790 revolt, Ogé and his lieutenants had their arms, legs, thighs, and spines broken, after which they were bound to wheels. When they died, their bodies were decapitated and their heads exposed on poles. See Earl Leslie Griggs and Clifford H. Prator, eds., *Henry Christophe and Thomas Clarkson: A Correspondence* (Berkeley: University of California Press, 1968), 12; C. L. R. James, *The Black Jacobins: Toussaint l'Ouverture and the San Domingo Revolution,* rev. ed. (New York: Vintage Books, 1963), 73–75.

58. W. C. C. Claiborne to Jean-Noël Destrehan, January 16 and 19, 1811, in Rowland, *Official Letter Books,* 5:101–100, 105–106.

59. Dorman, "Persistent Specter," 398–399, at 404; Rodriguez, "Rebellion on the River Road," 76–77.

60. Dorman, "Persistent Specter," 403. On the 2019 reenactment of the revolt on River Road from LaPlace to St. Rose, Louisiana, see Katy Reckdahl, "Reenacting Revolt," *New Orleans Times-Picayune*, November 8, 2019.

61. Lachance, "The 1809 Immigration of Saint-Domingue Refugees to New Orleans: Reception, Integration and Impact," *Louisiana History*, 29 (Spring 1988): 124.

62. Savary signs his name with the *fils* designation in Petition to Andrew Jackson from Joseph Savary et al., March 16, 1815, Livingston Papers, box 23, folder 41. "Savary, Charles-Joseph," in *African American National Biography*; Charles K. Gardner, *A Dictionary of All Officers, Who Have Been Commissioned, or Have Been Appointed and Served, in the United States* (New York, 1860), 395; Vanessa Mongey, "A Tale of Two Brothers: Haiti's Other Revolutions," *The Americas*, 69 (July 2012): 37, 49 note 36, 50; Arsène Lacarrière Latour, *Historical Memoir of the War in West Florida and Louisiana in 1814–15*, ed. Gene Allen Smith (New Orleans: Historic New Orleans Collection, 1999), xviii. The Attakapas region derives its geographic identity from the Atakapan-speaking people, whose tribal villages in southwest Louisiana were concentrated between Bayou Teche and the Sabine River circa 1700. See Goins and Caldwell, *Historical Atlas of Louisiana*, 17.

63. Vincent Nolte, *Fifty Years in Both Hemispheres or, Reminiscences of the Life of a Former Merchant* (New York: Redfield, 1854), 206.

2. INSURGENCY AND INVASION

1. Janet Polasky, *Revolutions without Borders: The Call to Liberty in the Atlantic World* (New Haven, CT: Yale University Press, 2015), 2–10, at 3–4 and 9.

2. Mongey, "Tale of Two Brothers," 37; Polasky, *Revolutions without Borders*, 10; Anne Pérotin-Dumon, "Les corsairs de la liberté," *l'histoire*, 43 (March 1982), 28–29.

3. Mongey, "Tale of Two Brothers," 37, 49 note 36, 50; Frank Lawrence Owsley Jr. and Gene A. Smith, *Filibusters and Expansionists: Jeffersonian Manifest Destiny, 1800–1821* (Tuscaloosa: University of Alabama Press, 1997), 41, 49, 51–52; David Head, *Privateers of the Americas: Spanish American Privateering from the United States in the Early Republic* (Athens: University of Georgia Press, 2015), 98; Jaime E. Rodriguez O, *The Independence of Spanish America* (Cambridge: Cambridge University Press, 1998), 209.

4. Bell, *Revolution*, 49–50; William C. Davis, *The Pirates Laffite: The Treacherous World of the Corsairs of the Gulf* (Orlando, FL: H. M. H. Books, 2005), 142; Polasky, *Revolutions*, 252–253.

5. Polasky, *Revolutions*, xvi, 270. Polasky also counts Humbert among the Atlantic world's itinerant revolutionaries. Bell, *Revolution*, 50; Pierre Larousse, ed., *Grand dictionnaire universel du XIXe siècle* (Paris, 1876), 15:289; William Theobald Wolfe Tone, ed., *Life of Theobald Wolfe Tone* (Washington, DC, 1826), 2:548.

6. Blaufarb, *Bonapartists*, 39; Head, *Privateers*, 16, 142; Mongey, "Tale of Two Brothers," 57; Owsley and Smith, *Filibusters*, 39–42.

7. Reilly, *British at the Gates*, 124, 170–171.

8. Dessens, *From Saint-Domingue to New Orleans*, 73; Casey, *Louisiana in the War*, 30, v, lxxi, and "Rosters of Louisiana Troops in War of 1812," n.p.

9. McConnell, *Negro Troops*, 5–14, 17–22, at 13; Hanger, *Bounded Lives*, 117–118, 125. The Spanish organized free Black militiamen on the basis of skin color, designating dark-complexioned soldiers as *morenos* and light-complexioned men as *pardos*.

10. Jefferson's notes on a cabinet meeting, October 4, 1803, in Thomas Jefferson Papers, Library of Congress; Aslakson, *Making Race*, 67; James Wilkinson to the Secretary of War, December 21, 1803, in Clarence Edwin Carter, ed., *The Territorial Papers of the United States*, vol. 9, *The Territory of Orleans, 1803–1812* (Washington, DC: US Government Printing Office, 1940), 139.

11. Aslakson, *Making Race*, 82–83; Joseph P. Stoltz III, "'The Preservation of Good Order': William C. C. Claiborne and the Militia of the Louisiana Provisional Government, 1803–1805," *Louisiana History*, 54 (Fall 2013): 429, 439.

12. Claiborne to James Madison, July 3, 1804, in Dunbar Rowland, ed., *Official Letter Books of W. C. C. Claiborne, 1801–1816* (Jackson: Mississippi Department of Archives and History, 1917), 2:234–235.

13. Claiborne to Madison, July 12, 1804, in *Official Letter Books*, 2:244–245. The 1805 population figures cited in the text are from Thomas Marc Fiehrer, "The African Presence in Colonial Louisiana: An Essay on the Continuity of Caribean Culture," in *Louisiana's Black Heritage*, ed. Robert R. MacDonald, John R. Kemp, and Edward F. Haas (New Orleans: Louisiana State Museum, 1979), 19.

14. McConnell, *Negro Troops*, 41–43; Stoltz, "Preservation of Good Order," 440.

15. Jennifer M. Spear, *Race, Sex, and Social Order in Early New Orleans* (Baltimore: Johns Hopkins University Press, 2009), 186–192, at 191; Aslakson, *Making Race*, 22, 52–54. In 1822, the legislature commissioned Moreau-Lislet, Pierre Derbigny, jurist and refugee of the French Revolution, and Edward Livingston, a politician and lawyer from New York, to author the Civil Code of Louisiana. The legislature would approve the comprehensive Civil Code of Louisiana in 1824. For the reference to the *New York Herald*, see Debien and Le Gardeur, "Saint-Domingue Refugees," 205; "Moreau-Lislet, Louis Casimir Elisabeth," in *Dictionary of Louisiana Biography*; Alain A. Levasseur, "A 'Civil Law' Lawyer: Louis Casimir Elisabeth Moreau Lislet," LSU Law Digital Commons, 234, https://digitalcommons.law.lsu.edu/faculty_scholarship/323.

16. Aslakson, *Making Race*, 3–5, 64; Spear, *Race, Sex, and Social Order*, 187–188. In 1850, one thousand free children of color attended school, representing 23 percent of the South's total Black schoolchildren. In 1860, the city possessed the largest number of free Black property owners in the South. Altogether, Louisiana's free Black population was by far the richest in the United States. With rare exceptions, wealthy free Blacks in Louisiana and elsewhere in the lower South were directly related either to whites or to free people of color whose white patrons had assisted them. This was the case in Louisiana, with the South's largest number of free Black planters. See Loren Schweninger, *Black Property Owners in the South, 1790–1915* (Urbana: University of Illinois Press, 1997), 71, 101, 129; and Ira Berlin, *Slaves without Masters: The Free Negro in the Antebellum South* (New York: The New Press, 1974), 130.

17. Quote in Annals of Congress, 9th Congress, 2nd session, 215, Library of Congress, hpps://memory.loc.gov. See also William T. Hatfield, *William Claiborne: Jeffersonian Centurion in the American Southwest* (Lafayette: University of Southwestern Louisiana, 1976), 159–161; Aslakson, *Making Race*, 64–66; Stoltz, "Preservation of Good Order," 436 note 38.

18. Quotes in W. C. C. Claiborne to Daniel Clark, May 23, 1807, and Claiborne to Thomas

Jefferson, June 12, 1807, in Thomas Jefferson Papers, Library of Congress. See also Hatfield, *William Claiborne*, 160–161, 352 note 57; *Louisiana Gazette*, May 20, 1807; McConnell, *Negro Troops*, 18, 43–45; Stoltz, "Preservation of Good Order," 436 note 38. In 1803, Claiborne himself had signed a law prohibiting dueling. The penalty for participating, either as a principal or second, was a $1,000 fine and a year in jail. In addition, participants were barred from holding a territorial office for five years.

19. For the number of free male émigrés of color in New Orleans in 1809 alone, see Lachance, "Repercussions," 213; Ira Berlin, *Many Thousands Gone: The First Two Centuries of Slavery in North America* (Cambridge, MA: Belknap Press of Harvard University Press, 1998), 374–375; McConnell, *Negro Troops*, 53–54.

20. Quotes in Claiborne to Jackson, August 12, 1814, in John Spencer Bassett, ed., *Correspondence of Andrew Jackson* (Washington, DC, 1926–1935), 6:435–436. See also Robert V. Remini, *The Battle of New Orleans: Andrew Jackson and America's First Military Victory* (New York: Penguin Viking, 1999), 15; Marcus Christian, *The Battle of New Orleans: Negro Soldiers in the Battle of New Orleans* (New Orleans: Battle of New Orleans, 150th Anniversary Committee of Louisiana, 1965), 25–26. For the distinction between Michel Fortier *père* and *fils* see Casey, *Louisiana in the War*, 33 and v.

21. McConnell, *Negro Troops*, 41. On the necessity of recruiting free men of color, see Jackson to Claiborne, September 21, 1814, in Bassett, *Correspondence of Andrew Jackson*, 2:56–57.

22. Reilly, *British at the Gates*, 203; *Courrier de la Louisiane*, September 23, 1814; *Louisiana Courier*, September 26, 1814.

23. *Courrier de la Lousiane*, September 23, 1814. Other members of the committee were state lawmaker Jean Blanque, judge of the parish court of New Orleans Jacques-François Pitot, and planter Pierre Foucher. "Hall, Dominick Augustine," "Morgan, David Bannister," "Pitot, James," and "Destrehan de Tours, Jean Noël," in *Dictionary of Louisiana Biography*; Grace King, *Creole Families of New Orleans* (New York: Macmillan, 1921), 379; Christian, *Battle of New Orleans*, 19; Nathan A. Buman, "Historiographical Examinations of the 1811 Slave Insurrection," *Louisiana History*, 53 (Summer 2012): 328; Claiborne to Vilerae [sic], January 16, 1811, *Official Letter Books*, 5:101; Claiborne to Jackson, October 17, 1814, in Bassett, *Correspondence of Andrew Jackson*, 2:76–77.

24. Claiborne to Jackson, October 28, 1814, in Rowland, *Official Letter Books*, 6:294.

25. Claiborne to Andrew Jackson, October 17, 1814, in Bassett, *Correspondence of Andrew Jackson*, 2:76–77; Christian, *Battle of New Orleans*, 19–20.

26. Claiborne to Jackson, October 17, 1814; McConnell, *Negro Troops*, 63. On distrust of white Saint-Domingue refugees, see Lachance, "Repercussions," 212–213; and White, *Encountering Revolution*, 196. The assertion that d'Aquin's opponents challenged his white identity rests on Marcus Christian's manuscripts written for the African American *Louisiana Weekly* between 1932 and 1957. Christian wrote that d'Aquin was removed from his post as an officer in the prestigious white Bataillon d'Orléans owing to a "rumor or an open charge of having Negro blood." See Christian, "Comments Here and There: Colonel Joseph Savary," Historical Manuscripts, Marcus Christian Collection, Earl K. Long Library, University of New Orleans. The substantive historical context in which the attack on d'Aquin occurred supports Christian's version of events.

27. Claiborne to Jackson, October 17, 1814, in Bassett, *Correspondence of Andrew Jackson*, 2:76; *Louisiana Gazette*, October 18, 1814.

28. Jackson to Claiborne, September 21, 1814, in Bassett, *Correspondence of Andrew Jackson*, 2:56–59.

29. Jackson to Claiborne, September 21, 1814, and Claiborne to Jackson, October 17, 1814, in Bassett, *Correspondence of Andrew Jackson*, 2:57, 77. Jackson's dispatches of September 27 were forwarded to Natchez, Mississippi, and did not reach Claiborne in New Orleans until October 15. Claiborne describes the cause of the delay in his October 17 response.

30. Latour, *Historical Memoir*, xv–xix, xxiv–xxv, 47, quote on 217; Robert V. Remini, *The Life of Andrew Jackson*, abridged ed. (New York: Harper Collins, 2001), 88–89; Reilly, *British at the Gates*, 214–215; Charles Gayarré, *History of Louisiana* (1903; reprint, New Orleans, 1965), 4:383; Casey, *Louisiana in the War*, 30–31.

31. Nolte, *Fifty Years in Both Hemispheres*, 206; *Biographical and Historical Memoirs of Louisiana* (Chicago, 1892), 1:63–64; Christian, "Comments Here and There." The rosters show that by December 16 d'Aquin had been moved from the Bataillon d'Orléans to the First Division of the Louisiana Militia. Casey, *Louisiana in the War*, i, xv, xvii, lix, lxi. Perhaps Alcée Fortier, a twentieth-century descendant of Michel Fortier, who also commanded free Black troops during the battle, had the racially charged attack on d'Aquin in mind when he defended his ancestor's white racial identity: "It is needless to say that Colonel Fortier and Major Lacoste were not colored men. They belonged to families which, in 1814, had been nearly a century in Louisiana. Fortier had served in [Bernardo de] Gálvez's army in his campaign against the English, . . . and had long been a captain of artillery in the militia service of Spain." Fortier offered no such defense of Major d'Aquin, the only other commanding officer of free troops of color, whose forebears, like Fortier's own, were among Louisiana's earliest colonists and served in the French campaigns against the Natchez. See Fortier, *History of Louisiana*, 3:267 note 8. Differing narratives about the racial identity of the d'Aquins have persisted within the city's Black community. Creole writer Alice Dunbar-Nelson wrote that officer d'Aquin was "probably regarded as a quadroon who had been accepted by the white race," and scholar Sybil Kein described Allain as an "Afro-French woman." For quotes, see Dunbar-Nelson, "People of Color of Louisiana," part 2, *Journal of Negro History*, 2 (January 1917), 59 note 20; and Kein, "The Use of Louisiana Creole in Southern Literature," in *Creole: The History and Legacy of Louisiana's Free People of Color* (Baton Rouge: Louisiana State University Press, 2000), 135.

32. Remini, *Life of Andrew Jackson*, 87–89, 91–92; Bernard Marigny, "Reflections on the Campaign of General Andrew Jackson in Louisiana in 1814 and '15," *Louisiana Historical Quarterly*, 4 (January 1923), 66, 73–74; Remini, *Battle of New Orleans*, 44–45, 47–48, 57–59.

33. For references to the French quatrain, see Stanley Clisby Arthur, *Old New Orleans: A History of the Vieux Carré, It's Ancient and Historical Buildings* (New Orleans, 1936), 70; Kein, "Use of Louisiana Creole," 145; and Christian, *Battle of New Orleans*, 29. Nankeen is a durable buff fabric made of cotton.

34. Remini, *Battle of New Orleans*, 42, 122; Reilly, *British at the Gates*, 349; Latour, *Historical Memoir*, 150.

35. Latour, *Historical Memoir*, xxv–xxvi, 229; Remini, *Life of Andrew Jackson*, 91–93; Remini, *Battle of New Orleans*, 58–59; Reilly, *British at the Gates*, 248; McConnell, *Negro Troops*, 66–67;

Jane Lucas de Grummond and Ronald R. Morazan, *The Baratarians and the Battle of New Orleans with Biographical Sketches of the Veterans of the Battalion of Orleans, 1814–1815* (Baton Rouge, LA: Legacy, 1979), 83–84.

36. Latour, *Historical Memoir*, 55. McConnell, *Negro Troops*, 69–71; Louisiana's 1810 census documents the presence of the elder Savary in New Orleans, indicating that he and his wife, Charlotte Lajoie, may have entered the city with the 1809 refugee movement. Lajoie's relation to Charles Savary is cited in *Acts Passed at the First Session of the Tenth Legislature of Louisiana, 1831*, Hathi Trust Digital Library, https://babel.hathitrust.org/cgi/pt?id=uc1.a0001917921&view=1up&seq=7, 106.

37. Andrew Jackson, April 4, 1815, New Orleans, Headquarters 7th District, Livingston Papers, box 23, folder 41; Lachance, "Repercussions," 222–223; Mongey, "Tale of Two Brothers," 49; McConnell, *Negro Troops*, 69–71.

38. Christian, *Battle of New Orleans*, 29; *Biographical and Historical Memoirs*, 1:64. According to Everett, "Emigres and Militiamen," 396, a number of whites signed up as commissioned officers in the battalions of color after Jackson promised soldiers of color the same bounty in pay and lands as the white soldiers. On Carrière, see Hanger, *Bounded Lives*, 51; and McConnell, *Negro Troops*, 68. For the soldiers' rankings, see Casey, *Louisiana in the War*, lxiv–lxv; Garrigus, *Before Haiti*, 80–81. On Sylvain d'Aquin, also see New Orleans city directories, 1822–1855; and 1820 US Census.

39. Remini, *Battle of New Orleans*, 63–65; Remini, *Life of Andrew Jackson*, 93–95; Davis, *Pirates Laffite*, 212; Reilly, *British at the Gates*, 205, 223, 251, 255.

40. Christian, *Battle of New Orleans*, 31.

41. Reilly, *British at the Gates*, 254–256; Remini, *Battle of New Orleans*, 69–70, 73–80; Remini, *Life of Andrew Jackson*, 95–96; McConnell, *Negro Troops*, 76–77; Latour, *Historical Memoir*, 82; Nolte, *Fifty Years in Both Hemispheres*, 211.

42. Remini, *Life of Andrew Jackson*, 97–104; McConnell, *Negro Troops*, 84–88; Remini, *Battle of New Orleans*, 140–155; "Savary, Charles-Joseph," in *African American National Biography*. Confusion over Belton Savary's rank and relationship to Major Savary are best resolved in Casey, *Louisiana in the War*, lxiv–lxv; *Acts Passed at the First Session of the Second Legislature of the State of Louisiana, 1814–1815*, xv; and "Savary, Joseph," in *Africana: The Encyclopedia of the African and African American Experience* (2005).

43. Reilly, *British at the Gates*, 225, 258, 322–329, at 323. For Jonathan Rees's rank, see Casey, *Louisiana in the War*, viii; Latour, *Historical Memoir*, 115–121.

44. Bell, *Revolution*, 59.

45. Latour, *Historical Memoir*, 246–247; Reilly, *British at the Gates*, 333.

46. Latour, *Historical Memoir*, xxxi, 115–119, quote on 299; Reilly, *British at the Gates*, 353–354.

47. Latour, *Historical Memoir*, 299; Remini, *Life of Andrew Jackson*, 95; Reilly, *British at the Gates*, 353–354.

48. Reilly, *British at the Gates*, 347–251; de Grummond and Morazan, *Baratarians*, 150–152; Remini, *Life of Andrew Jackson*, 109–110, quote on 109.

49. Latour, *Historical Memoir*, 229–230. McConnell, *Negro Troops*, 71, notes that d'Aquin's surname was Anglicized to Daquin during his stint in the US Army, as Jackson's quote indicates.

50. Latour, *Historical Memoir*, 56, 341.

51. Johnson, *Slavery's Metropolis*, 164–168, 176–200; Latour, *Historical Memoir*, 336.

52. McConnell, *Negro Troops*, 93–95; W. C. C. Claiborne to Jackson, February 1, 1815, in "Jackson Order Book," typescript copy, January 26, 1815–May 4, 1828 (Works Progress Administration, 1937), 49; Major Louis Daquin to Brigadier General Robert McCausland, February 15, 1815, in Andrew Jackson Papers, Library of Congress, Washington, DC.

53. Petition to Andrew Jackson from Joseph Savary et al., March 16, 1815, Livingston Papers, box 23, folder 41; Jackson to Lt. Col. Mathew Arbuckle, March 15, 1815, in Bassett, *Correspondence of Andrew Jackson*, 2:183.

54. Jackson to "Free Coloured Inhabitants of Louisiana," September 21, 1814, in Bassett, *Correspondence of Andrew Jackson*, 2:58; McConnell, *Negro Troops*, 104, 108–109.

3. THE TREE OF LIBERTY

1. James, *Black Jacobins*, 334. Jackson announced ratification of the Treaty of Ghent in New Orleans on March 6. See Reilly, *British at the Gates*, 350; Mongey, "Tale of Two Brothers," 50–51; Marixa Lasso, *Myths of Harmony: Race and Republicanism during the Age of Revolution, Colombia, 1795–1831* (Pittsburgh: University of Pittsburgh Press, 2007), 29, 34–36, 45–47. Lasso shows that between 1779 and 1825, Cartagena's slave population dropped by 50 percent. Fleeing Spanish planters who abandoned their slave workers contributed to the decline (19, 134).

2. Davis, *Pirates Laffite*, 298–299, 462; Blaufarb, *Bonapartists*, 39; Owsley and Smith, *Filibusters*, 171–173; Head, *Privateers*, 98, 135–136, 142–143. Head questions the presence of the entity known as the New Orleans Association, offering an extensive exploration of the name's origins (188 note 24). However, the presence of the covert coalition is broadly accepted and convincingly documented in the era's historiography. For a meticulously researched essay that refers to Watkin's involvement in the earlier Mexican Association, see Jerah Johnson, "Dr. John Watkins, New Orleans' Lost Mayor," in *Louisiana History*, 36 (Spring 1995), 195. Johnson's account dovetails with Stanley Faye's description of the amorphous coalition's origins among supporters of Spanish American independence, who organized the Mexican Association at the time of the Louisiana Purchase. That group gave rise to the Barataria Association, which in turn morphed into the New Orleans Association. See Faye, "The Great Stroke of Pierre Laffite," *Louisiana Historical Quarterly*, 23 (July 1940), 750. Anaya left New Orleans in 1815, and when Mexico gained its independence, he was elected to his new nation's congress. Gutiérrez became independent Mexico's governor of Texas. General Humbert returned to New Orleans, where he died in 1823.

3. Geggus, "Slavery, War, and Revolution," 15–16.

4. Pierre Force, *Wealth and Disaster: Atlantic Migrations from a Pyrenean Town in the Eighteenth and Nineteenth Centuries* (Baltimore: Johns Hopkins University Press, 2016), 132; Lancaster E. Dabney, "Louis Aury: The First Governor of Texas," *Southwestern Historical Quarterly*, 42 (July 1938–April 1939), 108–109; Owsley and Smith, *Filibusters*, 136; Faye, "Commodore," 611; Edgardo Pérez Morales, *No Limits to Their Sway: Cartagena's Privateers and the Masterless Caribbean in the Age of Revolutions* (Nashville: Vanderbilt University Press, 2018), 1–2.

5. Dabney, "Louis Aury," 110; Faye, "Commodore," 611–612; Morales, *No Limits*, 4–5.

6. Faye, "Commodore," 614–620, quotes on 692; Force, *Wealth*, 131–132; Lasso, *Myths of Harmony*, 74–75; Rodriguez O, *Independence of Spanish America*, 155–159; Morales, *No Limits*, 2, 171–172 note 2.

7. Force, *Wealth*, 127, quote on 134; Mongey, "Tale of Two Brothers," 51; Faye, "Commodore," 622–632, 638, 664; Fick, *Making of Haiti*, 205; Head, *Privateers*, 46.

8. Faye, "Commodore," 629–634; Davis, *Pirates Laffite*, 262, 303; Lachance, "Repercussions," 222–223. Cochineal is a scarlet or crimson dye derived from the cochineal insect.

9. Quotes in Head, *Privateers*, 143; Faye, "Commodore," 636–642; Dabney, "Louis Aury," 114; Owsley and Smith, *Filibusters*, 136–139, 170, 173–175; Davis, *Pirates Laffite*, 305–306, 322; Blaufarb, *Bonapartists*, 64–65; David P. Geggus, "Epilogue," in *Impact of the Haitian Revolution*, 250; Harris Gaylord Warren, "Mina, Francisco Xavier (1789–1817)," *Handbook of Texas Online*, Texas State Historical Association, https://tshaonline.org/handbook/online/articles/fmi46.

10. Landers, *Atlantic Creoles in the Age of Revolutions* (Cambridge, MA: Harvard University Press, 2010), 132–134, at 133; Blaufarb, *Bonapartists*, 65–67; Head, *Privateers*, 102–106; Faye, "Commodore," 643–645; Owsley and Smith, *Filibusters*, 135–137; Jane G. Landers, *Black Society in Spanish Florida* (Urbana: University of Illinois Press, 1999), 221, 245; William Earl Weeks, *John Quincy Adams and American Global Empire* (Lexington: University Press of Kentucky, 1992), 64.

11. Landers, *Atlantic Creoles*, 133–134; Landers, *Black Society*, 245.

12. Landers, *Atlantic Creoles*, 134.

13. Landers, *Black Society*, 220–227, at 246; Landers, *Atlantic Creoles*, 134.

14. Landers, *Atlantic Creoles*, 134–135.

15. Head, *Privateers*, 107–108.

16. Patrick W. Doyle, "Unmasked: The Author of Narrative of a Voyage to the Spanish Main in the Ship 'Two Friends,'" *Florida Historical Quarterly*, 78 (Fall 1999), 189–190, 192 note 16; [Joseph Freeman Rattenbury], *Narrative of a Voyage to the Spanish Main, in the Ship "Two Friends,"* (London, 1819), 96.

17. Head, *Privateers*, 108.

18. Landers, *Atlantic Creoles*, 110–111, at 111; Weeks, *John Quincy Adams*, 1–3, 27–29; Landers, *Black Society*, 220–221.

19. Landers, *Black Society*, 221–222, 226–227; Weeks, *John Quincy Adams*, 28–29.

20. James D. Richardson, ed., *A Compilation of the Messages and Papers of the Presidents, 1789–1897* (Washington, DC, 1875–1893), 2:13–14, at 14; Weeks, *John Quincy Adams*, 58, 62–66.

21. Weeks, *John Quincy Adams*, 63.

22. Landers, *Atlantic Creoles*, quote on 136–137. US forces remained in control of Amelia Island until the 1821 ratification of the 1819 Adams–Onís (or Transcontinental) Treaty, in which Spain ceded East Florida to the United States. See Robert E. May, *Manifest Destiny's Underworld: Filibustering in Antebellum America* (Chapel Hill: University of North Carolina Press, 2002), 8; Weeks, *John Quincy Adams*, 64.

23. Weeks, *John Quincy Adams*, 63–64. Adams quoted in Head, *Privateers*, 113.

24. Landers, *Black Society*, 246. Landers, 368 note 58, indicates that McIntosh's letter was widely published in a variety of venues both before and after its November appearance in the *Savannah Republican*.

25. Weeks, *John Quincy Adams*, 64, 66.

26. Head, *Privateers*, 146–147; Weeks, *John Quincy Adams*, 66–68.

27. Landers, *Atlantic Creoles*, 299 note 107.

28. Head, *Privateers*, 142, 147. On the basis of hearsay testimony in a legal proceeding, Head

also declares Savary a slaveholder. See the deposition of Mariano Gonzales, October 8, 1818, case no. 1227, in United States District Court, Louisiana, Eastern District, in *Conspicuous Cases in the United States District Court of Louisiana* (New Orleans: Survey of Federal Archives in Louisiana, 1940–1941). In addition to Monroe's misrepresentation of Aury, Head also references a 1928 essay, "MacGregor's Invasion of Florida," authored by T. Frederick Davis in the *Florida Historical Quarterly*, to disparage the French privateer. Though Aury, together with MacGregor, was among the most successful privateers in the cause of Spanish American independence, Davis diminished their accomplishments and resurrected the Monroe administration's groundless depiction of Aury as a slave trader. Davis attacked Aury for having "decided to lay aside his patriotism for the South Americans to become an outright pirate himself." At Galveston in 1816, Aury "collected a gang of desperate vagabonds, . . . together with a considerable body of vicious mulattoes from Santo Domingo Island"—Savary and other veterans of the Battle of New Orleans. "Slave ships," according to Davis, "were eagerly sought for as an especially valuable prize." With nearly two-thirds of his citations attributed to Charleston and Savannah newspapers and the remaining one-third to the Monroe administration's state papers, Davis can hardly be considered a fair judge of Aury and his itinerant revolutionary allies. Still, modern historians continue to reference his work. T. Frederick Davis, "MacGregor's Invasion of Florida," *Florida Historical Quarterly* 7 (1928), 31–32.

For instances in which Davis's negative depiction of Aury have reappeared, see Head, *Privateers*, chapter 4; Owsley and Smith, *Filibusters*, chapter 7; Landers, *Atlantic Creoles*, 135; Landers, "Franco/Spanish Entanglements in Florida and the Circumatlantic," *Journal of Transnational American Studies* 8 (2017), 58. For an account of the Monroe administration's unsubstantiated charges of piracy and slave trading, see Weeks, *John Quincy Adams*, 62–65.

29. Faye, "Commodore," 656, 676–677.

30. Ibid., 673, 676, 678–679; Ada Ferrer, "Haiti, Free Soil, and Antislavery in the Revolutionary Atlantic," *American Historical Review*, 117 (February 2012): 61.

31. Pérotin-Dumon, "Les corsairs de la liberté," 28–29; Faye, "Commodore," 613–614, 656, 672; Dabney, "Louis Aury," 108–111.

32. Ferrer, "Haiti, Free Soil, and Antislavery," 60; Nicholls, *From Dessalines to Duvalier*, 46–47; Mongey, "Tale of Two Brothers," 51.

33. Ferrer, "Haiti, Free Soil, and Antislavery," 60–61. For other works alleging Aury's extensive involvement in slave trading, see Owsley and Smith, *Filibusters*, 139, 164; Blaufarb, *Bonapartists*, 67; Landers, *Black Society*, 246; and Landers, *Atlantic Creoles*, 135.

34. Morales, *No Limits*, 151–155, at 152 and 155; Weeks, *John Quincy Adams*, 64; Vanessa Mongey, *Rogue Revolutionaries: The Fight for Legitimacy in the Greater Caribbean* (Philadelphia: University of Pennsylvania Press, 2020), 24. Also see Mongey, "Tale of Two Brothers," 46, 51–55, 59; Landers, *Atlantic Creoles*, 136; Landers, *Black Society*, 246; deposition of Mariano Gonzales; Faye, "Commodore," 656; Dabney, "Louis Aury," 116.

35. *L'Union*, December 6, 1862; Stanley Faye, "Privateersmen of the Gulf and Their Prizes," *Louisiana Historical Quarterly*, 22 (October 1939), 1068; Nolan, *Sacramental Records*, 13:393; Mc-Connell, *Negro Troops*, 102, 109; "Savary," Louisiana Digital Library, http://www.louisianadigtallibrary.org. Eugénie Pressot's designation as Savary's widow on a July 21, 1829, emancipation

petition, and the termination of his state pension payments in 1828, indicates that Savary likely died in either 1827 or 1828. See Petition 30882921, New Orleans Public Library, Records of the Parish Court, Emancipation Petitions 1813–1843, microfilm reel 98-5, frame 163; Stephen J. Ochs, *A Black Patriot and a White Priest: André Cailloux and Claude Paschal Maistre in Civil War New Orleans* (Baton Rouge: Louisiana State University Press, 2000), 71.

36. Fatima Shaik, *Economy Hall: The Hidden History of a Free Black Brotherhood* (New Orleans: Historic New Orleans Collection, 2021), 137–138, 228, at 137; Blassingame, *Black New Orleans*, 147.

37. Polasky, *Revolutions*, 2.

38. Christian, *Battle of New Orleans*, 44; Robin Blackburn, *The Overthrow of Colonial Slavery, 1776–1848* (London: Verso, 1988). Blackburn concludes that Aury and corsairs like him "caused great damage to Spanish sea communications" (345).

39. Lloyd Kramer, *Lafayette in Two Worlds: Public Cultures & Personal Identities in an Age of Revolutions* (Chapel Hill: University of North Carolina Press, 1996), 217–218, at 2 and 218; McConnell, *Negro Troops*, 100; A. Levasseur, *Lafayette in America in 1824 and 1825* (1829; reprint, New York: Research Imprints, 1970), 89–93. On Lafayette's request to meet with Savary and his cohorts, see his letter to his daughters, New Orleans, April 15, 1825, in Dean Lafayette Collection, no. 4611, Division of Rare and Manuscript Collections, Cornell University Library, https://digital.library.cornell.edu/catalog/ss:12591016; Francis P. Burns, "Lafayette Visits New Orleans," *Louisiana Historical Quarterly*, 29 (April 1946), 321.

40. Hanger, *Bounded Lives*, 130–132. Spain's King Charles III awarded Charles Simón a medal of honor for his service. See Sylvia Neely, *Lafayette and the Liberal Ideal, 1814–1824: Politics and Conspiracy in an Age of Reaction* (Carbondale: Southern Illinois Press, 1991), 72–73; John D. Garrigus, "'Thy coming fame, Ogé! Is sure': New Evidence on Ogé's 1790 Revolt and the Beginnings of the Haitian Revolution," in *Assumed Identities: The Meanings of Race in the Atlantic World*, ed. John D. Garrigus and Christopher Morris (Arlington: University of Texas at Arlington, 2010), 27–28, 38. Lafayette had designed the uniforms himself; see Polasky, *Revolutions*, 90.

41. Lafayette to his daughters, New Orleans, April 15, 1825; Kramer, *Lafayette*, 154–162; Wright quoted in Norman K. Risjord, *Representative Americans: The Romantics* (Lanham, MD: Rowman and Littlefield, 2001), 192.

42. Kramer, *Lafayette*, 82–97, 102, at 87.

43. J. L. Talmon, *Romanticism and Revolt: Europe, 1815–1848* (New York: Harcourt, Brace & World, 1967), 9.

44. McConnell, *Negro Troops*, 106, quotes on 107–108; Charles E. Kinzer, "The Band of Music of the First Battalion of Free Men of Color and the Siege of New Orleans, 1814–1815," *American Music*, 10 (Fall 1992), 361. New Orleans city directories (1822–1846) list Sylvain d'Aquin's occupation as a trader/mason/bricklayer.

45. For outstanding modern examples of this literary tradition, see Marcus Christian, *I Am New Orleans and Other Poems by Marcus B. Christian*, ed. Rudolph Lewis and Amin Sharif (New Orleans: Xavier Review Press, 1999); Brenda Marie Osbey, *History and Other Poems* (St. Louis: Time Being Books, 2012); Charles Edwards O'Neill, *Séjour: Parisian Playwright from Louisiana* (Lafayette: Center for Louisiana Studies, University of Southwestern Louisiana, 1995),

2–7, 26 note 24, 162; M. Lynn Weiss, "Introduction," in Victor Séjour, *The Jew of Seville*, trans. Norman R. Shapiro (Urbana: University of Illinois Press, 2002), xv–xvi, xxi; Roussève, *Negro in Louisiana*, 82 note 42; Juliane Braun, *Creole Drama: Theatre and Society in Antebellum New Orleans* (Charlottesville: University of Virginia Press, 2019), 152–154, with illuminating discussion of Séjour's views on slavery and abolition at 151–160; Sally McKee, *The Exile's Song: Edmond Dédé and the Unfinished Revolutions of the Atlantic World* (New Haven, CT: Yale University Press, 2017), 96.

46. Roussève, *Negro in Louisiana*, 82 note 42.

47. Bauer, *Creole Genesis*, 8–9, 26–31; Casey, *Louisiana in the War*, lxxi.

48. Nolan, *Sacramental Records*, 9:87, 10:111; "Moreau-Lislet, Louis Casimir Elisabeth," in *Dictionary of Louisiana Biography*.

49. Jean-Charles Houzeau, *My Passage at the New Orleans "Tribune": A Memoir of the Civil War Era*, ed. David C. Rankin, trans. Gerard F. Denault (Baton Rouge: Louisiana State University Press, 1984), 25–27, at 27, 25 note 3. Bauer refers to Jean-Baptiste Roudanez as "Eug. Roudanez." Bauer, *Creole Genesis*, 10, 73–74, 163 note 190; Mark Charles Roudané, "Race, Memory, and the World That Made New Orleans," *Roudanez History and Legacy*, 2015, https://roudanez.com/race-memory-and-the-world-that-made-new-orleans. Roudané graciously shared a certified "True Copy of Sacramental Record" he obtained from Saint Michael's Church in Convent, Louisiana; the Diocese of Baton Rouge Archive has the original. Also see Bell, "The Common Wind's Creole Visionary: Dr. Louis Charles Roudanez," *South Atlantic Review*, 73 (Spring 2008): 13, 19–23, 24 note 5; Blassingame, *Black New Orleans*, 164–165.

50. McConnell, *Negro Troops*, 111–112, at 112; Works Progress Administration, *Louisiana: A Guide to the State* (1941; reprint, New York: Hastings House, 1959), 493. Dedicated to Jackson and finally completed in 1908, the 110-foot Chalmette Monument was modeled after the Washington obelisk in the nation's capital.

51. McConnell, *Negro Troops*, 104, 106, 112–113.

52. Allain, *Souvenirs*, 14; New Orleans city directories (1822–1855); "Louis Daquin," in Collins C. Diboll Vieux Carré Digital Survey; King, *Creole Families*, 444–445.

4. UNE FAMILLE CRÉOLE

1. Allain, *Souvenirs*, 120–122, at 120, 122. Hélène d'Aquin Allain's death notice, Centre administratif, Ville de St-Germain-en-Laye, Yvelines, France, includes her birth date of January 22, 1833; Tinker, *Les Écrits*, 83; "Aquin" and "Daron" in Jamaican Family Search; Sullivan-Holleman and Cobb, *Saint Domingue*, 384–391; Maduell, "d'Aquin Family," 261; "Trouvailles," *Généalogie et Histoire de la Caraï*, 103 (April 1998), 2206.

2. d'Aquin et al., "Antiquity," part 2, 263–265; Allain, *Souvenirs*, 14–15, 20.

3. Knight, "Haitian Revolution," 113–114. The other two of the four largest slave rebellions in the Americas were in Barbados (1816) and Demerara (1823); Eric Williams, *Capitalism and Slavery* (1944; reprint, Chapel Hill: University of North Carolina Press, 1994), 202–208; Julius S. Scott, *The Common Wind: Currents of Afro-American Communication in the Era of the Haitian Revolution* (London: Verso, 2020), 10–12; Peter Linebaugh and Marcus Rediker, *The Many-Headed Hydra: Sailors, Slaves, Commoners and the Hidden History of the Revolutionary Atlantic* (Boston:

Beacon, 2000), 301; Geggus, "Slavery, War, and Revolution," 5–20, 46–49; Edward Bartlett Rugemer, *The Problem of Emancipation: The Caribbean Roots of the American Civil War* (Baton Rouge: Louisiana State University Press, 2008), 2–3, 47; Blackburn, *Overthrow,* 456–458; Eric Foner, *Nothing but Freedom: Emancipation and Its Legacy* (Baton Rouge: Louisiana State University Press, 1983), 16–17.

4. "Aquin," Jamaican Family Search; Debien and Le Gardeur, "Saint-Domingue Refugees," 117; Allain, *Souvenirs,* 13–14. Allain is mistaken regarding the location of Charles-Louis's marriage. See Raillicourt, *Filiations,* table 2.

5. Frances Trollope, *Domestic Manners of the Americans* (London: Whittaker, Treacher & Co., A. A. Knopf, 1832), 28; Auguste Viatte, *Histoire littéraire de l'Amérique française* (Québec: Presses Universitaires Laval, 1954), 243, quote on 276; Paul F. Lachance, "The Foreign French," in Hirsch and Logsdon, *Creole New Orleans,* 101–105, 130.

6. Palmer, Colton, and Kramer, *History of the Modern World,* 2:473–474; Emiliano Gil-Blanco, "Spanish Policy Towards the Abolition of Slavery in the Nineteenth Century," in *The Abolitions of Slavery: From Léger Félicité Sonthonax to Victor Schœlcher, 1793, 1794, 1848,* ed. Marcel Dorigny (New York: Bergahn Books, 2003), 293; Blackburn, *Overthrow,* 372–375.

7. Aptheker, *American Negro Slave Revolts,* quotes on 99, 282–283, 288; Merton L. Dillon, *Slavery Attacked: Southern Slaves and Their Allies, 1619–1865* (Baton Rouge: Louisiana State University Press, 1990), 145–146; W. Jeffrey Bolster, *Black Jacks: African American Seamen in the Age of Sail* (Cambridge, MA: Harvard University Press, 1997), 197; Lacey K. Ford, *Deliver Us from Evil: The Slavery Question in the Old South* (New York: Oxford University Press, 2009), 450.

8. Allain, *Souvenirs,* 127. Nineteenth-century New Orleans was a particularly dangerous disease environment for newcomers, with as many as 20 percent perishing annually in some immigrant neighborhoods. Yellow fever was the biggest killer, but Allain's father and sister would also have been vulnerable to cholera, influenza, consumption, typhoid, and plague. See Kathryn Olivarius, "Immunity, Capital, and Power in Antebellum New Orleans," *American Historical Review,* 124 (April 2019): 428, 434.

9. Olivarius, "Immunity," 428, 434. On the deaths of Louis-Charles and Elisabeth d'Aquin, see the Saint Louis Cemetery no. 1 death records, November 23, 1836, and the Saint Louis Cathedral Funeral Records, May 7, 1837.

10. Allain, *Souvenirs,* 127–128. Marie-Anne-Elisabeth Desmortiers Daron died on November 2, 1838. Tombstone index, New Orleans Cemeteries, Louisiana State Museum at the US Mint. Allain's paternal grandparents, Charles-Pierre and Marie-Louise-Victoire d'Aquin, remained in Jamaica and died there in 1834 and 1828, respectively. See "Aquin" in Jamaican Family Search.

11. For quotes, see "Prospectus of the Columbian Educational and Kindergarten Institute," 1880, Special Collections, Tulane University; and James William Mobley, "The Academy Movement in Louisiana," *Louisiana Historical Quarterly,* 30 (July 1947): 863. For the approximate date of the school's opening, see "Prospectus." Also see the New Orleans city directory (1843); Liliane Crété, *Daily Life in Louisiana 1815–1830,* trans. Patrick Gregory (Baton Rouge: Louisiana State University Press, 1978), 124–125; Mary Boykin Chesnut, *Mary Chesnut's Civil War,* ed. C. Vann Woodward (New Haven, CT: Yale University Press, 1981), xxxi–xxxii. Allain, *Souvenirs,* 171, uses the French term *quartier* for "barracks" in referring to her home at the corner of present-day Barracks and Chartres Streets. For street name changes, see Alphabetical and Numerical Indexes

of Changes in Street Names, Louisiana Division, New Orleans Public Library. For a description of the Daron residence, see "602–610 Barracks St.," in Collins C. Diboll Vieux Carré Digital Survey, Historic New Orleans Collection, Williams Research Center, New Orleans. For McDonogh's title to the property, see, "620–624 Chartres St.," in Collins C. Diboll Vieux Carré Digital Survey. In newspaper advertisements for the D'Aquin Institute, the Chartres Street address is listed as 155 Condé Street. The present-day address of the existing compound is 1235–37 and 1239–43 Chartres Street. For references to Saint Charles College, Grand Coteau, see Allain, *Souvenirs*, 127–128; G. Leighton Ciravolo, *The Legacy of John McDonogh* (Lafayette: Center for Louisiana Studies, University of Louisiana at Lafayette, 2002), 3; Donald E. DeVore and Joseph Logsdon, *Crescent City Schools: Public Education in New Orleans, 1841–1991* (Lafayette: Center for Louisiana Studies, University of Southwestern Louisiana, 1991), 33.

12. *New Orleans Daily Picayune*, September 5, 1858; Mobley, "Academy Movement," 863–864, 967–968.

13. Peter N. Stearns, *Priest and Revolutionary: Lamennais and the Dilemma of French Catholicism* (New York: Harper & Row, 1967), 19–20; Alec R. Vidler, *Prophecy and Papacy: A Study of Lamennais, the Church and the Revolution* (New York: Charles Scribner's Sons, 1954), 101, 268–269; Thomas Bokenkotter, *Church and Revolution: Catholics in the Struggle for Democracy and Social Justice* (New York: Crown Publishing, 1998), 40; Ciccarelli, "Introduction," 1, 4.

14. Frank Paul Bowman, "Specificity of French Romanticism," 80; Breckman, *European Romanticism*, 18–21.

15. Allain, *Souvenirs*, 369–370. While Joseph de Maistre traditionally has been portrayed as an inflexible ideologue and a precursor of fascism, the discovery of manuscripts in the Maistre family archives in the 1970s sparked a reassessment. The resulting scholarship recognizes Maistre's political conservatism while refuting the traditionalist depiction of him as an authoritarian extremist. The summary of his views expressed here reflects the new perspective, as set forth brilliantly in Carolina Armenteros, *The French Idea of History: Joseph de Maistre and His Ideas, 1794–1854* (Ithaca, NY: Cornell University Press, 2011). In paying close attention to Maistre's religious philosophy and his concept of "history as moral renewal," Armenteros offers crucial insights into his profound influence on Francophone Catholics like Allain. See Armenteros, *French Idea*, 6–10, 320.

16. Armenteros, *French Idea*, "Introduction," 113–114, 129, 155, 161–162, 206–207.

17. Allain, *Souvenirs*, 369. Allain's l'abbé Émile Bougaud quote is taken from *Histoire de sainte Chantal et des origenes de la Visitation* (Paris, 1861).

18. Allain, *Souvenirs*, 22–24.

19. Ibid., 369–370.

20. François-René de Chateaubriand, *The Genius of Christianity, or, the Spirit and Beauty of the Christian Religion*, ed. Charles I. White, 15th rev. ed. (Philadelphia, c1856), 51; Ellie Nower Schamber, *The Artist as Politician: The Relationship between the Art and the Politics of the French Romantics* (Lanham, MD: University Press of America, 1984), 28–29; Ciccarelli, "Introduction," 1; Armenteros, "Introduction," 117. For an insightful essay on Chateaubriand, see Peter Brooks, "Noble Memories," *New York Review* (April 19, 2018), 38–39.

21. "C'est magnifique, pensé comme M. de Maistre, écrit comme Rousseau, fort, vrai, élevé,

pittoresque, concluant, neuf, enfin tout." Vidler, *Prophecy,* 71–72 (my translation); see also 68–73, 148–151.

22. Stearns, *Priest and Revolutionary,* 38–45, at 45; David Owen Evans, *Social Romanticism in France, 1830–1848* (Oxford: Clarendon Press, 1951), 38–39, 90; Vidler, *Prophecy,* 148–151.

23. Vidler, *Prophecy,* 72, 101, 149, 267–269.

24. Ibid., 247–248, at 242; Armenteros, *French Idea,* 234–235; Stearns, *Priest and Revolutionary,* 138–142.

25. Vidler, *Prophecy,* 245, 251, also 244, 251 note 144; Emily Suzanne Clark, *A Luminous Brotherhood: Afro-Creole Spiritualism in Nineteenth-Century New Orleans* (Chapel Hill: University of North Carolina Press, 2016), 230 note 86.

26. Evans, *Social Romanticism,* 38–39; C. H. C. Wright, *The Background of Modern French Literature* (Boston: Ginn and Company, 1926), 84.

27. Armenteros, *French Idea,* 235, 309–311, at 311.

28. Ibid., 310.

29. Stearns, *Priest and Revolutionary,* 151–152; "Félicité de Lamennais," in *Encylopédie Larousse en ligne,* http://www.larousse.fr/encyclopedie/personnage.

30. C. H. C.Wright, *A History of French Literature* (1912; reprint, New York: Oxford University Press, 1969), 2:636–637; Clark, *Luminous Brotherhood,* 163–166, 190.

31. Allain's pride in her ethnic identity led her to publish *Souvenirs* under the pseudonym "Une Créole." For the usages of the term *créole,* see Joseph G. Tregle Jr., "Creoles and Americans" in Hirsch and Logsdon, *Creole New Orleans,* 137–139. Curiously, Tregle asserts that immigrants from Haiti and Saint-Domingue did not carry "their creole identity with them into Louisiana" (138 note 12). Allain and her family carried their Creole identity from Saint-Domingue to Jamaica, Louisiana, and France.

32. Allain, *Souvenirs,* 23–24; letter from Father Bavray, Paris, France, to Anthony Blanc, New Orleans, October 14, 1839, University of Notre Dame Archives, https://archives.nd.edu/search/calendar-search.htm; Chamber of Commerce of the New Orleans Area, *Decisions of the New Orleans Chamber of Commerce: From Its Formation in 1834 to August 4th, 1856* (New Orleans, 1857), 84–85; Edward L. Miller, *New Orleans and the Texas Revolution* (College Station: Texas A&M University Press, 2004), 232 note 53; "Aquin," in Jamaican Family Search; "Foreign Consuls," in the New Orleans city directory (1850); Henri-Charles D'Aquin, "Parallèle du Typhus et de la Fièvre Typhoide," Thèse pour le Doctorate en Médecine, Faculté de Médecine, April 26, 1856.

33. Allain, *Souvenirs,* 24. Allain's mention of "oratory" likely refers to a Catholic religious society.

34. Ibid., 24–25. Allain is mistaken with regard to the succession and number of her father's siblings. Louis-Charles was the eldest son in a family of eleven children. He had four older sisters, Cidele or Sidley (ca. 1792), Amélie (ca. 1793), Eveline-Marguerite (1799), and Victoire-Antoinette (1800). See d'Aquin et al., "Antiquity," part 2, 265; Sullivan-Holleman and Cobb, *Saint Domingue,* 384. On January 18, 1847, Eveline-Marguerite succumbed to her illness, within days of Allain's fourteenth birthday on January 22. See *l'Abeille,* January 19, 1847. After her death, her husband, Charles-Joseph Daron, married Louise de Bouligny. See Sullivan-Holleman and Cobb,

Saint Domingue Epic, 391. He continued to serve as the city's Catholic consul until his death in Bordeaux, France. *l'Abeille*, February 2, 1867, p. 1.

35. Allain, *Souvenirs*, 243–244. Also Sullivan-Holleman and Cobb, *Saint Domingue*, 386; "D'Aquin" in Jamaican Family Search.

36. Allain's citation: a Creole term for kettle.

37. Allain, *Souvenirs*, 244–245.

38. Ibid., 245–246; *l'Abeille*, January 19, 1847; Roger Baudier, *The Catholic Church in Louisiana* (New Orleans: A. W. Hyatt Stationery, 1939), 293.

39. Allain, *Souvenirs*, 246–247; "Dubreuil," in Jamaican Family Search.

40. Allain, *Souvenirs*, 246–247.

41. On Martha's enslaved status, see Allain, *Souvenirs*, 21; Caryn Cossé Bell, "Hermann-Grima House: A Window on Free Black Life and Urban Slavery in Creole New Orleans," *Louisiana Cultural Vistas*, 11 (Summer 2000), 71–72.

42. For a discussion of Latin European slave codes and the Catholic sacraments, see Judith Kelleher Schafer, *Slavery, the Civil Law, and the Supreme Court of Louisiana* (Baton Rouge: Louisiana State University Press, 1994), 1–3. Present-day St. Mary's Church at 1116 Chartres Street was originally the chapel for the eighteenth-century Ursuline Convent until 1824, when the order moved downriver from the city. In 1828, the renovated convent became the bishopric, with the chapel/church variously referred to as l'Archevêché (the chapel of the archbishopric), St. Mary's Church, and St. Mary's Italian Church. See Baudier, *Catholic Church*, 293, 312, 397.

43. Bell, *Revolution*, 73.

44. Ibid., 128–129; Mary Bernard Deggs, *No Cross, No Crown: Black Nuns in Nineteenth-Century New Orleans*, ed. Virginia Meacham Gould and Charles E. Nolan (Bloomington: Indiana University Press, 2001), xxxi–xxxii; Cyprian Davis, *Henriette Delille: Servant of Slaves, Witness to the Poor* (New Orleans: Archdiocese of New Orleans, 2004), 41, 43 note 18, 132–136; Aslakson, *Making Race*, 5; Acts of the State of Louisiana (1830), 92. For the marriage of Herriman Sr. and Eckel, see Michael Tisserand, "St. Mary's Catholic Church and the Herriman Family," *New Orleans Historical*, https://neworleanshistorical.org/items/show/1528. The couple were the grandparents of cartoonist George Herriman III, famed for his creation of *Krazy Kat*.

45. Davis, *Henriette Delille*, 27–28; George Abry, "Bearing Witness in Tremé: Saint Augustine Church," *Louisiana Cultural Vistas*, 13 (Summer 2002): 33; Deggs, *No Cross*, xxx.

46. Stephen J. Ochs, *Desegregating the Altar: The Josephites and the Struggle for Black Priests, 1871–1960* (Baton Rouge: Louisiana State University Press, 1990), 24–25; Fiehrer, "From La Tortue," 26.

47. Cathleen Medwick, *Teresa of Avila: The Progress of a Soul* (New York: Alfred A. Knopf, 1999), ix–xi, 3, 13; Davis, *Henriette Delille*, 104–110; Armenteros, *French Idea*, 21.

48. On spiritualism, see Clark, *Luminous Brotherhood*; and Melissa Daggett, *Spiritualism in Nineteenth-Century New Orleans: The Life and Times of Henry Louis Rey* (Jackson: University Press of Mississippi, 2017).

49. Deggs, *No Cross*, 91–92.

50. Allain, *Souvenirs*, 27.

51. Allain, *Souvenirs*, 26–27; Allain, *New-York et Paris*, 163–164. Allain is quoting François-René de Chateaubriand, *Mémoires d'outre-tombe* (Paris: Jean de Bonnet, 1860), 5:9.

52. Andro Linklater, *An Artist in Treason: The Extraordinary Life of General James Wilkinson* (New York: Walker Books, 2009), 323–324; Alcée Fortier, *Louisiana Studies. Literature, Customs and Dialects, History and Education* (New Orleans: F. F. Hansell, 1894), 15.

53. Allain, *Souvenirs*, 21. Allain speculated that the prefix *Villeras* derived from the custom of naming each son after their respective plantations or the particular Saint-Domingue locale in which they lived (11). In fact, the prefixes derived from titles bestowed upon the d'Aquins by the seventeenth-century French crown. See Raillicourt, *Filiations*, table 2.

54. Allain, *Souvenirs*, 21.

55. Ibid., 22.

56. Ibid., 21, 23–24.

57. Allain, *Souvenirs*, 25.

58. Ibid., 25–26. Lilia d'Aquin was born in 1811.

59. Angered by the city's lax social regimen, in 1786 Governor Esteban Miró enacted a so-called tignon law prohibiting "excessive attention to dress" by women of "pure or mixed African Blood." The women were barred from wearing feathers, jewels, or silks and were required to wear their hair bound in a tignon (kerchief) as a sign of their inferior status. The Rinck portrait demonstrates the defiant, eye-catching response, an intricately wrapped turban in a vibrant fabric. See Joan M. Martin, "*Plaçage* and the Louisiana *Gens de Couleur Libre*: How Race and Sex Defined the Lifestyles of Free Women of Color," in *Creole: The History and Legacy of Louisiana's Free People of Color*, ed. Sybil Kein (Baton Rouge: Louisiana State University Press, 2000), 62.

60. Allain, *Souvenirs*, 23.

61. For the striking Rinck portrait, see Edward C. C. Campbell Jr. with Kym S. Rice, eds., *Before Freedom Came: African-American Life in the Antebellum South* (Richmond: University of Virginia Press, 1991), xi, plate 4, 157–158, 200; Carolyn Morrow Long, *A New Orleans Voudou Priestess: The Legend and Reality of Marie Laveau* (Gainesville: University Press of Florida, 2006), 4–5, 138, 140.

62. Allain, *Souvenirs*, 17–18. Allain's observation regarding Dédé-Sophie's ethnicity is likely accurate. By 1789, two-thirds of enslaved Saint-Dominguans were African-born, with the Congolese representing one of the largest and most influential ethnic groupings. Furthermore, Congo peoples were especially prevalent in the West Province. See Fick, *Making of Haiti*, 25, 59. Also see Dubois, *Avengers*, 42.

63. Allain, *Souvenirs*, 18–19.

64. Ibid., 17–18.

65. Michael A. Gomez, *Exchanging Our Country Marks: The Transformation of African Identities in the Colonial and Antebellum South* (Chapel Hill: University of North Carolina Press, 1998), 39, 146, 150–151, 284.

66. White, *Encountering Revolution*, 21.

67. Paul F. Lachance, "The 1809 Immigration of Saint-Domingue Refugees to New Orleans: Reception, Integration and Impact," *Louisiana History*, 29 (Spring 1988): 112; White, *Encountering Revolution*, 167; Jean-Pierre Leglaunec, "Slave Migrations in Spanish and Early American Louisiana: New Sources and New Estimates," *Louisiana History*, 46 (Spring 2005): 202, 206–207, 185–209; Hall, "Formation of Afro-Creole Culture," 65, 68–69, 84–85.

68. Allain, *Souvenirs*, 171–172. The French Place d'Armes was renamed Jackson Square in

1851, and Clark Mills's equestrian bronze of Andrew Jackson was installed in 1856. The Pontalba Buildings were begun in spring 1849 and completed in fall 1850. Jerah Johnson, *Congo Square in New Orleans* (New Orleans: Louisiana Landmarks Society, 1995), 46. See Freddi Williams Evans, *Congo Square: African Roots in New Orleans* (Lafayette: University of Louisiana at Lafayette Press, 2011), 23–24 and chapter 9, for Congo Square's overarching historical significance, and 135–163 for the author's useful Congo Square timeline. See also Christina Vella, *Intimate Enemies: The Two Worlds of the Baroness de Pontalba* (Baton Rouge: Louisiana State University Press, 1997), 274, 277. Francophone *marguilliers* (church wardens) successively confirmed both the Spanish Sedella and the French Moni, beloved priests of the multiethnic Francophone laity, as pastors of St. Louis Cathedral. With Moni's 1842 death, Catholicism's Anglo-American-aligned ecclesiastical authorities in Baltimore triumphed over the marguilliers after a protracted struggle. Clark, *Luminous Brotherhood*, 87.

69. "Dance the calinda, boom boom!" My translation.

70. Allain, *Souvenirs*, 172. Influential healer Charles Lafontaine, popularly known as Doctor Jim Alexander, is described as employing song and bamboula dancing during his healing treatments. See Long, *New Orleans Voudou Priestess*, especially 111–113.

71. Gary A. Donaldson, "A Window on Slave Culture: Dances in Congo Square in New Orleans, 1800–1862," in *The Louisiana Purchase Bicentennial Series in Louisiana History*, ed. Vaughan Burdin Baker, vol. 15 (1984; reprint, Lafayette: Center for Louisiana Studies, University of Southwestern Louisiana, 2000), 634–635; Johnson, *Congo Square*, 36–37.

72. Allain, *Souvenirs*, 172–173. The term *calalou*, spelled "callaloo" in the Caribbean, refers to the callaloo plant. The Louisiana Creole aphorisms were translated by Professor Anne Malena.

73. Allain, *Souvenirs*, 171; Dubois, *Avengers*, 8–13, 40–41. For references to Allain's maternal great-great-grandparents Charles-Nicholas Bizoton and Marie-Elisabeth de Laborde, and the marriage of their daughter Marguerite Pierrette Bizoton to Antoine-Pierre d'Aquin, as well as references to Allain's great-grandfather Antoine-Pierre d'Aquin and the Saint-Marc marriage of his daughter Elisabeth-Charlotte Antoinette "Bonne" d'Aquin to Jean-Louis Rossignol des Dunes, see Moreau de Saint-Méry, *Description*, 2:798, 845, 897, 878, 899, and 3:1444, 1453.

74. For his classifications, see Moreau de Saint-Méry, *Description*, 3:1438.

75. Doris L. Garraway, *The Libertine Colony: Creolization in the Early French Caribbean* (Durham, NC: Duke University Press, 2005). See 247–252 for Garraway's ethnography of Creole.

76. Ibid., 250–252.

77. Ibid., 253, 255.

78. Allain, *Souvenirs*, 176, 129–130; 132 note 1 comments on Moreau's excerpt: "In Louisiana, whites alone are called Creole." By 1883, that was true of her Louisiana reading audience.

79. Allain, *Souvenirs*, 171, 173. For the pages Allain selected for reprint, see Moreau de Saint-Méry, *Description*, 34–83, 529. For Moreau's excerpt in *Souvenirs*, see 132–170. Anne Malena, "Hélène d'Aquin Allain: une identité inachevé," *Études francophones*, 18, no. 2 (Autumn 2003): 38, notes that the "mania" for the inclusion of letters, pamphlets, and book extracts was a peculiarity of the nineteenth-century autobiographical genre. Allain, in her nearly verbatim excerpt of Moreau's *Description*, makes one exception when she replaces Moreau's "une dégoûtante prostitution" (disgusting prostitution) on page 68 of *Description* with "le mal" (evil) on page 151 of *Souvenirs*. Garraway, *Libertine Colony*, 356 note 32, points out that the practice of worshipping

snakes, as described by Moreau in Allain's excerpt, disappeared in nineteenth-century Haiti. For a useful translation of Moreau's important description of the vaudoux ceremony, the passage excerpted by Allain, see Ned Sublette, *The World That Made New Orleans: From Spanish Silver to Congo Square* (Chicago: Lawrence Hill Books, 2008), chapter 15. Sublette's descriptions of African dances and instruments, and his discussion of vaudoux, are also insightful.

80. Moreau de Saint-Méry, *Description*, 68 (my translation); Allain, *Souvenirs*, 6.

81. Allain, *Souvenirs*, 173.

82. Ibid., 174–175.

83. Karen McCarthy Brown, "Afro-Caribbean Spirituality: A Haitian Case Study," in *Vodou in Haitian Life and Culture: Invisible Powers*, ed. Claudine Michel and Patrick Bellegarde-Smith (New York: Palgrave Macmillan, 2006), 1–2; Hall, *Africans in Colonial Louisiana*, 302; Hall, "Formation of Afro-Creole Culture," 85–86; Leslie Gerald Desmangles, "African Interpretations of the Christian Cross in Vodou," in Michel and Bellegarde-Smith, *Vodou in Haitian Life and Culture*, 39–41; Works Progress Administration, *Louisiana*, 313. See the historical marker commemorating Félicité at the Historical Marker Database, https://www.hmdb.org/m.asp?m=85048.

84. For more on the healer Charles Lafontaine, see Long, *New Orleans Voudou Priestess*, 98–101, 103–105, 111; and Olivarius, "Immunity," 426 note 4, 428, 434.

85. On J. B. Valmour's legal name, see Daggett, *Spiritualism*, 164 note 35.

86. Richard Brent Turner, "The Haiti-New Orleans Vodou Connection: Zora Neale Hurston as Initiate-Observer," in Michel and Bellegarde-Smith, *Vodou in Haitian Life and Culture*, 123.

87. The term *gris-gris* refers to a potent ritual vaudoux charm and derives from the Mende language of the Mandingo and Bambara people. In Louisiana Creole, the term is defined as casting a spell or putting a hex on someone. See Turner, "Haiti-New Orleans Vodou," in Michel and Bellegarde-Smith, *Vodou in Haitian Life and Culture*, 122; Valdman et al., *Dictionary of Louisiana French*; Long, *New Orleans Voudou Priestess*, 93, 117; Hall, *Africans in Colonial Louisiana*, 163.

88. Long, *New Orleans Voudou Priestess*, xxiii–xxiv, 36–37, 67; Ina Johanna Fandrich, *The Mysterious Voodoo Queen, Marie Laveaux: A Study of Powerful Female Leadership in Nineteenth-Century New Orleans* (New York: Routledge, 2005), 165–167, 173–174, 214; Martha Ward, *Voodoo Queen: The Spirited Lives of Marie Laveau* (Jackson: University Press of Mississippi, 2004), 12–13.

89. Long, *New Orleans Voudou Priestess*, chapter 8, quote on 137. Malcolm John "Mac" Rebennack (1941–2019), a New Orleans musician whose artistry captured the genius of the city's unique musical heritage, adopted the stage name Doctor John after Jean Montanée's moniker, owing to his possible descent from Pauline Rebennack, Montanée's coreligionist. See Long, *New Orleans Voudou Priestess*, 142.

90. Makandal, according to contemporaneous sources, was born into an Arabic-speaking family and raised in the Muslim religion. At the age of twelve, the precocious youth was taken prisoner and sold into slavery.

91. Sharla M. Fett, *Working Cures: Healing, Health, and Power on Southern Slave Plantations* (Chapel Hill: University of North Carolina Press, 2002), 112, 140–141; Karol K. Weaver, *Medical Revolutionaries: The Enslaved Healers of Eighteenth-Century Saint Domingue* (Urbana: University of Illinois Press, 2006), 1–3, 65, 89–91, 98, 104–112; Fick, *Making of Haiti*, 59–61, 72–73.

92. Bell, *Revolution*, 206, 214; Daggett, *Spiritualism*, 8–9, 13, 72–73, 75; Clark, *Luminous Brotherhood*, 3–5, 33, 165–166; also the useful "Index of Spirits," 259.

93. Long, *New Orleans Voudou Priestess*, 107.

94. Claude F. Jacobs and Andrew J. Kaslow, *The Spiritual Churches of New Orleans: Origins, Beliefs, and Rituals of an African-American Religion* (Knoxville: University of Tennessee Press, 1991), 26-27.

95. Walter Johnson, *Soul by Soul: Life Inside the Antebellum Slave Market* (Cambridge, MA: Harvard University Press, 1999), 2, 6-7, 19, 51.

96. Allain, *New-York et Paris*, 164.

97. Deggs, *No Cross*, 2, 20, quote on 46. In 1881, the school was renamed St. Mary's Academy for Girls and moved to Orleans Street.

98. Allain, *Souvenirs*, 239-240. Allain describes the *estomacs mulâtre*, as a "kind of ginger bread made with flour and cane syrup." "Aunt Sanité" could easily be Sanité Dédé, an influential voudou priestess and street vendor famed for her fried, sweetened rice balls called *calas*. Long, *New Orleans Voudou Priestess*, 21, 98-100. "Bayou Road" was a popular nineteenth-century designation for Hospital Street, later renamed Governor Nicholls Street. Throughout this book, Bayou Road is used.

99. Johnson, *Soul by Soul*, 128.

100. Solomon Northup, *Twelve Years a Slave*, ed. Sue Eakin and Joseph Logsdon (Baton Rouge: Louisiana State University Press, 1968), xi, 17-26, quote on 227; Mary Niall Mitchell, "All Things Were Working Together for My Deliverance," *Commonplace*, 14 (Winter 2014), 1-3; James Parton, *General Butler in New Orleans: History of the Administration of the Department of the Gulf*, 10th ed. (New York, 1865), 290; Catherine Chancerel, *l'homme du Grand Fleuve* (Paris: CNRS Éditions, 2014), 305-306.

101. Chanerel, *l'homme*, 518 note 3, 501-502. For more on the extraordinary Macarty, see William I. Horne, "Victor Eugène Macarty: From Art to Activism in Reconstruction-Era New Orleans," *Journal of African American History*, 103 (Fall 2018), 496-525.

5. PARIS IN NEW ORLEANS

1. Edwin Adams Davis, *The Story of Louisiana* (New Orleans: J. F. Hyer, 1960), 1:223-224.

2. Trévigne is referring to seventeenth- and eighteenth-century classical plays by Jean Racine (*Phèdra* and *Athalie*), Pierre Corneille (*Le Cid*), and Voltaire (*Mérope* and *Oreste*).

3. Amélie Fleury-Jolly, a soprano with the Théâtre d'Orléans, delighted audiences in New Orleans and New York in the 1840s and 1850s with her *opéra-comique* performances.

4. Paul Trévigne, letter to an anonymous Fisk University Librarian, July 28, 1902, in Southern Writer Series, Tulane University Libraries, New Orleans (my translation). I am indebted to documentary filmmaker Dawn Logsdon for bringing this letter to my attention. The clever couplet Trévigne quotes can be better appreciated in the original French:

J'aime beaucoup le drame qu'on renomme,
Où l'ingénue en feu dit au héros:
"Presse mon sein sur ta poitrine d'homme,
Chair de ma chair, toi les os de mes os."

Voilà comment d'un langage vulgaire,
On s'affranchit, grâce à Victor Hugo.
Laissons dormir et Racine et Voltaire
On n'en veut plus, fi donc, c'est rococo!

5. Schamber, *Artist as Politician,* 3–12, at 5–6, 14 note 11; Tom Reiss, *The Black Count: Glory, Revolution, Betrayal, and the Real Count of Monte Cristo* (New York: Crown Publishers, 2012), 54–56, 324–330.

6. Schamber, *Artist as Politician,* 6, 11; Rien Fertel, *Imagining the Creole City: The Rise of Literary Culture in Nineteenth-Century New Orleans* (Baton Rouge: Louisiana State University Press, 2014), 24.

7. Lilian R. Furst, Romanticism in Perspective: A Comparative Study of Aspects of the Romantic Movements in England, France and Germany (New York: St. Martin's Press, 1969), 27–28; Breckman, *European Romanticism,* 4–7.

8. Hall, "Formation of Afro-Creole Culture," 58–63, 87; Lachance, "Foreign French," 101–105.

9. François-René de Chateaubriand, *Atala and René,* trans. Rayner Heppenstall (London: Oxford University Press, 1963), 3. See also George D. Painter, *Chateaubriand: A Biography* (New York: Knopf, 1978), 137–138, 202–205.

10. Painter, *Chateaubriand,* 137.

11. Allain, *Souvenirs,* 238.

12. Painter, *Chateaubriand,* 136–137; Schamber, *Artist as Politician,* 30; Talmon, *Romanticism and Revolt,* 138; David Cairns, *Berlioz, 1803–1832: The Making of an Artist* (London: Sphere Books, 1989), 67–68.

13. Fertel, *Imagining the Creole City,* 34–35, 39; "Rouquette, Adrien Emmanuel," in *Dictionary of Louisiana Biography*; Stanley Clisby Arthur, *Old Families of Louisiana* (New Orleans: Harmanson, 1931), 121–123; Tinker, *Les Écrits,* 401–402.

14. Tinker, *Les Écrits,* 404–406, at 404. My translations. Ossian is the legendary Gaelic poet thought to have authored poems and ballads commemorating the heroic third-century exploits of his father, Fionn mac Cumhail. The Ossianic ballards were popularized, beginning in 1762, by Scottish poet James Macpherson.

15. Abbé Adrien Rouquette, *Wild Flowers, Sacred Poetry* (New Orleans: T. O'Donnell, 1848), 2.

16. Fertel, *Imagining the Creole City,* 47. Interestingly, Rouquette developed a close friendship with Civil War naval commander Admiral David G. Farragut. See "Adrien Emmanuel Rouquette," in *Dictionary of Louisiana Biography.*

17. Adrien-Emmanuel Rouquette [Chahta-Ima, pseud.], *La nouvelle Atala, ou la fille de l'esprit* (New Orleans, 1979), v; Tinker, *Les Écrits,* 404–406; Viatte, *Histoire littéraire,* 252–259; Works Progress Administration. *Louisiana,* 181, 445.

18. Viatte, *Histoire littéraire,* 253, 255; Tinker, *Les Écrits,* 417–419, 420–421, 431.

19. Although Tinker refers to Rouquette's supportive fellow Creole as "Natalie," with no surname, scholar Ulysses S. Ricard Jr. leaves no doubt that Natalie is Nathalie Populus. See Ricard, "Note from the Editor," *Chicory Review* (Fall 1988): 7. The surname Mello often appears after Populus in the historical literature. It may be that Mello derives from her mother's name,

Mélot. See Clint Bruce, ed. and trans., *Afro-Creole Poetry in French from Louisiana's Radical Civil War–Era Newspapers* (New Orleans: Historic New Orleans Collection, 2020), 188–189, note on 189; Tinker, *Les Écrits,* 420–421, 431; Roussève, *Negro in Louisiana,* 66.

20. Tinker, *Les Écrits,* 421. On Marie Couvent's maiden name, Camaire, see Mary Frances Berry, *"We Are Who We Say We Are": A Black Family's Search for Home Across the Atlantic World* (New York: Oxford University Press, 2015), 41–42. Also see the excellent scholarship of Elizabeth Clark Neidenbach, "The Life and Legacy of Marie Couvent: Social Networks, Property Ownership, and the Making of a Free People of Color Community in New Orleans," PhD diss., College of William & Mary; and Clark, *Luminous Brotherhood,* 29–30.

21. Viatte, *Histoire littéraire,* 260, 279–280; Davis, *Story of Louisiana,* 1:222–223.

22. *l'Album littéraire: Journal des jeunes gens, amateurs de littérature* (July 1843), 77. My translation.

23. "Horrors of the Day," *l'Album,* July 1843, 77–81, at 79, 80.

24. "Crime Everywhere," *l'Album,* August 1, 1843, 101–105, at 101, 103.

25. Mimi Sheller, *Democracy after Slavery: Black Publics and Peasant Radicalism in Haiti and Jamaica* (Gainesville: University Press of Florida, 2000), 112–113.

26. Sheller, *Democracy,* 113–115; Mongey, "Tale of Two Brothers," 46–47, chapter 3; Nicholls, *From Dessalines to Duvalier,* 60, 74.

27. Sheller, *Democracy,* 120–140, at 140.

28. Eric Hazan, *A History of the Barricade,* trans. David Fernback (London: Verso, 2015), 71–75, 78.

29. Hugues-Félicité Robert de Lamennais, *Words of a Believer* (New York: Charles de Behr, 1834), 34–35; Schamber, *Artist as Politician,* 105–106; Charles Boutard, *Lamennais: Sa vie et ses doctrines* (Paris: Perrin, 1913), 3:406 note 2, 409; Blackburn, *Overthrow,* 493–499; "Félicité-Robert de Lamennais," in *Dictionnarie des Lettres Françaises,* 46; Francis Arzalier, "Changes in Colonial Ideology in France Before 1848: From Slavery to Abolitionism," in Dorigny, *Abolitions of Slavery,* 265–266.

30. David McCullough, *The Greater Journey: Americans in Paris* (New York: Simon & Schuster, 2011), 187; "Félicité-Robert de Lamennais"; Stearns, *Priest and Revolutionary,* 152; Hazan, *History of the Barricade,* 94–95.

31. Palmer, Colton, and Kramer, *History of the Modern World,* 2:477–481; Schamber, *Artist as Politician,* 107; Michael Marrinan, *Romantic Paris: Histories of a Cultural Landscape, 1800–1850* (Stanford, CA: Stanford University Press, 2009), 381–387; O'Neill, *Séjour,* 16–18.

32. M. C. Boutard, ed., "Correspondance de Lamennais avec Madame Ligeret de Chazey," *La Revue hebdomadaire* (October 1909), 10; *Dictionnarie de Lettres Françaises,* 46.

33. Bell, *Revolution,* 166.

34. Ibid., 163–164.

35. Pierre-Aristide Desdunes, *Rappelez-vous concitoyens! La poésie de Pierre-Aristide Desdunes,* ed. Caryn Cossé Bell, trans. Clint Bruce (Shreveport, LA: Les Éditions Tintamarre 2010), 24–26.

36. DeVore and Logsdon, *Crescent City,* 42; Caryn Cossé Bell, "Pierre-Aristide Desdunes (1844–1918), Creole Poet, Civil War Soldier, and Civil Rights Activist: The Common Wind's Legacy," *Louisiana History,* 55 (Summer 2014): 289–290, 293–294; Fiehrer, "From La Tortue," 26; Mary Niall Mitchell, *Raising Freedom's Child: Black Children and Visions of the Future after Slavery*

(New York: New York University Press, 2008), 17–19; Mitchell, "'A Good and Delicious Country': Free Children of Color and How They Learned to Imagine the Atlantic World in Nineteenth-Century Louisiana," *History of Education Quarterly,* 40 (2000): 124–125.

37. J. Franklin Jameson, ed., "Correspondence of John C. Calhoun," in *Annual Report of the American Historical Association* (Washington, DC, 1900), 2:1189.

38. O'Neill, *Séjour,* 5; Desdunes, *Rappelez-vous,* 12; Judith Kelleher Schafer, *Becoming Free, Remaining Free: Manumission and Enslavement in New Orleans, 1846–1862* (Baton Rouge: Louisiana State University Press, 2003), 132; Desdunes, *Our People,* 53; Clark, *Luminous Brotherhood,* 27; Régine Latortue and Gleason R. W. Adams, eds. and trans., *Les Cenelles: A Collection of Poems by Creole Writers of the Early Nineteenth Century* (Boston: G. K. Hall, 1979), xiv.

39. Marrinan, *Romantic Paris,* 379–380, at 379; Nicholls, *From Dessalines to Duvalier,* 82.

40. Viatte, *Histoire littéraire,* 245–246, at 245; Arnold R. Hirsch and Joseph Logsdon, "Introduction," in *Creole New Orleans,* 91–100; Lachance, "Foreign French," 101–115; Tinker, *Les Écrits,* 29–30; Testut, *Portraits,* 173; Allain, *Souvenirs,* 196–197.

41. Allain, *Souvenirs,* 196–197, 235–238.

42. Boutard, "Correspondance," 5–6; Emma Lowndes, *Récits de femmes pendant la guerre franco-prussienne, 1870–1871* (Paris: l'Harmattan, 2013), 17, 33; Gordon A. Craig, *Europe, 1815–1914* (Hinsdale, IL: Dryden Press, 1972), 137; Jolanta T. Pekacz, "Poles in European Revolutions 1848–1849," *Encyclopedia of 1848 Revolutions* (February 24, 1997), http://www.ohio.edu/chastain/ip/poleurev.htm. Mieroslawski led a "people's army" in April 1849, after German activists appealed to the Polish Democratic Society for support of their revolution. In general command of the republican army in Baden, he won several victories before surrendering to the Prussians. The failure of the 1848 revolutions ended Polish independence aspirations for decades.

43. Boutard, "Correspondance," quote on 5; Evans, *Social Romanticism,* 38–39, at 39; Warren Breckman, *Marx, the Young Hegelians, and the Origins of Radical Social Theory: Dethroning the Self* (Cambridge: Cambridge University Press, 1999), 157.

44. Stearns, *Priest and Revolutionary,* 138–141; "Félicité de Lamennais," in *Encyclopedie Larousse en ligne,* 46; "Félicité-Robert de Lamennais," in *Dictionnarie des Lettres Françaises,* 46.

45. Boutard, "Correspondance," 5–7, at 6–7.

46. Boutard, "Correspondance," 5–7, quote on 11–12; Carl A. Brasseaux, *The "Foreign French": Nineteenth-Century French Immigration into Louisiana, 1840–1848* (Lafayette: Center for Louisiana Studies, University of Southwestern Louisiana, 1992), 2:214.

47. Boutard, "Correspondance," 5–6, quote on 41; Stearns, *Priest and Revolutionary,* 153.

48. Khaled J. Bloom, *The Mississippi Valley's Great Yellow Fever Epidemic of 1878* (Baton Rouge: Louisiana State University Press, 1993), 39; Henry M. McKiven Jr., "The Political Construction of a Natural Disaster: The Yellow Fever Epidemic of 1853," *Journal of American History,* 94 (December 2007), 735; Viatte, *Histoire littéraire,* 245–246; *Le Coup d'œil,* January 8, 1854; Tinker, *Les Écrits,* 99; Viatte, "Complement à la bibliographie louisianaise d'Edward Larocque Tinker," *Louisiana Review,* 3 (Winter 1974): 22.

49. Allain, *Souvenirs,* 231, quote on 211; *l'Abeille,* October 15, 1856; *New Orleans Times-Picayune,* December 9, 1884; Tinker, *Les Écrits,* 13; "Antonie Ligeret," in Chris Petteys, *Dictionary of Women Artists: An International Dictionary of Women Artists Born before 1900* (Boston: G. K. Hall, 1985).

50. Allain, *Souvenirs*, 208–210, 228, at 210; Lowndes, *Récits de femmes*, 48–50, at 49.

51. *l'Abeille*, October 15, 1856.

52. McPherson and Hogue, *Ordeal by Fire*, 65. For the origins of Anglo-America's negative perceptions of "Creole" identity, see Sean X. Goudie, *Creole America: The West Indies and the Formation of Literature and Culture in the New Republic* (Philadelphia: University of Pennsylvania Press, 2006), 7–9, and chapter 2.

53. Leon C. Soulé, "The Creole-American Struggle in New Orleans Politics, 1850–1862," *Louisiana Historical Quarterly*, 40 (January 1957): 60–79; Shirley Elizabeth Thompson, *Exiles at Home: The Struggle to Become American in Creole New Orleans* (Cambridge, MA: Harvard University Press, 2009), 28.

54. Soulé, "Creole-American Struggle," 60–79.

55. Rollin G. Osterweis, *Romanticism and Nationalism in the Old South* (1949; reprint, Baton Rouge: Louisiana State University Press, 1967), 66.

56. *Harper's New Monthly Magazine*, 11 (June 1855), 132.

57. Manoël de Grandfort [Marie Fontenay, pseud.], *L'Autre monde* (Paris: Librairie Nouvelle, 1855), quote on 228; Tinker, *Les Écrits*, 99. The second edition of *L'Autre monde*, published in Paris in 1857, is the same as the 1855 edition except for the designation "Membre de l'institut Canadien de Montréal" in subscript beneath the author's name on the title page. All subsequent quotes here are from that second edition. Grandfort's membership in l'institut likely resulted from her obsequious concluding tribute, "Le Canada, Lettre A Monsieur De La Rochefoucauld Duc De Doudeauville," in Grandfort, *l'Autre monde* (1857), 257–272. For Grandfort's comparison of Francophone Canada with New Orleans and Louisiana, see Anna Brickhouse, "The Writing of Haiti: Pierre Faubert, Harriet Beecher Stowe, and Beyond," *American Literary History*, 13 (Fall 2001), 422. More broadly, Brickhouse's essay is an insightful study of Grandfort's *L'Autre monde* in the context of Haitian and US literary history.

58. Frances M. Trollope, *Domestic Manners of the Americans*, ed. Donald Smalley (New York: Knopf, 1949). See especially Smalley's excellent introduction, vii–lxxvi.

59. *Harper's New Monthly Magazine*, 11 (June 1855), 132.

60. Clement Eaton, *The Freedom-of-Thought Struggle in the Old South* (1940; reprint, New York: Harper & Row, 1964), 337–338, 380; Works Progress Administration, *Louisiana*, 178, 182.

61. Grandfort, *L'Autre monde*, 6–7, 120.

62. For instances of Grandfort's ridicule of feminists, abolitionists, and socialists, see *L'Autre monde*, 31–34, 43–56, 89–91, 155–196.

63. Ibid., 68, 75, 77, 81.

64. Ibid., 76, 91.

65. Ibid., 85, 97.

66. Ibid., 109–110.

67. Ibid., 115–116.

68. "Translator's and Publisher Notice," concluding note in Manoël de Grandfort [Marie Fontenay, pseud.], *The New World: Translated from the French of Mme M. de Grandfort, by Edward C. Wharton* (New Orleans: Sherman Wharton, 1855); Grandfort, *l'Autre monde*, 117–118.

69. Grandfort, *l'Autre monde*, 212–245, quotes on 233–234, 254.

70. Ibid., 234–235, 256.

71. Tinker, *Les Écrits*, 99–100. For the Anglophone version, see Grandfort, *New World*.

72. Viatte, "Complement à la bibliographie," 22; *La Presse* (Paris), June 16 and 18, 1855; [Eléonore Ligeret de Chazey], *l'Inconnue à Mme de Grandfort et à Madame L**** (New Orleans, 1855); L. d'Ambrumenil, *l'Ombre de Mme de Grandfort* (New Orleans, 1855); *New Orleans Times-Picayune*, June 29, 1855.

73. Ambrumenil, l'Ombre, 5–6.

74. Ibid., 21, 40.

75. Ibid., 60.

76. Allain, *Souvenirs*, 177.

77. [Eléonore Ligeret de Chazey], *Les Créoles. Réponse à Madame de Grandfort* (New Orleans, 1855); Allain, *Souvenirs*, 185–207, 212–227.

78. Ligeret, *Les Créoles*, 41–42.

79. Ibid., 4–5.

80. *Harper's New Monthly Magazine*, 11 (June 1855), 130.

81. [de Chazey], *l'Inconnue*, 6.

82. *La Presse* (Paris), June 18, 1855.

83. For Grandfort's full quote, see *L'Autre monde*, 109–110.

84. Ligeret, *Les Créoles*, 20–21, 24–25.

85. Ibid., 6, 9–10.

86. Ligeret, *Les Créoles*, 13–14. Given her intellectual and religious predilections, Ligeret is undoubtedly using *lowly* in the same sense that Harriet Beecher Stowe used the term in *Uncle Tom's Cabin* (1852), to refer to those of every condition and ethnicity everywhere who suffered oppression. See Alfred Kazin, "Her Holiness," *New York Review* (December 1, 1994), 39.

87. In colonial Saint-Domingue, *hospitalière* designated enslaved women responsible for the care of enslaved patients and the daily administration of the plantation hospital. See Karol K. Weaver, *Medical Revolutionaries*, 48–49.

88. Fett, *Working Cures*, 112, 140–141.

89. Osterweis, *Romanticism and Nationalism*, 26.

90. Ibid., 15.

91. Ligeret, *Les Créoles*, 15.

92. Evans, *Social Romanticism*, 39. See Clark, *Luminous Brotherhood*, for numerous references to Lamennais among Afro-Creole spiritualists. Also see Daggett, *Spiritualism*, chapter 2.

93. For Allain's rewrite, see *Souvenirs*, 192. For Ligeret's original, see *Les Créoles*, 15–16.

94. Brickhouse, "Writing of Haiti," 421.

95. Bokenkotter, *Church and Revolution*, 43; Ligeret, *Les Créoles*, 40–41.

96. Tregle, "Creoles and Americans," 167–168.

6. LES DOCTEURS

1. McCullough, *Greater Journey*, 103, quote on 131. The name Paris Médicale appears to have fallen out of use in contemporary France. It may be that McCullough picked it up as a term used by the many nineteenth-century medical students whose letters he read. The students may have used it as a term of endearment for the wondrous Parisian world of hospitals, physicians, nurses,

patients, international students, and the celebrated Faculté de Médecine de Paris.

2. Michel Foucault, *The Birth of the Clinic: An Archaeology of Medical Perception*, trans. A. M. Sheridan Smith (New York: Vintage Books, 1973), 32–33, at 33; McCullough, *Greater Journey*, 106; Georges Lefebvre, *The French Revolution*, trans. Elizabeth Moss Evanson (London: Routledge & Kegan Paul, 1962), 1:225.

3. Houzeau, *My Passage*, 27–28, at 28. Jack D. Ellis, *The Physician-Legislators of France: Medicine and Politics in the Early French Republic, 1870–1914* (Cambridge: Cambridge University Press, 1990), 1–9; Palmer, Colton, and Kramer, *History of the Modern World*, 2:473–474.

4. McCullough, *Greater Journey*, 103–107, 115; W. Michael Byrd and Linda A. Clayton, *An American Health Dilemma: A Medical History of African Americans and the Problem of Race Beginnings to 1900* (New York: Routledge, 2000), 360.

5. Cauna, *L'Eldorado*, 334; de Grummond and Morazan, *Baratarians*, 83–84; Winston C. Babb, "French Refugees from Saint Domingue to the Southern United States, 1791–1810" (PhD diss., University of Virginia, 1954), 363.

6. Ada Ferrer and Marie Pascale Brasier-Iribarne, "La société esclavagiste cubaine et la revolution haïtiene," *Annales. Histoire, Sciences Sociales*, 58, no. 2 (2003), 343 note 27.

7. Kinzer, "Band of Music," quote on 356; "Faget, Jean Charles," in *Biographical Dictionary of Contemporary American Physicians and Surgeons* (Philadelphia, 1880); *Le Franc-Maçon*, New Orleans, May 1, 1846, 17–19; Stanley Clisby Arthur, *The Story of the Battle of New Orleans* (New Orleans: Louisiana Historical Society, 1915), 202, 249. For Faget's role in the founding of the New Orleans Philharmonic Society, see the Louisiana legislative bill approved on March 2, 1838. He died in New Orleans on April 3, 1862, at the age of eighty, just ahead of the arrival of Union forces in the city on April 25. St. Louis Cemetery No. 1 Interment Book, Archdiocese of New Orleans Archives.

8. Allain, *Souvenirs*, 235; "Faget, Jean-Charles," in John A. Garraty and Mark C. Carnes, eds., *American National Biography*, 24 vols. (New York: Oxford University Press, 1999); Tinker, *Les Écrits*, 197; "Faget, Jean Charles," in *Biographical Dictionary*.

9. Debien and Le Gardeur, "Saint-Domingue Refugees," 210–211; Marie Jenkins Schwartz, *Birthing a Slave: Motherhood and Medicine in the Antebellum South* (Cambridge, MA: Harvard University Press, 2006), 164–165; John Duffy, ed., *The Rudolph Matas History of Medicine in Louisiana* (Baton Rouge: Louisiana State University Press, 1962), 2:72–73, 380.

10. "Faget, Jean-Charles," in *American National Biography*. For an example of an affluent northerner denied anesthesia during childbirth, see Elaine Showalter, *The Civil Wars of Julia Ward Howe: A Biography* (New York: Simon and Schuster, 2016); and Jill Lepore, "'The Civil Wars of Julia Ward Howe,' by Elaine Showalter," book review, *New York Times*, February 29, 2016.

11. Jean-Charles Faget, *l'Art d'apaiser les douleurs de l'enfantement* (Paris, 1880), 7; Edmond Souchon, *Original Contributions of Louisiana to Medical Sciences: A Biographic Study* (New Orleans, 1915), 12.

12. Souchon, *Original Contributions*, 9, 11; J. C. Faget, *Etudes sur les bases de la science médicale et exposition sommaire de la doctrine traditionnelle* (New Orleans: Imprimerie Franco-Américaine, 1855), iii; Armenteros, *French Idea*, 102–103.

13. Souchon, *Original Contributions*, 11.

14. Deggs, *No Cross*, 20, 51–52, at 51. In 1867, Faget also treated three Baltimore nuns of color (members of the Oblate Sisters of Providence) who contracted yellow fever on a visit to the city. See Father Gilbert Raymond's letter to Archbishop John Oden, October 10, 1867, University of Notre Dame, https://archives.nd.edu/search/calendar-search.htm; Abry, "Bearing Witness," 31–33; Davis, *Henriette Delille*, 48–49; Baudier, *Catholic Church*, 397.

15. Charles was born in New Orleans in 1812, and like Delille and Gaudin, she was the daughter of a free woman of color and a white father. Her father was Joseph Charles, a German immigrant. The surname of her mother, Philomine, is unknown. Records indicate that the Charles family was close-knit and prosperous. See Deggs, *No Cross*, 21.

16. Deggs, *No Cross*, 2; Blassingame, *Black New Orleans*, 164–165.

17. Houzeau, *My Passage*, 27; Roudané, "Race, Memory, and the World That Made New Orleans"; *New Orleans Crusader*, March 22, 1890. For Marx's quote, see McCullough, *Greater Journey*, 187.

18. Hazan, *History of the Barricade*, 71–77, 85–86, at 75. See chapter 5 for a summary of the February revolt. Students and literati were largely absent from the ensuing June insurrection, which was fought by Parisian workers alone.

19. Louis-Charles Roudanez, "De l'Endocardite," thèse pour le docteur en médicine, Faculté de Mediciné de Paris, 1853, quote from title page; Houzeau, *My Passage*, 27–28.

20. Kahlil Chaar-Pérez, "A Revolution of Love": Ramón Emeterio Betances, Anténor Firmin, and Affective Communities in the Caribbean," *Global South*, 7 (Fall 2013), 11–12, 22–24, at 24; Jorge L. Chinea, "Betances y Alacán, Ramón Emeterio," *Encyclopedia of Emancipation and Abolition in the Transatlantic World*, 1 (2007), 70–71; Índice Anterior Siguiente, "El doctor Ramón Emeterio Betances, higienista social," paper presented at the Centro de Estudios Martianos, Havana, Cuba, September, 2002, http://scielo.sld.cu/scielo.php?script=sci_arttext&pid=S0045-91782004000100006.

21. "Roudanez, Louis Charles," in *Dictionary of Louisiana Biography*; Edward Larocque Tinker, *Pens, Pills and Pistols: A Louisiana Chronicle* (New York: Longmans, Green, 1934), 12.

22. "Velpeau, Alfred Armand Louis Marie," in *The American Annual Cyclopaedia and Register of Important Events of the year 1867* (1868), 755; *Catalogue from 1834 to 1872 of the Professors, Other Instructors, and Alumni with an Historical Sketch of the Medical College (from its Origin in 1834 to 1847), and of Its Successor, The Medical Department of the University of Louisiana* (New Orleans, 1871). For his tribute to Velpeau, see d'Aquin, "Parallèle du typhus et de la fièvre typhoëde"; McCullough, *Greater Journey*, 105–106, 125.

23. McCullough, *Greater Journey*, 115.

24. d'Aquin, "Parallèle du typhus et de la fièvre typhoëde." For an instance of their collaborative work, see H. C. D'Aquin, "Dengue, A Typical Eruptive Fever: Its Thermometrical Semeiology," *New Orleans Medical and Surgical Journal*, 2 (July 1874), 40; Duffy, *Rudolph Matas History*, 2:21–23. On the dengue fever epidemic of 1870–1873, with forty thousand cases reported in New Orleans, see "Dengue Fever," Louisiana Office of Public Health, Infectious Disease Epidemiology Section, 2017, http://ldh.la.gov/assets/oph/Center-PHCH/Center-CH/infectious-epi/Annuals/Dengue_LaIDAnnual.pdf.

25. Duffy, *Rudolph Matas History*, 2:380.

26. J. P. Boley, "The History of Caesarean Section," *Canadian Medical Association Journal* (May 1935; reprint, August 15, 1991), 320–321.

27. Nolan, *Sacramental Records*, 16:5, 307; 1840 US Federal Census; *l'Abeille*, November 11, 1863; Archives départementales des Côtes d'Armor, Registres paroissiaux et d'état civil, http://archives.cotesdarmor.fr/index.php?page=registres-paroissiaux. On Frédéric's nickname, see "Alphabetical Birth Indexes for Orleans Parish 1796–1900," USGenWeb Archives Project, Louisiana, Orleans Parish, http://www.usgwarchives.net/la/orleans/birth-alpha.htm.

28. M. Paul Reclus, "Éloge d'Alphonse Guérin," *Lancette française: Gazette des hôpitaux et militaries*, 69 (Paris, 1896), 574–575, at 575.

29. Allain, *Souvenirs*, 177.

30. Faget, *Etude médicale*, v. The Asile des Orphelins referenced by Faget was likely located in the Third District. A link between the orphanage and the Société française is noted in Félix Limet, *Historique de la société française de bienfaisance et d'assistance mutuelle de la Nouvelle-Orléans* (New Orleans, 1880), 31.

31. A. Le François, *Abrégé historique de la société française de bienfaisance et d'assistance mutuelle de la Nouvelle-Orléans* (New Orleans, 1903), 27; Duffy, *Rudolph Matas History*, 2:231; Roulhac Toledano and Mary Louise Christovich, *New Orleans Architecture*, vol. 6, *Fauburg Tremé and the Bayou Road* (Gretna, LA: Pelican, 1980), 82–83.

32. "Pierre Soulé," "Charles-Alfred Mercier," and "Jules-Placide-Armand Mericer," in *Dictionary of Louisiana Biography*.

33. Félix Limet, *Historique de la société française*, 7–9.

34. Le François, *Abrégé historique*, 5–6.

35. Souchon, *Original Contributions*, 10; Le François, *Abrégé historique*, 27; "Faget, Jean Charles," in *American National Biography*; "Faget, Jean Charles," in *Biographical Dictionary*. For a modern validation of Faget's conjecture concerning the microbe's entry into the city, see Bloom, *Mississippi Valley's Great Yellow Fever Epidemic*, 30–31. On Deléry, see Tinker, *Les Écrits*, 114–125.

36. Duffy, *Rudolph Matas History*, 2:95–97, at 96; James H. Cassedy, *Medicine in America: A Short History* (Baltimore: Johns Hopkins University Press, 1991), 51–52; "Cartwright, Samuel Adolphus," in *Dictionary of Louisiana Biography*.

37. On Soulé's political philosophy, see Bell, *Revolution*, 159–167.

38. Jacques-René Hébert, a journalist in the 1789 French Revolution who voiced the grievances of the Parisian working class.

39. Viatte, *Histoire littéraire*, 267–268.

40. Tinker, *Les Écrits*, 115, 120.

41. Victor A. McKusick, "Rouanet of Paris and New Orleans: Experiments on the Valvular Origin of the Heart Sounds 125 Years Ago," *Bulletin of the History of Medicine*, 32 (March–April 1958), 146–149, at 147. Jean-Nicolas Corvisart was a famed French cardiologist and one of the heads of the so-called Paris school in the city's sprawling system of hospitals and health care facilities known as the Paris Médicale.

42. Duffy, *Rudolph Matas History*, 2:57–58, 282–283, at 58; Tinker, *Les Écrits*, 122.

43. McKusick, "Rouanet of Paris," 148; Duffy, *Rudolph Matas History*, 2:95. For negative depictions of Rouanet, see Tinker, *Les Écrits*, 116.

44. Charles Boutard, "Correspondance de Lamennais avec Madame Ligeret de Chazey," *La*

Revue hebdomadaire (October 1909), 5; New Orleans city directory, 1849.

45. Sacramental Registers, no. 6, 1852–1866, St. Mary's Church, Archdiocesan Archives, New Orleans; Tinker, *Les Écrits*, 83.

46. Death certificates, 1858–1864, New Orleans Health Department, Louisiana State Archives, microfilm vol. 19; baptism, Sacramental Registers, no. 4, 1855–1867, St. Mary's Church.

47. *Le Courrier de la Louisiane,* September 8, 1858.

48. *Le Courrier de la Louisiane,* September 5, 1858, and *l'Abeille,* September 6, 1858; John Salvaggio, *New Orleans' Charity Hospital: A Story of Physicians, Politics, and Poverty* (Baton Rouge: Louisiana State University Press, 1992), 75.

49. *Le Courrier de la Louisiane,* September 1 and 5, 1858; Tinker, *Les Écrits,* 131.

50. Faget, *Etude Médicale,* vi–viii, 10–11, 84–85, 97–98, 112, at 98; Souchon, *Original Contributions,* 10–11; Bloom, *Mississippi Valley's Great Yellow Fever Epidemic,* 10–11. Bloom notes that during the relatively mild 1873 outbreak, not one New Orleanian of color died in an epidemic that claimed 226 lives. Still, Bloom writes, all human beings are susceptible to the virus, though people of West African ancestry benefit from a comparative resistance to yellow fever owing to countless generations of exposure to the disease in their ancestral homeland.

51. Faget, *Etude Médicale,* 84–85; Duffy, *Rudolph Matas History,* 2:18–19.

52. *Extraits de quelques unes des lettres sur la fievre jaune, publiées dans le Journal de la Medicale Société de la Nouvelle-Orléans* (New Orleans, 1859–1864), 22–23.

53. Tinker, *Les Écrits,* 117–119.

54. Father S. Rousselon, New Orleans, LA, to Archbishop John Mary Odin, Opelousas, LA, September 10, 1861; Odin to Rousselon, September 14; and Rousselon to Odin, Thibodaux, LA, September 21, 1861, University Notre Dame Archives; "Cartwright, Samuel Adolphus," in *Dictionary of Louisiana Biography*; US, Confederate Soldiers Compiled Service Records, 1861–1865, Ancestry.com.

55. Nemesis is the Greek goddess of divine retribution.

56. Tinker, *Les Écrits,* 118–119. Butler's spy network will be discussed in chapter 7.

57. Jo Ann Carrigan, "Yankees Versus Yellow Jack in New Orleans, 1862–1866," *Civil War History,* 9 (September 1963), 251–257, at 254.

58. Carrigan, "Yankees Versus Yellow Jack"; Jerah Johnson, "Yellow Fever and the Louisiana-Mississippi War of 1905," *Louisiana Cultural Vistas,* 11 (Fall 2000), 72.

59. "Faget, Jean Charles," in *Biographical Dictionary*; Duffy, *Rudolph Matas History,* 2:338–339.

60. "Faget, Jean Charles," in *Biographical Dictionary*; *New Orleans Times-Picayune,* obituary, December 9, 1884; Tinker, *Les Écrits,* 119; Caulfeild, *French Literature,* 182, 214–215.

61. Duffy, *Rudolph Matas History,* 2:325–326, at 326; Bloom, *Mississippi Valley's Great Yellow Fever Epidemic,* 4.

62. Bloom, *Mississippi Valley's Great Yellow Fever Epidemic,* 2, 4, 10–11, 20, 39, 279, 284. In terms of absolute mortality, New Orleans' worst yellow fever epidemic occurred in 1853. In the United States, yellow fever never again approached the scale of the 1878 epidemic. Just a few years later, in 1881, the Cuban physician Dr. Carlos Finlay identified the *Aedes aegypti* mosquito as the transmitter of the disease, though the yellow fever "germ" eluded detection until the late 1920s, when researchers identified its cellular pathology. In 1938, a practicable vaccine finally became available. On quinine's adverse effects on children, see Faget, *Etude Médicale,* 106. See

also Robert Florence, *City of the Dead: A Journey through St. Louis Cemetery #1* (Lafayette: Center for Louisiana Studies, University of Southwestern Louisiana, 1996); Limet, *Historique de la société française,* 26.

PART III.
CIVIL WAR AND RECONSTRUCTION

1. Bell, *Romanticism,* 2; Geggus, "Slavery, War, and Revolution," 13–14.

2. Oscar J. Dunn, chair of the Central Executive Commmittee of the Friends of Universal Suffrage, July 6, 1865.

7. REVOLUTION AND COUNTERREVOLUTION

1. James G. Hollandsworth Jr., *The Louisiana Native Guards: The Black Military Experience during the Civil War* (Baton Rouge: Louisiana State University Press, 1995), 1–2.

2. Hollandsworth, *Louisiana Native Guards,* 7–11, at 11; Lawrence Lee Hewitt, "An Ironic Route to Glory: Louisiana's Native Guards at Port Hudson," in John David Smith, ed., *Black Soldiers in Blue: African American Troops in the Civil War Era* (Chapel Hill: University of North Carolina Press, 2002), 78–79.

3. Michael D. Pierson, *Mutiny at Fort Jackson: The Untold Story of the Fall of New Orleans* (Chapel Hill: University of North Carolina Press, 2008), 1–3, at 3; Hans L. Trefousse, *Ben Butler: The South Called Him Beast* (New York: Octagon, 1974), 96–97. The Department of the Gulf included Alabama, Florida, Louisiana, and Mississippi. James K. Hogue, *Uncivil War: Five New Orleans Street Battles* (Baton Rouge: Louisiana State University Press, 2006), 5 note 5. In 1860, the population of the city was 168,000. In 1862, the antebellum state capital at Baton Rouge burned after Union forces occupied the city, and federal forces established New Orleans as the seat of state government until the constitution of 1872 returned the capital to Baton Rouge.

4. G. Howard Hunter, "The Politics of Resentment: Unionist Regiments and the New Orleans Immigrant Community, 1862–1864," *Louisiana History,* 44 (Spring 2003), 189; Pierson, *Mutiny,* 3.

5. John D. Winters, *The Civil War in Louisiana* (Baton Rouge: Louisiana State University Press, 1963), 125; Trefousse, *Ben Butler,* 105–109.

6. Adam Goodheart, *1861: The Civil War Awakening* (New York: Vintage Books, 2012), 295–296; William E. Gienapp, ed., *The Civil War and Reconstruction: A Documentary Collection* (New York: W. W. Norton, 2001), 115–116; McPherson and Hogue, *Ordeal by Fire,* 290. It is estimated that as many as two hundred thousand contrabands would contribute to the US Army as cattle drivers, stevedores, and pioneer laborers building roads and bridges, among other support activities. See John David Smith, "Let Us All Be Grateful That We Have Colored Troops That Will Fight," in Smith, *Black Soldiers in Blue,* 12; W. E. B. Du Bois, *Black Reconstruction in America, 1860–1880* (1935; reprint, New York: Atheneum, 1975), 63. Fortress Monroe was built at the site of a 1619 Virginia colony stockade after the War of 1812. The massive fortification was part of a coastal defense system drawn up by the US Army. Enslaved workers began construction of the

fort in 1829 and military convicts completed the structure in 1834. "Fort Monroe," Hampton Virginia, 2022, https://hampton.gov/1912/history.

7. Trefousse, *Ben Butler,* 338–339.

8. Goodheart, *1861,* 342; John Hope Franklin and Alfred A. Moss Jr., *From Slavery to Freedom: A History of African Americans,* 8th ed. (Boston: McGraw Hill, 2000), 222; McPherson and Hogue, *Ordeal by Fire,* 290.

9. Goodheart, *1861,* 340–341, at 341; Vincent Harding, *There Is a River: The Black Struggle for Freedom in America* (San Diego: Harcourt, Brace, 1981), 230.

10. Goodheart, *1861,* 333.

11. Parton, *General Butler,* 493. At the time, Parton was the nation's most famous biographer and an admirer of Butler, who gave the author access to his papers. The book was an immediate success. See Trefousse, *Ben Butler,* 139. Goodheart, *1861,* 333, points out that it became standard military practice to debrief contrabands, owing to the useful military intelligence they furnished.

12. Parton, *General Butler,* 334–335, 413, quotes on 493; Trefousse, *Ben Butler,* 113–114; Hollandsworth, *Louisiana Native Guards,* 17.

13. Winters, *Civil War,* 128; Parton, *General Butler,* 363–377.

14. Trefousse, *Ben Butler,* 125; "Pierre Gustave Toutant Beauregard," in *Dictionary of Louisiana Biography.*

15. Hollandsworth, *Louisiana Native Guards,* 20–21; Parton, *General Butler,* 529–531.

16. Joe Gray Taylor, *Louisiana Reconstructed, 1863–1877* (Baton Rouge: Louisiana State University Press, 1974), 17; Palmer, Colton, and Kramer, *History of the Modern World,* 2:538, 579.

17. C. Peter Ripley, *Slaves and Freedmen in Civil War Louisiana* (Baton Rouge: Louisiana State University Press, 1976), 13–14, chapter 2, quote on 28; Peyton McCrary, *Abraham Lincoln and Reconstruction: The Louisiana Experiment* (Princeton, NJ: Princeton University Press, 1978), 88–89.

18. McCrary, *Abraham Lincoln,* 89.

19. Jason Berry, *City of a Million Dreams: A History of New Orleans at Year 300* (Chapel Hill: University of North Carolina Press, 2018), 158–159; Desdunes, *Our People,* 119; McConnell, *Negro Troops,* 110–113.

20. Benjamin F. Butler to Edwin M. Stanton, May 25, 1862, in *The War of the Rebellion: A Compilation of the Official Records of the Union and Confederate Armies,* series 1, vol. 15 (Washington, DC, 1880–1901), 442.

21. Camp Parapet was near the present-day intersection of Causeway Boulevard and the river. See DeVore and Logsdon, *Crescent City,* 54.

22. Mary F. Berry, "Negro Troops in Blue and Gray: The Louisiana Native Guards, 1861–1863," in *The Louisiana Purchase Bicentennial Series in Louisiana History,* vol. 11, part B, ed. Charles Vincent (Lafayette: Center for Louisiana Studies, University of Louisiana at Lafayette, 2000), 25.

23. Hollandsworth, *Louisiana Native Guards,* 15–16; McCrary, *Abraham Lincoln,* 90.

24. Hollandsworth, *Louisiana Native Guards,* 16–18, at 18; Hewitt, "Ironic Route," 79.

25. James M. McPherson, *Battle Cry of Freedom: The Civil War Era* (New York: Oxford University Press, 1988), 500; Silvana R. Siddali, *From Property to Person: Slavery and the Confiscation Acts, 1861–1862* (Baton Rouge: Louisiana State University Press, 2005), 6. The second Confiscation Act punished rebels by confiscating all of their property, including their enslaved workers, who

"shall be deemed captives of war and shall be forever free." Loyal slaveholders were exempted from having to emancipate their enslaved workers.

26. Bell, *Revolution*, 233; Blassingame, *Black New Orleans*, 36; Hollandsworth, *Louisiana Native Guards*, 21; Berry, "Negro Troops," 26.

27. Berry, "Negro Troops," 26; Nathan W. Daniels, *Thank God My Regiment an African One: The Civil Diary of Colonel Nathan W. Daniels*, ed. C. P. Weaver (Baton Rouge: Louisiana State University Press, 1998), xvi. South Carolinian Martin Delany was the only other African American to achieve the rank of major. He was commissioned three months before the end of the war at the specific order of Secretary of War Edwin M. Stanton. See "Delany, Martin R," in Eric Foner, *Freedom's Lawmakers: A Directory of Black Officeholders during Reconstruction* (Baton Rouge: Louisiana State University Press, 1996).

28. For a complete list of commissioned officers, see Hollandsworth, *Louisiana Native Guards*, 117–124; McCrary, *Abraham Lincoln*, 143.

29. Du Bois, *Black Reconstruction*, 68. Ripley, *Slaves*, 37–39.

30. Roger A. Fischer, *The Segregation Struggle in Louisiana, 1862–77* (Urbana: University of Illinois Press, 1974), 30–31; Hollandsworth, *Louisiana Native Guards*, 31–32.

31. Fischer, *Segregation*, 30; DeVore and Logsdon, *Crescent City*, 55.

32. "Dumas, François Ernest," in *African American National Biography*.

33. Foner, *Freedom's Lawmakers*, 66; "Dumas, François Ernest," in *African American National Biography*.

34. "Dumas, François Ernest," in *African American National Biography*.

35. Desdunes, *Rappelez-vous*, 36. With regard to the absence of "scars" on Desdunes's body, physical examinations of Louisiana's formerly enslaved recruits would certainly have yielded different results. Dr. Wesley Humphrey described his observations in Corinth, Mississippi, on May 25, 1863: "I have been selected as the surgeon of the regiment of African descent, now forming here (not all black by any means), and during the past week had occasion to examine about seven hundred men in a *nude state*, preparatory to their being mustered into the United States services, and I then saw evidences of abuse and maltreatment perfectly horrifying to relate, and must be *seen* to fully understand the abuse to which they have been subjected. I think I am safe in saying that at *least one-half* of that number bore evidence of having been severely *whipped* and maltreated in various ways; some were *stabbed* with a knife; others shot through the limbs; some pounded with clubs, until their bones were broken. One man told me he had received for a trifling offense two thousand lashes; and, upon examination, I found seventy-five scars on his back and limbs, that rose above the skin the size of your finger, saying nothing of the smaller ones. Others had the cords of their legs cut (hamstrings, as they call them), to prevent their running off; and some were shot in resenting such insults. These were witnessed by the colonel, J. M. Alexander, lieutenant-colonel, major, &c., of the regiment." Parton, *General Butler*, 494.

36. Desdunes, *Rappelez-vous*, 12–14.

37. Ibid., 26–30, at 30.

38. Ibid., 38–42, at 38.

39. Matthew J. Clavin, *Toussaint Louverture and the American Civil War* (Philadelphia: University of Pennsylvania Press, 2010), chapter 7, at 154.

40. McPherson, *Battle Cry of Freedom,* 563–567, at 563 and 566.

41. Smith, "Let Us All Be Grateful," 46, 47.

42. *L'Union,* September 27, 1862; Bruce, *Afro-Creole Poetry,* 1, 18–19; Mark Charles Roudané, "Transfixed by Her Eyes: Race, Memory, and the World That Made New Orleans," *La Créole: A Journal of Creole History & Genealogy,* 10 (October 20, 2017), 37; Charles Vincent, *Black Legislators in Louisiana during Reconstruction* (Baton Rouge: Louisiana State University Press, 1976), 16; Richard H. Abbott, *For Free Press and Equal Rights: Republican Newspapers in the Reconstruction South,* ed. John W. Quist (Athens: University of Georgia Press, 2004), 14.

43. *l'Union,* October 18, 1862; Blackburn, *Overthrow,* 498–500.

44. Desdunes, *Rappelez-vous,* 54; McCrary, *Abraham Lincoln,* 153; Devore and Logsdon, *Crescent City,* 55; Abbott, *For Free Press*; Houzeau, *My Passage,* 72–75, 73 note 14. Tinchant served in the Union army until his disgust with the treatment of Black soldiers led him to emigrate to Mexico with his family in 1864. Rebecca J. Scott and Jean M. Hébrard, *Freedom Papers: An Atlantic Odyssey in the Age of Emancipation* (Cambridge, MA: Harvard University Press, 2012), 73, 77, 88, 92–95, 97–99, 108, quotes on 97–98. By 1860, he and his older brother Louis Tinchant ran a successful cigar manufacturing business, L. & J. Tinchant, with a retail store on St. Charles Avenue. McKee, *Exile's Song,* 72–73.

45. James McKaye, *The Mastership and Its Fruits: The Emancipated Slave Face to Face with His Old Master* (New York, 1864), 3–7, at 5–6; McCrary, *Abraham Lincoln,* 299; Eric Foner, *Reconstruction: America's Unfinished Revolution, 1863–1877* (New York: Harper & Row, 1988), 68.

46. "Trévigne, Paul," in *Encyclopedia of the Confederacy* (1993); Pierre Force, "The House on Bayou Road: Atlantic Creole Networks in the Eighteenth and Nineteenth Centuries," *Journal of American History* 100 (June 2013), 31–35, 40, 43. Casey, *Louisiana in the War,* lviii, lists José Antonio de Paula de Trebiño in his troop rosters as Antonio "Trèvine."

47. Daniels, *Thank God,* 16–17; Ochs, *A Black Patriot,* 4; Desdunes, *Rappelez-vous,* 43–44; Hollandsworth, *Louisiana Native Guards,* 32–36.

48. Trefousse, *Ben Butler,* chapter 11, at 124. Butler's greatest offense in New Orleans was that, in the words of President Lincoln, he was "a staunch friend of the [Black] race from the time you [Butler] first advised me to enlist them at New Orleans." For his alliance with Black Louisianians, according to W. E. B. Du Bois, Butler "brought down on himself the wrath and contempt, not simply of the South, but even of the North." Du Bois, *Black Reconstruction,* 68, 149.

49. Du Bois, *Black Reconstruction,* 132–140.

50. Hollandsworth, *Louisiana Native Guards,* 36, 38–41.

51. Rebecca J. Scott, *Degrees of Freedom: Louisiana and Cuba after Slavery* (Cambridge, MA: Harvard University Press, 2005), 31.

52. Trefousse, *Ben Butler,* 134, quote on 122.

53. Hollandsworth, *Louisiana Native Guards,* 51, 78, 117–124, quotes on 62, 82; Hunter, "Politics of Resentment," quote on 202; Smith, "Let Us All Be Grateful," 100. On continued resistance to African Americans in the US Army officer corps into the twenty-first century, see Helene Cooper, "For African-Americans in Uniform, It's Duty, Honor, Country. But Don't Expect to Lead," *New York Times* (May 25, 2020). For positive new assessments of Butler's Civil War and Reconstruction history and politics, see Adam Fairclough, *Bulldozed and Betrayed: Louisiana and*

the Stolen Elections of 1876 (Baton Rouge: Louisiana State University Press, 2021); and Elizabeth D. Leonard, *Benjamin Franklin Butler: A Noisy, Fearless Life* (Chapel Hill: University of North Carolina Press, 2022).

54. Hewitt, "Ironic Route," 82, 101 note 4; McCrary, *Abraham Lincoln,* 123; Daniels, *Thank God,* 15; Bell, *Revolution,* 238. Ultimately, military necessity forced Banks to reintroduce Butler's recruitment policy.

55. Daniels, *Thank God,* xvii, xxi, 14–15, 151 note 85, 153–154, 153 note 9, quote on 176; Hollandsworth, *Louisiana Native Guards,* 19 note 29, 121. For J. B. Valmour's surname, see Clark, *Luminous Brotherhood,* 22.

56. McCrary, *Abraham Lincoln,* 108–115, quote on 118; *l'Union,* December 25, 1862; Caryn Cossé Bell, "*Une Chimère*: The Freedmen's Bureau in Creole New Orleans," in *The Freedmen's Bureau and Reconstruction: Reconsiderations,* ed. Paul A. Cimbala and Randall M. Miller (New York: Fordham University Press, 1999), 144.

57. *L'Union,* August 31, 1865; McCrary, *Abraham Lincoln,* 110.

58. Houzeau, *My Passage,* 19 note 24.

59. *New Orleans Times,* November 6, 1863.

60. McCrary, *Abraham Lincoln,* 199–202, 210, at 202.

61. Hollandsworth, *Louisiana Native Guards,* 3, 4 note 10, 94, 121, quote on 73; Joan Abshear Brown, "A Tribute to Arnold Bertonneau," *La Créole: A Journal of Creole History and Genealogy,* 12 (October 25, 2019), 22.

62. McCrary, *Abraham Lincoln,* 53–53, 153–154, 230–231, at 231.

63. Boston *Liberator,* April 17, 1864; McCrary, *Abraham Lincoln,* 299.

64. McCrary, *Abraham Lincoln,* 207–209, 234–235, quotes on 209, 255.

65. Nick Douglas, *Finding Octave: The Untold Story of Two Creole Families and Slavery in Louisiana* (Createspace, 2013), 157–160; McCrary, *Abraham Lincoln,* 255–256, 299; Logsdon and Bell, "Americanization," 227–228; Brown, "Tribute to Arnold Bertonneau," 27–28.

66. Abbott, *For Free Press,* 15, 119; Tinker, *Pens, Pills & Pistols,* 12–13; Houzeau, *My Passage,* 23–25; McCrary, *Abraham Lincoln,* 296.

67. Bell, *Une Chimère,* 146–147; *New Orleans Tribune,* December 8, 1864.

68. McKaye, *Mastership and Its Fruits,* 36–37; McCrary, *Abraham Lincoln,* 231–232.

69. Clark, *Luminous Brotherhood,* 171; Dantes Bellegarde, "President Alexandre Pétion," *Phylon,* 2 (3rd quarter, 1941), 210–212, at 211. By 1940, Bellegarde concluded, Haitians owned three-quarters of their republic's lands. See Ferrer, "Haiti," 44; Foner, *Nothing but Freedom,* 12; Uncertainty surrounds the exact date of the *Tribune's* last issue. According to Mark Roudané, the last issue appeared in early 1870 in the form of a weekly edition. Roudané, *The New Orleans Tribune: An Introduction to America's First Black Daily Newspaper* (Minneapolis: Chicoté Graphics, 2014), 35. Rankin, *My Passage,* 56, writes that the paper closed down "sometime in 1871." Clint Bruce, however, has identified an October 18, 1870, public notice indicating the sale of the *Tribune's* press and materials. Bruce, *Afro-Creole Poetry,* 23, 322 note 36.

70. McCrary, *Abraham Lincoln,* 271, 295–296, 302; McPherson and Hogue, *Ordeal by Fire,* 503, A20–21. The Thirteenth Amendment was ratified December 18, 1865. Bell, *Une Chimère,* 148.

71. Bell, *Une Chimère*, 148–151, 155; Hogue, *Uncivil War*, 31–34; Houzeau, *My Passage*, 44.

72. Hogue, *Uncivil War*, 4, 30. For 1860 Louisiana population, see Berlin, *Slaves without Masters*, 136, 396–399.

8. RECONSTRUCTION AND COUP D'ÉTAT

1. James G. Hollandsworth Jr., *An Absolute Massacre: The New Orleans Race Riot of July 30, 1866* (Baton Rouge: Louisiana State University Press, 2001), 92–93, 96 note 33, 140, at 92; Hogue, *Uncivil War*, 34–35, 40–44, 42 note 24, quote on 31; McPherson and Hogue, *Ordeal by Fire*, 562.

2. Houzeau, *My Passage*, 131. The interesting Houzeau was a skilled astronomer at the Belgian Royal Observatory who was forced into exile because of his political radicalism. Trévigne and Dr. Roudanez hired him as the editor in chief in November 1864; *New Orleans Tribune*, August 31, September 1, 1866; Hollandsworth, *Louisiana Native Guards*, 107; Bruce, *Afro-Creole Poetry*, 21, 38–39, at 38.

3. Foner, *Reconstruction*, 261–263; McPherson and Hogue, *Ordeal by Fire*, 558–559, 562–567, 590–591. The Fourteenth Amendment disqualified from office all federal and state officials who had taken an oath to uphold the Constitution and later broke that oath by engaging in rebellion.

4. *New Orleans Tribune*, April 21, 1867.

5. Houzeau, *My Passage*, 140–141, 141 note 159, at 140; Fischer, *Segregation*, 34–41, 154; Bruce, *Afro-Creole Poetry*, 22–23.

6. Daniels, *Thank God*, 171–176, at 173; Bruce, *Afro-Creole Poetry*, 42; Ochs, *A Black Patriot*, 1; Daggett, *Spiritualism*, 78–80; Foner, *Reconstruction*, 68.

7. Daniels, *Thank God*, 172, quotes on 176; Daggett, *Spiritualism*, 34, 78–81; Johnson, "Yellow Fever," 72.

8. Fischer, *Segregation*, 54–55, at 54; Ted Tunnell, *Crucible of Reconstruction: War, Radicalism, and Race in Louisiana, 1862–1877* (Baton Rouge: Louisiana State University Press, 1984), 107–113.

9. Fischer, *Segregation*, chapter 3, at 51, 53–55; Hollandsworth, *Louisiana Native Guards*, 105, 121–122; Tunnell, *Crucible*, 117–119.

10. Bell, *Revolution*, 76–77, 88; Diana Irene Williams, "'They Call It Marriage': The Interracial Louisiana Family and the Making of American Legitimacy" (PhD diss., Harvard University, 2007), 1–4.

11. Vincent, *Black Legislators*, 68–69; Logsdon and Bell, "Americanization," 246; Blassingame, *Black New Orleans*, 212–213; Houzeau, *My Passage*, 47–51; Roudané, *New Orleans Tribune*, 35; Foner, *Freedom's Lawmakers*, 67.

12. Brian K. Mitchell, Barrington S. Edwards, and Nick Weldon, *Monumental: Oscar Dunn and His Radical Fight in Reconstruction Louisiana* (New Orleans: Historic New Orleans Collection, 2021), 142–143, 232 note 144; Williams, "They Call It Marriage," 306; Foner, *Reconstruction*, 352–354; Foner, *Freedom's Lawmakers*, 29, 65, 171, 181; Charles Vincent, "Aspects of the Family and Public Life of Antoine Dubuclet: Louisiana's Black State Treasurer, 1868–1878," in *Louisiana Purchase Bicentennial Series*, 186–187, 195 note 40; Du Bois, *Black Reconstruction*, 470. Dunn became the acting governor when Warmoth suffered a serious injury in 1871. By that time the

two men were bitter enemies, with Warmoth attempting to delegitimize Acting Governor Dunn by assigning the governor's office to one of his white political cronies. In 1872, Warmoth would later employ the same tactic to humiliate Lieutenant Governor Pinchback in his role as acting governor.

13. Hogue, *Uncivil War*, 1–8; Tunnell, *Crucible*, 153–161; Foner, *Reconstruction*, 307, 436; Mitchell, Edwards, and Weldon, *Monumental*, 230 note 98.

14. Foner *Reconstruction*, 385; Tunnell, *Crucible*, 169.

15. Fischer, *Segregation*, 68–69, 113–114, 131; Ron Chernow, *Grant* (New York: Penguin, 2017), 641; Mitchell, Edwards, and Weldon, *Monumental*, 104–109. For the correct date of the *Tribune's* reopening, see Bruce, *Afro-Creole Poetry*, 44; Devore and Logsdon, *Crescent City*, 68; Foner, *Reconstruction*, 367; Gienapp, *Civil War*, 389.

16. Devore and Logsdon, *Crescent City*, 70–76; Fischer, *Segregation*, 116, 119; Hogue, *Uncivil War*, 68–69.

17. Daggett, *Spiritualism*, 116–117; Vincent, *Black Legislators*, 150–151, 196; Devore and Logsdon, *Crescent City*, 76.

18. Fischer, *Segregation*, 109–110, 116, 131.

19. Tunnell, *Crucible*, 164–165; Taylor, *Louisiana*, 209–215.

20. Tunnell, *Crucible*, 165; Taylor, *Louisiana*, 218, 252; Vincent, *Black Legislators*, 134–135; Mitchell, Edwards, and Weldon, *Monumental*, 172.

21. Taylor, *Louisiana*, 219–220; Fischer, *Segregation*, 73–74.

22. Taylor, *Louisiana*, 235–236, at 236; Hogue, *Uncivil War*, 92; McPherson and Hogue, *Ordeal by Fire*, 553.

23. "Kellogg, William Pitt," in *Dictionary of Louisiana Biography*; Fischer, *Segregation*, 74; Taylor, *Louisiana*, 254; Foner, *Freedom's Lawmakers*, 8; Tunnell, *Crucible*, 230.

24. Taylor, *Louisiana Reconstructed*, 246–247; Vincent, *Black Legislators*, 140–142.

25. Taylor, *Louisiana Reconstructed*, 268–270; Tunnell, *Crucible*, 189; Hogue, *Uncivil War*, 109–112, 116; LeeAnna Keith, *The Colfax Massacre: The Untold Story of Black Power, White Terror, & the Death of Reconstruction* (New York: Oxford University Press, 2008), 37–38, 104, 109, 131–132, 149; McPherson and Hogue, *Ordeal by Fire*, 615–616; Foner, *Reconstruction*, 498, 530–531.

26. Tinker, *Les Écrits*, 118–119, at 119.

27. Caulfeild, *French Literature*, 173; Tinker, *Les Écrits*, 119–120; Foner, *Freedom's Lawmakers*, 8–9, 171–172.

28. Tinker, *Les Écrits*, 119–121, at 121. For Deléry's self-explanatory titles, see his bibliography, 122–125. Tinker, *Pens, Pills & Pistols*, 13–15, at 15; "Delery, Charles François," in *Dictionary of Louisiana Biography*.

29. Fischer, *Segregation*, 75–76, at 76; Vincent, *Black Legislators*, 167; Hogue, *Uncivil War*, 118–119.

30. Bell, *Revolution*, 278.

31. Fischer, *Segregation*, 76; Bell, *Revolution*, 279.

32. Abel, *Charles Testut's "Le Vieux Salomon,"* 69.

33. Foner, *Reconstruction*, 529–531, at 529; Hogue, *Uncivil War*, 123–124; Keith, *Colfax*, 135; McPherson and Hogue, *Ordeal by Fire*, 644.

34. Hogue, *Uncivil War*, 124; Keith, *Colfax*, 136; Foner, *Reconstruction*, 531.

35. Hogue, *Uncivil War*, 124–131; McPherson, *Battle Cry of Freedom*, 748 note 48. On the renaming of the Battle of Canal Street, see Tunnell, *Crucible*, 1–2.

36. Hogue, *Uncivil War*, 133–137, 143–144, at 133–134; "Penn, David Bradfute," in *Dictionary of Louisiana Biography*; Vincent, "Aspects of the Family and Public Life of Antoine Dubuclet," 190; Clark, *Luminous Brotherhood*, 32.

37. Hogue, *Uncivil War*, 144–146.

38. Hogue, *Uncivil War*, 122–127, 146–147; Devore and Logsdon, *Crescent City*, 76; Fischer, *Segregation*, 131.

39. Devore and Logsdon, *Crescent City*, 82–87, quote on 89.

40. Philip Dray, *Capitol Men: The Epic Story of Reconstruction through the Lives of the First Black Congressmen* (Boston: Houghton Mifflin, 2008), 151, 178; Trefousse, *Ben Butler*, 7–10.

41. Paul Trévigne, L. Roudanez, and J. B. Roudanez to Charles Sumner, May 22, 1870, New Orleans, in Charles Sumner Papers, reel 31, document 555, Houghton Library, Harvard University, Cambridge, Massachussetts.

42. Taylor, *Louisiana*, 303; Hogue, *Uncivil War*, 147; Goodheart, *1861*, 380–381.

43. Hogue, *Uncivil War*, 6, 176; McPherson and Hogue, *Ordeal by Fire*, 671.

44. Hogue, *Uncivil War*, 2–4.

45. Fischer, *Segregation*, 140–141; Devore and Logsdon, *Crescent City*, 88–89.

46. Fischer, *Segregation*, 146–148, quote on 152.

47. Desha P. Rhodes, *A History of Flint Medical College, 1889–1911* (New York: IUniverse, 2007), 1; Blassingame, *Black New Orleans*, 124–129, 163–166; "Roudanez, Louis Charles," in *Dictionary of Louisiana Biography*; Todd L. Savitt, "Straight University Medical Department: The Short Life of a Black Medical School in Reconstruction New Orleans," *Louisiana History* 41 (Winter 2000), 182–186, 201. A. P. Tureaud noted that Martinet practiced medicine before he practiced law, likely referring to his work in Straight's dispensary. Tureaud, "The Negro at the Louisiana Bar," paper presented at the National Bar Association in New Orleans, 1953, 2, A. P. Tureaud Papers, Amistad Research Center.

48. "Louis A. Martinet Records," Clerk of Civil District Court for the Parish of Orleans, http://www.orleanscivilclerk.com/martinet.htm; Williams, "They Call It Marriage," 319–320; Keith Weldon Medley, *We as Freemen: Plessy v. Ferguson* (Gretna, LA: Pelican Publishing, 2003), 112, 150–151; Blassingame, *Black New Orleans*, 126–128; Savitt, "Straight University," 178.

49. Devore and Logsdon, *Crescent City*, 84–87, 94, 114.

50. Editorial Committee, *Prospectus*, September 15, 1887, in A. P. Tureaud Papers, Amistad Research Center, Tulane University; Williams, "They Call It Marriage," 319–320; Carolyn Morrow Long, "The Family of Blanc François Joubert: Racial Determination in New Orleans, 1818–1916," *Louisiana History*, 41 (Fall 2020), 404; Desdunes, *Rappelez-vous*, 70; Joseph Logsdon with Lawrence Powell, "Rodolphe Lucien Desdunes: Forgotten Organizer of the *Plessy* Protest," in *Sunbelt Revolution: The Historical Progression of the Civil Rights Struggle in the Gulf South, 1866–2000*, ed. Samuel C. Hyde Jr. (Gainesville: University Press of Florida, 2003), 50.

51. Medley, *We as Freemen*, quote on 106, illustrations on 108–109; Scott, *Degrees of Freedom*, 80–87, 90. The bayou parishes include St. Mary, Terrebonne, Lafourche, Iberia, and St. Martin.

52. Logsdon and Powell, "Rodolphe Lucien Desdunes," 65 note 30.

53. Ibid., 52–53, 57, 65 note 30; "Martinet, Louis A.," in *Dictionary of Louisiana Biography, Ten-Year Supplement.*

54. Desdunes, *Rappelez-vous*, 74–76, at 76; *Year Book, Twenty-Seventh Session of New Orleans University, 1899–1900* (New Orleans, 1900), 9; Rhodes, *A History*, 12; Desdunes, *Our People*, 140–41; Logsdon and Powell, "Rodolphe Lucien Desdunes," 58; Scott, *Degrees*, 88–91.

55. Medley, *We as Freemen*, 135; Scott, *Degrees*, 89; Fischer, *Segregation*, 153–154.

56. Rhodes, *A History*, 14.

57. Rhodes, *A History*, 14; "Dartmouth College (Geisel)," *Nupepedia Wikia*, https://nupepedia. fandom.com/wiki/Dartmouth_College_(Geisel); Medley, *We as Freemen*, 173; L. A. Martinet, ed., *The Violation of a Constitutional Right* (New Orleans, 1893), reprint, *Chicory Review* (Spring 1989), 32, 35–41; University of New Orleans Department of Medicine and Surgery, *Catalogue of 1896–1897* (New Orleans, 1897).

58. Logsdon and Bell, "Americanization," 258–259; Desdunes, *Rappelez-vous*, 80–84.

59. Scott, *Degrees*, 190, 193; David W. Blight, "Trump Reveals the Truth About Voter Suppression," *New York Times* (April 11, 2020); Osterweis, *Romanticism and Nationalism*, 214–216; Bonnie Berkowitz and Adrian Blanco, "Confederate Monuments Are Falling, but Hundreds Still Stand. Here's Where," *Washington Post* (June 17, 2020); Eugene Robinson, "Trump Might Go Down in History as the Last President of the Confederacy," *Washington Post* (June 17, 2020).

CONCLUSION

1. Frank Paul Bowman, "The Specificity of French Romanticism," in Ciccarelli, Isbell, and Nelson, *People's Voice*, 76; Brothers of Christian Instruction and Pradel Pompilus, *Manuel Illustré d'Histoire de Littérature Haïtienne* (Port-au-Prince, 1961), 98; Logsdon and Powell, "Rodolphe Lucien Desdunes," 51; Nicholls, *From Dessalines to Duvalier*, 92.

2. For a description of the *Crusader* clippings in a scrapbook at Xavier University, New Orleans, see Lester Sullivan, "The Unknown Rodolphe Desdunes: Writings in the New Orleans *Crusader*," *Xavier Review*, 10 (1990), 1–17.

3. Breckman, *European Romanticism*, 189.

4. *New Orleans Times-Picayune* (December 9, 1884).

5. *Weekly Louisianian (New Orleans)*, January 4, 1879; Mark Charles Roudané, "Residence and Medical Practice of Dr. Louis Charles Roudanez and Family," *New Orleans Historical*, https:// neworleanshistorical.org/items/show/1542; Laura V. Rouzan, "Dr. Louis Charles Roudanez: Publisher of America's First Black Daily Newspaper," *South Atlantic Review*, 73 (Spring 2008), 54–58; Martinet, *Violation of a Constitutional Right*.

6. Trefousse, *Ben Butler*, 213–215; Goodheart, *1861*, 380–381; Foner, *Reconstruction*, 491; Dray, *Capitol Men*, 89; McPherson and Hogue, *Ordeal by Fire*, 615–616. For an image of the Tiffany medal, see "1801–1870: Expansion and Reform," Behring Center, National Museum of American History, https://americanhistory.si.edu/american-stories/1801-1870-expansion-and-reform.

7. Desdunes, *Rappelez-vous*, 86; Rachel L. Emanuel and Alexander P. Tureaud Jr., *A More Noble Cause: A. P. Tureaud and the Struggle for Civil Rights in Louisiana* (Baton Rouge: Louisiana State University Press, 2011). Tureaud's ancestral roots are discussed in chapter 3 of the present book.

8. James B. Borders IV, ed., *Marking Time, Making Place: An Essential Chronology of Blacks in New Orleans since 1718* (Silver Spring, MD: Beckham Publications, 2015), 111, 167. Quote from interview with Jacques Morial, September 29, 2019. Also see Contemporary New Orleans interview by Connie Zeanah Atkinson, PhD, Arnold Hirsch, and Eric Hardy, June 1, 2004, at Midlo Center for New Orleans Studies, "Jacques Morial Interview," September 27, 2017, YouTube video, 39:45, https://youtu.be/6FwLPCV1mfE; "Morial, Ernest 'Dutch,'" in *Dictionary of Louisiana Biography, Ten-Year Supplement.*

9. Toledano and Christovich, *New Orleans Architecture,* 6:83, 176–177, 183.

10. Williamjames Hull Hoffer, *Plessy v. Ferguson: Race and Inequality in Jim Crow America* (Lawrence: University Press of Kansas, 2012), 136–137, 139; Gillian Brockell, "Louisiana Board Votes to Pardon Homer Plessy of *Plessy v. Ferguson,*" *Washington Post* (November 12, 2021); Rick Rojas, "With a Pardon, Homer Plessy's Record Is Clear, but a Painful Legacy Endures," *New York Times* (January 5, 2022).

POSTSCRIPT

1. Allain, *New-York et Paris,* 167.

2. Allain, *Souvenirs,* 26.

3. Ibid., 251, 253, 372 note 1, 385.

4. John Merriman, *Massacre: The Life and Death of the Paris Commune* (New York: Basic Books, 2014), 1–11, 35, 139–224, 255; Hazan, *History of the Barricade,* 115; Allain, *Souvenirs,* 122.

5. Reiss, *Black Count,* 10–14, 36–37, 55–60. For Allain's travels, see New York Passenger Lists, 1820–1957, Ancestry.com.

6. Hélène d'Aquin Allain's death notice is number 77 in the Centre administrative, Ville de Saint-Germain-en-Laye, Yvelines. Tinker, *Les Écrits,* 14. For details of Frédéric Allain's death, see death certificate number 456, Cannes Town Hall, Alpes-Maritimes, dated September 18, 1937.

BIBLIOGRAPHY

PRIMARY SOURCES

Archival Materials

Amistad Research Center at Tulane University, New Orleans
    A. P. Tureaud Papers
    Nils R. Douglas Papers
Ancestry.com
    New York Passenger Lists, 1820–1957
Archdiocese of New Orleans Archives
    Sacramental Records
Archives départementales de la Haute-Garonne, Toulouse, France
    Census Records
    Newspapers
Archives départementales des Yvelines et de l'ancienne Seine et Oise, Montigny-le-Bretonneux, France
    Census Records
Archives du Maire, Centre administratif, Ville de Saint-Germain-en-Laye, Yvelines, France
    Death Certificates
Archives généalogiques Andriveau, Toulouse, France
    Genealogical Records
Archives nationales
    Ministère de la culture—Base Léonore
    Dossier: 19800035/0270/36191
    http://www2.culture.gouv.fr/LH/LH147/PG/FRDAFAN84_019800035v0529898.htm
Archives nationales d'outre-mer (ANOM)
    Instruments de recherché en ligne (IREL)
    Inventaires détaillés, Personnel colonial modern (fin XVIIE–XIXE S.)
Bibliothèque nationale de France
    Allain, Frédéric. "De l'apoplexie pulmonaire." Thèse pour le docteur en médicine, Faculté de Mediciné de Paris, 1855.
    Allain, Hélène d'Aquin. [Nihila, pseud.]. *New-York et Paris*. Paris, 1884.
    D'Aquin, Henri-Charles. "Parallèle du typhus et de la fièvree typhoïde." Thèse pour le docteur en médicine, Faculté de Mediciné de Paris, 1856.

Faget, Jean-Charles. "Quelques faits anatomiques en faveur de la cystotomie sus-pubienne chez les trés-jeunes enfants." Thèse pour le docteur en médicine, Faculté de Mediciné de Paris, 1844.

Grandfort, Mme Manoël de [Marie Fontenay, pseud.]. *L'Autre monde*. Paris, 1855.

Roudanez, Louis-Charles. "De l'Endocardite." Thèse pour le docteur en médicine, Faculté de Mediciné de Paris, 1853.

Cornell University Library, Ithaca, New York

    Arthur H. and Mary Marden Dean Lafayette Collection

Earl K. Long Library, University of New Orleans, Louisiana, Special Collections

    Allain, Hélène d'Aquin [une Créole, pseud.]. *Souvenirs d'Amérique et de France*. Paris, 1883.

    État détaillé des liquidations opérées à l'époque du 1er janvier (1829, 1830, 1831, and 1832).

    Marcus B. Christian Collection

    René Grandjean Collection

    Supreme Court of Louisiana Records

Firestone Library, Princeton University, New Jersey

    Rare Books and Special Collections, Edward Livingston Papers (C0280)

Hathi Trust Digital Library

    Garran de Coulon, Jean Phillippe. *Rapport sur les Troubles de Saint-Domingue, fait au nom de la Commission des colonies*. 4 vols. Paris, 1797–1799.

    Souchon, Edmond. *Original Contributions of Louisiana to Medical Sciences: A Biographic Study*. New Orleans, 1915.

Hill Memorial Library, Louisiana State University

    E. C. Wharton Papers

    Grima Family Papers

    Morgan Family Papers

    Reynes Family Papers

    Saint-Domingue Indemnity Records

The Historic New Orleans Collection, Williams Research Center, New Orleans

    The Collins C. Diboll Vieux Carré Digital Survey, https://www.hnoc.org/vcs

    Grima Family Papers

    P. A. Desdunes Ledgers

Houghton Library, Harvard University, Cambridge, Massachusetts

    Charles Sumner Papers

Jamaican Family Search Genealogy Research Library, http://www.jamaicanfamilysearch.com.

John Carter Brown Library, Brown University, Providence, Rhode Island

    Haiti Collection

    Traité de paix, entre les citoyens blancs & les citoyens de couleur, des quatorze paroisses de

la province de l'ouest, de la partie française de Saint-Domingue, https://archive.org/details/
traitdepaixentreoounkn

Library of Congress, Washington, DC

Thomas Jefferson Papers

Louisiana Digital Library, http//www.louisianadigitallibrary.org

"Jackson Order Book." Typescript copy. Works Progress Administration, 1937.

Louisiana National Guard Museum, New Orleans

Louisiana State Archives

Vital Records

Louisiana State Museum, US Mint, New Orleans

Courrier de la Louisiane/Louisiana Courier, 1814–1815

New Orleans Public Library, New Orleans

Alphabetical Index of Changes in Street Names, Old and New, http://archives.nolali
brary.org/~nopl/facts/streetnames/namesa.htm

Louisiana Biography & Obituary Index, http://archives.nolalibrary.org/~nopl/obits/
obits.htm

l'Inconnue à Mme de Grandfort et à Madame L*** [Ligeret]. New Orleans, 1855.

Tulane University Libraries, New Orleans

Ambruménil, L. d.' *l'Ombre de Mme de Grandfort.* New Orleans, 1855.

*Catalogue from 1834 to 1872 of the Professors, Other Instructors, and Alumni with an Histor-
ical Sketch of the Medical College (from its Origin in 1834 to 1847), and of Its Successor,
the Medical Department of the University of Louisiana.* New Orleans, 1871.

D'Aquin, H. C. "Dengue, A Typical Eruptive Fever: Its Thermometrical Semeiology."
New Orleans Medical and Surgical Journal, 2 (July 1874): 37–41.

*Extraits de quelques unes des lettres sur la fievre jaune, publiées dans le Journal de la Medi-
cale Société de la Nouvelle-Orléans.* New Orleans, 1859–1864.

Faget, J. C. *l'Art d'apaiser les douleurs de l'enfantement.* Paris, 1880.

———. *Etude medical de quelques questions importantes pour la Louisiane.* New Orleans,
1859.

Grima Family Papers

Joseph Jones Collection

Lambert Family Papers

La Société française Collection

Le François, A. *Abrégé historique de la société française de bienfaisance et d'assistance mutuelle de la Nouvelle-Orléans.* New Orleans, 1903.

[Ligeret de Chazey, Eléonore]. *Les Créoles. Réponse à Madame de Grandfort.* New Orleans, 1855.

Limet, Félix. *Historique de la société française de bienfaisance et d'assistance mutuelle de la
Nouvelle-Orléans.* New Orleans, 1880.

Paul Trévigne to Fisk University Librarian, in Southern Writers Series.

Rudolph Matas Library of the Health Sciences, Library Guides, *Tulane University's Contributions to Health Sciences Research and Education: A Guide—A–Z List of Notables*, https://libguides.tulane.edu/famousalumni

University of Notre Dame Archives, https://archives.nd.edu/search/calendar-search.htm

Xavier University, New Orleans

Archives & Special Collections, Desdunes Family Collection

Public Documents

Acts of the State of Louisiana

Acts Passed at the First Session of the Tenth Legislature of Louisiana, 1831, Hathi Trust Digital Library, https://babel.hathitrust.org/cgi/pt?id=uc1.a0001917921&view=1up&seq=7

A Compilation of the Messages and Papers of the Presidents, 1789–1897. Ed. James D. Richardson. 11 vols. Washington, DC, 1875–1893.

Tombstone index, New Orleans Cemeteries, Louisiana State Museum in the US Mint.

Newspapers and Periodicals

Boston Liberator
Comptes-Rendus de l'Athénée Louisianais (New Orleans)
Echo d'Paris (France)
Harper's New Monthly Magazine (New York)
Journal de Toulouse (France)
l'Album littéraire: Journal des jeunes gens, amateurs de littéraire
La Chronique (New Orleans)
La Presse (Paris)
La semaine littéraire du Courrier des États Unis (New York)
Le Coup-D'œil (New Orleans)
Le Franc-Maçon (New Orleans)
Le Moniteur de la Louisiane
l'Union (New Orleans)
Louisiana Courier/Le Courrier de la Louisiane (New Orleans)
New Orleans Bee (*l'Abeille de la Nouvelle-Orléans*)
New Orleans Crusader
New Orleans Daily Picayune
New Orleans Times-Picayune
New Orleans Tribune
New York Review of Books

New York Times
Washington Post
Weekly Louisianian (New Orleans)

Published Memoirs, Letters, Articles, Documents,
Literary Works, and Historical Narratives

Allain, Hélène d'Aquin [une Créole, pseud.]. Souvenirs d'Amérique et de France. Paris: Perisse Frères, 1883.

———. [Nihila, pseud.]. New-York et Paris. Paris, 1884.

———. Paris-Rapide, 1884.

Ardouin, Beaubrun. Études sur l'Histoire d'Haiti. 11 vols. Paris: Dezobry et E. Magdeleine, 1853–1860.

Bassett, John Spencer, ed. Correspondence of Andrew Jackson. 6 vols. Washington, DC: Carnegie Institution of Washington, 1926–1935.

Biographical and Historical Memoirs of Louisiana. Chicago, 1892.

Boutard, M. C., ed. "Correspondance de Lamennais avec Madame Ligeret de Chazey." La Revue hebdomadaire (October 1909): 5–41.

Bruce, Clint, ed. and trans. Afro-Creole Poetry in French from Louisiana's Radical Civil War–Era Newspapers. New Orleans: Historic New Orleans Collection, 2020.

Carter, Clarence Edwin, ed. The Territorial Papers of the United States. Vol. 9, The Territory of Orleans, 1803–1812. Washington, DC: US Government Printing Office, 1940.

Chamber of Commerce of the New Orleans Area. Decisions of the New Orleans Chamber of Commerce: From Its Formation in 1834 to August 4th, 1856. New Orleans, 1857.

Chateaubriand, François-René de. Atala and René. Trans. Rayner Heppenstall. London: Oxford University Press, 1963.

———. The Genius of Christianity, or, the Spirit and Beauty of the Christian Religion. Ed. Charles I. White. 15th rev. ed. Philadelphia, 1856.

———. Mémoires d'outre-tombe. 6 vols. Paris: Jean de Bonnet, 1860.

Chesnut, Mary Boykin. Mary Chesnut's Civil War. Ed. C. Vann Woodward. New Haven, CT: Yale University Press, 1981.

Daniels, Nathan W. Thank God My Regiment an African One: The Civil War Diary of Colonel Nathan W. Daniels. Ed. C. P. Weaver. Baton Rouge: Louisiana State University Press, 1998.

Deggs, Sister Mary Bernard. No Cross, No Crown: Black Nuns in Nineteenth-Century New Orleans. Ed. Virginia Meacham Gould and Charles E. Nolan. Bloomington: Indiana University Press, 2001.

Desdunes, Pierre-Aristide. Rappelez-vous concitoyens! La poésie de Pierre-Aristide Desdunes. Ed. Caryn Cossé Bell. Trans. Clint Bruce. Shreveport, LA: Les Éditions Tintamarre, 2010.

Desdunes, Rodolphe Lucien. *Our People and Our History*. Ed. and trans. Sister Dorothea Olga McCants. Baton Rouge: Louisiana State University Press, 1973.

Destrehan Plantation. *The 1811 Slave Revolt and Trial at Destrehan Plantation*. 2 vols. Destrehan, LA: Author, 1999.

Faget, Jean-Charles. *Etude medical de quelques questions importantes pour la Louisiane*. New Orleans: Imprimerie Franco-Américaine, 1859.

Gardner, Charles K. *A Dictionary of All Officers, Who Have Been Commissioned, or Have Been Appointed and Served, in the United States*. New York, 1860.

Gayarré, Charles. *History of Louisiana*. 1903. Reprint, New Orleans, 1965.

Grandfort, Manoël de [Marie Fontenay, pseud.]. *L'Autre monde*. Paris: Librairie Nouvelle, 1855.

———. *The New World: Translated from the French of Mme M. de Grandfort, by Edward C. Wharton*. New Orleans: Sherman, Wharton, 1855.

Houzeau, Jean-Charles. *My Passage at the New Orleans "Tribune": A Memoir of the Civil War Era*. Ed. David C. Rankin. Trans. Gerard F. Denault. Baton Rouge: Louisiana State University Press, 1984.

Jameson, J. Franklin, ed. "Correspondence of John C. Calhoun." In *Annual Report of the American Historical Association*. Washington, DC, 1900.

Lamennais, Hugues Félicité Robert de. *Words of a Believer*. New York: Charles de Behr, 1834.

Larousse, Pierre, ed. *Grand dictionnaire universel du XIXe siècle*. Paris, 1876.

Latour, Arsène Lacarrière. *Historical Memoir of the War in West Florida and Louisiana in 1814–15*. Ed. Gene Allen Smith. New Orleans: Historic New Orleans Collection, 1999.

Levasseur, A. *Lafayette in America in 1824 and 1825; or Journal of a Voyage to the United States*. 1829. Reprint, New York: Research Reprints, 1970.

Ligeret de Chazey, Eléonore. *Les Créoles. Réponse à Madame de Grandfort*. New Orleans, 1855.

———. *l'Inconnue à Mme de Grandfort et à Madame L****. New Orleans, 1855.

Martinet, L. A., ed. *The Violation of a Constitutional Right*. New Orleans, 1893, in Nils R. Douglas Papers, Amistad Research Center, Tulane University, New Orleans.

McKaye, James. *The Mastership and Its Fruits: The Emancipated Slave Face to Face with His Old Master*. New York, 1864.

Miller, Edward L. *New Orleans and the Texas Revolution*. College Station, TX: Texas A&M University Press, 2004.

Moreau de Saint-Méry, Médéric-Louis-Élie. *Description topographique, physique, civile, politique et historique de la partie française de l'isle Saint-Domingue*. 3 vols. 1796. Reprint, Paris: Librairie Larose, 1958.

Nolan, Charles E., ed. *Sacramental Records of the Roman Catholic Church of the Archdiocese of New Orleans*. 19 vols. New Orleans: Archdiocese of New Orleans, 1987–2004.

Nolte, Vincent. *Fifty Years in Both Hemispheres or, Reminiscences of the Life of a Former Merchant.* New York: Redfield, 1854.

Northup, Solomon. *Twelve Years a Slave.* Ed. Sue Eakin and Joseph Logsdon. Baton Rouge: Louisiana State University Press, 1968.

Parton, James. *General Butler in New Orleans: History of the Administration of the Department of the Gulf.* 10th ed. New York, 1864.

[Rattenbury, Joseph Freeman]. *Narrative of a Voyage to the Spanish Main, in the Ship "Two Friends."* London: Printed for J. Miller, 1819.

Rouquette, Abbé Adrien. *Wild Flowers, Sacred Poetry.* New Orleans: T. O'Donnell, 1848.

Rouquette, Adrien-Emmanuel [Chahta-Ima, pseud.]. *La nouvelle Atala ou la fille de l'esprit.* New Orleans: Catholique Propagateur, 1879.

———. *La pour le docteur en Atala, ou la Fille de l'Esprit.* New Orleans: Catholique Propagateur, 1879.

Rowland, Dunbar, ed. *Official Letter Books of W. C. C. Claiborne, 1801–1816.* 6 vols. Jackson: Mississippi Department of Archives and History, 1917.

Saint-Simon, Louis de Rouvroy duc de. *Saint-Simon at Versailles.* Ed. and trans. Lucy Norton. New York: Hamish Hamilton, 1980.

Séjour, Victor. *The Fortune-Teller.* Trans. Norman R. Shapiro. Urbana: University of Illinois Press, 2002.

———. *The Jew of Seville.* Trans. Norman R. Shapiro. Urbana: University of Illinois Press, 2002.

Trollope, Frances. *Domestic Manners of the Americans.* London: Whittaker, Treacher & Co., A. A. Knopf, 1832.

———. *Domestic Manners of the Americans.* Ed. Donald Smalley. New York: Knopf, 1949.

University of New Orleans Department of Medicine and Surgery. *Catalogue of 1896–1897.* New Orleans, 1897.

United States District Court, Louisiana, Eastern District. *Conspicuous Cases in the United States District Court of Louisiana: Transcriptions of the Case Papers and other Interesting Documents Pertaining to Trials and Indictments, Dating from the Establishment of the Federal Court in 1806.* New Orleans: Survey of Federal Archives in Louisiana, 1940–1941.

The War of the Rebellion: A Compilation of the Official Records of the Union and Confederate Armies. Washington, DC: US Government Printing Office, 1880–1901.

Warren, Harris Gaylord, ed. and trans. "Documents Relating to the Establishment of Privateers at Galveston, 1816–1817." *Louisiana Historical Quarterly,* 21 (October 1938): 1086–1109.

Wharton, Edward C. *The New World: Translated from the French of Mme M. de Grandfort.* New Orleans: Sherman, Wharton, 1855.

SECONDARY SOURCES

Books and Pamphlets

Abbott, Richard. *For Free Press and Equal Rights: Republican Newspapers in the Reconstruction South.* Ed. John W. Quist. Athens: University of Georgia Press, 2004.

Abel, Sheri Lyn. *Charles Testut's "Le Vieux Salomon": Race, Religion, Socialism, and Freemasonry.* Lanham, MD: Rowman & Littlefield, 2009.

Aptheker, Herbert. *American Negro Slave Revolts.* 6th ed. New York: International Publishers, 1993.

Armenteros, Carolina. *The French Idea of History: Joseph de Maistre and His Heirs, 1794–1854.* Ithaca, NY: Cornell University Press, 2011.

Arthur, Stanley Clisby. *Old Families of Louisiana.* New Orleans: Harmanson, 1931.

———. *The Story of the Battle of New Orleans.* New Orleans: Louisiana Historical Society, 1915.

Aslakson, Kenneth R. *Making Race in the Courtroom: The Legal Construction of Three Races in Early New Orleans.* New York: New York University Press, 2014.

Baudier, Roger. *The Catholic Church in Louisiana.* New Orleans: A. W. Hyatt Stationery, 1939.

Bauer, Craig A. *Creole Genesis: The Bringier Family and Antebellum Plantation Life in Louisiana.* Lafayette: University of Louisiana at Lafayette Press, 2011.

Bell, Caryn Cossé. *Revolution, Romanticism, and the Afro-Creole Protest Tradition in Louisiana, 1718–1868.* Baton Rouge: Louisiana State University Press, 1997.

Bennett, James B. *Religion and the Rise of Jim Crow in New Orleans.* Princeton, NJ: Princeton University Press, 2005.

Berlin, Ira. *Many Thousands Gone: The First Two Centuries of Slavery in North America.* Cambridge, MA: Belknap Press of Harvard University Press, 1998.

———. *Slaves without Masters: The Free Negro in the Antebellum South.* New York: The New Press, 1974.

Berry, Jason. *City of a Million Dreams: A History of New Orleans at Year 300.* Chapel Hill: University of North Carolina Press, 2018.

Berry, Mary Frances. *"We Are Who We Say We Are": A Black Family's Search for Home Across the Atlantic World.* New York: Oxford University Press, 2015.

Blackburn, Robin. *The Making of New World Slavery: From the Baroque to the Modern, 1492–1800.* London: Verso, 1997.

———. *The Overthrow of Colonial Slavery, 1776–1848.* London: Verso, 1988.

Blassingame, John W. *Black New Orleans, 1860–1880.* Chicago: University of Chicago Press, 1973.

———. *The Slave Community: Plantation Life in the Antebellum South.* 1972. Revised and enlarged ed. New York: Oxford University Press, 1979.

Blaufarb, Rafe. *Bonapartists in the Borderlands: French Exiles and Refugees on the Gulf Coast, 1815–1835.* Tuscaloosa: University of Alabama Press, 2005.

Bloom, Khaled J. *The Mississippi Valley's Great Yellow Fever Epidemic of 1878.* Baton Rouge: Louisiana State University Press, 1993.

Bokenkotter, Thomas. *Church and Revolution: Catholics in the Struggle for Democracy and Social Justice.* New York: Crown Publishing, 1998.

Bolster, W. Jeffrey. *Black Jacks: African American Seamen in the Age of Sail.* Cambridge, MA: 1997.

Borders, James B., IV, ed. *Marking Time, Making Place: An Essential Chronology of Blacks in New Orleans since 1718.* Silver Spring, MD: Beckham Publications, 2015.

Boutard, Charles. *Lamennais: Sa vie et ses doctrines.* 3 vols. Paris: Perrin, 1913.

Brasseaux, Carl A. *The "Foreign French": Nineteenth-Century French Immigration into Louisiana, 1840–1848.* 3 vols. Lafayette: Center for Louisiana Studies, University of Southwestern Louisiana, 1992.

Brasseaux, Carl A., and Glenn R. Conrad, eds. *The Road to Louisiana: The Saint-Domingue Refugees, 1792–1809.* Lafayette: Center for Louisiana Studies, University of Southwestern Louisiana, 1992.

Braun, Juliane. *Creole Drama: Theatre and Society in Antebellum New Orleans.* Charlottesville: University of Virginia Press, 2019.

Breckman, Warren. *European Romanticism: A Brief History with Documents.* Boston: Bedford/St. Martin's, 2008.

———. *Marx, the Young Hegelians, and the Origins of Radical Social Theory: Dethroning the Self.* Cambridge: Cambridge University Press, 1999.

Brothers of Christian Instruction and Pradel Pompilus. *Manuel illustré d'histoire de littérature haitienne.* Port-au-Prince: H. Deschamps, 1961.

Buckley, Veronica. *The Secret Wife of Louis XIV: Françoise d'Augigne Madame de Maintenon.* New York: Farrar, Straus and Giroux, 2008.

Byrd, W. Michael, and Linda A. Clayton. *An American Health Dilemma: A Medical History of African Americans and the Problem of Race Beginnings to 1900.* New York: Routledge, 2000.

Cairns, David. *Berlioz, 1803–1832: The Making of an Artist.* London: Sphere Books, 1990.

Campbell, Edward C. C., Jr., with Kym S. Rice, eds. *Before Freedom Came: African-American Life in the Antebellum South.* Richmond: University of Virginia Press, 1991.

Casey, Powell A. *Louisiana in the War of 1812.* Baton Rouge: Self-published, 1963.

Cassedy, James H. *Medicine in America: A Short History.* Baltimore: Johns Hopkins University Press.

Caulfeild, Ruby Van Allen. *The French Literature of Louisiana.* New York: Institute of French Studies, Columbia University, 1929.

Cauna, Jacques de. *l'Eldorado des Aquitains: Gascons, Basques et Béarnais aux Iles d'Amérique, XVIIe–XVIIIe siècles.* Biarritz: Atlantica, 1998.

Chancerel, Catherine. *l'homme du Grand Fleuve.* Paris: CNRS Éditions, 2014.

Chernow, Ron. *Grant.* New York: Penguin, 2017.

Christian, Marcus. *The Battle of New Orleans: Negro Soldiers in the Battle of New Orleans.* New Orleans: Battle of New Orleans, 150th Anniversary Committee of Louisiana, 1965.

————. *I Am New Orleans and Other Poems by Marcus B. Christian.* Ed. Rudolph Lewis and Amin Sharif. New Orleans: Xavier Review Press, 1999.

Ciccarelli, Andrea, John C. Isbell, and Brian Nelson, eds. *The People's Voice: Essays on European Romanticism.* Melbourne: Monash Romance Studies, 1999.

Cimbala, Paul A., and Randall M. Miller, eds. *The Freedmen's Bureau and Reconstruction: Reconsiderations.* New York: Fordham University Press, 1999.

Ciravolo, G. Leighton. *The Legacy of John McDonogh.* Lafayette: Center for Louisiana Studies, University of Louisiana at Lafayette, 2002.

Clark, Emily Suzanne. *A Luminous Brotherhood: Afro-Creole Spiritualism in Nineteenth-Century New Orleans.* Chapel Hill: University of North Carolina Press, 2016.

Clavin, Matthew J. *Toussaint Louverture and the American Civil War.* Philadelphia: University of Pennsylvania Press, 2010.

Clements, J. Clancy, Thomas A. Klingler, Deborah Piston-Hatlan, & Kevin J. Rottet, eds. *History, Society, and Variation: In Honor of Albert Valdman.* Amsterdam: John Benjamins, 2006.

Craig, Gordon A. *Europe, 1815–1914.* Hinsdale, IL: Dryden Press, 1972.

Crété, Liliane. *Daily Life in Louisiana, 1815–1830.* Trans. Patrick Gregory. Baton Rouge: Louisiana State University Press, 1978.

Daggett, Melissa. *Spiritualism in Nineteenth-Century New Orleans: The Life and Times of Henry Louis Rey.* Jackson: University Press of Mississippi, 2017.

Daguillard, Fritz. *A Jewel in the Crown: Charles Sumner and the Struggle for Haiti's Recognition.* Washington, DC: Haitian Embassy, 1999.

Davis, Cyprian. *Henriette Delille: Servant of Slaves, Witness to the Poor.* New Orleans: Archdiocese of New Orleans, 2004.

Davis, Edwin Adams. *The Story of Louisiana.* 3 vols. New Orleans: J. F. Hyer, 1960.

Davis, William C. *The Pirates Laffite: The Treacherous World of the Corsairs of the Gulf.* Orlando, FL: H. M. H. Books, 2005.

Delany, Francis X. *A History of the Catholic Church in Jamaica.* New York: Jesuit Mission Press, 1930.

Dessens, Nathalie. *From Saint-Domingue to New Orleans: Migration and Influences.* Gainesville: University Press of Florida, 2007.

De Ville, Winston. *The Territory of Orleans, 1803–1812.* Ville Platte, LA: W. De Ville, 1987.

Devore, Donald E., and Joseph Logsdon. *Crescent City Schools: Public Education in New Orleans, 1841–1991.* Lafayette: Center for Louisiana Studies, University of Southwestern Louisiana, 1991.

Dillon, Merton L. *Slavery Attacked: Southern Slaves and Their Allies, 1619–1865.* Baton Rouge: Louisiana State University Press, 1990.

Dorigny, Marcel, ed. *The Abolitions of Slavery: From Léger Félicité Sonthonax to Victor Schœl-cher, 1793, 1794, 1848.* New York: Bergahn Books, 2003.

Douglas, Nick. *Finding Octave: The Untold Story of Two Creole Families and Slavery in Louisiana.* Createspace, 2013.

Dray, Philip. *Capitol Men: The Epic Story of Reconstruction through the Lives of the First Black Congressmen.* Boston: Houghton Mifflin, 2008.

Dubois, Laurent. *Avengers of the New World: The Story of the Haitian Revolution.* Cambridge, MA: Belknap Press of Harvard University Press, 2004.

Dubois, Laurent, and John D. Garrigus, eds. *Slave Revolution in the Caribbean, 1789–1804: A Brief History with Documents.* Boston: Bedford/St. Martin's, 2006.

Du Bois, W. E. B. *Black Reconstruction in America, 1860–1880.* 1935. Reprint, New York: Atheneum, 1975.

Duffy, John, ed. *The Rudolph Matas History of Medicine in Louisiana.* 2 vols. Baton Rouge, Louisiana State University Press, 1962.

Eakin, Sue. *Rapides Parish History.* Alexandria: Historical Association of Central Louisiana, 1976.

Eaton, Clement. *The Freedom-of-Thought Struggle in the Old South.* 1940. Reprint, New York: Harper & Row, 1964.

Ellis, Jack D. *The Physician-Legislators of France: Medicine and Politics in the Early French Republic, 1870–1914.* Cambridge: Cambridge University Press, 1990.

Emanuel, Rachel L., and Alexander P. Tureaud Jr. *A More Noble Cause: A. P. Tureaud and the Struggle for Civil Rights in Louisiana.* Baton Rouge: Louisiana State University Press, 2011.

Evans, David Owen. *Social Romanticism in France, 1830–1848.* Oxford: Clarendon Press, 1951.

Evans, Freddi Williams. *Congo Square: African Roots in New Orleans.* Lafayette: University of Louisiana at Lafayette Press, 2011.

Fairclough, Adam. *Bulldozed and Betrayed: Louisiana and the Stolen Elections of 1876.* Baton Rouge: Louisiana State University Press, 2021.

Fandrich, Ina Johanna. *The Mysterious Voodoo Queen, Marie Laveaux: A Study of Powerful Female Leadership in Nineteenth-Century New Orleans.* New York: Routledge, 2005.

Fertel, Rien. *Imagining the Creole City: The Rise of Literary Culture in Nineteenth-Century New Orleans.* Baton Rouge: Louisiana State University Press, 2014.

Fett, Sharla M. *Working Cures: Healing, Health, and Power on Southern Slave Plantations.* Chapel Hill: University of North Carolina Press, 2002.

Fick, Carolyn E. *The Making of Haiti: The Saint Domingue Revolution from Below.* Knoxville: University of Tennessee Press, 1990.

Fischer, Roger A. *The Segregation Struggle in Louisiana, 1862–77.* Urbana: University of Illinois Press, 1974.

Florence, Robert. *City of the Dead: A Journey through St. Louis Cemetery #1*. Lafayette: Center for Louisiana Studies, University of Southwestern Louisiana, 1996.

———. *New Orleans Cemeteries: Life in the Cities of the Dead*. New Orleans: Batture Press, 1997.

Foner, Eric. *Freedom's Lawmakers: A Directory of Black Officeholders during Reconstruction*. Baton Rouge: Louisiana State University Press, 1996.

———. *Nothing but Freedom: Emancipation and Its Legacy*. Baton Rouge: Louisiana State University Press, 1983.

———. *Reconstruction: America's Unfinished Revolution, 1863–1877*. New York: Harper & Row, 1988.

Force, Pierre. *Wealth and Disaster: Atlantic Migrations from a Pyrenean Town in the Eighteenth and Nineteenth Centuries*. Baltimore: Johns Hopkins University Press, 2016.

Ford, Lacy K. *Deliver Us from Evil: The Slavery Question in the Old South*. New York: Oxford University Press, 2009.

Fortier, Alcée. *A History of Louisiana*. 4 vols. New York: Manzi, Joyant, 1904.

———. ed. *Louisiana: Comprising Sketches of Parishes, Towns, Events, Institutions, and Persons*. 3 vols. Madison, WI: Century Historical Association, 1914.

———. *Louisiana Studies. Literature, Customs and Dialects, History and Education*. New Orleans: F. F. Hansell, 1894.

Foucault, Michel. *The Birth of the Clinic: An Archaeology of Medical Perception*. Trans. A. M. Sheridan Smith. New York: Vintage Books, 1973.

Franklin, John Hope, and Alfred A. Moss Jr. *From Slavery to Freedom: A History of African Americans*. 8th ed. Boston: McGraw Hill, 2000.

Furst, Lilian R. *Romanticism in Perspective: A Comparative Study of Aspects of the Romantic Movements in England, France and Germany*. New York: St. Martin's Press, 1969.

Garraway, Doris. *The Libertine Colony: Creolization in the Early French Caribbean*. Durham, NC: Duke University Press, 2005.

Garrigus, John D. *Before Haiti: Race and Citizenship in French Saint-Domingue*. New York: Palgrave Macmillan, 2006.

Garrigus, John D., and Christopher Morris, eds. *Assumed Identities: The Meanings of Race in the Atlantic World*. Arlington: University of Texas at Arlington, 2010.

Gaspar, David Barry, and David Patrick Geggus, eds. *A Turbulent Time: The French Revolution and the Greater Caribbean*. Bloomington: Indiana University Press, 1997.

Geggus, David P., ed. and trans. *The Haitian Revolution: A Documentary History*. Indianapolis, IN: Hackett, 2014.

———. ed. *The Impact of the Haitian Revolution in the Atlantic World*. Columbia: University of South Carolina Press, 2001.

———. *Slavery, War, and Revolution: The British Occupation of Saint Domingue 1793–1798*. Oxford: Oxford University Press, 1982.

Gienapp, William E., ed. *The Civil War and Reconstruction: A Documentary Collection*. New York: W. W. Norton, 2001.

Goins, Charles Robert, and John Michael Caldwell. *Historical Atlas of Louisiana*. Norman: University of Oklahoma Press, 1995.

Gomez, Michael A. *Exchanging Our Country Marks: The Transformation of African Identities in the Colonial and Antebellum South*. Chapel Hill: University of North Carolina Press, 1998.

Goodheart, Adam. *1861: The Civil War Awakening*. New York: Vintage Books, 2012.

Goudie, Sean X. *Creole America: The West Indies and the Formation of Literature and Culture in the New Republic*. Philadelphia: University of Pennsylvania Press, 2006.

Greenwald, Erin M. *Purchased Lives: New Orleans and the Domestic Slave Trade, 1808–1865*. New Orleans: Historic New Orleans Collection, 2015.

Griggs, Earl Leslie, and Clifford H. Prator, eds. *Henry Christophe and Thomas Clarkson: A Correspondence*. Berkeley: University of California Press, 1968.

Grummond, Jane Lucas de, and Ronald R. Morazan. *The Baratarians and the Battle of New Orleans with Biographical Sketches of the Veterans of the Battalion of Orleans, 1814–1815*. Baton Rouge: Legacy, 1979.

Hall, Gwendolyn Midlo. *Africans in Colonial Louisiana: The Development of Afro-Creole Culture in the Eighteenth Century*. Baton Rouge: Louisiana State University Press, 1992.

———. *Afro-Louisiana History and Genealogy, 1719–1820*, http://www.ibiblio.org/laslave.

Hall, Stephen G. *A Faithful Account of the Race: African American Historical Writing in Nineteenth-Century America*. Chapel Hill: University of North Carolina Press, 2009.

Hanger, Kimberly S. *Bounded Lives, Bounded Places: Free Black Society in Colonial New Orleans, 1769–1803*. Durham, NC: Duke University Press, 1997.

Harding, Vincent. *There Is a River: The Black Struggle for Freedom in America*. San Diego: Harcourt, Brace, 1981.

Hatfield, Joseph T. *William Claiborne: Jeffersonian Centurion in the American Southwest*. Lafayette: University of Southwestern Louisiana, 1976.

Hazan, Eric. *A History of the Barricade*. Trans. David Fernback. London: Verso, 2015.

Head, David. *Privateers of the Americas: Spanish American Privateering from the United States in the Early Republic*. Athens: University of Georgia Press, 2015.

Hirsch, Arnold R., and Joseph Logsdon, eds. *Creole New Orleans: Race and Americanization*. Baton Rouge: Louisiana State University Press, 1992.

Hoffer, Williamjames Hull. *Plessy v. Ferguson: Race and Inequality in Jim Crow America*. Lawrence: University Press of Kansas, 2012.

Hogue, James K. *Uncivil War: Five New Orleans Street Battles and the Rise and Fall of Radical Reconstruction*. Baton Rouge: Louisiana State University Press, 2006.

Hollandsworth, James G., Jr. *An Absolute Massacre: The New Orleans Race Riot of July 30, 1866*. Baton Rouge: Louisiana State University Press, 2001.

————. *The Louisiana Native Guards: The Black Military Experience during the Civil War*. Baton Rouge: Louisiana State University Press, 1995.

Horton, James Oliver, and Lois E. Horton. *Slavery and the Making of America*. New York: Oxford University Press, 2005.

Hugo, Victor. *Oeuvres Complètes de Victor Hugo*. 70 vols. Paris, 1888–1893.

Hunt, Alfred N. *Haiti's Influence on Antebellum America: Slumbering Volcano in the Caribbean*. Baton Rouge: Louisiana State University Press, 1988.

Hunt, Lynn. *Inventing Human Rights: A History*. New York: W. W. Norton, 2007.

Hyde, Samuel C., Jr., ed. *Sunbelt Revolution: The Historical Progression of the Civil Rights Struggle in the Gulf South, 1866–2000*. Gainesville: University Press of Florida, 2003.

Jacobs, Claude F., and Andrew J. Kaslow. *The Spiritual Churches of New Orleans: Origins, Beliefs, and Rituals of an African-American Religion*. Knoxville: University of Tennessee Press, 1991.

James, C. L. R. *The Black Jacobins: Toussaint l'Ouverture and the San Domingo Revolution*. Rev. ed. New York: Vintage Books, 1963.

Johnson, Jerah. *Congo Square in New Orleans*. New Orleans: Louisiana Landmarks Society, 1995.

Johnson, Rashauna. *Slavery's Metropolis: Unfree Labor in New Orleans during the Age of Revolutions*. New York: Cambridge University Press, 2016.

Johnson, Walter. *Soul by Soul: Life Inside the Antebellum Slave Market*. Cambridge, MA: Harvard University Press, 1999.

Kein, Sybil, ed. *Creole: The History and Legacy of Louisiana's Free People of Color*. Baton Rouge: Louisiana State University Press, 2000.

Keith, LeeAnna. *The Colfax Massacre: The Untold Story of Black Power, White Terror, & the Death of Reconstruction*. New York: Oxford University Press, 2008.

King, Grace. *Creole Families of New Orleans*. New York: Macmillan, 1921.

King, Stewart R. *Blue Coat or Powdered Wig: Free People of Color in Pre-Revolutionary Saint Domingue*. Athens: University of Georgia Press, 2001.

Klingler, Thomas A. *If I Could Turn My Tongue Like That: The Creole Language of Pointe Coupee Parish, Louisiana*. Baton Rouge: Louisiana State University Press, 2003.

Knight, Franklin W., ed. *General History of the Caribbean*. London: UNESCO Publishing, 1997.

Kramer, Lloyd. *Lafayette in Two Worlds: Public Cultures & Personal Identities in an Age of Revolutions*. Chapel Hill: University of North Carolina Press, 1996.

Landers, Jane G. *Atlantic Creoles in the Age of Revolutions*. Cambridge, MA: Harvard University Press, 2010.

————. *Black Society in Spanish Florida*. Urbana: University of Illinois Press, 1999.

Lasso, Marixa. *Myths of Harmony: Race and Republicanism during the Age of Revolution, Colombia, 1795–1831*. Pittsburgh: University of Pittsburgh Press, 2007.

Latortue, Régine, and Gleason R. W. Adams, eds. and trans. *Les Cenelles: A Collection of Poems by Creole Writers of the Early Nineteenth Century.* Boston: G. K. Hall, 1979.

Lefebvre, Georges. *The French Revolution.* Trans. Elizabeth M. Evanson. 2 vols. London: Routledge & Kegan Paul, 1962.

Leonard, Elizabeth D. *Benjamin Franklin Butler: A Noisy, Fearless Life.* Chapel Hill: University of North Carolina Press, 2022.

Levin, Kevin M. *Searching for Black Confederates: The Civil War's Most Persistent Myth.* Chapel Hill: University of North Carolina Press, 2019.

Linebaugh, Peter, and Marcus Rediker. *The Many-Headed Hydra: Sailors, Slaves, Commoners and the Hidden History of the Revolutionary Atlantic.* Boston: Beacon, 2000.

Linklater, Andro. *An Artist in Treason: The Extraordinary Life of General James Wilkinson.* New York: Walker Books, 2009.

Long, Carolyn Morrow. *A New Orleans Voudou Priestess: The Legend and Reality of Marie Laveau.* Gainesville: University Press of Florida, 2006.

Lowndes, Emma. *Récits de femmes pendant la guerre franco-prussienne (1870–1871).* Paris: l'Harmattan, 2013.

Lowndes, Marie Belloc. *"I, Too, Have Lived in Arcadia": Mrs. Belloc Lowndes.* London: Macmillan, 1941.

MacDonald, Robert, R., R. Kemp, and Edward F. Haas, eds. *Louisiana's Black Heritage.* New Orleans: Louisiana State Museum, 1979.

Marrinan, Michael. *Romantic Paris: Histories of a Cultural Landscape, 1800–1850.* Stanford, CA: Stanford University Press, 2009.

May, Robert E. *Manifest Destiny's Underworld: Filibustering in Antebellum America.* Chapel Hill: University of North Carolina Press, 2002.

McConnell, Roland C. *Negro Troops of Antebellum Louisiana: A History of the Battalion of Free Men of Color.* Baton Rouge: Louisiana State University Press, 1968.

McCrary, Peyton. *Abraham Lincoln and Reconstruction: The Louisiana Experiment.* Princeton, NJ: Princeton University Press, 1978.

McCullough, David. *The Greater Journey: Americans in Paris.* New York: Simon & Schuster, 2011.

McKee, Sally. *The Exile's Song: Edmond Dédé and the Unfinished Revolutions of the Atlantic World.* New Haven, CT: Yale University Press, 2017.

McKivigan, John R., and Stanley Harrold, eds. *Antislavery Violence: Sectional, Racial, and Cultural Conflict in Antebellum America.* Knoxville: University of Tennessee Press, 1999.

McPherson, James M. *Battle Cry of Freedom: The Civil War Era.* New York: Oxford University Press, 1988.

McPherson, James M., and James K. Hogue. *Ordeal by Fire: The Civil War and Reconstruction.* 4th ed. New York: McGraw Hill, 2009.

Medley, Keith Weldon. *We as Freemen: Plessy v. Ferguson.* Gretna, LA: Pelican Publishing, 2003.

Medwick, Cathleen. *Teresa of Avila: The Progress of a Soul.* New York: Alfred A. Knopf, 1999.

Melville, Annabelle M. *Louis William DuBourg: Bishop of Louisiana and the Floridas, Bishop of Montauban, and Archbishop of Besançon, 1766–1833.* 2 vols. Chicago: Loyola University Press, 1986.

Merriman, John. *Massacre: The Life and Death of the Paris Commune.* New York: Basic Books, 2014.

Michel, Claudine, and Patrick Bellegarde-Smith, eds. *Vodou in Haitian Life and Culture: Invisible Powers.* New York: Palgrave Macmillan, 2006.

Mitchell, Brian K., Barrington S. Edwards, and Nick Weldon. *Monumental: Oscar Dunn and His Radical Fight in Reconstruction Louisiana.* New Orleans: Historic New Orleans Collection, 2021.

Mitchell, Mary Niall. *Raising Freedom's Child: Black Children and Visions of the Future after Slavery.* New York: New York University Press, 2008.

Mongey, Vanessa. *Rogue Revolutionaries: The Fight for Legitimacy in the Greater Caribbean.* Philadelphia: University of Pennsylvania Press, 2020.

Morales, Edgardo Pérez. *No Limits to Their Sway: Cartagena's Privateers and the Masterless Caribbean in the Age of Revolutions.* Nashville: Vanderbilt University Press, 2018.

Neely, Sylvia. *Lafayette and the Liberal Ideal, 1814–1824: Politics and Conspiracy in an Age of Reaction.* Carbondale: Southern Illinois Press, 1991.

Nicholls, David. *From Dessalines to Duvalier: Race, Colour, and National Independence in Haiti.* 1979. Reprint, New Brunswick, NJ: Rutgers University Press, 1996.

Ochs, Stephen J. *A Black Patriot and a White Priest: André Cailloux and Claude Paschal Maistre in Civil War New Orleans.* Baton Rouge: Louisiana State University Press, 2000.

———. *Desegregating the Altar: The Josephites and the Struggle for Black Priests, 1871–1960.* Baton Rouge: Louisiana State University Press, 1990.

O'Neill, Charles Edwards. *Séjour: Parisian Playwright from Louisiana.* Lafayette: Center for Louisiana Studies, University of Southwestern Louisiana, 1995.

Osbey, Brenda Marie. *History and Other Poems.* St. Louis: Time Being Books, 2012.

Osterweis, Rollin G. *Romanticism and Nationalism in the Old South.* 1949. Reprint, Baton Rouge: Louisiana State University Press, 1967.

Owsley, Frank Lawrence, Jr., and Gene A. Smith. *Filibusters and Expansionists: Jeffersonian Manifest Destiny, 1800–1821.* Tuscaloosa: University of Alabama Press, 1997.

Painter, George D. *Chateaubriand: A Biography.* New York: Knopf, 1978.

Palmer, Jennifer L. *Intimate Bonds: Family and Slavery in the French Atlantic.* Philadelphia: University of Pennsylvania, 2016.

Palmer, R. R., Joel Colton, and Lloyd Kramer, eds. *A History of the Modern World.* 2 vols. 9th ed. New York: Alfred A. Knopf, 2003.

Petteys, Chris. *Dictionary of Women Artists: An International Dictionary of Women Artists Born before 1900.* Boston: G. K. Hall, 1985.

Pierson, Michael D. *Mutiny at Fort Jackson: The Untold Story of the Fall of New Orleans.* Chapel Hill: University of North Carolina Press, 2008.

Polasky, Janet. *Revolutions without Borders: The Call to Liberty in the Atlantic World.* New Haven, CT: Yale University Press, 2015.

Raillicourt, D. Labarre de. *Filiations et notices généalogiques de Familles Notables Françaises.* Paris: Self-pubished, 1965.

Reilly, Robin. *The British at the Gates: The New Orleans Campaign in the War of 1812.* 1974. Reprint, Toronto: Robin Brass Studio, 2003.

Reinders, Robert C. *End of an Era: New Orleans, 1850–1860.* New Orleans: Pelican Publishing, 1964.

Reiss, Tom. *The Black Count: Glory, Revolution, Betrayal, and the Real Count of Monte Cristo.* New York: Crown Publishers, 2012.

Remini, Robert V. *The Battle of New Orleans: Andrew Jackson and America's First Military Victory.* New York: Penguin Viking, 1999.

———. *The Life of Andrew Jackson.* Abridged ed. New York: Harper Collins, 2001.

Rhodes, Desha P. *A History of Flint Medical College, 1889–1911.* New York: IUniverse, 2007.

Ripley, C. Peter. *Slaves and Freedmen in Civil War Louisiana.* Baton Rouge: Louisiana State University Press, 1976.

Risjord, Norman K. *Representative Americans: The Romantics.* Lanham, MD: Rowman and Littlefield, 2001.

Rodriguez O., Jaime E. *The Independence of Spanish America.* Cambridge: Cambridge University Press, 1998.

Roudané, Mark Charles. *The New Orleans Tribune: An Introduction to America's First Black Daily Newspaper.* Minneapolis: Chicoté Graphics, 2014.

Roussève, Charles Barthelemy. *The Negro in Louisiana: Aspects of His History and His Literature.* New Orleans: Xavier University Press, 1937.

Rugemer, Edward Bartlett. *The Problem of Emancipation: The Caribbean Roots of the American Civil War.* Baton Rouge: Louisiana State University Press, 2008.

Salvaggio, John. *New Orleans' Charity Hospital: A Story of Physicians, Politics, and Poverty.* Baton Rouge: Louisiana State University Press, 1992.

Schafer, Judith Kelleher. *Becoming Free, Remaining Free: Manumission and Enslavement in New Orleans, 1846–1862.* Baton Rouge: Louisiana State University Press, 1994.

———. *Slavery, the Civil Law, and the Supreme Court of Louisiana.* Baton Rouge: Louisiana State University Press, 2003.

Schamber, Ellie Nower. *The Artist as Politician: The Relationship between the Art and the Politics of the French Romantics.* Lanham, MD: University Press of America, 1984.

Schwartz, Marie Jenkins. *Birthing a Slave: Motherhood and Medicine in the Antebellum South.* Cambridge, MA: Harvard University Press, 2006.

Schweninger, Loren. *Black Property Owners in the South, 1790–1915.* Urbana: University of Illinois Press, 1990.

Scott, Julius S. *The Common Wind: Afro-American Currents in the Age of the Haitian Revolution.* London: Verso, 2020.

Scott, Rebecca J. *Degrees of Freedom: Louisiana and Cuba after Slavery.* Cambridge, MA: Harvard University Press, 2005.

Scott, Rebecca J., and Jean M. Hébrard. *Freedom Papers: An Atlantic Odyssey in the Age of Emancipation.* Cambridge, MA: Harvard University Press, 2012.

Shaik, Fatima. *Economy Hall: The Hidden History of a Free Black Brotherhood.* New Orleans: Historic New Orleans Collection, 2021.

Sheller, Mimi. *Democracy after Slavery: Black Publics and Peasant Radicalism in Haiti and Jamaica.* Gainesville: University Press of Florida, 2000.

Siddali, Silvana R. *From Property to Person: Slavery and the Confiscation Acts, 1861–1862.* Baton Rouge: Louisiana State University Press, 2005.

Smith, John David, ed. *Black Soldiers in Blue: African American Troops in the Civil War Era.* Chapel Hill: University of North Carolina Press, 2002.

Spear, Jennifer M. *Race, Sex, and Social Order in Early New Orleans.* Baltimore: Johns Hopkins University Press, 2009.

Stearns, Peter N. *Priest and Revolutionary: Lamennais and the Dilemma of French Catholicism.* New York: Harper & Row, 1967.

Stein, Robert Louis. *Léger Félicité Sonthonax: The Lost Sentinel of the Republic.* Rutherford, NJ: Fairleigh Dickinson University Press; London: Associated University Presses, c1985.

Sublette, Ned. *The World That Made New Orleans: From Spanish Silver to Congo Square.* Chicago: Lawrence Hill Books, 2008.

Sullivan-Holleman, Elizabeth, and Isabel Hillery Cobb. *The Saint Domingue Epic: The de Rossignol des Dunes and Family Alliances.* Bay St. Louis, MS: Nightingale Press, 1995.

Talmon, J. L. *Romanticism and Revolt: Europe, 1815–1848.* New York: Harcourt, Brace & World, 1967.

Taylor, Joe Gray. *Louisiana Reconstructed, 1863–1877.* Baton Rouge: Louisiana State University Press, 1974.

Thompson, Shirley Elizabeth. *Exiles at Home: The Struggle to Become American in Creole New Orleans.* Cambridge, MA: Harvard University Press, 2009.

Thrasher, Albert. *"On to New Orleans!": Louisiana's Heroic Slave Revolt.* New Orleans: Cypress Press, 1996.

Tinker, Edward Larocque. *Creole City: Its Past and Its People.* New York: Longmans, Green, 1953.

———. *Les Écrits de langue française en Louisiane au XIX siecle.* Paris: Librairie Ancienne Honoré Champion, 1932.

———. *Pens, Pills and Pistols: A Louisiana Chronicle.* New York: Longmans, Green, 1934.

Toledano, Roulhac, and Mary Louise Christovich. *New Orleans Architecture.* Vol. 6, *Faubourg Tremé and the Bayou Road.* Gretna, LA: Pelican, 1980.

Trefousse, Hans L. *Ben Butler: The South Called Him Beast*. 1957. Reprint, New York: Octagon, 1974.

Tunnell, Ted. *Crucible of Reconstruction: War, Radicalism, and Race in Louisiana, 1862–1877*. Baton Rouge: Louisiana State University Press, 1984.

Usner, Daniel H., Jr. *Indians, Settlers & Slaves in a Frontier Exchange Economy: The Lower Mississippi Valley before 1783*. Chapel Hill: University of North Carolina Press, 1992.

Valdman, Albert, Kevin J. Rottet, Barry Jean Ancelet, Richard Guidry, Thomas A. Klingler, Amanda LaFleur, Tamara Lindner, Michael D. Picone, and Dominique Ryon, eds. *Dictionary of Louisiana French: As Spoken in Cajun, Creole, and American Indian Communities*. Jackson: University of Mississippi Press, 2010.

Vella, Christina. *Intimate Enemies: The Two Worlds of the Baroness de Pontalba*. Baton Rouge: Louisiana State University Press, 1997.

Viatte, Auguste. *Histoire littéraire de l'Amérique Française des origines à 1950*. Québec: Presses Universitaires, 1954.

Vidler, Alec R. *Prophecy and Papacy: A Study of Lamennais, the Church and the Revolution*. New York: Charles Scribner's Sons, 1954.

Vincent, Charles. *Black Legislators in Louisiana during Reconstruction*. Baton Rouge: Louisiana State University Press, 1976.

———, ed. *The Louisiana Purchase Bicentennial Series in Louisiana History*. Vol. 11, part B. Lafayette: Center for Louisiana Studies, University of Louisiana at Lafayette, 2000.

Ward, Martha. *Voodoo Queen: The Spirited Lives of Marie Laveau*. Jackson: University Press of Mississippi, 2004.

Weaver, Karol K. *Medical Revolutionaries: The Enslaved Healers of Eighteenth-Century Saint Domingue*. Urbana: University of Illinois Press, 2006.

Weeks, William Earl. *John Quincy Adams and American Global Empire*. Lexington: University Press of Kentucky, 1992.

White, Ashli. *Encountering Revolution: Haiti and the Making of the Early Republic*. Baltimore: Johns Hopkins University Press, 2010.

Williams, Eric. *Capitalism and Slavery*. 1944. Reprint, Chapel Hill: University of North Carolina Press, 1994.

Winters, John D. *The Civil War in Louisiana*. Baton Rouge: Louisiana State University Press, 1963.

Works Progress Administration. *Louisiana: A Guide to the State*. 1941. Reprint, New York: Hastings House, 1959.

Wright, C. H. C. *The Background of Modern French Literature*. Boston: Ginn and Company, 1926.

———. *A History of French Literature*. 2 vols. 1912. Reprint, New York: Oxford University Press, 1969.

Articles

Abry, George. "Bearing Witness in Tremé: Saint Augustine Church." *Louisiana Cultural Vistas*, 13 (Summer 2002): 26–39.

Bell, Caryn Cossé. "The Common Wind's Creole Visionary: Dr. Louis Charles Roudanez." *South Atlantic Review*, 73 (Spring 2008), 10–25.

———. "Hermann-Grima House: A Window on Free Black Life and Urban Slavery in Creole New Orleans." *Louisiana Cultural Vistas*, 11 (Summer 2000): 68–78.

———. "Pierre-Aristide Desdunes (1844–1918), Creole Poet, Civil War Soldier, and Civil Rights Activist: The Common Wind's Legacy." *Louisiana History*, 55 (Summer 2014): 282–312.

———. "*Une Chimère:* The Freedmen's Bureau in Creole New Orleans," in *The Freedmen's Bureau and Reconstruction: Reconsiderations*, ed. Paul A. Cimbala, and Randall M. Miller, 140–160. New York: Fordham University Press, 1999.

Bellegarde, Dantes. "President Alexandre Pétion." *Phylon*, 2 (3rd quarter, 1941): 205–213.

Berkowitz, Bonnie, and Adrian Blanco. "Confederate Monuments Are Falling, but Hundreds Still Stand. Here's Where." *Washington Post*, June 17, 2020.

Berry, Mary Frances. "Negro Troops in Blue and Gray: The Louisiana Native Guards, 1861–1863," in *The Louisiana Purchase Bicentennial Series in Louisiana History*, vol. 11, part B, ed. Charles Vincent, 21–38. 1967. Reprint, Lafayette: Center for Louisiana Studies, University of Louisiana at Lafayette, 2000.

Blight, David W. "Trump Reveals the Truth About Voter Suppression." *New York Times*, April 11, 2020.

Boley, J. P. "The History of Caesarean Section." *Canadian Medical Association Journal*, May 1935. Reprint, August 15, 1991, 319–322.

Brickhouse, Anna. "The Writing of Haiti: Pierre Faubert, Harriet Beecher Stowe, and Beyond." *American Literary History*, 13 (Fall 2001): 407–444.

Brooks, Peter. "Noble Memories." *New York Review*, (April 19, 2018), 38–40.

Brown, Joan Abshear. "A Tribute to Arnold Bertonneau." *La Créole: A Journal of Creole History and Genealogy*, 12 (October 25, 2019): 19–30.

Bryan, Patrick. "Émigrés, Conflict and Reconciliation: The French Émigrés in Nineteenth-Century Jamaica." *Jamaica Journal*, 7 (September 1973), 13–19.

Burns, Francis P. "Lafayette Visits New Orleans." *Louisiana Historical Quarterly*, 29 (April 1946): 296–340.

Carrigan, Jo Ann. "Yankees Versus Yellow Jack in New Orleans, 1862–1866." *Civil War History*, 9 (September 1963): 248–260.

Chaar-Pérez, Kahlil. "A Revolution of Love": Ramón Emeterio Betances, Anténor Firmin, and Affective Communities in the Caribbean." *Global South*, 7 (Fall 2013): 11–36.

Dabney, Lancaster E. "Louis Aury: The First Governor of Texas Under the Mexican Republic." *Southwestern Historical Quarterly*, 42 (July 1938–April 1939): 108–116.

D'Aquin, Count François, Joseph d'Aquin, Jude d'Aquin, and Charles R. Maduell Jr. "The Antiquity of the D'Aquin Family." *New Orleans Genesis*, part 1, 18 (March 1979): 129–134.

———. "The Antiquity of the D'Aquin Family." *New Orleans Genesis*, part 2, 18 (June 1979): 261–268.

Davis, T. Frederick. "MacGregor's Invasion of Florida, *Florida Historical Quarterly*, 7 (1928): 1–71. https://stars.library.ucf.edu/fhq/vol7/iss1/5/.

Donaldson, Gary A. "A Window on Slave Culture: Dances in Congo Square in New Orleans, 1800–1862," in *The Louisiana Purchase Bicentennial Series in Louisiana History*, ed. Vaughan Burdin Baker, vol. 15 (1984). Reprint, Lafayette: Center for Louisiana Studies, University of Southwestern Louisiana, 2000.

Dormon, James H. "The Persistent Specter: Slave Rebellion in Territorial Louisiana." *Louisiana History*, 18 (Fall 1977): 393–394.

Doyle, Patrick W. "Unmasked: The Author of *Narrative of a Voyage to the Spanish Main in the Ship 'Two Friends.'*" *Florida Historical Quarterly*, 78 (Fall 1999): 189–206.

Dubois, Laurent. "Going to the Territory." *American Historical Association* (June 2020): 917–920.

Everett, Donald E. "Emigres and Militiamen: Free Persons of Color in New Orleans, 1803–1815." *Journal of Negro History* (October 1953): 377–402.

Fandrich, Ina J. "The Birth of New Orleans' Voodoo Queen: A Long-Held Mystery Resolved." *Louisiana History*, 46 (Summer 2005): 293–309.

Faye, Stanley. "Commodore Aury." *Louisiana Historical Quarterly*, 25 (July 1941): 611–697.

———. "Privateersmen of the Gulf and Their Prizes." *Louisiana Historical Quarterly*, 22 (October 1939): 1012–1094.

Ferrer, Ada. "Haiti, Free Soil, and Antislavery in the Revolutionary Atlantic." *American Historical Review*, 117 (February 2012): 40–66.

Ferrer, Ada, and Marie Pascale Brasier-d'Iribarne. "La société esclavagiste cubaine et la révolution haïtienne." *Annales. Histoire, Sciences Sociales*, 58 no. 2 (2003): 333–356. http://www.jstor.org/stable/27587177.

Foner, Laura. "The Free People of Color in Louisiana and St. Domingue: A Comparative Portrait of Two Three-Caste Slave Societies." *Journal of Social History*, 3 (Summer 1970): 406–430.

Force, Pierre. "The House on Bayou Road: Atlantic Creole Networks in the Eighteenth and Nineteenth Centuries." *Journal of American History*, 100 (June 2013): 21–45.

Horne, William I. "Victor Eugène Macarty: From Art to Activism in Reconstruction-Era New Orleans." *Journal of African American History*, 103 (Fall 2018): 496–525.

Hunter, G. Howard. "The Politics of Resentment: Unionist Regiments and the New Orleans Immigrant Community, 1862–1864." *Louisiana History*, 44 (Spring 2003): 185–210.

Johnson, Jerah. "Dr. John Watkins, New Orleans' Lost Mayor." *Louisiana History*, 36 (Spring 1995): 187–96.

———. "Yellow Fever and the Louisiana–Mississippi War of 1905." *Louisiana Cultural Vistas,* 11 (Fall 2000): 71–79.

Kinzer, Charles E. "The Band of Music of the First Battalion of Free Men of Color and the Siege of New Orleans, 1814–1815." *American Music,* 10 (Fall 1992): 348–369.

Knight, Franklin W. "The Haitian Revolution." *American Historical Review,* 105 (February 2000): 103–115.

Lachance, Paul F. "The 1809 Immigration of Saint-Domingue Refugees to New Orleans: Reception, Integration and Impact." *Louisiana History,* 29 (Spring 1988): 109–141.

———. "The Politics of Fear: French Louisianians and the Slave Trade, 1786–1809." *Plantation Society,* 1 (June 1979): 162–197.

Landers, Jane. "Franco/Spanish Entanglements in Florida and the Circumatlantic." *Journal of Transnational American Studies,* 8 (2017): 1–18.

Le Glaunec, Jean-Pierre. "German Coast (Louisiana) Insurrection of 1811." In *Encyclopedia of Antislavery and Abolition,* vol. 1, ed. Peter Hinks and John McKivigan, 534–537. Westport, CT: Greenwood, 2007.

———. "Slave Migrations in Spanish and Early American Louisiana: New Sources and New Estimates." *Louisiana History,* 46 (Spring 2005): 185–209.

Long, Carolyn Morrow. "The Family of Blanc François Joubert: Racial Determination in New Orleans, 1818–1916." *Louisiana History,* 41 (Fall 2020): 357–405.

Maduell, Charles R., Jr. "d'Aquin Family." *New Orleans Genesis,* 10 (June 1971): 256–263.

Malena, Anne. "Hélène d'Aquin Allain: une identité inachevé." *Études francophones,* 18, no. 2 (Autumn, 2003): 37–52.

McKiven, Henry M., Jr. "The Political Construction of a Natural Disaster: The Yellow Fever Epidemic of 1853." *Journal of American History,* 94 (December 2007): 734–742.

McKusick, Victor A. "Rouanet of Paris and New Orleans: Experiments on the Valvular Origin of the Heart Sounds 125 Years Ago." *Bulletin of the History of Medicine,* 32 (March–April, 1958): 137–151.

Mitchell, Mary Niall. "'A Good and Delicious Country': Free Children of Color and How They Learned to Imagine the Atlantic World in Nineteenth-Century Louisiana." *History of Education Quarterly,* 40 (2000): 123–144.

———. "All Things Were Working Together for My Deliverance." *Commonplace,* 14 (Winter 2014). http://commonplace.online/article/all-things-were-working-together-for-my-deliverance.

Mobley, James William. "The Academy Movement in Louisiana." *Louisiana Historical Quarterly,* 30 (July 1947): 738–978.

Mongey, Vanessa. "A Tale of Two Brothers: Haiti's Other Revolutions." *The Americas,* 69 (July 2012): 37–60.

Olivarius, Kathryn. "Immunity, Capital, and Power in Antebellum New Orleans." *American Historical Review* 124 (April 2019): 425–455.

Paquette, Robert L. "'A Horde of Brigands?' The Great Louisiana Slave Revolt of 1811 Reconsidered." *Historical Reflections/Réflexions Historiques*, 35 (Spring 2009): 72–96.

———. "German Coast Slave Insurrection of 1811." *64 Parishes*, January 10, 2011. https://64parishes.org/entry/slave-insurrection-of-1811.

Paxton, Robert O. "The Bloodiest Urban Revolution." *New York Review* (February 9, 2014): 26–28.

Pérotin-Dumon, Anne. "Les corsairs de la liberté." *l'histoire*, 43 (March 1982): 24–29.

Ricard, Ulysses S., Jr. "Note from the Editor." *Chicory Review*, 1 (Fall 1988): 6–7.

Robinson, Eugene. "Trump Might Go Down in History as the Last President of the Confederacy," *Washington Post*, June 11, 2020.

Roudané, Mark Charles. "Race, Memory, and the World That Made New Orleans." *Roudanez: History and Legacy*, 2015. https://roudanez.com/race-memory-and-the-world-that-made-new-orleans.

———. "Residence and Medical Practice of Dr. Louis Charles Roudanez and Family." *New Orleans Historical*, https://neworleanshistorical.org/items/show/1542.

Rouzan, Laura V. "Dr. Louis Charles Roudanez: Publisher of America's First Black Daily Newspaper." *South Atlantic Review*, 73 (Spring 2008): 54–58.

Savitt, Todd L. "Straight University Medical Department: The Short Life of a Black Medical School in Reconstruction New Orleans." *Louisiana History*, 41 (Winter 2000): 175–201.

Soulé, Leon C. "The Creole-American Struggle in New Orleans Politics, 1850–1862." *Louisiana Historical Quarterly*, 40 (January 1957): 54–83.

Stoltz, Joseph F. III. "'The Preservation of Good Order': William C. C. Claiborne and the Militia of the Louisiana Provisional Government, 1803–1805." *Louisiana History* (Fall 2013): 424–447.

Thompson, Thomas Marshall. "National Newspaper and Legislative Reactions to Louisiana's Deslondes Slave Revolt of 1811." *Louisiana History*, 33 (Winter 1992): 5–29.

Tisserand, Michael. "St. Mary.s Catholic Church and the Herriman Family." *New Orleans Historical*, Auguste 22, 2019. https://neworleanshistorical.org/items/show/1528.

Viatte, Auguste. "Complement à la bibliographie louisianaise d'Edward Larocque Tinker." *Louisiana Review*, 3 (Winter 1974): 13.

Villeré, Sidney L. "The Enterprising Career of Don Pablo Lanusse in Colonial New Orleans." *New Orleans Genesis*, 2 (June 1963): 243–248.

Warren, Harris Gaylord. "Mina, Francisco Xavier (1789–1817)." *Handbook of Texas Online*. Texas State Historical Association. https://tshaonline.org/handbook/online/articles/fmi46.

Dissertations and Theses

Babb, Winston C. "French Refugees from Saint Domingue to the Southern United States, 1791–1810." PhD diss., University of Virginia, 1954.

Fiehrer, Thomas Marc. "The Baron de Carondelet as Agent of Bourbon Reform: A Study of Spanish Colonial Administration in the Years of the French Revolution." PhD diss., Tulane University, 1977.

Meadows, Darrell R. "The Planters of Saint-Domingue, 1750–1804: Migration and Exile in the French Revolutionary Atlantic." PhD diss., Carnegie Mellon University, 2004.

Neidenbach, Elizabeth Clark. "The Life and Legacy of Marie Couvent: Social Networks, Property Ownership, and the Making of a Free People of Color Community in New Orleans." PhD diss., College of William & Mary, 2015.

Scott, Julius S. "The Common Wind: Currents of Afro-American Communication in the Era of the Haitian Revolution." PhD diss., Duke University, 1986.

Williams, Diana Irene. "'They Call It Marriage': The Interracial Louisiana Family and the Making of American Legitimacy." PhD diss., Harvard University, 2007.

INDEX

Note: Page numbers in *italics* refer to illustrations; those followed by "n" indicate endnotes.

abolition. *See under slavery*
Académie Saint-Barbe, 125
Adams, John Quincy, 66–67
Adams, Thomas E., 201
Adams–Onís (Transcontinental) Treaty (1819), 255n22
Adéle v. Beauregard, 40–41
African ethnic groups, 107
Africanized culture, 105–13
agrarian reform, 199–200
Agricultural and Mechanical College, Louisiana, 212
Aliquot, Marie-Jeanne "Sister Aliquot," 98, 156–57
Allain, Albert-Louis, 166
Allain, Frédéric Constant François Joseph, 138, 160–61, 165–67
Allain, Frédéric Marie François Joseph, 166, 239–40
Allain, Hélène-Marie-Joseph d'Aquin: about, 3, 12; ancestral past and, 11–12; arrival in New Orleans, 82; on Bouny salon, 135; Creole identity and, 92–93; education, 87, 137–39, 160–61; Grandfort's *l'Autre monde* and, 146; later life and death of, 238–40; marriage and widowhood, 138, 165–66; on Native Americans, 122; *Souvenirs d'Amérique et de France par une Créole,* 1–5, 146, 149; as teacher, 166. *See also* New Orleans, daily life in
Allain, Pierre, 160
Ambruménil, L. d', 144–45, 150

Amelia Island, 62–69, 255n22
American Anti-Slavery Society, 138
American Freedmen's Inquiry Commission, 189, 196, 206
American Revolution, 38, 49
Anaya, Juan Pablo de, 37, 57–58
Andrew, John A., 197
Andry, Manuel, 30
Antoine, C. C., 209, 214, 217–18, 228
Aquin, Saint-Domingue, 16
Ardouin, Beaubrun, 127, 232
Ardouin, Coriolan, 127, 186
Asile de la Société française (French Hospital), 161–63, 166–67, 171, 232–35
Aslakson, Kenneth R., 31
Association of Colored Veterans, 181
Atlantic, Francophone: circum-Caribbean historical model, 4; d'Aquin family and, 5, 239; Enlightenment, humanitarianism, and, 84; Romantic movement and, 3. *See also* Catholicism; family alliances; Haitian Revolution; New Orleans; Romanticism, French; Saint-Domingue; slavery
Audige, Alfred, 70
Auger, Adéle, 41
Aunt Sanité, 115, 266n98
Aury, Louis-Michel, 58–60, 127, 256n28
Autre monde, l' (Grandfort), 140–50, 270n57
Avernière, Sabarot de l', 152

Badger, Algernon S., 221
Bailly, Pierre, 27
Baker, Frank, 177–78
Banks, Nathaniel P., 170, 191–99
Baron, Noel Auguste, Jr., 29, 75
Barousse, Marie, 137

Barousse, Prosper, 134, 137, 144
Barthet, Joseph, 112
Bass, Samuel, 115–16
Bataillon d'Orléans, 28, 37–39, 47, 50–51, 53
Batallion of Free Men of Color, First: in Battle of New Orleans, 48–55; Claiborne on, 34; Militia Corps of Free Morenos and Pardos, 38–39; mustered officially, 48; recruitment under Jackson, 42–46
Batallion of Free Men of Color, Second, 48–51, 53–55, 74
Battle of New Orleans, 46–55
"Battle of New Orleans" (1874 coup attempt), 220–21
Bauvais, Louis-Jacques, 22
Beauregard, P. G. T., 139, 179, 217
Beaurocher, Frederick, 41
Beckwith, J. R., 219
Bell, Joseph M., 178
Belloc, Jean-Hilaire, 135, 138
Benigne, Josephine-Charlotte, 74
Benoit, Marie Louise, 225
Béranger, Pierre-Jean, 124
Bertonneau, E. Arnold, 195–98, 203, 223–24
Bertonneau v. New Orleans Board of School Directors, 224
Betances, Ramón Emeterio, 157–58
Bienville, Jean-Baptiste de, 14, 37, 190
Bizoton, Marguerite-Charlotte, 15–17, 19–20, 25–26, 244n26
Black Codes, 201, 214
Blair, Montgomery, 178
Blanque, Jean, 36, 251n23
Blassingame, John W., 4
Blineau, Olivier, 166
Bloomer, Amelia, 142
Bohn, Auguste, 218
Boisdoré, François, 188, 195
Bolívar, Simón, 58, 63, 68–69
Boston, MA, 197–98
Bougaud, Émile, 89
Bouillaud, Jean-Baptiste, 157–58, 164
Bouligny, Louise de, 261n34

Bouny, Nancy, 134–35
Bouny, Zélie, 135
Boyer, Jean-Pierre, 127–28
Bradley, Joseph P., 219–20
Brickell, D. Warren, 159–60
Bringer, Elisabeth, 76
Bringier, Marius Pons, 28–29, 74–76
Bringier, Marius Ste. Colombe, 75
Bringier, Michel Doradou, 28–29, 37, 74–75
Bringier, Paul-Louis, 29, 37, 74
Brissot, Jacques-Pierre, 35, 71
Britain and the British: abolition in Caribbean colonies, 83; invasion of Saint-Domingue, 24–25; War of 1812 and Battle of New Orleans, 37, 42, 46–55. See also Jamaica
Brizeux, Auguste, 123
Brown, John, 188
Brown, William G., 209, 212
Bruslé, Camille, 47, 49
Bruslé, Théodat Camille, 26, 74
Butler, Benjamin F., 169–70, 176–84, 190–94, 197, 205–7, 215–16, 222, 233–34

Calhoun, John C., 132, 133–34
Camaire, Marie Justin, 125
"Campaign of 1814–15, The" (Castra), 73
Carillon, Le, 217
Carrière, Noel, 49
Carroll, William, 52
Cartagena, Republic of, 56–60, 63, 68
Cartwright, Samuel A., 163, 169
Castra, Hippolyte (pseud.), 72–73
Catholicism: French Revolution and, 88; Mechanics' Institute memorial and, 206; Romanticism and radical spiritual/mystical reform philosophies, 79–80, 87–92, 99, 156; slavery and, 96, 97, 100; US Civil War and, 99–100
Caulfeild, Ruby Van Allen, 4–5
Cayol, Jean-Bruno, 156
Cazabat, Alphonse, 215
cénacles (literary societies), 72–74, 127
Cenelles, Les (Lanusse), 5, 132, 232

Chapman, Maria Weston, 138

Charles (enslaved *commandeur* and rebellion leader), 30–31

Charles, Josephine, 156, 273n15

Charles X, 26, 120, 128–29, 161

Chase, Salmon P., 181

Chateaubriand, François-René de: Allain on, 100; *Atala*, 122–24; Catholic reformism and, 3, 87–88, 98; *Génie du christianisme*, 3, 90–91, 99; Grandfort's attack on, 141–42; Lammenais and, 90–91; *Les Natchez*, 122; *René*, 122–23

Chauveau, Jean-Jacques, 37, 74

Chesnut, Mary Boykin, 5

Chevarre, Henry, 70

Choctaw Native Americans, 47, 50, 111, 123–24, 241n7

Christian Mission Baptist Church, New Orleans, 235

Citizens' Committee (Comité des Citoyens), New Orleans, 228–30, 233

Civil Rights Act of 1869 (LA), 211

Civil Rights Act of 1871 (Ku Klux Klan Act) (US), 222, 234

Civil Rights Act of 1875 (US), 222–24

Civil Rights Cases, 224

Civil War and occupation of New Orleans: Afro-Creole delegation to Washington, 195–97; appeasement policy, 191–94; under Banks, 191–99; Black informants, network of, 178–79; Butler, arrival of, 176–77; under Butler, 176–84, 190–94; Catholic churches and, 99–100; Confederate veterans and Black Codes, 200–201; Confiscation Acts, 177, 182–84, 277n25; contraband-of-war strategy, 177–79, 276n6; desegregation, 184; doctors and, 168–69; Dumas as agent of liberation, 185; foreign consuls and, 179–80, 191; Freedmen's Aid Association, 200; Freedmen's Bureau, 200; freedom-seeking refugees and exclusion order, 180; free state movement, 195–96; interracial

dinner parties under Butler, 184–85; Johnson's Amnesty Proclamation, 200; labor systems, 183, 189, 194, 198–99; Lincoln's amnesty proclamation and Ten Percent Plan, 195; Native Guard (Black regiments) and Black officers, 175–76, 181–83, 185–87, 190–93, 279n41; number of Black soldiers in US Army, 183; onset of Civil War, 175; plantation lands, redistribution of, 199–200; Port Hudson campaign, 192–93; reactions of conservative southerners, 186–87; slave resistance and, 180–81; suffrage demands, 194–98; *l'Union* newspaper, 187–90, 194–95; work program, 183–84

Claiborne, W. C. C., 28, 31–33, 34, 38–39, 40–46, 55, 74

Clark, Daniel, 39, 40–41

Clarkson, Thomas, 71

Clay, Henry, 66

Clinton, Catherine, 5

Cochrane, Alexander, 54

Colfax Massacre (1873), 215–16

Colombia, Republic of, 69

Comité des Citoyens (Citizens' Committee), New Orleans, 228–30, 233

Committee of Defense, New Orleans, 44, 45, 53

Communards, 239

Compagnie des Mulâtres et Nègres Libres, La, 37–38

Concordat of October 1791, 22

Condorcet, Marquis de, 71

Confederacy. *See* Civil War and occupation of New Orleans

Confiscation Acts, 177, 182–83, 277n25

Congolese identity, 103–5, 263n62

Conner, H. W., 133

Conseil de Paix et d'Union de Saint-Marc, 22–24

constitution, Louisiana: 1863 convention, 194–95; 1864 convention, 203; 1867 convention, 207–8; 1868 constitution, 208, 224; 1898 constitution, 230

Constitution, US: Fifteenth Amendment, 202, 204, 227; Fourteenth Amendment, 202, 204, 219, 224, 227, 281n3
contraband-of-war strategy, 177–79, 276n6
Conway, Thomas W., 211–13
Cornish, Dudley Taylor, 187
Corvisart, Jean-Nicolas, 274n41
Coup d'œil, Le (journal), 137, 146
court cases: Adéle v. Beauregard, 40–41; Bertonneau v. New Orleans Board of School Directors, 224; Civil Rights Cases, 224; Plessy v. Ferguson, 202, 205, 224, 228, 229, 232, 235–37; Slaughterhouse Cases, 219–20; Tureaud v. Board of Supervisors, 235; United States v. Andrew Jackson, 53–54; United States v. Cruikshank, 219–20
Courtois, Joseph, 127–28
Courtois, Juliette, 127–28
Courtois, Sévère, 33, 35–36, 48–49, 55, 57, 60–61, 68, 69, 127–28
Cousin, Louise, 123
Couturié, Amedée, 179
Couvent, Bernard, 125
Couvent School (Institution Catholique des orphelins indigents), 125–26, 132–33, 186, 190, 226
Creole culture in New Orleans, 83; Grandfort's attack on, 143–44, 149–50; political struggle against Anglo-Americans, 139–40; Romanticism and, 121–22
Creole identity, 92–93, 107–9, 261n31
Cruikshank, William, 219
Cuba: Bolívar revolutionary conspiracy, 69; emigration of people of color from New Orleans to, 44, 46; Rigaud's soldiers in, 33; Saint-Dominguan refugees in, 30, 153–54
Custom House faction, 213–14

Daggett, Melissa, 212
Dain, Charles, 188
Dames Hospitalière, 97
Daniels, Henrietta "Etta," 206–7

Daniels, Nathan W., 187, 190, 193, 206–7
d'Aquin, Adophe, 77
d'Aquin, Althée (Marie Althée Josephine), 77
d'Aquin, Amélie, 89, 94–95, 98, 261n34
d'Aquin, Antoine, 13–14
d'Aquin, Antoine-Benoist/Benoit, 14, 17, 122
d'Aquin, Antoine-Pierre, 14–17, 122
d'Aquin, Célina, 77
d'Aquin, Charles-Antoine, 244n26
d'Aquin, Charles-Louis: in Bataillon d'Orléans, 28, 33, 37, 47; in Battle of New Orleans, 49, 51, 54–55; business dealings, 29–30; Francophone network of, 74–76; in Kingston, 25–26; migration to New Orleans, 26–27; racial identity questioned, 45, 251n26, 252n31; in revolutionary Saint-Domingue, 20–22; Savary family and, 11; slavery and, 101
d'Aquin, Charles-Pierre, 16–17, 19–20, 26, 82–83, 259n10
d'Aquin, Cidele (Sidley), 261n34
d'Aquin, Elisabeth, 82, 86
d'Aquin, Elisabeth-Charlotte-Antoinette "Bonne," 26
d'Aquin, Elisabeth Josephine, 75
d'Aquin, Elmire, 104
d'Aquin, Eveline-Marguerite-Françoise, 82, 83, 85, 93–95, 100, 101, 102–3, 261n34
d'Aquin, François, 77
d'Aquin, François-Louis, 26
d'Aquin, Henri-Charles, 82, 86, 87, 93, 138, 158–61, 165, 171
d'Aquin, Léocadie, 77
d'Aquin, Lilia, 102–3, 238
d'Aquin, Louis-Charles, 26, 77, 82, 85, 261n34
d'Aquin, Louise-Adèle, 101, 102, 238
d'Aquin, Louise-Marie-Thérèse Elmire, 82
d'Aquin, Louis-Henri-Thomas, 13
d'Aquin, Louis-Jules, 101
d'Aquin, Louis-Thomas, 101
d'Aquin, Lucile, 77
d'Aquin, Marie Thérèse, 29, 75
d'Aquin, Paul-Joseph George, 82, 87

d'Aquin, Philippe, 12–13

d'Aquin, Pierre, 13–14

d'Aquin, Pierre-François, 19–20, 244n26

d'Aquin, Pierre-Thomas, 26

d'Aquin, Sylvain (Silvano), 22–25, 45, 49, 73

d'Aquin, Thomas, 77

d'Aquin, Uranie, 77

d'Aquin, Victoire-Antoinette, 261n34

Daquin Brothers Bakery, New Orleans, 77

D'Aquin Institute (school), 86–87, 137, 166

d'Aquino, Antonio, Baron de Grotta-Minanda, 12

Daron, Charles-Joseph-Edouard, 82, 83, 85, 93–94, 95, 100, 261n34

Daron, George-Paul, 20

Daron, Jean-Paul, 20, 82, 103

Daron, Marie-Anne-Elisabeth, 82, 86–87, 93, 95, 104, 137, 139, 166, 259n10

Daron, Pierre-Elie-Theodore, 82

Daron, Théodore, 104

Davis, Edgar, 181

Davis, Jefferson, 187, 191

Decoudreau, Charles, 190

Decoudreau, Françoise, 190

Decoudreau, Joséphine, 190

Dédé, Sanité, 111, 266n98

Dédé-Sophie, 18–20, 103–5, 109

De Forest, John W., 184–85

Deggs, Mary Bernard, 99–100, 115, 156

Delany, Martin, 278n27

Deléry, Charles François, 162–65, 168–70, 216–19

Delille, Henriette, 97–98, 114–15, 156

Delrieu, Leon Raymond, 167, 169

Democrats vs. Republicans. See Reconstruction

Denison, George S., 181–82

Department of the Gulf, 176, 191, 276n3

de Puèch, Ernest Auguste, 77

de Puèch, Louis, 77

Derbigny, Pierre, 250n15

Desbrosses, Nelson, 133–34

Description . . . de la partie française de l'isle Saint-Domingue (Moreau), 107–9, 264n79

Desdunes, Alcibiade, 185–86

Desdunes, Daniel, 228

Desdunes, Pierre-Aristide, 132–33, 185–86, 190, 226, 231–32, 278n35

Desdunes, Rodolphe Lucien, 1, 132–33, 226, 228–32

Deslondes, Anne Baude Paumet, 30

Desmortiers, François-Raymond-Alexis, 20

Desmortiers, Hélène Lessard, 17–18, 109

Desmortiers, Marie-Anne-Elisabeth, 18–20, 82, 103, 109

Desmortiers, Pierre, 17

Dessalines, Jean-Jacques, 25

Destrehan, Jean-Noël, 32, 44

d'Eynaut, Célinie Adelaïde, 26, 28–29, 75

d'Eynaut, Marie-Josephine Alix, 26, 75

Diégarias (Séjour), 73

Dimitry, Alexander, 139

doctors. See medicine and doctor profiles

Domestic Manners of the Americans (Trollope), 84, 140–41

Dormenon, Pierre, 24

Douglass, Frederick, 197

Dray, Philip, 222

Duane, William, 66

Dubois, Laurent, 26

Du Bois, W. E. B., 183–84

DuBourg, Abbé William, 28–29

DuBourg, Mme. J., 90

DuBourg, Joseph Patrice, 74

DuBourg, Louise Elizabeth Algaé, 28, 74

DuBourg, Louis William, 17, 28

DuBourg, Pierre, 17, 28

DuBourg, Pierre-François, 28–29, 31, 37, 74–75

Dubreuil, Charles-Eugene, 95–96

Dubreuil, Claude Joseph, 190

Dubreuil, Gaspard-François, 95

Dubreuil, Nanette, 190

Dubuclet, Antoine, 209, 221

Dubuclet, Auguste, 209, 221

Dubuclet, François Louis "Petit," 112, 209–10, 221

Dumas, Alexandre, 91, 120, 127, 132, 185, 239–40; *The Count of Monte Cristo,* 240; *Henri III et sa cour,* 120

Dumas, François Ernest, 183, 184–85, 193, 208–9

Dumas, P. A., 184–85

Dumas, Thomas-Alexandre, 120, 239–40

Dunn, Oscar J., 202, 207, 209–11, 213–14, 225

Dupérier, Frederick H., 110

Durel, J. M., 217

Dutty, Boukman "Zamba," 18

Eckel, Louisa, 97–98

École du Peuple, L' (Deléry), 217

Edwards, John Bel, 236–37

election of 1868, 208–9

election of 1872, 214–15

election of 1876, 223

Enard (free person of color), 21

Enlightenment, 3, 84, 90

Essai sur l'indifférence en matière de religion (Lamennais), 90–91

Estèves, Arthur, 226, 228

Etudes sur les bases de la science médicale (Faget), 156, 167

Étude sur les passions (Deléry), 163–64

Eulalie (free person of color), 115

Euphémie (free person of color), 115

Fabre, Albert, 144

Faculté de Médecine de Paris, 153–60, 164

Faget, Gladys, 135, 138, 154

Faget, Jean-Baptiste, 153–54, 216, 233

Faget, Jean-Charles, 98, 136, 138, 150–51, 153–59, 162–71, 273n14

Faget, Jean, 153

family alliances: d'Aquin transatlantic network, 26; Daron/d'Aquin, 82; DuBourg/Bruslé/Bringier/d'Aquin, 17, 29, 74–75; Roudanez/Bringier/Tureaud, 75–76; Savary/d'Aquin, 11, 22–23

Farragut, David G., 176, 192

Faustin I (Faustin-Élie Soulouque) of Haiti, 134

Faye, Stanley, 67

Félicité (enslaved worker), 110

feminism: Grandfort's attack on, 142, 147; Ligeret's *Paroles d'une femme,* 136

Ferguson, John H., 228, 236

Ferguson, Phoebe, 236–37

Ferrero, Bernardo, 67–68

Feuille du Commerce (journal), 127–28

Fiehrer, Thomas, 4

Fifteenth Amendment, 202, 204, 227

Finlay, Carlos, 275n62

Fleurs d'Amérique (Rouquette), 124–25

Flood, William, 36

Florida (East Florida and Republic of Florida), 62–69, 255n22

Foner, Eric, 220

Fontanges, General Viscount de, 20

Force, Pierre, 58

Forrest, Nathan Bedford, 220

Fortier, Michel, 252n31

Fortière, Marthe, 97

Foucher, Pierre, 251n23

Fourier, Charles, 142

Fourteenth Amendment, 202, 204, 219, 224, 227, 281n3

France: 1848 February Revolution and Second Republic, 79, 129–34, 157, 160, 163–64, 188–89; Bloody June Days (1848), 130–31; Franco-Prussian War, Bloody Week, and Third Republic, 238–39; Paris Médicale and Faculté de Médecine de Paris, 153–60, 164, 171, 229, 271n1; Second Empire, 134. *See also* French Revolution (1789); Napoléon I; Napoléon III

Francis de Sales, 98–99

Franco-Prussian War, 238–39

Freedmen's Aid Association, 200

Freedmen's Bureau, 200, 206

Freemasonry, 154, 161–62

free people of color: banned from entering New Orleans, 33; chosen as slave man-

agers, 21; citizenship in U.S., struggle
for, 40–41, 55; citizenship rights under
Louis XVI, 23; Haitian refugees arriving
in New Orleans, 30, 34, 40; Lyceum Hall
mass meeting, New Orleans (1863), 196;
Native Guard (Black regiments in Civil
War), 175–76, 181–83, 185–87, 190–93;
numbers in Saint-Domingue, 15; risk
of being abducted into slavery, 115–16;
Saint-Dominguan soldiers of color in Louisiana, 32–33, 39–40; in Saint-Domingue,
21–22; soldiers in Saint-Domingue,
14–15; two-tiered vs. three-tiered racial
orders and, 40–41; in wars of Latin American independence, 57–69. *See also* Civil
War and occupation of New Orleans;
Haitian Revolution; Reconstruction
free statement movement, 195–96
Free Woman of Color, New Orleans, 1844
(Rinck), 103, 263n59
French Hospital (Asile de la Société
française), 161–63, 166–67, 171, 232–35
French Revolution (1789): Catholic Church
and, 88; ideals of, 27; medical modern-
ization and, 152–53; Romanticism and,
3; Saint-Domingue and, 17; the Terror,
64, 90

Galveston, 61–62, 65–66
Gálvez, Bernardo de, 38, 49, 252n31
Garibaldi, Giuseppe, 185
Garland, J. P., 193
Garnier, Jeanne-Renée, 14
Garraway, Doris, 107
Garrison, William Lloyd, 138, 177, 197
Gaudet, F., 155
Gaudin, Juliette, 97–99, 114–15, 156
Gautier, Théophile, 120
Geggus, David P., 27, 58
Génie du christianisme (Chateaubriand), 3,
90–91, 99, 122–23
Glapion, Marie, 111
godparentage, 29

Goodheart, Adam, 177–78
Grandfort, Madame de (Marie Barousse),
134–35, 140–50, 270n57
Grandfort, Manoël de, 137, 144
Grant, Ulysses S., 211, 213, 215–17, 221, 223,
234
Greeley, Horace, 213
Grégoire, Henri-Baptiste, 71
Gregory XVI, Pope, 91–92, 136
Gual, Pedro, 63
Guérin, Alphonse-François-Marie, 160
Guérin, Jules, 152
Guilbaud, Tertulien, 186
Guillaud, Claudius, 30
Guillot, Marcelin, 33, 48–49, 55, 69
Gurowski, Adam, 177
Gutiérrez de Lara, José Bernardo, 35, 37, 49,
57–58

Hahn, Michael, 197
Haiti: 1843 Revolution, 128–29; abolition of
slavery and free soil policy, 68; Faustin
I dictatorship, 134; indemnity placed by
Charles X on, 26, 128; land redistribution
in, 199; Latin American wars of independence, role in, 58; Romantic literary art
and commentary in, 127–29; U.S. dip-
lomatic recognition of, 246n40. *See also*
Saint-Domingue
Haitian Revolution (1791): civil war, 24–26,
33; impact on U.S. and Louisiana, 26–27,
30, 32–33; Latin American revolutionary
movements, impact on, 58; October 1791
Concordat, 22; Ogé revolt (1790), 32,
248n57; refugees in Jamaica, 19, 25–26,
82; refugees in Louisiana, 30; slave revolt
and onset of, 18–22
Halevy, Léon, 116
Hall, Dominick Augustine, 44, 53–54
Hall, Gwendolyn Midlo, 4
Halleck, Henry W., 182
Hampton, Wade, 31
Hanes, Lewis, 187

Harding, Vincent, 173
Harlan, John Marshall, 236
Hatch, Cora L. V., 206–7
Hayes, Rutherford B., 223
Head, David, 67, 256n28
healers, Afro-Creole, 110–12
Hérard, Charles Rivière-, 128–29
herbalists, 110–12
Herrera, José Manuel de, 57–58, 60–63
Herriman, George, 97–98
Heurtelou, Eugène, 188
Hidalgo y Costilla, Miguel, 30, 35
Hollandsworth, James G., Jr., 176
Holmes, Oliver Wendell, 159
hospitalières, 97, 110, 147–48, 271n87
Houzeau, Jean- Charles, 203, 281n2
Hubbard, Ruggles, 63–64
Hugo, Victor, 91, 118–20, 124, 127, 131, 132, 188
humanitarianism, 3, 84, 116–17, 150, 163
Humbert, Jean-Joseph-Amable, 36–37, 52, 57–58
Humphrey, Wesley, 278n35

Iberville, Pierre Lemoyne, Sieur d', 14
Ignace (Black crewman), 60–61
Ingraham, James H., 207–8
Institution Catholique des orphelins indigents (Couvent School), 125–26, 132–33, 186, 190, 226
Irwin, Jared, 63–64
itinerant revolutionaries, 35

Jackson, Andrew, 34, 46–55, 74, 76–77, 85, 182, 258n50
Jackson, Thomas J. "Stonewall," 215
Jamaica: Haitian refugees in, 19, 25–26, 82, 103; slave resistance in, 20, 82–83
Janssens, Francis, 99
Jean (slave magnetizer), 112
Jean-Baptiste (vaudoux papalwa), 186
Jefferson, Thomas, 38, 65
Jérôme (slave magnetizer), 112

Johnson, Andrew, 200–201, 204, 210
Johnson, Henry S., 71
Johnson, Reverdy, 191
Jonau, Pierre Antoine, 70
Jugeant, Pierre, 50
Julien (slave magnetizer), 112
justice system, Black access to, 178

Kant, Immanuel, 3
Keane, John, 50
Kelley, William D., 196–97
Kellogg, William Pitt, 214–15, 219–21
Kentucky militiamen, 47–48
Knights of Peter Claver, 234
Kramer, Lloyd, 72
Ku Klux Klan, 210, 216, 219, 234

labor systems, 183, 189, 194, 198–99
Lacoste, Pierre, 42–43, 50, 54, 252n31
Lafayette, Gilbert du Motier de, 70–72
Lafitte brothers (Jean and Pierre), 33, 46, 47, 50, 57, 62, 66
Lafontaine, Charles (Doctor Jim Alexander), 111
Lajoie, Charlotte, 253n36
Lake Borgne, 48
Lamarque, Marie-Thérèse-Françoise, 95
Lamartine, Alphonse de, 79, 90–91, 123, 127, 131–33, 142, 149, 186, 188
Lamennais, Félicité de: 1848 French Revolution and, 79; in Boisdoré's "Liberty," 188; death of, 137; egalitarianism and, 127; Essai sur l'indifférence en matière de religion, 90–91; Lanusse and, 132; in legislature, 130; Ligeret and, 135–37; Paroles d'un croyant, 91–92, 130, 135–36, 148–49; Rouquette and, 123; Spiritualism and, 113
Lamennais, Hugues-Félicité Robert de, 88
Lanthenas, François, 152
Lanusse, Armand, 5, 125–26, 132; l'Album littéraraire, 126, 232; Les Cenelles, 5, 132, 232
Laraillet, Marguerite Antoinette, 153–54
Latin American independence movements:

abolition and, 68, 84; Cartagena, Republic of, 56–60, 63, 68; Colombia, Republic of, 69; East Florida, Amelia Island, and Republic of Florida, 62–69; Galveston base, 61–62, 65–66; Haiti's role in, 58; Mexico, Republic of, 57–58, 60–61, 68; New Granada, 59–60, 68; privateers and, 58–62, 65–69

Latour, Arsène Lacarrière, 46, 48, 51–52, 54

Latrobe, Benjamin, 106

Laveau, Marie, 111, 113

Le Bon de Lapointe, Marie-Louise-Victoire, 82–83, 101, 259n10

Leclerc, Victor Emanuel, 36

Leroux, Pierre, 92

Lespinasse, Beauvais, 127

Lessard, Etienne Marafret, 17, 122

Lessard, Hélène Fasende, 17

Levasseur, Auguste, 153

Lewis, John L., 176

Ligeret de Chazey, Antonia, 135, 138, 146

Ligeret de Chazey, Éléonore Bénard, 131, 135–36, 144, 146–50, 165

Ligeret de Chazey, Jacques-François, 135, 165

Limet, Félix, 162

Lincoln, Abraham, 157–58, 191–92, 195, 197, 199–200, 206, 279n49

Lincoln, Mary Todd, 206

Livingston, Edward, 46, 57, 250n15

Longstreet, James, 212, 215, 220–21

Lost Cause mythology, 230

Louaillier, Philip, 53

Louisiana: Baton Rouge as capital, 276n3; Black population of, 201; Civil Code of, 250n15; Congolese-Angolan population in, 105; constitutional conventions, 194–95, 203, 207–8; constitution of 1868, 208, 224; constitution of 1898, 230; coup attempts, 215, 220–21; coup d'état (1877), 223; d'Aquin migration to, 25, 26; Haitian refugees in, 30; Iberville mission and founders of, 14; Pointe Coupée slave conspiracies (1795), 27; revolutionaries in,

26–27; Saint-Dominguan soldiers of color in, 32–33; two-tiered and three-tiered racial orders, 40–41. See also Civil War and occupation of New Orleans; New Orleans; Reconstruction

Louisiana State University, 212, 225

Louisiana Unification Movement, 217–18

Louis-Phillippe, 92, 121, 129, 135–36, 157

Louis XIV, 13–14, 239

Louis XVI, 17, 23

Louverture, Toussaint, 33, 40, 56, 186

Luxemberg, C. A., 164

Macarty, Victor Eugène, 116

MacGregor, Gregor, 62–63, 256n28

Madison, James, 28, 31, 65

Maintenon, Françoise d'Aubigné de, 13

Maistre, Claude Paschal, 206

Maistre, Joseph de, 87–92, 99, 156, 260n15

Makandal, François, 111–12, 265n90

malarial fever, 162, 167–68, 171

Mallory, Sheppard, 177–78

Marciacq, Jean-Louis, 126

Marie de' Medici, Queen, 13

Marks, Isaac, 218

Marr, R. H., 220

marriages: anti-miscegenation laws, 208, 226; arranged, 28–29; of free people of color, women witnessing, 97; Louisiana 1830 law on racial classes, 97–98; slave, 96, 114; Suzanne's wedding, 102–3

Marshall, Thurgood, 235

Martha (enslaved worker), 96, 100, 103

Martineau, Harriet, 96–97

Martinet, Hippolite, 225

Martinet, Louis André, 225–26, 283n47

Martyre du Coeur, Le (Séjour), 73–74

Marx, Karl, 131

Mary, Aristide, 217–18, 225, 228

Mathieu, Louisy, 188

Mauger, Madame de, 21

Mazuline, Victor, 188

McCrary, Peyton, 195

McDonogh, John, 87
McEnery, John, 214–15
McIntosh, John Houston, 64–65
McKaye, James M., 189, 196, 198–99, 206
McKinney, Jesse, 216
McPherson, James M., 187
Mechanics' Institute attack (1866), 202–6, 223
medicine and doctor profiles: Afro-Creole
    healers, 110–12; Allain, 160–61; Civil War
    and, 168–69; Dames Hospitalière, 97;
    d'Aquin (Henri-Charles), 158–61; Deléry,
    162–65, 168–70; Faculté de Médecine de
    Paris, 153–60, 164; Faget, 153–57, 162–71;
    Faget's sign (diagnostic method), 168;
    French Hospital and La Société française
    de bienfaisance, 161–63, 166–67, 171,
    232–35; French Revolution and modern-
    ization of, 152–53; infectious school vs.
    contagionist school, 162–65; malarial
    fever, 162, 167–68, 171; Martinet, 225–26;
    medical schools in Louisiana, 224–26,
    227–29; obstetrics and cesarean sections,
    154–55, 159–60, 171; Paris Médicale,
    151–53, 171, 229, 271n1; Rouanet, 164–65;
    Roudanez (George), 229; Roudanez
    (Louis-Charles), 157–58; states' rights
    medicine, theory of, 163, 167–68; typhoid
    fever, 159; yellow fever, 137, 150, 161–71,
    207, 275n50, 275n62
Mercier, Armentine, 161
Meschacébéenes (Rouquette), 124
mesmerism, 112
Mexican independence, war of, 35–37
Mexico, Republic of, 57–58, 60–61, 68
Michelet, Jules, 232
Mieroslawski, Ludwik, 135, 269n42
Militia Corps of Free Morenos and Pardos,
    38–39
Miller, Samuel F., 219
Mina, Francisco Xavier, 62
Miró, Esteban, 263n59
Moni, Louis Aloysius Leopold (Abbé Mouni),
    105–6, 264n68

Monroe, James, 54, 55, 65, 67
Monroe, John T., 176–78, 201, 204
Montanée, Jean ("Doctor John"), 111, 113
Montespan, Marquise de, 13
Montgolfier, Adélaïde de, 135, 138
Moore, Thomas D., 175–76
Moore, Thomas, 123
Morand, Louis Dauquemenil de, 190
Moreau de Saint-Méry, Médéric-Louis-Elie,
    4, 107–9, 250n15, 264n79
Moreau-Lislet, Louis, 40–41, 75
Morelos, José María, 68
Morgan, David B., 44, 51–54
Morial, Ernest Nathan "Dutch," 235
Morial, Jacques, 235

Napoléon I (Napoléon Bonaparte), 25, 36
Napoléon III (Louis-Napoléon Bonaparte),
    74, 112, 131, 134, 160, 238–39
Nash, Christopher C., 215
Natchez Native Americans, 11, 14, 37, 122
National Association for the Advancement of
    Colored People (NAACP), 234–35
Native Americans, 122–25
Native Guard (Black regiments in Civil War),
    175–76, 181–83, 185–87, 190–93, 203,
    279n41
Nau, Emile, 127
Nau, Ignace, 127
negros rebeldes de Santo Domingo, los, 153–54
New Orleans: 1848 French Revolution and,
    131–34; African and African-American
    population of, 39, 42, 84, 105, 171, 201;
    Africanized culture in, 105–13; ban on
    entry of free Black males, 33; Black health
    crisis and medical schools in, 224–26;
    Caribbean refugees arriving in, 30, 34,
    40, 83, 154; Christian Mission Baptist
    Church, 235; Congo Square, 106, 205;
    Creole/Anglo-American political struggle
    for control of, 139–40; Crescent City
    White League, 220; French Market, 169–
    70; French Romanticism and Catholic re-

form in, 79–80; German Coast rebellion and, 31; itinerant revolutionaries in, 35; Jackson Square, 105, 139, 263n68; Lafayette in, 70–71; as Louisiana state capital, 200, 276n3; Lyceum Hall Black mass meeting (1863), 196; martial law in, 31, 48, 53; Mechanics' Institute attack (1866), 202–4, 206; ordinance restricting assembly (1858), 113; population of, 276n3; religious orders in, 89, 94–95, 97–99, 156–57; school board, 211–12; segregation and desegregation, 184; slave market, 113–16; Spanish Texas and, 36–37; St. Augustine Church, 97, 112, 233; St. Louis Cathedral, 96–97, 124, 132, 264n68; St. Mary's Catholic Church, 96–100, 166, 262n42; Third African Church, 199–200; yellow fever epidemic, 137, 150, 161–71, 207, 275n50, 275n62. *See also* Civil War and occupation of New Orleans; Reconstruction

New Orleans, daily life in: Catholic spiritual/mystical reform philosophies, 87–92, 99; in Civil-War era, 99–100; Congo Square, 106; Creole culture and identity, 83, 92–93, 107–9; Daron household, 83, 93–96; education, 86–87; Francophone community, 83; literary portraits of Suzanne and Dédé Sophie, 100–105; religious orders, 94–95, 97–99; St. Mary's Catholic Church, 96–100; vaudoux and Spiritualism, 108–13, 134

New Orleans Association, 57–58, 60–63, 254n2

New Orleans Crusader, 227–30

New Orleans University medical school, 227–29

Nicholls, Francis T., 222–23, 228

Northup, Solomon, 115–16

Nouvelle Atala ou la fille de l'esprit, La (Rouquette), 124

Oblate Sisters of Baltimore, 98, 273n14

Ogden, Frederick N., 220

Ogden, Henry D., 176

Ogé, Vincent, 32, 71, 248n57

Old Providence Island, 69

O'Reilly, Alejandro, 17, 38

Orléans, Marie-Adélaïde d', 135

Our People and Our History (Desdunes), 232

Owen, Robert Dale, 206

Owen, Robert, 142

Packard, Stephen B., 223

Paine, Thomas, 70

Pakenham, Edward Michael, 51–52

Pallières, Georges Martin des, 20

Pandelly, George, 139

Paris Médicale, 151–53, 171, 229, 271n1

Paroles d'un croyant (Lamennais), 91–92, 130, 135–36, 148–49

Paroles d'une femme (Ligeret), 136

Parton, James, 178, 277n11

Paula de Trebiño, Francisco de, 190

Paula de Trebiño, José Antonio de, 190

Pazos, Vicente, 63, 67

Peire, Henry D., 61–62

Penn, D. B., 221

Pepe, Félicité Caroline, 160

Père Antoine (Antonio de Sedella), 75

Périer, Étienne, 37

Pérotin-Dumon, Anne, 68

Pérrinon, François-Auguste, 188

Pétion, Alexandre Sabès, 22, 58, 60, 68–70, 127–28, 158, 186, 199, 232

Phelps, John W., 181–82

Philipeau (free person of color), 21

Phillips, Wendell, 177, 197

Picornell, Mariano, 36

Pinchback, P. B. S., 207–9, 214–15, 217, 226, 282n12

Pinchinat, Pierre, 22

Pitot, Jacques-François, 251n23

plantation land redistribution, 199–200

Plauché, Jean Baptiste, 50–51, 154

Plessy, Homer Adolphe, 228, 236–37

Plessy, Keith M., 236–37

Plessy & Ferguson Foundation, 236
Plessy v. Ferguson, 202, 205, 224, 228–29, 232, 235–37
Polasky, Janet, 35
Polvérel, Étiénne, 23–25
Populus, Nathalie Formento, 125–26, 267n19
Pory-Papy, Pierre-Marie, 188
Potens, Aimée, 75
Poydras, Julien, 100
Pressot, Eugénie (Presand/Presot), 69, 256n35
Prévost, François-Marie, 154–55
privateers, 58–62, 65–69
protest literature, Afro-Creole, 72–74
Puerto Rico, 157–58

Questy, Joanni, 125–26

racial order: anti-miscegenation laws, 226; Grandfort on, 140–44, 146–47; legal ostracisim of racially mixed children, 226; Louisiana law against violating caste distinctions, 126; Savary's assistance in Louisiana, 69–70; three-tiered, 40–41, 107; two-tiered Anglo-American, 40–41, 76–77, 99–100, 208, 218–19; white supremacism, 139, 141–43, 148, 210–13, 215–24, 227
Randolph, William, 218
Rapp, Eugène, 181
Rattenbury, Joseph Freeman, 65
Rebennack, Malcolm John "Mac" ("Doctor John"), 265n89
Rebennack, Pauline, 265n89
Reconstruction: 1867 constitutional convention and 1868 constitution (LA), 207–8, 209; 1898 constitution (LA), 230; anti-miscegenation laws and, 208, 226; Civil Rights Act of 1869 (LA), 211; Civil Rights Act of 1875 (US), 222–24; Civil Rights Cases, 224; Colfax Massacre (1873), 215–16; Comité des Citoyens, 228–30; coup attempts in New Orleans, 215,

220–21; coup d'état (1877), 223; Custom House Republican faction and, 213–14; elections, 208–9, 210, 214–15, 223; health care and medical schools in New Orleans, 224–25, 227–29; Lost Cause mythology and, 230; Louisiana Unification Movement, 217–18; Mechanics' Institute attack (1866), 202–6, 223; Memphis violence (1866), 204; Plessy v. Ferguson, 202, 205, 224, 228–29, 232, 235–37; Reconstruction Acts (1867), 204–5; school desegregation, 211–13, 221–22, 224, 226; Slaughterhouse Cases and U.S. v. Cruikshank, 219–20; transportation segregation, 205, 228, 229; l'Union Louisianaise, 226–27; voting rights, barriers to, 230; white supremacist actions against, 210–13, 215–24, 227
Rees, Jonathan, 51
Register, R. C., 215
Reinders, Robert C., 5
Religieuses du Sacre Coeur, 94–95
religious orders in New Orleans, 89, 94–95, 97–99, 156–57
Republicans vs. Democrats. See Reconstruction
Rey, Barthélemy, 112
Rey, Henri-Louis, 112–13, 181, 193, 209–10, 212
Reynaud de Barbarin, Auguste, 239
Reynaud de Barbarin, Jean-Baptiste, 82
Reynaud de Barbarin, Marie-Charlotte-Zélie d'Aquin, 82
Rhea, John, 66
Ricord, Philippe, 157
Rigaud, André, 22, 23, 33, 60, 245n34
Rinck, Adolph, 103, 263n59
Romanticism, French: 1789 French Revolution and, 3; 1848 French Revolution and, 79; Age of Revolution and, 127; Allain and, 3; Catholic reform philosophies and, 79–80, 88; classicism, struggle with, 119–20; defined, 3, 121; education in New Orleans and, 125–26, 132–33; Grandfort's attack on, 141–49; in Haiti, 127–29;

Lafayette and, 72; New Orleans and embrace of, 119, 121–27; Southern white supremacist version of, 141–42, 148, 230. *See also specific authors*

Rossignol-Desdunes, Jean Louis de, 26

Rouanet, Joseph, 164–65

Roudanez, Albert Francis, 229

Roudanez, George Alexandré, 229, 233

Roudanez, Jean-Baptiste, 75–76, 187, 194–98, 211, 222

Roudanez, Jean-Louis, 75

Roudanez, Louis-Charles: background, 75–76; Citizens' Committee and, 228–29; constitutional convention and, 207–8; Dunn's sudden death and, 213; equal rights, work for, 171; later life and death of, 233; Louisiana Unification Movement and, 217–18; medical training and career, 157–58; at Straight University, 225; Sumner's Civil Rights bill and, 222; *Tribune* and, 198, 205, 207, 211; *l'Union* and, 187–89, 194

Roudanez, Louis-Charles II, 229

Roudanez, Marie Anne "Nanene," 75

Rouquette, Adrien-Emmanuel (Chahta-Ima), 123–24

Rouquette, Dominique, 123

Rouquette, François-Dominique, 123–26

Rouquette, Térence, 123–24, 126

Rousseau, Jean-Jacques, 90

Rousselon, Etienne, 97–98

Roussève, Charles Barthélémy, 1–2, 4

Sacriste, Rose Agnès, 112

Saint-Domingue: acquired by France, 14; British invasion of, 24–25; civil war, 24–26; Conseil de Paix et d'Union de Saint-Marc, 22–24; d'Aquin family escapes from, 18–20; emancipation and abolition in, 23–24; free soldiers of color in, 14–15, 23; mesmerism in, 112; Moreau on ethnic groups in, 107; Polvérel's agricultural code, 23; population of, 17; racial mixing

in, 21, 22; slave regime and conditions in, 15, 21. *See also* Haitian Revolution

Saint-Rémy, Joseph, 232

Saloppé, Marie, 111

Sand, George, 92, 135

Saulay, Célie, 158

Sauvinet, Joseph, 60

Sauzy, Charles Eugene, 138

Savanes, poésies américaines, Les (Rouquette), 123

Savary, Belton, 22, 49, 51

Savary, Charles, *aîné,* 11, 22–25, 33, 48, 245n31, 253n36

Savary, Jean, 245n31

Savary, Joseph, *fils:* as advocate for Louisiana's people of color, 69–70; arrival in Louisiana, 33; in Battle of New Orleans, 48–51, 54–55; Courtois and, 127; d'Aquin/Savary alliance and, 11, 22; death of, 257n35; Lafayette and, 71; Mexican independence movement and, 35–36, 60–64

Schoelcher, Victor, 129–30

school segregation and desegregation, 184, 211–13, 221–22, 224, 226

Scott, David W., 206

Scott, Sir Walter, 141, 148

Sedella, Antonio de (Père Antoine), 75, 105–6, 264n68

segregation and desegregation: schools, 184, 211–13, 221–22, 224, 226; transportation, 184, 205, 228, 229

Séjour, Louis, 73, 133

Séjour, Ruojès-Louis, 133

Séjour, Victor, 73–74, 119, 125, 131, 133

Séligny, Michel, 125

Separate Car Act (LA), 228, 229

Seven Years' War, 16

Shaw, Daniel, 215

Sheller, Mimi, 128–29

Shepley, George F., 196

Sheridan, Philip H., 207, 210, 216, 221

Simón, Charles (Carlos), 71

Simón, Louis (Luis), 71

Sisters of the Holy Family, 98–99, 112, 114–15, 156–57
Sisters of the Presentation, 98
Slaughterhouse Cases, 219–20
slave rebellions and revolts: 1791 Saint-Domingue, 18–22; 1795 Pointe Coupée conspiracies, 27; 1810 Louisiana plantation workers, 30; 1811 German Coast, 30–32, 44; 1829–1831 Louisiana river region, 84–85; 1829 Christmas slave conspiracy, New Orleans, 85; 1831 Nat Turner, 85; Jamaica, 20, 82–83; in US Civil War, 180–81; War of 1812, siding with the English in, 54. *See also* Haitian Revolution
slavery: abolished by France's Second Republic, 79; abolished in British Caribbean, 83; Amelia Island and, 63, 66–67; ban on importation in Louisiana, 28; Catholicism and, 96, 100; Davis order on captured former slaves, 187; Emancipation Proclamation, 192; French and British Nationals during US Civil War and, 179–80; French Commission on Slavery and abolition decree (1848), 129–30; Grandfort on, 142–43; Haitian abolition and Pétion's free soil policy, 68; harsh Anglo-American regime, 97; Lafayette and Wright on, 71–72; Latin American independence and abolition, 68, 84; Ligeret on, 147–48; Moreau's slave classifications, 107; Napoleon's campaign to restore, 25; "naturalized," Moreau's theory of, 107–8; numbers in New Orleans, 39; numbers in Saint-Domingue, 17; privateering and, 66–67; in Saint-Domingue, 15, 21, 23–24; scars and evidence of abuse, 278n35; slave market, New Orleans, 113–16; urban slave quarters in New Orleans, 96; US abolitionism, 84. *See also* Civil War and occupation of New Orleans
Snaër, Louis A., 207
Société d'economie et d'assistance mutuelle, 70

Société des Artisans, La, 72–74, 76, 181
Société française de bienfaisance, La, 161–63, 166–67, 171, 232–35
Society for the Rights of Man and the Citizen, 128
Soirées de Saint-Pétersburg, Les (Maistre), 88–89
Sonthonax, Léger Félicité, 23–24, 244n29
Souchon, Edmond, 155–56, 162
Soulé, Armentine, 134–35, 233
Soulé, Pierre, 116, 131–32, 134, 161–63
Southern University, 226
Spanish colonial independence movements. *See* Latin American independence movements
Spiritualism, 112–13, 134, 206
Stafford, Spencer H., 178, 183, 184, 190, 193, 206
Stanton, Edwin M., 181–82, 198, 278n27
states' rights medicine, theory of, 163, 167–68
St. Augustine Church, New Orleans, 97, 112, 233
Stevens, Thaddeus, 204
St. Louis Cathedral, New Orleans, 96–97, 124, 132, 264n68
St. Mary's Catholic Church, New Orleans, 96–100, 166, 262n42
Stone, Lucy, 142
Stowe, Harriet Beecher, 100, 116, 138, 141, 142, 271n86
Straight University, 224–26
Strother, David H., 194
Subileau, Joseph, 233
suffrage, African American, 194–98, 230
Suffren, Charles, 70
Sumner, Charles, 151–52, 177–78, 189, 191, 196–97, 199, 211, 222, 224
Supervielle, Eugene, 126
Sutherland, Harriet Leveson-Gower, Duchess of, 116, 142
Suzanne (free Afro-Creole), 89, 94, 96, 101–103, 105, 146
Swanton-Belloc, Louise, 135, 138

Talvande, Ann Marsan, 86
Taylor, Joe Gray, 180
Télémaque (enslaved bakery worker), 30
Télémaque (slave magnetizer), 112
Teresa of Avila, 98–99
Testut, Charles, 1, 84
Texas and Mexican independence, 35–37, 61–62
Théodore (enslaved worker), 30
Thierry, Camille, 126
Third African Church of New Orleans, 199–200
Thomas, Pierre Frédéric, 164
Thompson, C. H., 225
Tinchant, Joseph, 188–89, 279n44
Tinker, Edward Larocque, 5, 125, 164, 216–17, 240, 267n19
Tone, Theobald Wolfe, 36
Tone, William Theobald Wolfe, 36
Touatre, Just, 170
"Toussaint Louverture à l'aspect de la flotte française, 1802" (Buildbaud), 186
Townsend, James, 177–78
Treaty of Ghent, 53, 56–57
Trévigne, Paul, 119–20, 125–26, 187, 190, 207, 211, 222, 223–24, 226–27
Tribune de la Nouvelle-Orléans/New Orleans Tribune, 198–200, 203–7, 209, 211
Trollope, Frances, 84, 140–42
Tureaud, A. P., 234–35
Tureaud, Augustin Dominique, 76
Tureaud v. Board of Supervisors, 235
Turner, Nat, 85
Twain, Mark, 148
typhoid fever, 159

Uncle Tom's Cabin (Stowe), 100, 116, 138, 141, 271n86
Union, l' (Black newspaper), 187–90, 194–95, 198
Union Association of New Orleans, 194–95

Union Louisianaise, l', 226–27
United Provinces of New Granada, 59–60, 68
United States: Florida, takeover of, 64–67; Haiti, diplomatic recognition of, 246n40; Haitian Revolution, impact of, 26–27, 30, 32–33; War of 1812, 37, 42, 46–55. See also Civil War and occupation of New Orleans; Louisiana; New Orleans
United States v. Andrew Jackson, 53–54
United States v. Cruikshank, 219–20
US Sanitary Commission, 170

Valmour, J. B. (John B. Averin), 111–13, 193
vaudoux, 80, 108–13, 134, 186
Velpeau, Alfred-Armand-Louise-Marie, 158–59
Villeré, Gabriel, 48, 50, 52–54
Villeré, Jacques Philippe, 44, 48, 50, 53
Vincent, 109
Vincent de Paul, 98–99
voting rights, 194–98, 230

Walker, David, 84–85
Walker's Appeal . . . to the Coloured Citizens of the World (Walker), 84–85
Waples, Rufus, 206
Warburg, Eugène, 116
Warmoth, Henry Clay, 208–11, 213–14, 217, 225, 282n12
War of 1812, 37, 42, 46–55
Wharton, Edward C., 143–44, 149
White Leagues, 216, 220–21, 227
Wild Flowers, Sacred Poetry (Rouquette), 124
Wilkinson, James, 38, 100
Williams, P. M., 225
Wiltz, Victor, 139
Woods, W. B., 224
Wright, Frances "Fanny," 71–72

yellow fever epidemic, 137, 150, 161–71, 207, 275n50, 275n62

www.ingramcontent.com/pod-product-compliance
Lightning Source LLC
Chambersburg PA
CBHW030921150426
42812CB00046B/449